Reading Instruction Through Content Teaching

EARL H. CHEEK Jr.
Louisiana State University

MARTHA COLLINS CHEEK
Louisiana State University

Charles E. Merrill Publishing Company
A Bell & Howell Company
Columbus Toronto London Sydney

Published by
Charles E. Merrill Publishing Company
A Bell & Howell Company
Columbus, Ohio 43216

Photographs: p. 5 (© 1983 Richard Khanlian), p. 18 (© C. Quinlan), p. 29 (Strix Pix), p. 32 (Michael Hayman/Corn's Photo Service), p. 46 (Paul M. Shrock), p. 76 (© C. Quinlan), p. 96(Vivienne della Grotta), p. 118 (© Joanne Meldrum), p. 126 (Paul Conklin), p. 150 (Rick Smolan), p. 172 (© C. Quinlan), p. 208 (© C. Quinlan), p. 210 (© Richard Khanlian), p. 239 (Paul Conklin), p. 243 (Strix Pix), p. 260 (© C. Quinlan), p. 264 (Strix Pix), p. 290 (Michael Hayman/Corn's Photo Service), p. 312 (© Phillips Photo Illustrators), p. 316 (© Richard Khanlian), p. 332 (Paul M. Shrock), p. 334 (Paul Conklin).

This book was set in Souvenir Light and Serif Gothic Heavy.
Cover photo by Jean Greenwald.
Cover design by Tony Faiola.

Library of Congress Catalog Card Number: 82-062868
International Standard Book Number: 0-675-20026-1

Printed in the United States of America

1 2 3 4 5 6 7 8 9 10 — 87 86 85 84 83

To Our Students and Friends—

Thanks for your continuing support and encouragement.

CONTENTS

CHAPTER 6

Organizational Patterns for Content Learning 200

CHAPTER 7

Organizing and Managing Content Instruction 228

CHAPTER 8

Using Material for Content Instruction 248

Special Notes for Special Folks   349

APPENDIXES

Preface

This book has emerged during the years that one of us worked as a secondary social studies teacher and the other as a reading specialist in a middle school. It was evident that reading had to be incorporated into these middle and secondary classes—but how? We began pooling our knowledge and as the years passed, we refined and expanded our initial ideas. Now, as a result of our work as classroom teachers and reading specialists, and finally from our experiences as university teachers observing and interacting with undergraduate and graduate students, we realized that a text emphasizing an organized, step-by-step approach to integrating reading into the content classroom was needed. This book is our attempt to share our model for content reading instruction.

Content teachers are faced daily with the problem of providing appropriate instruction for students reading at different levels. Pre- and in-service activities offer techniques that might be used in teaching. Yet, while teachers want to try new ideas in content teaching, they are frequently unsure of what to add where. This text provides teachers with an organized way of enhancing content learning and improving reading at the middle and secondary school levels. This book is a guide that can be adapted to complement their teaching styles. It provides practical techniques that content teachers can use to achieve their goal of giving the right kind of instruction to every student.

Chapter 1 deals with content teaching and reading instruction. It also stresses the need for integrating reading into the various content areas and introduces a five-step model for implementing content reading instruction.

Step One (Chapter 2) defines concept teaching and assists content teachers in identifying concepts. Step Two (Chapter 3) identifies reading skills and discusses their relationship to concepts. Appropriate skill areas such as word identification, comprehension, and study skills are defined and discussed in depth.

Step Three (Chapter 4) focuses on the importance of diagnosis to content instruction. Formal and informal diagnostic procedures that are practical for use in the content classroom are discussed.

Step Four (Chapters 5–11) is concerned with instruction. Chapter 5 covers techniques for teaching content reading, with emphasis on relating concepts, skills, and diagnosis. In Chapter 6 the importance of organizational patterns in content materials is presented. Techniques for organizing and managing content instruction are shown in Chapter 7, and suggestions are given for using materials and determining readability of content materials in Chapter 8. Chapter 9 is a compilation of lessons developed to show how the Directed Learning Activity procedure can be applied to the various content areas. In Chapter 10 suggestions for teaching students with special needs in the content areas are discussed. Special students identified in this chapter are poor readers, mainstreamed students, language-varied students, and gifted students. Chapter 11 is concerned with motivating students. The identification of problems is undertaken with suggestions for alleviating them.

In Step Five (Chapter 12) the need for integrating reading instruction through content teaching is summarized, and assistance is given the teacher in putting all the parts together.

Each chapter is preceded by questions which suggest its objectives as well as a list of vocabulary terms that are important in understanding the material. Each chapter contains a summary, discussion questions, and a list of other suggested readings. Scattered throughout the chapters are special notes or extra bits of information under the heading "Lagniappe" (lan-yap). (This French term is commonly used in Louisiana to indicate something given gratuitously along with other information or a purchase.) Also included in each chapter are "Reflections," designed to encourage readers to think about previously studied materials and to relate the ideas to experiences in the content classroom.

Between the final chapter and the appendixes is a special section of notes for content teachers. The appendixes themselves include activities for skill development in various content areas; a list of commercially available diagnostic tests; guidelines for administering and interpreting an informal reading inventory; sample structured overviews, pattern guides, concept guides, and three-level study guides; plus a list of activity books. A glossary of terms is also provided.

These introductory remarks would be incomplete without saying thanks to all of our students and professional colleagues who, through the years, helped develop this model. Your reactions, suggestions, contributions, and encouragement are appreciated. We have learned that an idea is but a dream until it is applied, revised, adapted, and becomes a usable vehicle for improving student learning.

We also wish to thank our reviewers who gave us constructive criticisms and comments. A special thanks goes to Professor William Rupley of Texas A & M University for his encouragement, understanding, and critiques as the manuscript developed. Thanks also to the reviewers: Dan Pearce of Western Illinois University, Marilyn Fairbanks of West Virginia University, and Mike Angelotti of Texas Technical University. Acknowledgments are extended to Karla Lemoine who typed the manuscript drafts, regardless of circumstance.

Because of all of you, our ideas have reached a reality that we hope will assist content teachers to become successful in their work with content learners.

CHAPTER ONE

CONTENT TEACHING AND READING INSTRUCTION

The bell rings and hundreds of students move through the halls to different teachers and assorted content classrooms. As these students enter their rooms, the teacher faces a divergent population representing many levels of psychological, sociological, and cognitive development. Although all of these areas of development are important to the learning process, cognitive development, especially reading, has been promoted in recent years as a major responsibility of all educators.

Public concern over declining test scores, the inability of some students to demonstrate basic reading skills to prospective employers, the recognized need for the use of higher level thinking skills in today's society, and reports by parents and teachers regarding poor student performance in elementary and secondary classrooms, has led to additional interest in reading instruction at all levels. It has given vitality to the incorporation of reading into content teaching. Thus, the development of more pre- and in-service courses in content reading instruction, state certification changes requiring such courses for undergraduate and graduate education majors, and numerous professional publications relating reading instruction to content teaching have resulted.

This book is written to assist middle and secondary school content teachers in their work with students. The ideas emphasize the incorporation of reading instruction into the content classroom in order to better meet the cognitive as well as the psychological and sociological needs of the students. Classroom experiences in the content areas have shown that as students are instructed at appropriate levels and taught how to study content information, their learning improves, as does their self-concept and attitude toward learning. This book presents a model that has been used by the authors to integrate reading and content instruction. The model outlines a step-by-step procedure which may be followed or adapted to meet individual teaching styles.

STUDY QUESTIONS

1. What is meant by content teaching and reading instruction?
2. Why is content reading so important in middle and secondary school education?
3. What factors affect the reading of content materials?
4. Why are the middle and secondary school curricula important in incorporating reading instruction in the content classroom?
5. What are the various staff responsibilities in incorporating content reading into the middle and secondary school curricula?
6. What steps should the content teacher follow to teach the content concepts and improve reading?

VOCABULARY

Content reading
Content teaching
Readability level

Reading instruction
Specialized vocabulary
Technical vocabulary

CONTENT READING INSTRUCTION: WHY?

Middle and secondary school content teachers know that students' reading levels normally range from six to eight years, and that these differences significantly affect the learning of the content information. The problem becomes more complex each year as societal forces exert a greater impact on school-age students. Alterations in the family structure, increased use of drugs, instability of the economy, increased mobility, changes in discipline in the home, learning experiences through travel and the media, and a rapidly changing society contribute to more diversity in the psychological and sociological levels in the classroom. While these areas definitely affect cognitive learning and cannot be ignored, the content teacher is nonetheless charged with the responsibility of cognitive development or teaching content information.

The problem has been compounded by a lack of continued reading instruction in the middle and secondary grades. Learning to read effectively is a developmental process which is not complete with the teaching of the basic reading skills in the elementary grades. The higher level thinking and study skills must be expanded in the upper grades and students taught to apply these skills in content learning. Reading in middle and secondary content classrooms is a curriculum adjustment that may be received either negatively or positively depending on the attitude of the administration, willingness of the teachers to adjust instruction, knowledge and assistance from support personnel and parents, motivation and attitude of the students, and appropriate use of instructional procedures and materials. These elements involve all persons in the school. Reading instruction in the middle and secondary content classroom is not the responsibility of an isolated few.

LAGNIAPPE

"The development of reading competence is best achieved when the student's focus is on the content of the material and not on the reading itself. Psychology of learning has long pointed out that what is taught is most effective within the context in which it is used."

William S. Palmer, "Teaching Reading in Content Areas," *Journal of Reading* (October 1975): 44.

In content instruction, teachers consider as their primary responsibility the guiding of students in learning the content material. Because content teachers have encountered problems in teaching their content information due to the students' difficulty in using the textbook, the terms *reading instruction* and *content reading* have become important ideas in the middle and secondary school curricula. As content teachers attempt to teach basic concepts in their specialized content areas, they immediately recognize student differences in learning the material. Some students know how to read the materials and understand the concepts being taught. Others are unable to grasp even a rudimentary understanding of the content information because they are unable to read the content material. This difficulty may be due to the poor reading skills of the student, but more likely it is because students have not been taught *how* to read the specialized content materials. Teaching *how* to read the materials then

Content teachers help students to read specialized information.

becomes the responsibility of the teacher. This type of reading instruction is known as *content reading*.

Content reading differs from general reading instruction in that content reading is provided in conjunction with content teaching, while *reading instruction* is usually thought of as instruction given in a special reading class or an elementary classroom. General reading instruction places emphasis on skill development and independent reading, while content reading relates reading instruction to specific content materials.

As content teachers, reading teachers, and administrators approach the inclusion of reading in the content classroom, they must remember that the content teacher is primarily responsible for content teaching. However, content teaching is most effective when the need for reading instruction via content reading is recognized.

Although many middle and secondary school content teachers have successfully used content reading techniques in their daily teaching, some teachers continue to ask why they, as content specialists, must consider reading instruction. Why must content teachers be concerned about reading instruction when they already have more than a hundred students a day for content instruction? Why do students come from the elementary grades unable to apply their reading skill knowledge to content materials? Why is it so important for content teachers to be included in reading instruction? Questions such as these are asked by content teachers every day. There are no simple answers, but a basis, at least, for determining logical conclusions is developed when content teachers understand *why* content instruction and reading instruction must be interrelated.

Some content teachers assume that they must teach reading because content classrooms are filled with so many students who cannot read the content textbook. This may be true. Although test data indicate that students on the whole are reading better today than in the past,[1] many individual students continue to experience difficulty in reading content materials. While test data indicate greater improvement in reading in the primary grades than in the upper levels, the problems students encounter in reading content materials will always exist, no matter how much reading instruction improves in elementary schools. This factor exists for two basic reasons: (1) because students possess different abilities and individual distinctions, they enter elementary school at a variety of levels and continue to develop as unique learners; and (2) although students may demonstrate an understanding of the reading skills taught in the elementary school, many of them must continuously be shown how to apply these skills in specialized content instruction. As teachers in the elementary grades attempt to prepare students better for middle and secondary school, content teachers may find that their classes contain students with a greater range of differences in reading levels. This happens as teachers strive to help students reach their maximum level of performance rather than to read "at grade level." Therefore, as students continue to improve in reading at the elementary school level, the inclusion of reading in the middle and secondary content curriculum becomes more essential.

The importance of content reading instruction may be better understood as teachers realize that reading is a developmental process, introduced in the primary grades, refined in the upper elementary grades, and applied exclusively to learning situations at the middle and secondary school levels. Reading has no content, only the learning and application of skills for gaining information and enjoyment. Materials used in reading instruction in the elementary grades are written in a narrative manner, their major objective being the development of an understanding of the reading skills. Only secondarily are activities provided that help students learn to apply these skills to their content reading. Students experience difficulty in transferring their learning from elementary reading materials to content materials. Materials in each of the content areas have their own organizational format, technical vocabulary, and unique written style—even the best readers need content reading instruction in order to maximize their content learning. Thus, content teachers must provide the necessary instruction so that students can learn how to read specialized content information.

Content reading strategies must be applied to specialized materials. This can be identified in any content classroom. In order to understand mathematics, students must understand the different symbols, such as $+$, $\times$, $>$, or $=$. Additionally, the students must comprehend how the wording of written problems directs them to perform various mathematical computations. In reading history materials, students should be taught that historical information is often organized in a chronological order or sequence, and that the understanding of these ideas is enhanced by recognizing and remembering the sequence. The sciences contain technical terms that are essential to grasping the concepts. Therefore, content teachers should introduce these terms as they teach the concepts. These simple examples serve only to show how important reading instruction is to the learning of content information. Content teachers expect students to achieve and become independent learners of content information. However, if this is to occur, the importance of content reading instruction must be accepted and implemented in the content classroom.

CONTENT READING: A HISTORICAL PERSPECTIVE

The need for reading in the various content areas was first discussed in the mid-1920s, with the application of these ideas coming much later. It was in the late 1940s that basal readers began to incorporate stories using social studies and science content with suggestions in the teachers' guides indicating ways reading could be integrated with the subject areas.[2] Secondary schools were encouraged to develop reading programs by the publication in 1948 of the Forty-Seventh Yearbook, Part II, of the National Society for the Study of Education, *Reading in the High School and College*. Previously, most reading instruction at this level was remedial reading; however, William S. Gray and Guy Bond suggested the inclusion of a developmental program for all secondary students as well as continuing the remedial teaching for the poorer readers.

In this developmental program the concerns about reading in the special content fields were addressed, although Harris suggested that content reading was a special type of problem which differed from basic reading instruction necessary for the learning of all material. To enhance this emphasis on secondary reading instruction, the first two professional books on reading in the secondary school were published, each devoting space to the topic of reading in the content fields, namely literature, social studies, science, and mathematics.[3]

LAGNIAPPE

Guy L. Bond and Eva Bond wrote the first professional book on reading in the secondary school. The book, *Developmental Reading in High School*, was published by Macmillan in 1941. In 1946, *Problems in the Improvement of Reading* by Ruth Strang, Constance McCullough, and Arthur Traxler was published by McGraw-Hill.

Interest in reading in the content areas continued because of research studies such as those by Artley, Norwell, Swenson, McCallister and Lessenger.[4] This moderate interest in secondary reading persisted until the early 1950s. At this time the national interest in reading exploded because reading was recognized as a necessary tool for developing the literate society considered essential for national preservation. Thus, reading in the content areas became more important. This importance continued to escalate in the production of research and in the evidence of need for more emphasis on implementing the theory of reading in the content in the classroom.[5] In 1961, Gray suggested several considerations regarding the future of reading. Among his suggestions was the following statement.

> I wish to refer to the urgent need for reading in the content fields. Herein lies one of the great possibilities for developing mature, competent readers in the future.[6]

Strang reinforced this need for specific instruction through content reading.

> One direction in which we should move is toward a more intensive analysis of the reading processes that are actually used by students with varying back-

grounds and degrees of ability when they read different kinds of materials for different purposes. Instruction in reading has been much too general.[7]

Thus, the importance of incorporating reading instruction into content class-rooms was recognized for many years prior to the attempt to implement the concept. Why this time delay in putting into practice ideas which seemed to be such a viable way to improve both content learning and reading achievement? Burton is probably correct in pointing the finger at colleges, suggesting that the academic departments in the colleges did not encourage or provide such train-ing.[8] While the interest in secondary reading and reading instruction in the con-tent classroom had existed for many years, it was not until the mid 1960s that educators became concerned about the implementation of these ideas.

From the mid-1960s to the present, reading instruction in content teaching has become a major concern of middle and secondary school programs. As teacher education programs have improved, teachers are now more aware of the individual differences of students as well as the necessity of reading in learn-ing content material. To ease the integration of reading and content instruction many states are requiring training in this field for all teachers.[9] Additionally, pro-fessional books have been produced which deal exclusively with reading in the content areas. An early book of this type was *Teaching Reading in the Content Areas* by Harold Herber.[10] This book was followed by others, such as those of Estes and Vaughan, Singer and Donlan, Forgan and Mangrum, Thomas and Robinson, Robinson, and Smith, Smith and Mikulecky, that have provided con-tent teachers with ideas on how reading instruction can assist content teaching.

Additionally, a review of the *Journal of Reading,* 1957–1977, indicated that while reading in the content areas was not the category in which the most arti-cles were published, the number of articles increased steadily from nine appear-ing in Volumes 1–7 to thirty-seven related to content reading in Volumes 15–20. Summers predicted that the number of articles in this category would rise even more "as the increased activity in this area in recent years is translated into journal content."[11]

Content teachers' attitudes toward teaching reading also seem to be chang-ing. In a survey of secondary teachers regarding their attitudes toward teaching reading in high school, Jackson found that "nearly three-quarters of the respon-dents felt that content teachers could be reading teachers, more than two-thirds felt that they were reading teachers, and more than three-quarters were willing to take a course in teaching reading."[12] This finding as compared to Karlin's, in which secondary teachers indicated that the responsibility for teaching reading belonged to the elementary teacher,[13] suggests that secondary teachers are now accepting the responsibility of providing content reading instruction.

Although content teachers as a whole seem more willing to incorporate read-ing into their content classrooms, the degree of willingness varies among con-tent areas. Using an instrument designed by Vaughan to assess teacher attitudes toward teaching reading in the content classroom,[14] O'Rourke found that Eng-lish teachers scored "positive" on the instrument, while the other groups— math, science, and social studies—scored "average."[15] These findings reflect an optimistic view that content teachers are accepting reading as a tool that enhances the learning of content material, and as a developmental process, rather than as an isolated group of skills taught in the elementary school.

LAGNIAPPE

"The content teacher is the best-qualified person in the school for teaching reading in his subject. He is the one who (1) is most capable in teaching the new vocabulary in his subject, (2) is most knowledgeable in setting purposes for reading, (3) is most able in developing and motivating student interest, (4) is most adept in identifying important concepts to be arrived at, (5) is most conversant with multi-resources, their use and value in developing background experiences, and (6) is familiar enough with the text to know how to best read and study it."

H. Alan Robinson and Ellen Lamar Thomas, eds., *Fusing Reading Skills and Content* (Newark, Del.: International Reading Association, 1969), p. 19.

Thus, as the need for content reading has been recognized, the 1970s have seen it become a reality in many classrooms. The trend for the 1980s is one of refining and expanding the original ideas to develop more carefully planned programs at these upper levels. Such planning is necessary if reading instruction is to incorporate not only the introduction of skills in the primary grades, but also the application and utilization of the skills in the content classrooms at the upper elementary, middle, and secondary levels. Research indicates that, while elementary teachers can teach the reading skills and show how they are used in the content areas, the content teacher must be sure the students can apply the specific reading skills in their particular subject.[16] Therefore, the current trend in reading instruction in the middle and secondary schools is to organize a school program in reading so that every teacher assumes this responsibility and is indeed a teacher of reading in order to broaden content learning.

REFLECTION

Think about your middle and secondary school experiences and identify the instructional emphasis as well as the types of materials used. Then think about a middle or secondary class that you have recently taught or observed. How has the content classroom changed through the years?

FACTORS AFFECTING CONTENT INSTRUCTION

In emphasizing the importance of content reading instruction, content teachers must recognize that many factors create the need for additional help in reading content materials. These factors relate to three major components of the content classroom—the reader, the material, and the management of instruction. Students enter the content classroom with different reading levels, personalities, interests, as well as psychological, sociological, and cognitive needs. These differences are present when students begin school, and become greater as they grow in the school and home environments. Content teachers may better understand the vast differences in students when they visit a kindergarten or first grade classroom. Although all children in the first grade may have a chronological age of about six, some have a mental age or ability to understand comparable to a three-year-old, while others may have a mental age of a seven-

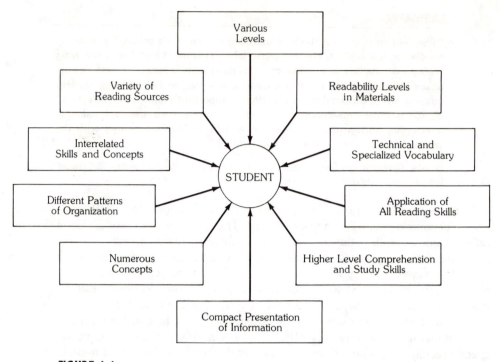

FIGURE 1.1

Factors Contributing to the Difficulty of Content Reading

or eight-year old. Regardless of the additional instructional assistance given through the years, the child with a mental age of three often never catches up with the average student. This difference in learning continues into the middle and secondary levels, and becomes an important factor for the content teacher in providing instruction in the classroom. Dealing with individual differences and various levels of students is a major factor which affects content teaching. In considering ways to deal with this problem, the content teacher should be aware of other factors that affect the students' ability to learn content material. These factors are summarized in Figure 1.1 and discussed in the following pages.

Learning content information and using content materials present many difficulties to the student. Whether the student is considered a good reader or a poor one, there are contributing factors that content teachers must recognize in their instruction. Of major concern is the readability level of content materials. The problem is twofold: (1) the readability levels within a single content textbook vary greatly due to the vocabulary used and the information given, and (2) the reading levels of the students in the content classrooms range from far below grade level to far above grade level. This variation in both materials and students causes problems because, generally speaking, they tend to vary in different directions. The readability levels of the materials are usually at or above the assigned grade level, while the reading levels of many students are at or below their assigned grade level. Additionally, the variations of readability levels within a single text present a problem in using a single text in a classroom. Therefore, the use of a variety of sources is encouraged to meet the different reading levels in the class. More ideas on assessing and adjusting the readability levels of content materials are given in Chapter 8.

Another difficulty encountered in reading content material is that of understanding the specialized and technical vocabulary. *Specialized vocabulary* is vocabulary which changes in meaning from one content area to another. For example, the word *root* means a part of a plant in botany, while in mathematics the word refers to a quality (number) which when multiplied by itself a certain number of times produces another quality. Likewise, the word *root* may be used in language to refer to a base word before a suffix or prefix is added. Therefore, the student must be taught the meaning of this word in relation to the content area in which it is used.

Technical vocabulary is that which is essential to the understanding of a specific content area. Such words relate to only one content area and are crucial to understanding. An example is the word *pollen*. To understand a lesson on plants, students must first learn the technical words and their meanings. An example of a technical word in social studies is *embargo*. To understand an embargo on U.S. trade with Cuba, students must first know the meaning of embargo. Content teachers should note that vocabulary instruction is essential to successful content reading and must, therefore, become integral to the instructional program. Information on vocabulary instruction is given in Chapter 5.

In learning content information, students must be able to apply all reading skills. Such application is a critical part of the transition from reading "reading books" in the elementary grades to reading content materials in the middle and secondary school levels. The reading of content materials requires that students know the reading skills and be able to use them appropriately instead of being told which skill to use when, as they were at elementary levels. Content reading calls for the application of reading skills without first identifying that skill. An automatic response is needed to make easy the understanding of content material. The application of reading skills to content materials is actually a basic reason for reading; therefore, students who seemingly know the skills but are unable to use them have not achieved a fundamental goal in reading instruction. Because the application of these skills varies from one content area to another, teachers must accept this variable as a prime reason for incorporating reading into their content instruction. Specific suggestions are given in Chapters 3, 5, 6, and 9.

Content materials not only require the application of all previously taught reading skills, they also demand a thorough knowledge and application of the higher level comprehension and study skills which generally receive only cursory instruction in the elementary grades. In elementary reading more emphasis seems to be placed on lower-level literal comprehension and on word identification than on study skills and interpretive and critical reading. With research in comprehension stressing the need for more emphasis on meaning at all levels of reading instruction, the gap between the comprehension skills taught and those needed for content reading will, it is hoped, narrow.

At present the content teacher will find it necessary to offer instruction in the higher level reading skills, as well as provide tips on how to use them in understanding content material. Without teacher assistance, the condition leads to frustration for student and teacher alike. The result can often cause a decline in the students' performance and a corresponding decline in their self-esteem and attitude toward the content area. More information on reading skills is given in Chapter 3.

Another factor bearing on content instruction is the compact presentation of information in the content textbook. Content textbooks present many new ideas and facts in a few pages, as compared to the limited concepts in the basal readers with which most students are familiar. This compact presentation, along with what many students see as a mass of unrelated facts, causes difficulty in reading a content textbook. Likewise, content teachers are confronted with the added problem of teaching students how to better understand the content textbook. Suggestions for dealing with concepts and the presentation of information are presented in Chapters 2, 5, 6, and 9.

The presentation of numerous concepts in content learning is another factor that causes difficulty in content reading. Many new ideas or concepts are presented briefly without thorough explanation. The content teacher, therefore, must carefully identify the ideas to be learned, must provide instruction covering these ideas, and must guide reading to ensure that the information is understood. Unless students grasp new concepts and retain them, they can soon become lost in a deluge of obscure information. In content materials one concept builds on another, but each must be properly understood before the concept cluster can become a meaningful structure. More information on identifying and teaching concepts is presented in Chapters 2 and 5.

Content materials offer a variety of different organizational patterns as compared to materials used in elementary grades. The result is that these patterns not only present problems in understanding the format of the information, but also create difficulty for students as they transfer their reading skills from a reading book to a content text. For example, in reading narrative information commonly used in elementary reading materials, students are often asked to identify the sentence in a paragraph or selection that states the main idea. The students may have been instructed previously that the main idea is usually given in the first or last sentence, although sometimes it may be within the paragraph. However, content materials are more likely to be written in a different literary style, such as enumerative or explanatory. These seldom contain an explicitly stated main idea. Usually the reader must glean the main idea from stated information or rely on subheadings. Therefore, these different organizational patterns must first be identified so that the structure of information can be understood. Next, students should be shown how to apply their reading skills in order to comprehend the various literary styles. Chapter 6 presents information on the different organizational patterns used in each content area.

While content materials present much unrelated information and each content area material uses different organizational formats, there also exist many relationships among the various content subjects. Interestingly, the lack of understanding of these relationships causes students problems in reading content materials. For example, while there are different study procedures which can be used for various subject areas, students should realize that the use of a study procedure is necessary in all areas. Likewise, in learning inferential comprehension skills, the student should realize that the skill remains the same regardless of the content area. In reading social studies materials the student must study maps and graphs which correspond to the printed information. Using a legend on the map or interpreting the figures on the graph in the social studies book involves the same skills as would be necessary to acquire the information from similar figures in a science or mathematics book. Thus, the skills needed in content reading are interrelated, although the student may need to be reminded about the application of the skill in each subject. Similarly, the concepts in the different content areas are interrelated. For example, the understanding of poems or novels in American literature may be enhanced as students learn about the history of the country at the time these works were written. Likewise, knowledge of certain mathematical concepts such as metric units makes it easier to understand science concepts. From these limited examples, the teacher can see that the content areas are interrelated. Successful learning in one class will improve learning in another, while failure to relate learning experiences will create redundancy, frustration, and boredom in the content classroom.

In managing content reading instruction, teachers often find that students must read from a variety of sources in order to learn more about concepts or different ideas. For some students reading from various sources is a new experience, as their previous content instruction may have come from a single textbook. Difficulty in using many sources occurs not only because of the change in teaching materials, but also because of the varied writing styles and philosophies of the authors. Additionally, the student must be aware of the differences in the organization of the materials. Alternating from one material to another may add variety to content learning and serve to motivate students *if* they know how to adjust to these differences in materials. However, if students attempt to read all materials alike without regard to style, philosophy, and organization, they may well become confused, and little new learning will occur.

In considering the use of a variety of sources, content teachers should know the approximate readability level of the different materials, and then try to provide materials that are close to the students' reading level. More information on selecting materials for content instruction is provided in Chapter 8.

As teachers guide students in using different sources, they must note that poor readers cannot deal with materials in the same manner as better readers. In reading reference materials, for example, the poor reader needs careful guidance and assignments that require a less detailed analysis of the information. Content teachers should realize that the use of a variety of materials in a class may be a new and intimidating experience for some students. However, students can and should be encouraged to use a variety of sources in content reading—this helps them learn to seek out information on their own and become independent learners.

Content teachers must be aware that these various influences may help or hinder content instruction. The factors should be viewed as potential obstacles to student learning and must be considered in instructional planning. With necessary adjustments and the incorporation of reading instruction into the content classroom, these factors become suggestions for improving content learning.

REFLECTION

Consider the factors affecting content instruction that are identified in this chapter. Think about a content classroom in which you have observed, taught, or been a student. Which of these factors do you think may have had a negative impact on the learning of content in this class? Did you see the teacher attempting to overcome any of these factors to make content reading easier? If so, how?

READING AND THE CURRICULUM

The middle and secondary school curricula of the 1980s reflect a fast-moving society in which vast amounts of knowledge must be imparted to develop a more literate and capable future generation. Inherent in this movement are problems that may occur, such as:

All students are not able to keep pace with the rapid dissemination of content information;

So much new information is occurring each day in our fast-moving society that students cannot learn *all* of the facts about a content area; and

Teachers are uncertain what students should learn in order to function as leaders in coming years.

Thus, the content teacher must meet these challenges by teaching the student *how* to learn content information rather than to absorb mere facts presented in a textbook. The middle and secondary curricula must continue to adjust to these changing times.

Thirty or more years ago content teaching did not consider these problems and designed school curricula for students enrolled at the high school level. The range of differences in reading levels was narrow or reduced because (a) students who did not achieve at grade level were not promoted to high school or dropped out of school; (b) students were tracked or grouped according to their ability or performance level; (c) poor readers avoided, and still do not enroll in, classes with heavy and difficult reading assignments, and (d) teachers taught to the slowest group through lecture or reading to the class.[17]

Along with a reduced reading range in the content classroom, the secondary school had a narrow curriculum. Basic subjects such as English, history, math, and science formed the curriculum. The textbook and the teacher were the instructional tools. However, as school attendance became compulsory, enrollments grew, with elementary and secondary schools becoming overcrowded. Today, along with a more diverse student population, content teachers are now faced with more content information and a more diverse curriculum. Adjustments in the school curricula have been made for many reasons. The current times include busing, unemployment, mainstreaming, mass media, as well as a knowledge explosion. Thus, today's more varied curriculum prepares students with marketable communication abilities and possibly trade skills or preliminary learning opportunities leading to a profession.

Changes in the school curriculum must acknowledge the rapidly increasing wealth of knowledge and prepare the students for continuous learning. *Future Shock* and 1984 are here. Students must, as Alvin Toffler suggests, know the processes for learning rather than just remembering the content itself.[18] This suggests that students must be taught how to gain information from content materials, how to stay abreast of new information, and how to use knowledge for further learning. Quite possibly the curriculum of which Toffler wrote includes content reading instruction.

Much has been written about the relationship of reading to content teaching and the necessity for including reading in the secondary curriculum. Palmer

summarizes these ideas by giving four reasons for including reading in the secondary curriculum.[19]

1. Print is the dominant form of communication of ideas in the secondary
   school curriculum;
2. Content textbooks are too difficult for many students to comprehend yet
   they serve as the principle source of school learning;
3. Reading facilitates and reinforces other factors involved in learning; and
4. Reading is a unique mode of learning.

LAGNIAPPE

The percentage of students dropping out of school in the last decade has
declined from 8 to 2%. Since 1947 the percentage of youth enrolled in college has risen from 13 to 30, and the percentage of workers employed in
white collar jobs has risen from 36 to 50.

John R. Bormuth, *SLATE Newsletter* (August 1979).

Although content teachers would agree with these reasons, instruction in
many middle and secondary content classrooms continues to be dictated by the
textbook. The content of the curricula in many schools is the textbook. Because
many students cannot read the textbook and because the textbook represents
only one tool for learning content information, teachers and administrators must
consider the use of a variety of materials to assist students in learning concepts
identified as important in the curriculum. The school curriculum must be
designed so that content teachers can identify what the students are to learn in
the specific area, and then are allowed to use various materials to teach the
identified concepts. The use of a variety of materials does not mean that a textbook is not used. The textbook may well continue to serve as a guide for
instruction. Through the use of a variety of materials, however, the content
teacher can better meet the students' reading levels and skill needs. In addition,
the availability of different materials allows more opportunity for reteaching
some students while challenging the more advanced learners. Another advantage is that students learn to use different sources for obtaining information.
They become more independent learners and understand how content learning
involves more than a single textbook. Therefore, inherent in planning for reading instruction in the middle and secondary school curricula is the design of a
curriculum which considers the students' current and future needs in a rapidly
changing society.

If the middle and secondary school curricula are to prepare the current generation of students to deal with the unknown problems of tomorrow, the students must know how to learn from printed materials. This involves the inclusion of reading in the content classroom and requires that the curriculum
become more attuned to student needs. Flexibility will enhance content instruction by helping the student focus on how to learn content information, rather
than on the recall of factual textbook material.

As middle and secondary schools incorporate content reading into the classrooms, teachers and administrators must work as a team to develop an effective
curriculum. To develop a viable middle and secondary school reading program,
these seven items should be considered:

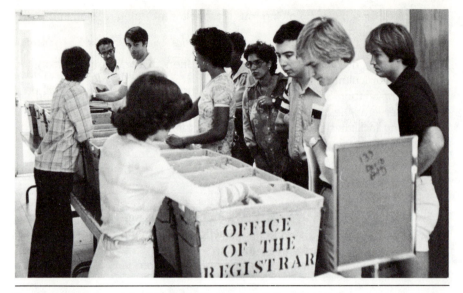

Fewer students drop out of school and more enroll in college today.

1. There should be evidence that all content teachers are teaching the reading skills which are unique to their particular areas.
2. Meaningful in-service should be provided for all faculty members to upgrade their reading instructional skills.
3. The secondary reading program that is established should be a logical part of a K−12 skills and competencies sequence that is applicable for the total school district.
4. All secondary reading programs should make instructional provisions for meeting the needs of students with widely varying reading abilities.
5. The costs of the program should be reasonable and defensible for the number of students who are served.
6. A well constructed reading program should receive both periodic as well as continuous evaluation to determine if the total offerings are producing desired results in terms of student reading achievement.
7. There should be ample evidence that there has been some type of community involvement in the construction, implementation, and evaluation of the reading program.[20]

Using these ideas as guides, schools can develop and evaluate their progress in including reading in the middle and secondary school curricula.

REFLECTION

Think about the curriculum in your high school or a school in which you have recently observed or taught. What was done to encourage flexibility in learning content materials? What was done to assist the students in learning to read content materials? List suggestions that you could give middle or secondary school principals to assist them in designing a curriculum which would facilitate content reading instruction.

STAFF RESPONSIBILITIES IN CONTENT READING

The successful implementation of a total school content reading program is heavily dependent upon the attitudes and cooperation of the staff. A crucial element is the administration in a particular school. Principals set the general tone for the school. Their receptiveness to the notion of content reading will go a long way toward ensuring the program's success. Principals must communicate to their teachers their desire for the successful integration of reading in the content areas. A positive tone indicates to the teachers that the administration not only favors the program, but will lend support to it. Administrative support persuades the teachers that the program will be given a reasonable opportunity to succeed.

Content teachers carry the major responsibility for day-to-day implementation of the content reading program. Content teachers must cooperate, coordinate, determine students' strengths and deficiencies, and initiate an appropriate instructional program designed to meet the needs of each student. In the final analysis, the success or failure of the content reading program lies with the content teacher.

Perhaps the most helpful member of the middle and secondary school team is the reading specialist. A competent, well-trained, experienced reading specialist is a welcome addition to any school and can be especially effective working with content teachers. The expertise of the reading specialist goes a long way toward assisting content teachers in developing and furthering their instructional programs. Staff development and coordinating reading activities in each content area and among all content areas are principal responsibilities of the reading specialist. Other responsibilities include assisting in the assessment of students' strengths and deficiencies, planning instructional activities, locating supplementary materials for use in the content classroom, and maintaining a close working relationship with each content teacher.

Another important member of the school's support personnel is the librarian. The librarian provides much-needed assistance in locating books and other reading material written on levels that afford all students an opportunity to read. Assistance in locating interesting material and instructing students in the appropriate use of study skills is a useful service rendered by the librarian. Competent librarians make the school library an enjoyable and interesting place to visit and encourage students to read. This greatly helps content instruction and enables students to obtain additional content-related materials to read.

Guidance counselors in middle and secondary schools also play an important role in assisting content teachers as they incorporate reading into their content instruction. While they do not necessarily deal with direct instruction in the content classroom, they serve to support the teacher by investigating personal problems of the students that may impede learning, promoting communication among the faculty regarding instructional needs of students, and assisting in arranging for and conducting parent-teacher or teacher-student conferences. This assistance helps to develop a more positive learning environment and often encourages the communication that is vital in a content reading program.

In order for a middle or secondary school to implement a total program whereby reading skills are taught in the content classroom, all personnel must assume their responsibilities. However, individual content teachers must realize that getting total school support and involvement in such an effort is slow.

The librarian is an important member of the school's support staff.

Therefore, one should not wait for all to accept their responsibilities. Individual teachers can incorporate content reading instruction in their classrooms—this helps the idea become contagious as others actually see changes in content learning. As more faculty become involved in adopting a content reading program, the staff will realize that each person has an important role that must be fulfilled if goals are to be achieved. The school curriculum will reflect the strengths and the weaknesses of the school staff and will only be as strong as the administration and faculty want it to be.

A MODEL FOR CONTENT READING INSTRUCTION

For many content teachers the ideas that have been presented to this point represent nothing new and different. Experienced teachers recognize the need for content reading instruction, and the problems inherent in reading content materials. The question that content teachers ask is what can be done to incorporate reading instruction into content teaching? This is not an easy question to answer because each content classroom represents a unique situation. However, the authors believe that by following a basic procedure in the content classroom the teacher and students can experience a greater feeling of success in content learning. Thus, the remainder of this book will present a step-by-step procedure that content teachers may follow in incorporating reading instruction into the content classroom. Within each step many options will be presented to allow teacher flexibility and to meet unique situations in classrooms at different levels. This model for content reading instruction is shown in Figure 1.2.

Step I involves the identification of the concepts that are to be taught in a lesson or unit. Concept identification is the responsibility of the content teacher so that the ideas students are expected to learn can be carried out. In *Step II*, the reading skills necessary in learning the concepts are selected. The purpose of this step is to specify which reading skills the student must know and use in reading the material.

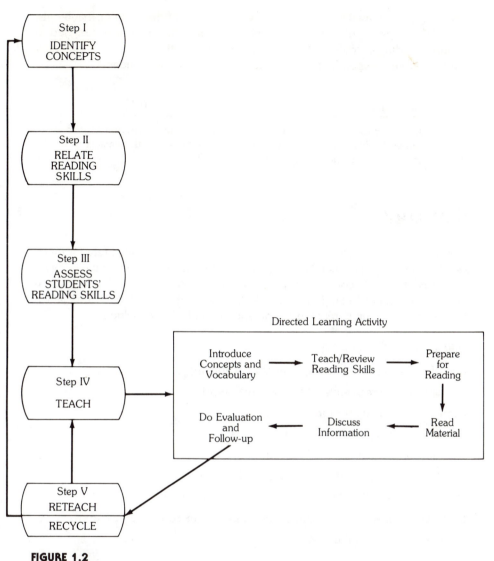

FIGURE 1.2

Model for Content Reading Instruction

Step III is the assessment stage. At this point the content teacher must determine if the students actually know the reading skills and can apply them to the content materials. In this step the teacher may use various assessment procedures ranging from observations to more complex inventories. Information obtained in this step will greatly assist the teacher as Step IV is begun. In *Step IV* the actual teaching begins, using a Directed Learning Activity format. Reading instruction and content teaching are integrated in order to increase content learning.

Step V is considered the recycle stage. At this time, reteaching of concepts not learned occurs, or, if all concepts are learned, the teacher begins again at Step I in presenting new information. This model for instruction is outlined in a structured manner for the content teacher who wishes to follow each step.

Other teachers may want to use initially only a few of the steps or maybe just some of the ideas provided in the text. Regardless, this model is designed to improve reading instruction through content teaching thereby developing better readers, more independent learners, and superior content students.

REFLECTION

Consider the five-step model for content reading instruction that is introduced in this chapter. Which steps do you think are the easiest to implement? Which are the most difficult? Why?

SUMMARY

The theory of reading in content areas has been discussed in literature for many years. However, only recently has the real importance of implementing this idea been recognized. As content teachers attempt to incorporate reading instruction into their content teaching, they should be aware of the various factors which influence the students' reading of content material. These include

Differencies in students' abilities;

Use of much technical and specialized vocabulary;

Knowledge of interpretive and critical reading skills;

Compact presentation of information;

Numerous concepts presented in materials;

Inclusion of a variety of reading sources;

Varied readability levels in the textbook;

Different organizational patterns in content materials;

Interrelationships of skills and concepts in different content areas; and

Application of all reading skills.

To further assist students in learning content information, the content curriculum must be reviewed and designed to include the necessary concepts rather than just information from the textbook. The content teacher is the principal ingredient in the curriculum—the key to implementing content reading in the classroom. Thus, emphasis should be placed on assisting content teachers in understanding how and why content reading is important for content learning.

In a content reading program, all school staff personnel have special responsibilities. The principal is the person who sets the tone for the program. Administrative leadership and support are crucial as teachers attempt to establish new instructional strategies. The content teacher is primarily responsible for providing content reading instruction with the reading teacher, librarian, and guidance counselor serving to support and assist as necessary.

To help the content teacher incorporate reading instruction into content teaching, a model for content reading instruction is outlined. This model includes five basic steps: concept identification, relating concepts and reading skills, assessment, instruction, and recycling. These steps form the five sections of this book.

FOR DISCUSSION

1. As a content teacher you are asked to incorporate reading instruction into your classes. What is your initial reaction? Why do you feel as you do?
2. According to the information provided in this chapter, why is content reading so important in the middle and secondary classroom?
3. Differentiate between content reading instruction and reading instruction provided in the elementary grades. How are these types of instruction interrelated?

OTHER SUGGESTED READINGS

Anders, Patricia L. "Dream of a Secondary Reading Program? People Are the Key." *Journal of Reading* 24 (January 1981):316–20.

Cassidy, Jack. "Good News About American Education." *The Reading Teacher* 32 (December 1978):294–96.

Cassidy, Jack. "Project C.A.R.E. (Content Area Reading Enrichment)." *Journal of Reading* 17 (December 1973):192–94.

Dillner, Martha H., and Olson, Joanne P. *Personalizing Reading Instruction in Middle, Junior, and Senior High Schools.* New York: Macmillan, 1977.

Dubbs, Mary Wray. "How Good were Readers in the Good Old Days? Replication of Two Studies." *The Reading Teacher* 32 (May 1979):933–39.

Dulin, Kenneth L. "Skill Training for All Secondary Teachers." *Journal of Reading* 15 (November 1971):109–14.

Dupuis, Mary M., and Askov, Eunice N. "Content Area Differences in Attitudes Toward Teaching Reading." *The High School Journal* 62 (November 1978):83–88.

Estes, Thomas H., and Vaughan, Joseph L. *Reading and Learning in the Content Classroom.* Boston: Allyn and Bacon, 1978.

Forgan, Harry W., and Mangrum, Charles T. *Teaching Content Area Reading Skills,* 2nd ed. Columbus, Ohio: Charles E. Merrill, 1981.

Herber, Harold H. *Teaching Reading in Content Areas,* 2nd ed. Englewood Cliffs, N.J.: Prentice-Hall, 1978.

Lamberg, Walter J. "Required Preparation in Reading for Secondary Teachers." *Reading Horizons* 18 (Summer 1978): 305–7.

Lamberg, Walter J., and Lamb, Charles E. *Reading Instruction in the Content Areas.* Chicago: Rand McNally, 1980.

Lipton, Jack P., and Liss, Jody A. "Attitudes of Content Area Teachers Towards Teaching Reading." *Reading Improvement* 15 (Winter 1978):294–300.

Rauch, Sidney J. "Administrators' Guidelines for More Effective Reading Programs." *Journal of Reading* 17 (January 1974):297–300.

Readence, John E.; Baldwin, R. Scott; and Dishner, Ernest K. "Establishing Content Reading Programs in Secondary Schools." *Journal of Reading* 23 (March 1980):522–26.

Rupley, William H. "ERIC-RCS Report: Content Reading in the Elementary Grades." *Language Arts* 52 (September 1975):802–7.

Smith, Carl B; Smith, Sharon L.; and Mikulecky, Larry. *Teaching Reading in Secondary School Content Subjects.* New York: Holt, Rinehart, and Winston, 1978.

Usova, George M. "Analysis of Attitudes Toward Reading Among Secondary Content-Area Teachers." *The Clearing House* 52 (September 1978):22–24.

Wolf, Ronald E. "Using Subject-Matter Areas ro Raise Reading Achievement Scores." *Reading Improvement* 15 (Winter 1978):242–45.

NOTES

1. See, for example, Roger Farr, Leo Fay, and Harold Negley, *Then and Now: Reading Achievement in Indiana (1944–45 and 1976)* (Bloomington, Ind.: School of Education, Indiana University, 1978); Education Commission of the States. *National Assessment of Educational Progress: A Project of the Education Commission of the States* (Washington, D.C.: National Center for Educational Statistics, 1977); Robert J. Tierney and Diane Lapp, eds. *National Assessment of Educational Progress in Reading* (Newark, Del.: International Reading Association, 1979); Paul Copperman, "The Achievement Decline of the 1970's," *Phi Delta Kappan* 60 (June 1979):736–39; Donald Fisher. *Functional Literacy and the Schools* (Washington, D.C.: National Institute of Education, 1978); John J. Micklos, Jr., "The Facts, Please, about Reading Achievement in American Schools," *Journal of Reading* 24 (October 1980):41–45.
2. Nila Banton Smith, *American Reading Instruction* (Newark, Del.: International Reading Association, 1965), pp. 288–89.
3. Nila Banton Smith, *American Reading Instruction,* p. 273.
4. A. Sterl Artley, "A Study of Certain Relationships Existing Between General Reading Comprehension and Reading Comprehension in a Specific Subject-Matter Area," *Journal of Educational Research* 37 (February 1944):464–73; George W. Norwell, "Wide Individual Reading Compared with the Traditional Plan of Studying Literature," *School Review* 49 (October 1941):603–13; James M. McCallister, "Determining the Types of Reading in Studying Content Subjects," *School Review* 40 (February 1932):115–23; Esther J. Swenson, "A Study of the Relationships Among Various Types of Reading Scores on General and Science Material," *Journal of Education Research* 36 (1942):81–90; W. E. Lessenger, "Reading Difficulties in Arithmetical Computations," *Journal of Educational Research* 11 (1925):287–91.
5. Nila Banton Smith, *American Reading Instruction,* pp. 298–318.
6. William S. Gray, "Looking Ahead in Reading," *Educational Digest* 26 (February 1961):26–28.
7. Ruth Strang, "Progress in the Teaching of Reading in High School and College," *The Reading Teacher* 16 (December 1962):173.
8. D. L. Burton, "Some Trends and Emphasis in High School Reading and Literature," in *Changing Concepts of Reading Instruction,* ed. J. A. Figurel (Newark, Del.: International Reading Association Conference Proceedings, 1961), pp. 265–69.
9. *Certification Requirements in Reading,* 3rd edition (Newark, Del.: International Reading Association, 1981).
10. Harold L. Herber, *Teaching Reading in the Content Areas* (Englewood Cliffs, N. J.: Prentice-Hall, 1970).
11. Edward G. Summers, "Information Characteristics of the *Journal of Reading* (1957–1977)," *Journal of Reading* 23 (October 1979):39–49.
12. James E. Jackson, "Reading in the Secondary School: A Survey of Teachers," *Journal of Reading* 23 (December 1979):232.
13. Robert Karlin, "What Does Research in Reading Reveal About Reading and the High School Student?" in *What We Know About High School Reading,* ed. M. Agnella Gunn (Urbana, Ill.: National Council of Teachers of English, 1969), pp. 19–28.

14. Joseph L. Vaughan, Jr., "A Scale to Measure Attitudes toward Teaching Reading in Content Classrooms," *Journal of Reading* 20 (April 1977):605–9.

15. William J. O'Rourke, "Research on the Attitude of Secondary Teachers Toward Teaching Reading in Content Classrooms," *Journal of Reading* 23 (January 1980):337–39.

16. A. Sterl Artley, "A Study of Certain Relationships Existing Between General Reading Comprehension and Reading Comprehension in a Specific Subject-Matter Area," pp. 464–73; George D. Spache, "Who is Responsible for Reading in the Content Fields?," *Toward Better Reading* (Champaign, Ill.: Garrard Publishing Company, 1963), pp. 273–97; Bernice E. Leary, "Meeting Specific Reading Problems in the Content Fields," in *Reading in the High School and College,* Forty-seventh Yearbook, National Society for the Study of Education, Part II (Chicago: University of Chicago Press, 1948), pp. 136–79; Russell J. Call and Neal A. Wiggins, "Reading and Mathematics," *Mathematics Teacher* 59 (February 1966):157.

17. Harry Singer and Dan Donlan, *Reading and Learning from Text* (Boston: Little, Brown, 1980), pp. 3–4.

18. Alvin Toffler, *Future Shock* (New York: Bantam, 1970).

19. William S. Palmer, "Toward a Realistic Rationale for Teaching Reading in Secondary School," *Journal of Reading* 22 (December 1978):236–39.

20. Donald C. Cushenberry, "Principles for Establishing Effective Secondary Reading Programs," *Reading Horizons* 19 (Summer 1979):320–23.

IDENTIFYING CONCEPTS

The first step in the model for content reading is a planning stage in which concepts are identified. Teachers first select the ideas that are most important in the unit of study. Teaching is then based on the identified concepts. Concept teaching encourages the teacher to specify what is to be learned rather than to rely only on the textbook. Using concepts as the basis for content teaching also encourages the use of materials at different reading levels and differentiation of learning activities based on the students' levels. Concept identification, therefore, is the beginning point in an instructional program that includes content reading.

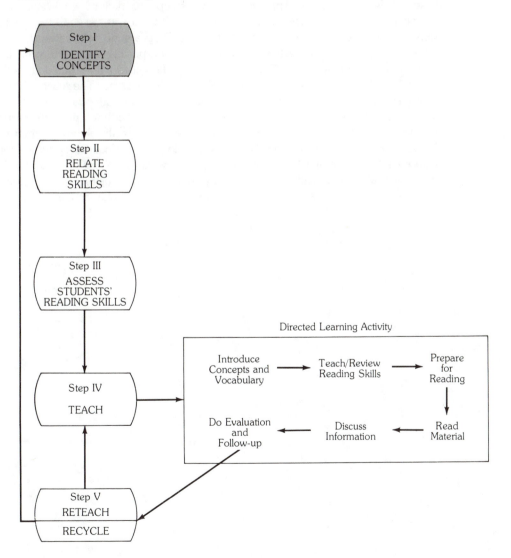

CHAPTER TWO

CONCEPT TEACHING IN CONTENT INSTRUCTION

A theory, an idea, a thought, a view or consideration, an abstraction, a concept—all c these words relate to concept teaching. A concept, as defined by Webster, is "ar abstract idea generalized from particular instances."[1] Concepts are goals that are formec from several pieces of interrelated information. They are not objectives, but are the foundation upon which objectives are based. Their purpose is to identify generalization or ideas that are to be taught. Content material is often filled with abstract ideas that ar so unrelated to students' experiences that learning is hindered. The teacher, therefore must first carefully analyze what is to be taught and then outline the concepts in some logical order. For example, a section of the social studies textbook presents informatior on different political systems. Rather than following the textbook, the content teacher should decide what concepts the students should learn about political systems. Using the textbook information, teacher knowledge, and other resources, the concepts for the uni can be specified. This outline then serves to guide content instruction. It also helps ir developing vocabulary and comprehension skills—two essential content reading skills.

STUDY QUESTIONS

1. What is concept teaching?
2. How does concept teaching differ from other instructional strategies?
3. Why is the identification of concepts important in content instruction?
4. How does the content teacher identify concepts?
5. How are concepts organized for instruction?

VOCABULARY

Concept development
Concept identification
Concepts

Concept teaching
Learning hierarchy
Prerequisite concepts

WHAT IS CONCEPT TEACHING?

The understanding of concepts begins early as children learn the names of objects and compare and contrast things that happen around them. This concept knowledge is basic to comprehending spoken or written language. Students come to school with an understanding of simple concepts, but as new information is introduced, new concepts must be taught. Concept learning for young children is a discovery process using information given by adults and relating it to their daily experiences. An example is that of the young child learning about dogs. A mother tried to teach her little boy the word *dog* by introducing him to a German shepherd named Kristy. The child patted the dog and the mother said *dog*, occasionally adding the name Kristy. Shortly, a poodle appeared whereupon the boy said, "Kristy." The child had confused two labels, a common misunderstanding in the early learning of basic concepts. This problem, however, is easily overcome by reteaching without adding other confusing labels. Nonetheless, concept development becomes more complex as children begin to compare and contrast information.

Again using the example, the boy learned to associate the word *dog* with a four-legged, furry animal. Then he saw a cat across the street. Here was another animal that met the criteria that the child had observed about dogs, so—he called it a dog. How confused young children must become when their understanding of a concept is corrected by giving it another name, in this case *cat*. Why is this animal a cat and not a dog? Through continuous experiences, children learn basic concepts and vocabulary as they associate names with objects and later compare information about abstract concepts or ideas. So, for young children, concept teaching is usually done through various experiences, some planned and others incidental. Children simply learn through experiences and the need to learn.

Concept teaching frequently changes when children enter school. As students, they are expected to learn specific information at definite times. Because all students have not learned the same concepts before coming to school, the teacher must include certain concepts that are prerequisite for learning other information. Elementary teachers do much concept teaching as students are learning to read, since this is essential for developing comprehension. For example, in order for primary grade students to be able to follow simple directions, they must learn concepts such as "draw a circle," "under the table," "mark the first box," and other directional ideas. As students progress, the concepts become more complex, with the ideas of sequence, time, space, and location (community, state, nation, and world) becoming crucial to the understanding of much elementary content information.

The difference in concept teaching before and after students enter school is that the concepts students learn in school are more abstract and are usually less meaningful to their immediate needs. Before entering school, students have no definite curriculum that their parents are expected to teach. Concepts are taught as needed to help understanding. Learning experiences are relevant to the child's immediate need for information. Many concepts taught in school are not given in a relevant manner. Therefore, students have difficulty in understanding and applying the information. A student quickly learns the concept of sales tax when he has saved to buy a radio, only to discover that he has only enough money for the radio and nothing for sales tax. This concept may take hours of

Students must understand a concept in terms of its characteristics.

class time for students to understand, unless they recognize the relationship to a present experience.

Concept teaching is defined as the identification of ideas essential to the understanding of content information and the provision of instruction to ensure the learning of the concept. For many years researchers in education and psychology have suggested the importance of identifying and teaching concepts in order to enhance learning. Bruner and his colleagues studied concept learning in terms of how individuals discovered concepts.[2] Piaget's works have suggested the notion of spontaneous concepts or that concepts are learned from external sources with the child's developmental stages affecting the learning of school concepts.[3] Smith suggests that learning involves not only receiving information from print but also using information that is already in the brain.[4] This is called nonvisual information and is important to understanding content materials. The comprehension of subject matter information not only requires the decoding of the printed symbols and the processing of the visual information, but students must also have a background of understanding or concept knowledge.

Gagné stresses the importance of learning concepts as a means of learning how to group information or ideas in order to develop intellectual skills that will assist in future learning.[5] Gagné's work in concept learning suggests that in the teaching of concepts several components should be considered.

1. *Teach the concept.* Students must know more than the definition of a word. They must understand the concept in terms of its characteristics, positive and negative aspects of the concept; in essence to know a concept suggests that the student can demonstrate the meaning rather than just verbalizing

information. In order for students to reach this level of understanding, teachers must provide, appropriate instruction.

2. *Concepts may be combined to form rules for problem solving.* As students learn different concepts, they learn also that some concepts can be combined to form rules. These rules do not have to be memorized as verbal statements; however, the student should be able to use the rule to assist in problem solving. For example, in mathematics, students learn the concepts of rectangle, width, and height. By understanding these concepts the student then understands the rule of multiplying width times height to find the area of a rectangle. This rule then can be used for problem-solving.

3. *Concept teaching must consider learning hierarchies.* All learning is based on the understanding of some prerequisite knowledge. In teaching, one must determine what knowledge is prerequisite to understanding the concept which is being taught. If, for example, a social studies teacher wanted the students to understand certain concepts about the causes of World War II, the teacher must be sure that the students have assimilated the prerequisite concepts such as varying philosophies of different governments, worldwide economic instability, territorial aspirations of various countries, and failure of negotiating bodies to achieve peace. Gagné suggests that teachers develop a learning hierarchy in order to plan an appropriate sequence of instruction.[6]

Further application of the importance of concept teaching in content areas was shown by Shavelson.[7] This research indicated, through the use of concept association tasks, that physics students who acquire concepts early in instruction consolidate more of the learning and achieve greater success in problem solving. Herber found that when students were given instruction on the development and use of concepts in physics, they improved significantly in their achievement in the subject.[8] In a study using a traditional lecture procedure and a technique emphasizing reading and concept understanding for a college calculus class, Lovelace and McKnight found that concept knowledge enhanced performance on the final exam, indicating a positive impact on long-term problem-solving skills.[9]

So, while the idea of concept teaching is not new in education and the value of such teaching consistently indicates improved learning of content materials, much content instruction continues to rely exclusively on the textbook. Because student needs and experiences vary so dramatically in each content classroom, concept teaching emphasizes the use of many techniques designed to promote the understanding of content information.

IDENTIFYING CONCEPTS FOR CONTENT READING INSTRUCTION

As teachers consider using concept teaching to enhance learning in their classes, the first concern is that of how to identify necessary concepts. Teachers must recognize that concepts may be identified at different levels. General concepts may be selected for an entire unit of study with specific concepts identified for daily lessons. Thus, the teacher should note the level of the identified concept—general or specific.

This section considers several ideas to help with concept identification. Because content textbooks are used in most middle and secondary schools, the first part of this discussion presents suggestions for identifying concepts from a textbook. The latter part offers ideas concerning concept identification independent of the text. The two procedures for identifying the concepts are basically the same with the major difference being that in the latter, teachers are deciding what is to be taught rather than following the textbook. Remember that concepts are generalized ideas, and in order for teachers to help students understand content materials, these generalized ideas must first be identified and organized before planning appropriate instruction.

In using a content textbook, teachers are usually provided with a teacher's guide that outlines the goals or objectives for a chapter as well as terms used and possible teaching strategies. Many of the newer texts also identify concepts, thus saving teacher time. For example, in a unit on plants for students in the sixth level of the textbook, the teacher's guide identifies five concepts that should be learned at various stages in the lesson. This example is provided in Table 2.1.

TABLE 2.1

Concept Identification in Textbooks: The World of Plants

Objectives	Conceptual Content
At the end of this cluster, the student should be able to 1. Identify some of the effects of humans on plant populations such as ginkgoes. 2. Describe some of the habitats of ferns.	a. Some plant populations are very successful, as evidenced by their survival for millions of years. b. The ginkgo is considered a successful population because it has survived for a long time and has adapted to a polluted environment. c. Ancient ferns slowly changed into what we now know as coal. d. Ferns are plants with unique parts that can be readily identified. e. Ferns grow in sequential stages.

Adapted from *Houghton Mifflin Science*, Teacher's Edition, Level 6 (Boston: Houghton Mifflin, 1979), pp. T106–T107.

In looking at the information in Table 2.1, teachers should carefully note the concepts that are suggested and determine if the students have the necessary prerequisite concepts. For these newly identified concepts to be learned, the students must understand other concepts such as

The world has changed over the years.
A polluted environment causes changes in living things.

Additionally, the teacher may need to teach other terms to clarify the concepts. The decisions about what concepts and terms need to be identified for preteaching purposes can only be decided by the teacher, as this decision must be based on the individual student and class needs. The objectives and con-

Teachers must identify appropriate concepts and correctly sequence them before teaching.

cepts in a teacher's guide should be used only as one source, possibly a beginning point, for the planning of content instruction.

When concepts are already identified within the textbook, the teacher must carefully consider them in light of the three ideas suggested by Gagné. In addition to the basic concept, teachers should determine if any concepts may be combined to form rules. Considerations should also be given to the learning hierarchy. Thus, even with concepts identified in the text, teachers are responsible for studying the concepts to ensure that those identified are appropriate for the emphasis of the class and the needs of the students, and that they are correctly sequenced for better understanding.

While it has been noted that some teachers' guides identify concepts, many others, especially at the secondary level, do not specifically outline the concepts to be taught in a chapter or unit. These texts usually provide the teacher with objectives, lesson summaries, questions, and student activities but no specific concepts. With guides of this type teachers must identify the concepts from careful study of the material, their background knowledge, as well as ideas from other sources in order to give the preteaching so essential to student success with content materials.

In identifying concepts from such a textbook, content teachers should first determine the lesson's objectives and then specify the concepts or generalized ideas needed to achieve the objectives. For example, in a literature class the content teacher sets up the following objective and concepts for a part of a chapter on short stories:

Objective: The students will identify the characteristics of a short story.

Concepts:
Short stories contain a single plot that is developed quickly through a rising action, climax, and resolution.

The number of characters in a short story is small, and all characters are involved in the major plot.

The action occurs in one basic setting.

Using the short stories and content in the textbook, the teacher then assists the students in understanding these generalizations by applying them to the information read.

Following a similar procedure, content teachers may decide to determine topics and concepts without relying on a textbook. Tenth grade world history teachers, for example, in one school or school system may get together to discuss the concepts that are to be taught during the term. As noted earlier, the identification of concepts by teachers allows the teacher to direct the instructional program rather than the textbook. By identifying and sequencing these concepts, the curriculum for a course is outlined. The teachers can then identify many materials such as library books, the textbook, reference materials, pamphlets and brochures, films, and resource persons to be used to teach the concepts.

LAGNIAPPE

"**Teacher knowledge is the key to it all. Materials, or texts, by definition, aim at a mythical average child who is probably unlike few if any real children.**

Tests, likewise, fail to represent the reality of a child's reading ability. If anything they are even farther away from reality than are texts, simply because they are forced, by definition, to sample even smaller chunks of reality for measurement purposes. This is bad enough, but much current testing is so far off base that the results are at best, counterproductive.

This leaves us, then, with what a teacher knows as the key to good instruction."

Roger W. Shuy, "What the Teacher Knows is More Important Than Text or Test." *Language Arts* (November–December 1981): 928.

This use of various materials assists content teaching in several ways. First, teaching becomes more creative and learning becomes more exciting when there is variety. Textbooks tend to be boring and cause teachers to get into a rut of assigning chapters and questions. By identifying concepts and using a unit approach to content instruction, the teacher exposes students to numerous materials as well as resources and encourages the learning of ideas rather than the study of a single textbook. Second, the different reading levels of students can be dealt with by assigning materials appropriate for the students' reading levels. By using a variety of materials written at different levels, all students learn the identified concepts. Finally, content teaching becomes student oriented rather than textbook oriented. In order for students to learn content information and to learn "how to learn" on their own, teachers must teach them content information in a meaningful way. By identifying the concepts and helping students study various related materials and ideas, the teacher is not only teaching content, but also showing students that they can learn and continue to learn more ideas on their own.

Regardless of the sources teachers use for specifying concepts, the same basic procedure should be followed. These procedures are summarized in Figure 2.1 and discussed on pages 34–36.

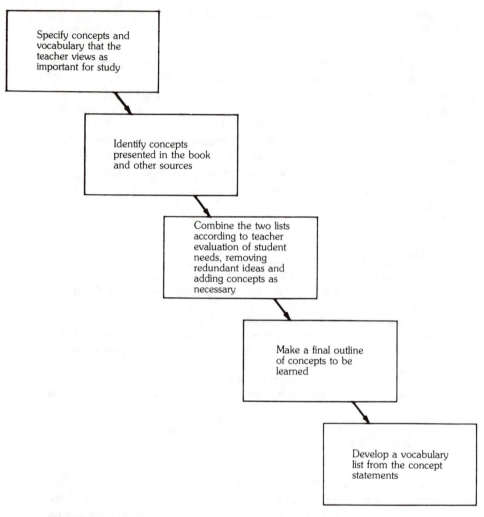

FIGURE 2.1

Considerations for Identifying Concepts

Make a list of what the students should know when they finish studying the chapter in the text or in the unit. This list may consist of terms, facts, and generalizations. The list will be longer if an entire unit is considered, but regardless of the length, this is the time that the teachers should identify everything they want the students to understand—not just the concepts or the information from the book.

Review the information in the teacher's guide about the material to be taught. By studying the objectives and summaries in the text, the teacher can determine the emphasis and scope of the information. Make a list of the information which seems to be most important.

Review the lists to see which ideas may be redundant or should be merged with other statements. Often terms will be included in a generalized statement or facts may be classified within a generalization. Be cautious. Essential elements should not be discarded, but avoid redundancy. For example, in an English unit on complex sentences the following lists of concepts, terms, ideas, or generalizations may be identified as necessary for understanding the content:

Information identified by the teacher
Complex sentence
Independent clause
Dependent clause
A complex sentence has one independent clause and one or more dependent clauses.
A complex sentence uses a comma to set off the clauses that interrupt the flow of the sentence.
There are different types of clauses used in forming a complex sentence.
Complex sentences often add interest in written communication.
Certain words are indicators of the different types of clauses.
Compound sentences can be reworded to become complex sentences.

Information identified in the textbook
Complex sentence
Adjective clause
Adverb clause
Noun clause
Subordinate conjunction
Relative pronoun
Use of an adjective clause may be more effective than a compound sentence.
A clause differs from a phrase in that a clause has a subject and a predicate and the phrase has neither.
A complex sentence differs from a compound sentence in that a compound sentence has two independent clauses.
A subordinate conjunction connects a dependent clause with an independent clause.
An adjective clause, an adverb clause, or a noun clause may be used to form a complex sentence.
Prepositional phrase
Participial phrase
Gerund phrase
Infinitive phrase

To eliminate the redundancy, a single list may include:

> Complex sentence
> Independent clause
> Dependent clause
> Adjective clause
> Adverb clause
> Noun clause
> A complex sentence has one independent clause and one or more dependent clauses.
> A complex sentence uses a comma to set off the clauses.

An adjective clause, an adverb clause, or a noun clause may be
used to form a complex sentence.
A clause differs from a phrase.
Writing can be made more interesting through the use of clauses.

Identify the concepts and write them out to serve as a guide for teaching.
Remember, a concept is an abstract idea generalized from several pieces of
related specific information. A concept is a theory, an idea, a view about facts—
a goal; it is not an objective. Concepts are necessary in order to specify the generalizations or ideas that are to be taught. Some teachers use another step by
detailing the facts that are needed to develop an understanding of the concept.
This is helpful, especially when many sources other than the textbook are used.
To look again at the example for the unit in English, the following concepts can
be identified:

A complex sentence has one independent clause and one or more
dependent clauses.
A complex sentence uses commas to set off the clauses that interrupt
the flow of the sentence.
An adjective clause, an adverb clause, or a noun clause may be used to
form a complex sentence.
A clause differs from a phrase in that a clause has a subject and a predicate, and the phrase has neither.
Clauses may be used to make writing more varied and interesting.

Make a vocabulary list. Terms that are basic to the reading of materials should
be noted from the final concept statements. This is the time to pull the key terms
together into a special list. These words should be taught to help students
understand the concepts before reading the materials. More ideas on identifying
vocabulary are given in Chapter 5.

REFLECTION

Look at the teacher's guide for an older content textbook and a more
recent edition. Does either identify the concepts to be taught? If not, how
could you use the information that is given to identify the concepts? Then
select a chapter in a content textbook that does not have the concepts
identified. Review the chapter and identify four concepts that you should
teach.

As teachers look at this process for identifying concepts, many recognize that
this is usually what they do mentally as they prepare for instruction. They realize
how concept identification benefits instruction. Others may react negatively,
feeling that additional time-consuming paper work is created, and that as a content teacher they already know what is to be taught. There is virtually no dis-
agreement that content teachers know what they want to teach, and know it so
well that they usually do not need to use the text. The problem is that students
are not on the same knowledge level as teachers, and therefore they must be
prepared to learn the information. Concept identification is a plan to help teachers organize instruction. By specifying concepts, teachers can decide how best

to use the text and what prerequisite concepts must be taught to build a foundation for understanding the new information. By organizing in this manner, time is often saved in instruction and student learning is increased.

Initially, this discussion on identifying concepts may appear to have little to do with teaching reading in the content areas. However, in order to incorporate reading into content teaching, we believe the planning idea to be the crucial first step. This is a time to organize the ideas that are to be taught and to consider the experiences and needs of the students for whom the instruction is being planned. Often, as teachers consider the concepts they hope to teach, they will be able to predict areas in which students will encounter difficulties with learning. Steps can then be taken to preteach ideas that help students become more successful learners. Is this the way to teach reading? Definitely. By teaching students how to understand information, acquire vocabulary and knowledge, and to provide ideas of what they are expected to learn, these students will become not only better readers but also more enthusiastic learners of content information.

REFLECTION

Think about your many experiences in learning content information. Were you ever taught the concepts before you were asked to read the materials? How did it help you (or would it have) to understand what you read?

SUMMARY

The necessity for identifying concepts prior to instruction is the focus of this chapter. Emphasis is placed on the need for concept teaching and ways of identifying concepts.

Concept teaching begins as parents teach their children about the world around them. This type of concept teaching does not follow a set plan and evolves as the child discovers new objects or ideas. However, when students enter school, teachers are responsible for teaching them specific information. In order for the students to learn, they must not only understand the prerequisite concepts, but they must also receive instruction relating to the concepts.

Teachers must give careful consideration to what is taught in the content classroom. Because students have such diverse backgrounds, it is necessary to determine before beginning a content lesson what the students need to learn about the topic and what they know that will help in understanding the information. Concepts must be identified and teaching strategies determined prior to the start of a lesson, chapter, or unit. This is one aspect of organizing for content instruction. With the identification and teaching of concepts, students' understanding of content materials is greatly helped.

Researchers in education and psychology have long noted the importance of concept teaching. It is now recognized as the responsibility of the content teacher to develop those concepts for reading content materials. Thus, the identification of concepts to be taught is the first step in incorporating reading instruction into content teaching.

FOR DISCUSSION

1. Compare concept teaching in a middle or secondary content classroom with the teaching of content information using only a textbook. What do you see as the strengths and weaknesses of each?
2. Identify the steps that a content teacher may follow to select concepts in a content area. Discuss what should be done in each step.
3. Why must concepts be organized for instruction? How might the concepts be organized?

OTHER SUGGESTED READINGS

Arnold, Martha Thompson. "Teaching Theme, Thesis, Topic Sentences, and Clinchers as Related Concepts." *Journal of Reading* 24 (February 1981):373–76.

Eggen, Paul D.; Kauchak, Donald P.; and Harder, Robert J. *Strategies for Teachers.* Englewood Cliffs, N.J.: Prentice-Hall, 1979.

Eggen, Paul D.; Kauchak, Donald P.; and Kirk, Sandra. "The Effect of Hierarchical Cues on the Learning of Concepts from Prose Materials." *The Journal of Experimental Education* 46 (Summer 1978):7–11.

Gagné, Ellen D., and Memory, David. "Instructional Events and Comprehension: Generalization Across Passages." *Journal of Reading Behavior* 10 (Winter 1978):321–35.

Henry, George H. *Teaching Reading as Concept Development.* Newark, Del.: International Reading Association, 1974.

Macklin, Michael D. "Content Area Reading is a Process for Finding Personal Meaning." *Journal of Reading* 22 (January 1979):212–15.

Pella, Milton O. "Concept Learning in Science," *The Science Teacher* 33 (December 1976):31–34.

Vaughan, Joseph L.; Estes, Thomas H.; and Curtis, Sperry L., "Developing Conceptual Awareness." *Language Arts* 52 (November–December 1975):1141–44.

NOTES

1. *Webster's New Collegiate Dictionary* (Springfield, Mass.: G. & C. Merriam, 1981), p. 231.
2. Jerome S. Bruner, J. J. Goodnow, and G. A. Austin, *A Study of Thinking* (New York: Wiley, 1956).
3. Jean Piaget, *Science of Education and the Psychology of the Child* (New York: Viking, 1971).
4. Frank Smith, *Understanding Reading*, 2nd ed. (New York: Holt, Rinehart, and Winston, 1978), pp. 4–5.
5. Robert M. Gagné, *The Conditions of Learning*, 3rd ed. (New York: Holt, Rinehart, and Winston, 1977); Robert M. Gagné and Leslie J. Briggs, *Principles of Instructional Design*, 2nd ed. (New York: Holt, Rinehart and Winston, 1979).
6. Benjamin B. Lahey and Martha S. Johnson, *Psychology and Instruction* (Glenview, Ill.: Scott, Foresman, 1978), pp. 92–93.
7. R. J. Shavelson, "Learning from Physics Instruction," *Journal of Research in Science Teaching* 10 (1973): 101–11.

8. Harold L. Herber, "Teaching Reading and Physics Simultaneously," in *Improvements of Reading Through Classroom Practice* (Newark, Del.: International Reading Association, 1964).
9. Terry L. Lovelace and Conrad K. McKnight, "The Effects of Reading Instruction on Calculus Students' Problem Solving," *Journal of Reading* 23 (January 1980): 305–8.

RELATING CONCEPTS TO READING SKILLS

The learning of concepts through content instruction is dependent on the students' skill in reading. Content learning requires the application of many different reading skills. Although students are taught these skills in the elementary grades, they often have difficulty in transferring their knowledge to content materials. Therefore, content teachers must be aware of the different reading skills in order to help students use them in content learning. The goal is to teach so that students understand the concepts and enjoy learning. Incorporating reading skills instruction into teaching greatly enhances reaching that goal.

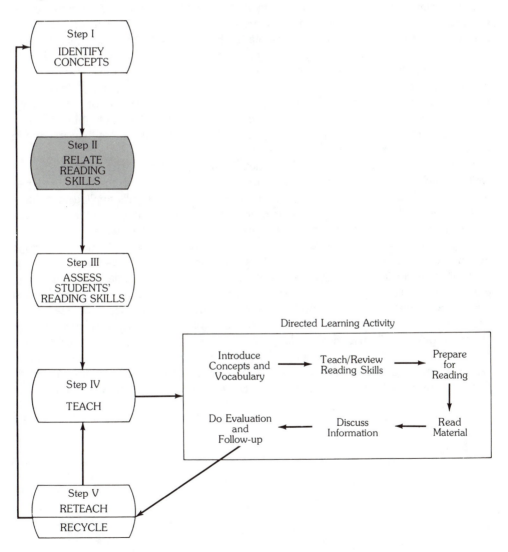

CHAPTER THREE

READING SKILLS: WHAT AND WHY?

"Me—teach reading? Never. I'm a math teacher. That's not my job." These comments and others are heard as the idea of reading in the content areas is discussed in the teachers' lounge, at faculty meetings, and in university classes. Although such complaints are common, more content teachers now recognize that theirs is the responsibility for teaching content reading or developing reading skills needed for content learning.

In exploring the ways that reading instruction is incorporated into the content areas, one essential element relates to the application of reading skills. Reading skills are as much a part of the teaching of reading as addition is to the teaching of mathematics. Knowledge of the reading skills gives students the key to learning content information. Failure of students to apply their reading skills effectively results in less than maximum performance and creates mounting frustration.

Elementary teachers spend much of their instructional time in teaching reading as well as emphasizing the development of specific reading skills, with the basal reader as the primary material used. Only occasionally are the reading skills applied to content material, either through a story in the reader or in the elementary content lessons. As a result, many students demonstrate a knowledge of reading skills when working with story type information in the basal reader, but are often unable to apply their knowledge in reading complex content materials. This problem becomes worse when students attempt to understand the advanced content material in the middle and high school grades. Therefore, helping students apply reading skills to all types of materials must become an integral part of content instruction. In order for this to occur, content teachers should incorporate reading skill development into their content instruction. This chapter provides a discussion of reading instruction and the various reading skills helpful to teachers. The major skill areas are divided within the chapter. Word identification skills, including vocabulary development and word analysis procedures, are in Part A. Comprehension skills are presented in Part B, with study skills discussed in Part C.

STUDY QUESTIONS

1. What is reading instruction and how does it relate to reading skills?
2. What are the reading skill areas?
3. How do these skills relate to the different content areas?
4. How do concepts and reading skills fit together?

VOCABULARY

Cognates
Comprehension
Contextual analysis
Critical reading skills
Interpretive comprehension
Literal comprehension
Organizational patterns
Organizational skills

Reading instruction
Reading skills
Reference skills
Sight words
Specialized study skills
Study skills
Structural analysis skills
Word identification skills

THE RELATIONSHIP OF READING INSTRUCTION TO SKILL DEVELOPMENT

The reading act involves essentially a series of complex thought processes through which a person interprets written or printed symbols as meaningful sounds, and comprehends these sounds as thought units in order to understand the message being presented. Therefore, *reading may be defined as an active process in which meaning is conveyed from one person to another using graphic symbols*. Reading instruction includes the actual teaching of how these symbols are decoded and comprehended. Specific instructional procedures for use in content reading are discussed in Chapter 5. Reading skills are the foundations on which much reading instruction is based, and involve learning procedures or strategies necessary for understanding the meaning of printed symbols.

REFLECTION

"Every teacher is a teacher of reading" is a common cliché. As a content teacher, what is your perception of reading and your role as a teacher of reading?

Content reading instruction incorporates teaching concepts and vocabulary, and using materials appropriate to the students' reading levels along with the development of necessary reading skills. Thus, reading skills represent one part of content reading instruction; however, for students who cannot apply these skills, it is a major part that may be overlooked by an unknowing content teacher. In content reading instruction, teachers should recognize that many skills are needed as students try to learn content information. These skills can be grouped according to three main categories: *word identification, comprehension*, and *study skills*. Word identification skills must be applied to help students recognize content words. More importantly, students must be taught how to understand printed information by applying appropriate comprehension skills. As students are expected to study their text as well as other related materials, content reading instruction should include the teaching or review of necessary study skills.

Each of these skill areas encompasses many specific subskills that are introduced to students at various points in their learning experiences. These skill areas and specific subskills are discussed in the following sections, with emphasis on those skills that are most useful in content instruction. Content teachers should note that all of the skill areas are interrelated and overlap in the instructional process, although they are separated in this chapter for discussion purposes.

This interrelated development of skills is outlined in Figure 3.1. Preschool experiences and prereading skills form the basis for the development of other reading skills. With instruction in the primary grades, students develop certain prereading skills, such as auditory and visual discrimination and listening comprehension, that build readiness for learning word identification and comprehension skills. As students begin to recognize words, reading comprehension becomes involved so that students learn to associate meanings with words they recognize, and can likewise comprehend sentences and paragraphs that they read. As students read various materials, study skills are taught to help them use books and other materials to locate information. Thus, when all of the reading

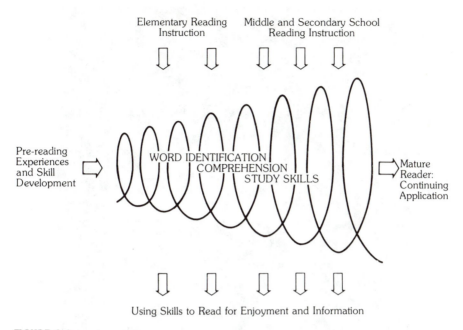

Elementary Reading Instruction   Middle and Secondary School Reading Instruction

Pre-reading
Experiences
and Skill
Development

WORD IDENTIFICATION
COMPREHENSION
STUDY SKILLS

Mature
Reader:
Continuing
Application

Using Skills to Read for Enjoyment and Information

FIGURE 3.1

Interrelationships in Reading Skill Development

skills are taught and students learn to apply them in different situations, the result is mature readers who continue to read for content as well as for enjoyment.

Applying students' reading skills is an essential part of reading instruction, for without it, many students would not understand why this ability is so important in their daily lives. Content reading is a vital component of reading instruction, and reading for information is a fundamental part of classroom learning.

Moreover, the content classroom can assist in another goal of reading instruction—reading for enjoyment. As students become familiar with reading skills and understand how these skills are used in content learning, new interests develop. Books and articles about different countries, science fiction, building additions to a house, or the use of the metric system become more than reading content materials or teacher assignments, they become new interests that can be explored through print. Students then begin to use their reading skills to fill leisure hours. They become self-motivated to read, and their attitudes toward learning are improved tremendously.

Thus, reading instruction is more than teaching reading skills at the elementary school level. Reading instruction involves this basic skill plus the application of skills in content learning and recreational reading. Reading instruction only begins in the elementary grades. Its success or failure depends on its continuation at the middle and secondary levels, for it is here that students either learn how to apply their previous knowledge or begin to forget it. Without continued reading instruction, students may become frustrated with content learning and lose interest. Other students may make the transfer of reading skills to the content classroom on their own, but become bored with the instruction because they are not challenged to use higher level skills. To overcome these possibili-

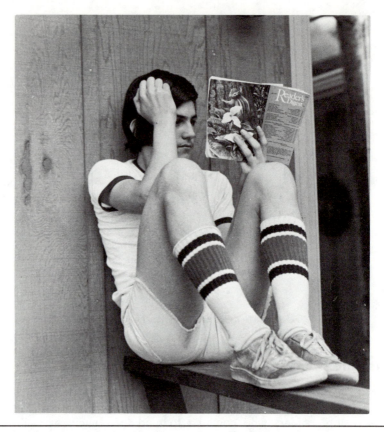

As students' reading skills develop, they read more in their leisure time.

ties, teachers must include skill development as part of their content reading instruction as one way to help maintain interest in content learning.

LAGNIAPPE

Many studies indicate that unless content teachers involve themselves in developing students' reading skills, the students will be robbed of both the opportunity to reach their potential in learning the content information as well as a chance to become active participants in the ongoing learning process.

THE READING SKILL AREAS

As previously defined, reading skills are the foundation on which reading instruction is based, and involve the learning of strategies necessary for identifying and understanding printed symbols.

To better understand these skills, the following pages contain a discussion of word identification, comprehension, and study skills. Contained in each are specific skills that are necessary for satisfactory student performance. Table 3.1 (pp. 47–49) shows the various skills as related to each content area. This list may not represent all skills needed, but the most common ones are included.

TABLE 3.1

Summary Chart of Reading Skills for Various Content Areas

Skill	Math	Science	Social Studies	English	Business Education	Vocational Education	Physical Education	Health	Art	Music	Foreign Language
Word Identification											
Structural analysis	X	X	X	X	X	X		X	X		X
Contextual analysis	X	X	X	X	X	X	X	X	X	X	X
Symbols, abbreviations, etc.	X	X	X	X	X	X	X			X	
Cognates											X
Sight words	X	X	X	X	X	X	X	X	X	X	X
Comprehension											
Details	X	X	X	X	X	X	X	X	X	X	X
Following directions	X	X	X	X	X	X	X	X	X	X	X
Contrast/comparisons	X	X	X	X	X	X	X	X	X	X	X
Reading for a purpose	X	X	X	X	X	X	X	X	X	X	X
Paraphrasing	X	X		X		X					
Interpreting symbols	X	X	X	X	X	X				X	
Sequence	X	X	X	X	X	X	X		X	X	X
Cause/effect relationships	X	X	X	X	X	X		X	X		X
Main idea	X	X	X	X	X	X	X	X	X	X	X

TABLE 3.1 (continued)

Skill	Math	Science	Social Studies	English	Business Education	Vocational Education	Physical Education	Health	Art	Music	Foreign Language
Character traits and actions			X	X							X
Mood				X						X	X
Predicting outcomes	X	X	X	X		X					X
Drawing conclusions	X	X	X	X		X		X	X	X	X
Perceiving relationships	X	X	X	X		X	X	X	X	X	X
Summarizing information	X	X	X	X		X	X	X	X	X	X
Synthesizing information	X	X									
Generalizations		X	X	X		X		X	X	X	X
Figurative language				X						X	X
Problem-solving	X	X	X	X		X			X		X
Author reliability	X	X	X	X	X	X	X	X	X	X	X
Propaganda			X	X							X
Relevant and irrelevant information	X	X	X	X	X	X	X	X	X	X	X
Fact/opinion			X	X				X			X
Fallacies in reasoning	X	X	X	X	X	X	X	X	X	X	X

48

TABLE 3.1 (continued)

Skill	Math	Science	Social Studies	English	Business Education	Vocational Education	Physical Education	Health	Art	Music	Foreign Language
Study Skills											
Parts of the book	X	X	X	X	X	X	X	X	X	X	X
Maps, tables, charts, etc.	X	X	X	X	X	X	X	X	X	X	
Skimming/scanning	X	X	X	X	X	X		X	X		X
Reading rate	X	X	X	X	X	X	X	X	X	X	X
Study techniques	X	X	X	X	X	X	X	X	X	X	X
Reference materials	X	X	X	X	X	X	X	X	X	X	X
Outlining		X	X	X							
Underlining	X	X	X	X	X	X	X	X	X	X	X
Note-taking	X	X	X	X	X	X	X	X	X	X	X
Test-taking	X	X	X	X	X	X	X	X	X	X	X

WORD IDENTIFICATION

Word identification skills help readers recognize words and comprehend their meanings. One word identification skill is that of recognizing *sight words*. These are words that a reader recognizes automatically without any phonic, structural or contextual analysis. Sight word recognition also is used in learning technical words—students recognize and pronounce them automatically. When teaching sight words, content teachers should introduce the words in the context of a sentence to help associate the correct meaning with the word. Here is an aid that may be used to reinforce learning.

EXAMPLE

Recognizing Sight Words

Provide students with a word search puzzle containing terms related to their unit of study. Ask that the word in each line be circled.

1.	b	f	r	a	c	t	i	o	n	m	s	t
2.	s	a	h	f	o	u	r	t	h	v	l	e
3.	d	m	r	o	i	c	l	o	h	a	l	f
4.	l	r	a	n	s	n	i	t	h	i	r	d
5.	s	i	x	t	h	g	o	g	a	s	u	h
6.	p	t	o	n	u	m	e	r	a	t	o	r
7.	m	d	e	n	o	m	i	n	a	t	o	r

These hints should help you find the words:

1. A number that compares part of a set with the whole set _ _ _ _ _ _ _ _

2. $\frac{1}{4}$ = "one _ _ _ _ _ _."

3. One part of two parts equals one _ _ _ _ _ .

4. ⊘ = ⦂ = one _ _ _ _ _ _ .

5. ⊞ = ⦂⦂⦂⦂ = one _ _ _ _ _ _ .

6. $\frac{5}{12}$ is called the _ _ _ _ _ _ _ _ _.

7. $\frac{4}{11}$ is called the _ _ _ _ _ _ _ _ _ _ _.

From Sharon Kossack, "Aids for Teaching Mathematics Vocabulary," *The Reading Clinic* (November 1975): 7.

In learning a foreign language, word identification comes first. Once students have a basic sight word knowledge and an understanding of the syntax used in the new language, other word recognition strategies may be used.

Another type of word identification skill involves using a decoding procedure, whereby the word is broken into sound-symbol correspondence. This procedure is called *phonics*. While the teaching of word identification skills through phonic analysis is relatively popular in the elementary grades, Boyd found that even though students experienced growth in phonics skills at the second and third grade levels, their development at the higher grades was slower.[1] Content teachers should note that students at the upper levels not only learn phonics at a slower rate, but they seem to lose some phonics skills that were previously learned.[2] Thus, the evidence shows that content teachers should not be concerned with phonics instruction but should rely instead on other types of word identification skills to help students learn new vocabulary words.

Two other types of word identification skills that are most important to content teachers are *structural analysis* and *contextual analysis skills*. Structural analysis includes decoding plural forms, analyzing words with prefixes and suffixes, and using syllabication generalizations. Structural analysis techniques of looking at letter clusters and parts of words appear to be the primary method of word recognition for older students.[3] Research findings suggest that as students get older, they rely more heavily on structural analysis rather than phonics because it is a faster reading technique. However, because a few older students may continue to analyze new words by sounding out individual letters rather than word parts, content teachers must help them ease the transition to structural analysis by showing them how. For example, in introducing a word like *hemisphere,* the teacher should give the prefix "hemi" and the base word "sphere," giving pronunciations and meanings of both. Thus, the structure of the word is shown, as is its use in determining its meaning and possibly the meaning of other words with the same prefix or root. A list of the more common prefixes and suffixes is shown in Table 3.2 (p. 52).

Analyzing words according to their prefixes and suffixes can be used in identifying many technical words in content reading. By dividing the words into prefixes or suffixes plus a root word, students are often able to recognize the word and develop a strategy for use in pronouncing other words as they read, should clues be needed to aid their memory. Additionally, these structural analysis skills help students in determining the meaning of the words, if the meanings of the parts are taught. Technical terms such as *microorganism, epicenter, altimeter, iconoscope, phosphorescence,* and *antibiotics* are found in science reading, and can be more easily pronounced and defined using structural analysis skills. For example, "iconoscope" is composed of the prefix "icon" meaning an image and "scope" meaning to see; thus, the word has something to do with seeing an image.

TABLE 3.2

Common Prefixes and Suffixes

Prefixes	*Suffixes*
ab- (from)—abnormal	-ness (state of being)—nerviness
ad- (to)—adhesion	-ment (object or agent of)—encampment
be- (on, over)—becloud	-ance (action or process)—protuberance
com-, con-, col- (with)—collinear	-tion (state of being)—hydration
de- (from)—decentralize	-ant (one who or thing that)—coolant
dis-, di- (apart)—dissect	-able (capable or worthy of)—perishable
en- (in)—encircle	-al or -ial (belonging to)—coastal
epi- (upon)—epilogue	-ful (full of)—peaceful
ex- (out from)—excavate	-ive (having nature or quality of)—
hemi- (half)—hemispheroid	reproductive
in- (not)—inactive	-ous (abounding in)—poisonous
inter- (between)—intercoastal	
mis- (wrong)—misalliance	
mono- (alone, one)—monobasic	
poly- (many)—polysemia	
pre- (before)—precook	
pro- (in front of)—procercoid	
re- (again)—reproduction	
sub- (under)—subocular	
trans- (across, beyond)—transcontinental	
un- (not)—unconscious	

In Spanish the gender of the noun is noted by the prefix "el" for masculine singular and "la" for feminine singular:

$$\begin{array}{ll} \text{la sopa} = \text{soup} & \text{los sopas} = \text{soups} \\ \text{el ojo} = \text{eye} & \text{los ojos} = \text{eyes} \end{array}$$

In French, similar prefixes are used to note gender.

$$\begin{array}{lll} \text{le professeur} = \text{professor} & \text{(masculine)} \\ \text{la table} = \text{table} & \text{(feminine)} \end{array}$$

Many suffixes, prefixes, and inflectional endings used in English words also appear in German, French, and other Romance languages. The suffix *age,* as in *bandage,* is found in French and English. Similarly, German forms the comparative adjective with the inflectional ending *er,* as in *gut/besser (good/better).*[4]

EXAMPLE

Prefixes and Suffixes

Using vocabulary words that contain prefixes, suffixes, or roots, students may be asked to determine the pronunciation or meaning of the words.

1. microscope—an instrument used to see small objects
2. mutation
3. cardiology
4. chronometer
5. dermatology
6. subterranean

LAGNIAPPE

Common Prefixes, Suffixes, and Root Words in Science

Prefixes	*Root Words*	*Suffixes*
alti- (height)	aqua (water)	-ology (study of)
anti- (against)	scope (sight)	-er (one who)
sub- (under)	bio (life)	-or (the state of)
micro- (small)	geo (earth)	-con (the act of)
tele- (far)	carn (flesh)	-y (to make)
proto- (first)	gen (race, kind)	-ation (the act of)
chrono- (time)	mute (change)	-ism (the state of)
inter- (between)	cardi (heart)	-ous, ious (full of)
intra- (within)	derm (skin)	
mal- (bad)	path (feeling, disease)	
contri- (center)	psych (mind)	
	zo (animal)	
	scien (knowledge)	
	terra (earth)	
	anthropo (man)	
	petri (rock)	
	meter (measure)	
	graph (write)	

Another structural analysis skill, *syllabication,* is useful to teachers as they introduce new vocabulary and also to some students in decoding unknown words. However, syllabication seems to be a skill that is better used for spelling or writing after the students can pronounce the word rather than as an aid to them in pronunciation.[5] This belief is reinforced by Weaver as she notes that syllabication principles are of decreasing value in recognizing words. The reasons for minimizing instruction in syllabication include: (1) the rules of syllabication create confusion in word recognition; (2) written syllables do not always conform to spoken syllables, thus words may be mispronounced when divided into syllables; and (3) research studies suggest that rule-oriented syllabication instruction does not improve word recognition skills or comprehension. Weaver does suggest that teachers consider instruction in letter clusters or spelling patterns instead of syllabication as an aid in word identification.[6] Thus, the content teacher should realize that syllabication techniques are helpful in presenting new words to students, but that students seldom use this procedure on their own to decode an unknown word. Likewise, in teaching students to recognize words using syllabication, content teachers should instruct students to analyze the structure of the word first, and then use contextual analysis to determine its meaning in order to know when a correct pronunciation is ascertained.[7] Other research reinforces the view that syllabication skills must be taught in a realistic reading situation rather than as isolated or independent rules.[8] For example, syllabication could be used to aid students in pronouncing the term "chromatography." The teacher may write the word on the board in syllables

　　　　chro-ma-tog-ra-phy

and if additional help is needed the word may be rewritten using syllables plus the phonetic respelling:

　　　　kroh-muh-tahg'-ruh-fee

Syllabication does not aid students in knowing the meaning of a new word, but it is an aid in teaching them to pronounce an unknown term.

EXAMPLE

Syllabication

Using five index cards, write a geographical term on each one, leaving enough space between the syllables to cut the cards at that point. Mix both halves of the cards, then let the student match the correct word parts to find the missing term.

trans-	-humance
perman-	-post
out-	-back
mid-	-lands
con-	-tour

After the activity is completed, put the words on the board and ask the students to pronounce each word and determine its meaning either from the book, dictionary, or class discussion.

　　　　Contextual analysis skills are applied as students use other words in a sentence or passage to determine the pronunciation or meaning of an unknown word. The use of context clues as a word identification technique is, to a great extent, dependent on the students' having the words in their speaking or listening vocabularies. This skill is usually applied in conjunction with phonics or structural analysis skills. Smith found that using a combination of context with limited graphic clues is sufficient for decoding the majority of words in the reader's speaking or listening vocabulary.[9]

　　　　The development of contextual analysis skills as a word identification strategy is also important to increasing speed in reading. Students who must phonetically or structurally analyze each unknown word are usually slow readers who tire of reading before they finish. Samuels, Begy, and Chen as well as Klein, Klein, and Vigoda have studied competence in reading as related to the use of context clues to analyze words.[10] Their findings suggest that better readers make greater use of context clues for word identification. Content teachers should also note that while other word identification skills become less valuable as the reader matures, contextual analysis skills become more useful.[11] Thus, instructional activities must be included to strengthen the use of this skill in the content classroom.

An example of the use of context clues in reading social studies materials is shown in the following sentence:

> Newfoundland, Prince Edward Island, New Brunswick, and Nova Scotia, located in Eastern Canada and referred to as the *Maritime* Provinces, rely upon fishing as their primary source of income.

In this example, the word "Maritime" is defined for the student through context. From prior information, the student notes that the provinces mentioned border the Atlantic Ocean. This is further reinforced by that part of the sentence that indicates fishing is the main source of income. Thus, using only the clues given in this sentence, the student could determine the meaning of the term "Maritime."

Another example of the use of contextual analysis to determine the meaning of terms in a science text is shown below:

> One of the major uses of sulfuric acid is in the production of *fertilizers* or nutrients for growing plants. The mineral called *rock phosphate* (calcium phosphate), which is quarried in large quantities in Florida and Tennessee, will not readily dissolve in the soil moisture. However, when it is treated with sulfuric acid, it becomes *superphosphate* and dissolves readily. This process makes available important phosphate compounds as fertilizers for growing plants.

From George R. Tracy, Harry E. Tropp, and Alfred E. Friedl, *Modern Physical Science* (New York: Holt, Rinehart, and Winston, 1979), p. 65.

In looking at this paragraph, contextual analysis may be used to determine the meaning of fertilizers, rock phosphate, and superphosphate. Within the paragraph these words are defined through the context of the sentences. Several activities that content teachers may use to help students develop their contextual analysis skills are given in the following pages.

ACTIVITIES

Modified Cloze Technique

Use a modified cloze technique to encourage students to use surrounding words to fill in the blanks. When the students have completed the activity, put them in groups of two or three to discuss the different words used to complete the selection.

The word decimal comes from the _____1_____ word _____2_____, which means _____3_____. Our system of writing _____4_____ to represent numbers is based on _____5_____ by tens and thus is called the _____6_____ system.

Since we _____ by tens in the _____ system, we say that the
                    7   8
_____ of the system is _____ or that it is a _____ sys-
            9   10   11
tem. By using ten as a _____ and the idea of _____ value, the
                                12   13
Hindu-Arabic _____ are the only _____ needed to write
                    14   15
_____ for every whole _____ .
        16   17

KEY: 1. Latin   7. group   13. place
          2. decem   8. decimal   14. digits
          3. ten   9. base   15. symbols
          4. numerals   10. ten   16. numerals
          5. grouping   11. base ten   17. number
          6. decimal   12. base

Passage from Robert E. Eicholz et. al., *School Mathematics* II (Menlo Park, Calif.: Addison-Wesley, 1967),
p. 6.

Reinforcing Vocabulary

Provide a crossword puzzle such as the one below with clues that reinforce the vocabulary previously taught. Students can also develop their own puzzles that may be used
with other students.

ACROSS:
1. The oval path of one body revolving around another is called an _____ .
2. _____ is a granular igneous rock composed chiefly of feldspars and quartz.
3. The abbreviation for the Atomic Energy Commission is _____ .
4. _____ is a metal-bearing mineral or rock.
5. A unit of length that is equal to 1/12 foot is called an _____ . (plural form)
6. A body of coherent matter with an indefinite shape and of considerable size may be
   called a _____ .

DOWN:
1. Any living thing is known as a _____ .
2. Gases which have component parts that are relatively separated are considered to be
   _____ gases.

3. An _____ is an electrically charged atom or group of atoms.
4. Radio tubes containing a grid, cathode, and plate are known as _____.
5. The abbreviation for an electric current that reverses directions at regular intervals is _____.
6. A rock which is composed chiefly of pumice or other volcanic material is known as _____.

Introducing New Terms

Introduce the following terms to the students: platen, tabulator, line retainer, impression control, and page gauge. After placing those terms on the board or overhead projector and discussing their meanings with the students, use a modified cloze procedure to determine their understanding of the terms.

1. A device used for indentations such as paragraphs, columns, forms, and date and signature position is called a _____.
2. The _____ helps to keep the margins at the bottom of the page uniform.
3. Controlling the force with which the keys strike the paper is a device known as the _____.
4. Holding the paper in the typewriter is a roller, often referred to as a _____.
5. A device that allows for temporary changes of line spacing when you want to return to your original typing line is called a _____.

Choosing Definitions

Ask the students to choose the correct definition of each italicized word by examining clues from the rest of the sentence. They should not use dictionaries for this activity.

1. Cardiologists are continuing research to find ways to reduce pulmonary difficulties as a result of people's becoming more *sedentary* or leading less active lives.
   a. eating too much
   b. sitting too much
   c. smoking too much
   d. exercising too much
2. The *heir* discovered after the man's death that his wealth had decreased considerably in recent years.
   a. the man's lawyer
   b. the man's daughter
   c. a close friend of the man
   d. the person chosen to receive the man's assets
3. *Sherry,* an alcoholic drink made from grapes, is produced primarily in Spain.
   a. wine
   b. beer
   c. whiskey
   d. liqueur

Matching Terms and Definitions

Using a series of sentences, underline one term in each sentence. At the end of the activity, include definitions for the terms. Ask students to match the correct definition with the underlined term. After completing the activity, go over the pronunciation and meaning of each term with the class.

1. Los Angeles receives much of its water supply through an *aqueduct* that originates at the Colorado River.
2. *Autobahns* speed German citizens from one city to another.
3. Two characteristics of *conifers* that make them unusual are that they grow year-round and produce cones.
4. In Brazil, coffee, cotton, and sugar are grown on *fazendas*.
5. In Norway, *fiords* transport people from place to place.

Definitions

1. Plantations
2. Long narrow waterways
3. Limited access superhighway
4. Open channel used to transport water from one place to another
5. Evergreens that grow needle-shaped leaves

In foreign languages, contextual analysis skills may be used initally with picture clues to help students in reading the new language. For example,

Son dos sombreros

Using the pictures and the Spanish sentence the students can understand that the sentence says "There are two hats." Picture clues should be deleted as soon as possible and students encouraged to rely on the sentence context alone. In the following sentence, the student may understand the underlined words using the other words as clues.

Para los ninos, el agua es mejor que el vino.
For the children, water is _____ wine.

Mejor que can be translated as "better than" to complete the sentence.

In learning new vocabulary, students may use a combination of structural and contextual analysis skills to help in understanding technical and specialized words in many content areas. For example, in a health class the meaning of the word "botulism" may be recognized and understood by applying these skills in the following manner: using structural analysis skills, the student may look at the parts of the word initially in order to pronounce it. Knowing that "ism" is a suffix which denotes a state or condition should be helpful in understanding the word. The initial part of the word, "botul," comes from the word *botulin* meaning a toxin formed from a bacterium in spoiled food. Putting these parts together the student could conclude that botulism is an illness caused from eating spoiled foods. However, students may not know the meaning of botulin and need further clues. Contextual analysis then becomes a helpful skill. For example, after reading the word in the following sentence, the student can use the context to understand the meaning.

> The illness was diagnosed as *botulism*, caused from eating beans that were improperly canned.

Using only stuctural analysis skills with many technical terms such as *iconoscope* gives only an idea of the meaning of the word. However, using the word in a sentence helps the student determine a more exact meaning. For example:

> The television picture was blank because the *iconoscope* did not work on the camera.

After reading this sentence, students can use the context to learn that an inconoscope is a part of a television camera that helps to transmit the image to the screen.

Another example is the term "diagonal bracing" in a vocational education lesson. Students may recognize that *di* means two and *agonal* is an angle. They may further conclude that "diagonal bracing" means providing a support or brace using two objects, such as boards, to extend from one edge to the opposite edge. However, this term is greatly clarified when used in a context such as

> The fence was supported by diagonal braces that looked like a big X in each section.

Contextual analysis must also be used to determine the meaning of specialized vocabulary used in content reading. Because specialized vocabulary meanings change from subject to subject, students must rely on context to determine the real meaning. For example, the word *plane* varies in meaning from subject to subject. To determine the correct meaning of the word in the following sentences, the student must use the context along with previous knowledge.

> I will use a *plane* to level the board.
>
> *Plane* figures are dealt with in geometry.
>
> We took the *plane* on our last trip.

In reading mathematics materials, students frequently use contextual analysis for this purpose. For example,

$$3A \cdot \frac{1}{3}C = b^3$$

Context helps the student know the meaning and pronunciation of the numbers in the equation. Using context, the student reads the sentence as "Three *A* times one-third *C* equals *b* cubed." Without contextual analysis students would not know the different meanings of the numeral 3.

Students may also use contextual analysis in some content areas primarily to determine the meaning of technical words rather than the pronunciation. Content materials are filled with technical terms that are essential to understanding and with which students have no familiarity. In the following sentences the technical words can be defined from the context.

> *Aqua regia*, a mixture of nitric and hydrochloric acids, will dissolve gold.

> The Spanish divided their South American territory into three areas called *vice-royalties* that were governed by representatives of the Spanish king.

> A *noun cluster* is a group of words in which a noun is preceded, followed, or preceded and followed by one or more modifiers.

In science reading, contextual analysis skills seem to help students determine the meanings of the words more than the pronunciation. This is true because students often are not acquainted with these technical terms in their listening or speaking vocabularies; therefore, context clues do not help students to pronounce a completely unknown word. They can, however, determine the meaning of a word, even if they cannot properly pronounce the word. Because meaning is the most important aspect of all reading, contextual analysis skills are of tremendous assistance in understanding content information. Additional information on the use of context clues as aids in vocabulary development is given in Chapter 5.

LAGNIAPPE

Types of Context Clues

1. Language experience or familiar expression
2. Modifying phrases or clauses
3. Definition or description
4. Words connected in a series
5. Comparison or contrast clues
6. Synonym clues
7. Tone, setting, and mood clues
8. Referral clues
9. Association clues
10. Main idea and supporting detail pattern
11. Question-answer pattern in paragraph
12. Preposition clues
13. Nonrestrictive clauses or appositive phrases
14. Cause-effect pattern of sentence or paragraph

W. S. Ames, "The Development of a Classification Schema of Contextual Aids," *Reading Research Quarterly* II (1966):57–82.

Another word identification skill is that of identifying abbreviations, symbols, and acronyms. Content materials include many abbreviated terms that must be pronounced and have a meaning associated with the identified terms. Symbols such as $+$ and $=$ are necessary to understanding math. Similarly, abbreviations such as O_2 combined with symbols form equations in science such as

$$2 \, ZnS + 3O_2 \, 2ZnO + 2SO_2$$

that must be understood in order to comprehend the symbols. Acronyms such as UNESCO and NATO abound in social studies materials. These terms must be properly identified if students are to understand their meaning. To identify these abbreviated word forms, students may also use contextual analysis. For example, in mathematics

$$2 \text{ in.} + 5 \text{ ft.} = \underline{\qquad}''$$

The context assists the student in remembering the meaning of the $''$ symbol, thereby indicating a need to change the 5 ft. to inches to compute the answer.

LAGNIAPPE

Common Symbols and Abbreviations in Mathematics

Symbols		*Abbreviations*	
$-$	minus, less, take away	cm	centimeter
$+$	plus, add	cot	cotangent
$\times$	times, multiplied by	dz	dozen
$\div$	divided by	ft	foot
$>$	greater than	lb	pound
$\neq$	is not equal to	in	inch
$\sqrt{}$	square root	km	kilometer
σ	standard deviation	mph	miles per hour
$=$	is equal to	qts	quarts
$<$	less than	cos	cosine
$\leq$	less than or equal to	fl	fluid
$\approx$	approximately	oz	ounces
$\parallel$	parallel	pt	pint
$\perp$	perpendicular	gal	gallon
$\sqrt[3]{}$	cube root	bu	bushel
$\pm$	plus or minus	pk	peck
$\cdot$	times, multiplied by	l	liter
$\ngtr$	is not greater than	mm	millimeter
$\nless$	is not less than	dm	decimeter
x^2	exponent	m	meter
$\angle$	angle	kg	kilograms
$\triangle$	triangle	gm	grams
$\bigcirc$	circle	ac	acre
π	pi	mi	mile

ACTIVITIES

Converting Word Sentences to Math

Ask the students to read each sentence and then rewrite the sentence into a mathematical equation. Provide one answered question as in item #1.

1. A certain number is less than 12 and is greater than 7.

$$x < 12$$
$$x > 7$$

2. A number is greater than another, which in turn is greater than a third number.
3. Six is less than x, and x is less than ten.
4. Eight times a number less two equals twenty-two.
5. Twenty less five times a number minus one equals twenty-nine.

The Chemical Elements

Each student is given a card containing the abbreviation for a chemical element. Using various reference materials, each student locates the assigned element, notes the chemical for which the abbreviation stands, when and where it was discovered and by whom, as well as any other significant information. A large wall chart in the classroom can be used by students to record their findings. A copy can then be made for each student to use as a reference.

Abbreviation	Element	When	Discovered By Whom	Where	Other Information
Na	Sodium				Occurs in nature only in combined state

Identifying Math Symbols

Ask students to match each symbol with its meaning by placing the correct letter in the space at the left.

_____ 1. $+$
_____ 2. $\parallel$
_____ 3. $\cdot$
_____ 4. $\neq$
_____ 5. $\sqrt{\ }$
_____ 6. $\leq$
_____ 7. σ
_____ 8. $\angle$
_____ 9. $\geq$
_____ 10. $\approx$

a. is not equal to
b. square root
c. angle
d. plus, add
e. standard deviation
f. is greater than or equal to
g. times, multiplied by
h. less than or equal to
i. approximately
j. parallel

One of the most helpful ways to identify new words in a second language is to recognize that many *cognates* exist in languages. Using cognates helps students to read more rapidly and gives additional clues that may be used along with context clues.

LAGNIAPPE

Cognates Which Assist Reading In Foreign Languages

English	Spanish	French	Latin
arm		arme	armus
grave	grave	grave	gravis
color	color	couleur	color
auto	auto	auto	
family	familia	famille	familia
herb	hierba	herbe	herba
rose	rosa	rose	rosa
professor	professor	professeur	professor
plate	plato	plat	platus
final	fin	final	finalis

If the content teacher is doubtful of the students' knowledge of the words or ability to use word identification skills to decide on pronunciation, then the words must be taught as new vocabulary words. Students should be encouraged to use various identification strategies to decode unknown words in content materials. The content teacher, however, is not responsible for introducing the basic word identification skills, but rather is expected to help students learn to apply the appropriate skills. Related ideas for vocabulary development are presented in Chapter 5, and other examples of word identification activities are found in Appendix A.

REFLECTION

As an adult reader, what strategy or strategies do you use to help you pronounce unfamiliar words? When were you taught to use these strategies? Were you taught any word identification skills in your content classes? If so, what type?

PART B

COMPREHENSION

Meaning, the primary goal of reading, understanding—these are terms used to define comprehension. Word identification skills are merely a means for helping students understand printed symbols. But comprehension is the real area of emphasis in content reading instruction. Herber defines reading comprehension as a three-level process:[12]

1. The reader examines the words of the author to determine what is being said.
2. The reader looks for relationships among statements to derive additional meaning.
3. Taking what the author said (literal understanding) and the relationships inferred (interpretive understanding), the reader moves to a third level in which the information is applied to other knowledge.

The applied level in Herber's three-level process is discussed by other writers using different labels. Smith calls it the elaborative level in which new thought processes are stimulated.[13] The emphasis in this level is on creating ideas of one's own. Other writers such as Lamberg and Lamb and Roe, Stoodt, and Burns give this level the labels of critical/creative or evaluative reading.[14] Regardless of the label, the highest level of comprehension involves reading for application, analysis, synthesis, and evaluation. This is the level that most content teachers want their students to use in reading content materials. Unfortunately, students are often functioning at the lower levels of understanding. This difference in teacher desires and student performance may cause both to become frustrated with content learning experiences. Thus, content teachers must recognize the different levels of comprehension and consider the levels that students are expected to use. They must also determine students' actual levels of comprehension, and then bridge the gaps through reading instruction.

Pearson and Johnson identify a number of factors that influence comprehension.[15] They subdivide these factors into two categories—internal factors, things that happen inside the head, and external factors that are affected by things outside the mind. These categories are not mutually exclusive and separate in that all of the factors interact with one another. An awareness of the factors, however, will help content teachers understand the relationship of comprehension to learning content information.

Among internal factors, *linguistic competence*, such as phonological, syntactic, and semantic knowledge, assists students in identifying words, understanding the organization of words in sentences, and knowing the meanings of words. These areas of linguistic competence interact to form the basis of comprehension. *Interest*, another internal factor, affects comprehension in that students better understand topics that are of high interest to them,[16] and which relate to their background knowledge.[17] Thus, content teachers may improve comprehension by generating interest in a topic using various instructional techniques and materials. *Motivation* is both intrinsic and extrinsic although initially the student must be self-motivated and receive reinforcers and incentives from others in order to maintain interest in content learning. When students are motivated to learn, comprehension is enhanced. *Reading ability* affects comprehension because students who have difficulty in identifying words will also have difficulty comprehending. However, as students begin to understand words that are recognized, they can use their understanding of the context to identify other words. Overall reading ability is thereby enhanced as comprehension is improved.

LAGNIAPPE

_____

A study of the interrelationship of IQ, reading comprehension scores, and amount of TV viewing among American middle schoolers (grades 6 through 9) showed that among low IQ students, heavy TV viewing (over 5.5 hours per day) was associated with higher reading scores for girls but had no effect for boys, although both boys and girls in the low IQ group reported reading less than did light viewers. Among medium IQ students, medium TV viewers (3 to 5 hours per day) had the highest reading comprehension scores; heavy viewing was associated with a slight drop in scores for girls, a severe drop (10 percentile points) for boys. Among high IQ students, the heavy viewers showed reading scores about 10 percentile points below those of either light or medium TV viewers.

_____

See "Television Viewing and Reading: Does More Equal Better?" by Michael Morgan, *Journal of Communication* (Winter 1980): 159–65.

External factors that influence comprehension include the written message and the reading environment. The *written message* can augment or deter comprehension. Words, sentences, structure, and thematic information must be considered to determine their impact on the message that students must understand. Organizational patterns used in the various content areas are discussed in Chapter 6. The *reading environment*—home and school—can affect comprehension either negatively or positively. Parents who read and encourage reading at home usually heighten their child's comprehension. Teachers influence comprehension positively through instruction, creating an atmosphere for reading, and serving as a reading model.

These factors affect comprehension at all levels, from initial comprehension instruction in the primary grades as students first learn to identify words and associate meaning with the printed symbol, to the content classroom where all comprehension skills must be applied. As comprehension instruction has been studied, many significant findings have been reported.

Taba, for example, found that teachers tend to expect students to learn and recite much factual information using a low level of questioning.[18] Guszak later substantiated the theory that questioning techniques in the lower grades were mainly on a literal level. He found that 78.8 percent of all questions in the second grade, 64.7 percent of all questions in the fourth grade, and 57.8 percent of all questions in the sixth grade were primarily recall type questions. Only 20 percent of the time were the questions at a higher level.[19] A study by Durkin is even more alarming in regard to comprehension and content reading instruction in the elementary grades. In a study of comprehension instruction in reading and social studies in grades 3-6, she found:

1. Practically no comprehension instruction.
2. A lack of other types of reading instruction in social studies.
3. Elementary teachers are assignment-givers with many transition and noninstruction activities.
4. None of the observed teachers saw the social studies period as a time to improve children's comprehension abilities.[20]

With such depressing research findings, content teachers are forced to become more knowledgeable about comprehension skills and ways of helping students respond to questions in order to learn content information. Fortunately, current researchers are investigating the schemata, organizational patterns or structure used in text materials. Indications are that readers recall or comprehend more information when they are aware of the schemata being used. Readers make inferences consistent with their schemata, and they recall more text information important to their schemata.[21] This research on schemata has significant implications for developing comprehension in the content classroom and possibly simplifying comprehension instruction. Sheridan suggests that schemata theory provides evidence that comprehending textual material is a holistic process.[22] Comprehension skills instruction would be necessary, but in relation to the schemata, rather than as isolated skills. Teaching comprehension in this manner would assist students in understanding the structure or organizational pattern used in content materials, thereby showing them how to apply the various comprehension skills directly related to their content learning. More specific information regarding the organizational patterns needed in learning information in the various content areas is presented in Chapter 6. Because instruction in using the different organizational patterns is dependent upon content teachers' understanding of the more specific reading skills, the remainder of this section on comprehension discusses the identification and development of the skills. The following pages contain information on the three levels of comprehension—literal, interpretive, and critical—as well as the more specific skills which relate to these different categories.

To help in this understanding and application of comprehension skills, a review of some of the taxonomies for cognitive learning is necessary. Content teachers are often more familiar with the language used in the various taxonomies than the terminology frequently used by reading teachers in discussing comprehension. This difference in terminology is due to the emphasis of many secondary methods courses in teacher training programs. Therefore, in designing comprehension questions as well as enhancing the development of comprehension skills, content teachers may be more comfortable thinking about the various levels in the taxonomies. Table 3.3 presents three widely used taxonomies and their correlation to three levels of comprehension. The more specific skills within each level are presented in Tables 3.4, 3.5, and 3.6.

Literal skills require that the reader examine carefully what is presented in the material. This is often considered the lowest level of thinking. At this level the student is not to make judgments, analyze, or evaluate. The student reads only for specific information, perhaps to locate explicitly stated details. An example of a question at this level is: "What are the steps in replacing a spark plug?" A list of literal skills and sample questions is found in Table 3.4 (p. 68).

TABLE 3.3

Relating Taxonomies to Levels of Comprehension

Levels of Comprehension	Bloom	Taxonomies[23] Sanders	Barrett
Literal	Knowledge Comprehension	Memory Translation	Recognition Recall
Interpretive (Inferential)	Application Analysis Synthesis	Interpretation Application Analysis Synthesis	Inference
Critical	Evaluation	Evaluation	Evaluation Appreciation

Content materials are filled with details and facts that must be remembered. The foremost skill in reading mathematics is that of recognizing and recalling details. In reading word problems, explanations, or even simple equations, students must note details like the symbols indicating addition or multiplication, the numbers involved in the problem, and the number of steps needed to complete the computations. Students who ignore these details are often accused of making careless mistakes, when in fact the mistake is that of not noting the details. Because math materials are written so compactly, every word is important to solving the problem. Therefore, every word, symbol, or abbreviation is significant and must be remembered.

Science materials are also filled with details and facts. A first reading is not the time to read for specifics. Students should, instead, read materials initially to identify any relationships, comparisons, or sequences that are important to understanding how the information is organized. With this type of overview, students then reread to note the details. Specifics are more easily remembered when organized in some way, possibly according to the text's pattern.

Physical education students must grasp details in order to develop a better understanding of the sport being studied. Rules, directions, and discussions of physical education concepts are examples of details that must be remembered. The understanding of the specifics in health materials forms the basis for students to make generalizations about a concept, and to see the relationships that exist among various ideas. For example, in studying the heart, students would have to learn that the auricle is one of two upper chambers of the heart, and the ventricle one of the two lower chambers. These basic details would then help students understand generalizations and relationships about the heart, such as damage to one of the chambers forcing the other chambers to work harder. Applying these three comprehension skills enhances the understanding of many health concepts.

TABLE 3.4

Literal Comprehension Skills

Skill	Meaning	Sample Question/Statement
Recall details	The skill of identifying who, what, when, where, and how information when given in a passage.	What was the size of the country?
Follow written directions	The skill of completing a task according to the given directions.	After reading the directions, find the information in the appropriate book.
Remember stated sequence of events	A skill that requires the reader to recall ideas and put them in a specific order.	In what order must you do the four steps in the experiment?
Select stated cause-effect relationships	The skill that requires that the reader identify the given relationship between two events or situations.	Why was the king exiled to another country?
Contrast and compare information	A skill requiring that the likenesses and differences of words, objects, or ideas be determined.	How are the Asian and European nations similar and different in terms of their cultures?
Paraphrasing	The skill of restating information in different words which mean the same as those of the author.	What did the author say to describe the old lady? Tell it in your own words.
Read for a stated purpose	A skill of determining information to be learned from reading material, formulating this into a question or questions, then reading to answer these questions.	Read these pages to find out how plants grow from seeds.
Understand symbols, abbreviations, and acronyms.	The skill of translating abbreviated forms of words into a meaningful unit.	In the problem, what word does *lb.* represent?
Identify stated main idea	The skill that requires the reader to select a sentence that tells what the paragraph or selection is about.	Which sentence tells what this selection is about?
Identify character traits and actions.	A skill that necessitates the student recalling the character and describing the personality features based on the given information.	One of the leading characters in this play was Jerome. What type of person is he described to be? What did he do in the story to reinforce this idea?

Questions to Guide Reading

In giving students a passage to read, purpose-setting questions should be used to guide their reading. These questions may also be used for discussion after reading. A sample passage with questions is given below.

> Our joints are surrounded by small fluid-filled sacs which allow more tendon flexibility and serve as a cushion to the joint. Each of the sacs is called a bursa. Bursas can become inflamed and sore due to an injury or too much continued pressure. When this happens additional fluid builds up in the bursa resulting in swelling and pain. This is bursitis. To treat bursitis one should rest the irritated joint. Additionally, a doctor can prescribe a pain reliever or give steroird injections. If severe swelling exists, excess fluid may be withdrawn or surgery may be necessary.

Details:
1. What surrounds our joints?
2. What is the sac called that cushions the joint?
3. What is bursitis?
4. How is bursitis treated?

Generalizations:
1. How could you try to prevent getting bursitis?
2. Why could bursitis be a crippling handicap?

Relationships:
1. What effects could bursitis have on your daily life if you should have it?
2. You read about arthritis last week, now compare bursitis and arthritis.

Similarly, as art materials are studied, students must be alert to details for they form the basis for the application of other reading skills. Details are needed to contrast or compare pieces of art or art techniques. They are needed to make generalizations about an artist's work or to go from an example of how to make a clay pot to making another piece of pottery.

In reading music materials, the major comprehension skill that is crucial to the application of other comprehension skills is that of recalling details. Noting details is important in understanding musical notations, remembering significant information about the history of the time, a theoretical idea, or the lyrics of a song. As details are noted, students can then compare and contrast information that delineates the similarities and differences in composers' works as well as periods of history.

When reading literature, students should try to find important details in the selection. One of the purposes for reading is that of recalling details. Because details support the main idea, students should use them to clarify it.

In reading social studies materials, recalling details is imperative. This is often a tedious task that many students would prefer to eliminate altogether; however, details are essential for adding substance to the concepts and generalizations presented. As noted previously, the skill of recalling details is associated with understanding the main idea. In reading social studies materials, locating and understanding the main idea with its supporting details are essential to understanding social studies concepts, since this is a common organizational pattern used in many texts.

Details must be remembered, not memorized; therefore, students should paraphrase the information or put the details in their own words. Students often have difficulty with this skill for two reasons: (1) they do not understand the information well enough to put it in their own words, or (2) they are not accustomed to restating what the book says. Content teachers can assist with this problem by carefully reviewing the concepts prior to assigning the material. The concepts and text information must first be understood before students can paraphrase any content material.

Another skill that is used in all types of content materials is that of reading for a purpose. Students must decide why they are reading a science material and what information they hope to gain before beginning to read. If a purpose is not established, students may try to remember everything in one reading. As pointed out previously, there is so much information in science materials that several readings are often necessary. Thus, different purposes should be established depending on the information sought. To encourage the application of this skill, content teachers may initially give students a purpose for reading, and encourage them to develop the habit of determining their purpose before reading.

As students read mathematical materials, they must also establish a purpose for reading. If the material consists of word problems, the first purpose for reading the problem may be to understand the situation in the problem. The second rereading would call for a different purpose, possibly to note the operations to be performed. By establishing specific purposes for reading the material, students can continuously assess their understanding in light of their purpose.

Comprehension is further enhanced in reading a foreign language if teachers provide students with purpose-setting questions to guide their reading. Thomas and Robinson suggest that foreign language teachers help students read fiction by giving them an easy preview to aid their understanding of the story.[24] The use of study strategies includes a preview or purpose-setting stage. This is the appropriate time for students to receive the teacher's help.

Skill in following directions is required in every content-learning area. In science, students must carefully follow directions in performing experiments. Similarly, this skill is needed in math, vocational and business education classes like home economics and typing, as well as in physical education and music. In learning to follow directions, students must also identify and understand the main idea and details supporting the main idea. As students learn to remember details, they are better able to follow directions because directions are usually filled with details like numbers, facts, names, etc. Additionally, following directions requires that students note sequence. Remembering details in directions means little if they are not remembered in the proper order. Thus, to understand the directions given in business education courses, students must apply sequence and detail skills. Sequencing skills are evident in music as students remember lyrics of songs in the correct order, and in physical education when game rules are followed. Again this requires the remembering of specifics to aid sequential recall.

Sequence understanding is also important in social studies, as it is an organizational pattern as well as a comprehension skill that is frequently used. In social studies materials, information is usually sequenced with dates as reference points.

In order to understand history, students must learn the proper sequence in which events occurred. This gives them a frame of reference around which to develop their understanding of the material. Many works of literature are written with intricate plots requiring a clear understanding of the sequence of events in the book as well as the cause-and-effect relationships among those events. The reader must recognize why a particular situation occurred as it did, and what the effect of the occurrence will be, based on when the event occured.

ACTIVITIES

Following Directions in Sports

Provide students with a printed set of directions for a sport. Ask them to discuss the directions with a friend and then teach the rules to another group.

Rules for Table Tennis

1. The table should be 9 feet long and 5 feet wide, with the surface thirty inches above the floor.
2. The table is divided in the center with a net parallel to the end lines.
3. The top side of the net is six inches above the playing surface.
4. The first server is decided by a coin toss.
5. The first server makes five consecutive serves.
6. The serve is made by releasing the ball and striking it with a paddle outside the boundary of the court near the server's end.
7. If the ball touches the net or its supports and then lands in the receiver's court it is called a let ball and does not count for scoring.
8. One point is awarded when the receiver fails to return the ball.
9. The winner of a match is the player who first scores 21 points. If both players have 20 points, one player must gain a two point lead to win.

Following Directions in Baking

Ask students to use a recipe such as the following to make strawberry shortcake:

    2 cups sifted all-purpose flour
    2 tablespoons sugar
    3 teaspoons baking powder
    1/2 teaspoon salt
    1/2 cup butter or margarine
    1 beaten egg
    2/3 cup light cream
    3 to 4 cups sugared sliced strawberries
    1 cup whipping cream, whipped

Sift dry ingredients adding butter until mixture is coarse, then combine egg and cream and add to dry ingredients, stirring only to moisten. For individual shortcakes, turn dough out on floured surface, knead gently for 1/2 minute. Roll to 1/2 inch, cut 6 shortcakes with floured 2-1/2 inch cutter. Bake on ungreased sheet at 450° for 10 minutes. Split and fill with strawberries and cream.

Ask students to read the entire recipe before they begin. After reading the recipe, the teacher may ask questions such as the following to be sure that students recognize sequence as well as directions:

1. Is the whipping cream mixed with the flour and sugar? Why or why not?
2. How much baking powder is called for in the recipe?
3. List the steps that must be followed after the ingredients are mixed and before the dough is put in the oven.
4. At what temperature should the shortcake bake? For how long?

Using a Time Line

Ask students to place these events in the order in which they occurred.

Review for *The Diary of Anne Frank*

Directions: Place these events on the time line in the order in which they occurred.

A. Anne's diary is published.
B. Hitler occupies Holland.
C. The Frank family moves to Amsterdam.
D. Hitler invades Poland.
E. The Franks and the Van Daans are arrested.
F. The office in the spice factory is burglarized.
G. Mr. Kraler is hospitalized.
H. Peter's cat disappears.
I. The Franks and the Van Daans go into hiding.
J. The Frank children are expelled from school because they are Jewish.
K. Anne dies.
L. Mrs. Frank dies.
M. Peter marches off with the Nazi soldiers.
N. Mr. Frank returns to Amsterdam after the war.

Activity courtesy of Betty Archambeault, Catholic High School, Baton Rouge, Louisiana.

Identifying Cause-and-Effect Relationships

Using a passage such as the one below, ask students to draw one line under the sentence that describes an effect. Then they can draw two lines under the sentence that describes the cause of that effect. Lastly, they should make a circle around the words or sentences that answer the questions that follow the passage.

> People with the disease emphysema have lost the elasticity in their lungs. This makes it very difficult for the person to breathe, especially to exhale. Emphysema is a common disease among smokers and people who breathe "dirty" air.

William L. Ramsey et al. *Life Science: Resource Book* (New York: Holt, Rinehart, and Winston, 1978).

1. What part of the body is affected by emphysema?
2. Who seems to get emphysema?
3. How does emphysema affect a person?

Cause-effect relationships are also used in studying art. As students study art history or art appreciation, they learn how different events or periods in history affected the art. Similarly, in creating pottery objects students learn that too much water in the clay results in a poor product and that different colors stimulate unique mood reactions. Thus, understanding cause-effect relationships is extremely important in the art class. In social studies materials, especially history, students must be able to understand cause-effect relationships because these relationships occur not only as skills, but also predominate as a pattern of organization used in many materials. Students must learn to anticipate this style of organization, and to become adept at identifying cause-effect relationships. Learning to recognize a specific cause that led to a specific event increases the likelihood that students can effectively understand the social studies information.

ACTIVITY

Cause-Effect Relationships in Sports

When teaching a sport, identify some of the problems that may occur. Ask students to tell why this problem occurred or what effect it would have on the game.

Problem	Cause-Effect
A pass was thrown, but the receiver was not watching the ball.	
The catcher forgot to pull down his mask.	
The girl kept the ball and tried to shoot every time she had it.	
The player continuously hit the ball into the net.	

Science materials also contain many relationships which are used to present varying ideas. Cause-effect relationships must be understood in discussions of how a chemical element reacts when mixed with another element or the effect of light frequency on the concept of color. Cause-effect relationships are also analyzed using comparison and contrast skills. For example, to understand the relationship of like and unlike magnetic poles, students must compare data to determine the similarities and differences. By understanding these relationships, students are better able to comprehend the concepts.

When presented with likenesses and differences of information in social studies materials, students should also use the skill of comparing and contrasting. By noting likenesses or differences, the materials are more easily interpreted and evaluated for adequacy and accuracy. Comparing and contrasting information is also important in home economics, where consumer education is taught, and in vocational agriculture, where deciding the type of corn to grow or the type of fertilizer to use may be crucial to a successful crop.

ACTIVITIES

Cause-Effect Sequence

Ask students to read the following passage about energy. After they have read the passage, ask them to speculate about the availability of oil in the future.

There is a worldwide energy shortage. This was not always true. For many years oil was plentiful and inexpensive. The United States produced more than enough to meet its needs, but oil companies were always exploring for more. In the 1920s and 1930s oil was discovered in the Middle East. During World War II, many countries had to ration oil and gas. After the war was over, economies expanded, production increased and more oil was expended. This continued into the 1950s and 1960s. During this period, the United States began to import oil. Suddenly, in the early 1970s, a shortage occurred, prices increased dramatically, and panic spread. People viewed the 1980s with trepidation.

Cause-Effect:
Why has the price of oil increased so dramatically?

Understanding Sequence:
Ask students to develop a time line indicating the order in which the events in the passage occurred.

Comparing and Contrasting in Order to Evaluate

Ask students to use their knowledge of different parts of the country and the descriptions of three types of strip cropping to decide which one is most suitable to Kansas; to Georgia; to Montana.

Contour Strip Cropping

1. Crops grown in strips across the slope of land and on the contour.
2. Densely growing crops such as hay are alternated with clean tilled row crops such as corn.
3. Strips of densely growing crops and row crops are same width.

Field Strip Cropping

1. Row and densely growing crops alternated and planted in narrow strips of the same width across the slope of the land but not parallel to the true contour of land.
2. Can be used on land with a consistent slope.

Wind Strip Cropping

1. Designed to prevent loss of soil by wind.
2. Crops grown in narrow parallel strips transversing the direction of the prevailing winds.

Comparing and Contrasting in Order to Generalize

Ask students to supply the appropriate information in the following chart by using reference materials in the class or library.

United States	Situation	Soviet Union
	Type of government	
	Ability to feed population	
	Energy	
	Population	
	Size	

Making Generalizations:
Which of the two countries do you think is the more affluent?

Content teachers should be aware that the skills identified in this section as being at a literal or recall level may also be categorized as inferential skills dependent on information in the content material. For example, a selection may include a stated cause-effect relationship whereby the student must only recall the information. Another selection may have a stated cause and an implied effect; thus, students must use inferential thinking to understand the effect. By being familiar with the different skills, and the information that students read, content teachers can determine what level of understanding is necessary to answer their content questions.

Another level of comprehension includes the *interpretive* or *inferential skills*. At this level, the reader is assimilating information in an effort to interpret the author's meaning. The reader must be able to locate and verify essential details, in order to make some generalization concerning their relationship. An example of a question at this level is: Was the Japanese attack on Pearl Harbor the direct cause of the United States entering World War II, or was it a contributory cause? Why? For a list of other interpretive skills and sample questions, see Table 3.5 (pp. 77–78).

Two extremely important interpretive comprehension skills that students must develop for understanding literary materials, especially poetry, are inter-

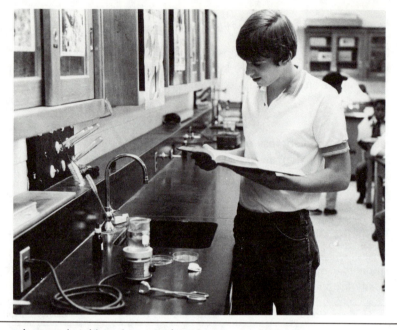

The reader must be able to locate and verify essential details.

preting figurative language and understanding mood and emotional reaction. Without these skills students experience great difficulty in understanding the author's point of view or purpose in poetry and other literary genres. These skills are also important in understanding song lyrics. Just as in writing poetry, song writers express their ideas in a poetic manner through the use of figurative language and symbolism. Many such implications must be understood. This is especially true in music. Protest songs of the late '60s and early '70s as well as many current popular songs use this type of language. For example, a song by Joan Baez, "If I Knew,"[25] contains ideas and phrases that tell of a person who is opposed to killing, and is considered "not to be a man." The person is, in fact, in prison due to his protest against, and refusal to serve in, the Vietnam War. Only through careful analysis of the words and an awareness of the singer's background could the listener understand this implied meaning. As language is interpreted in the lyrics of songs, students begin to understand moods and emotions being expressed by composer and singer. Likewise, feelings are expressed in music which has no lyrics. Using tempo and instrumentation, the composer communicates a mood. These feelings must be understood in order to comprehend and appreciate music.

In studying art materials, especially in the evaluation of art from different periods of history, or the work of various artists, students must learn to perceive relationships. For example, although each of Norman Rockwell's drawings was different, the commonalities in style can be recognized as unique characteristics of his work. By looking at his various drawings, students see relationships and learn to identify his work. These relationships are important in understanding information in many content areas. In literature, students must perceive the relationships of the writings of various periods in history. In science and social studies, too, students need this skill to understand the interrelationships of concepts.

TABLE 3.5

Interpretive Comprehension Skills

Skill	Meaning	Sample Question/Statement
Predict outcomes	A skill for which the reader must relate elements within a passage to one another in order to determine the result.	Read the news clippings and articles relating to U.S. economic conditions. Then predict what the economic situation will be next year.
Draw conclusions	A skill requiring that given facts be evaluated and that a judgment be made as to a possible conclusion.	If a person uses drugs, stops eating properly, and drops out of school, what may be the outcome of his/her life?
Make generalizations	The skill in which the reader takes the given facts and applies reasoning in order to make a decision.	Look at the data on the chemical changes of the compound during the last week. Based on this, what do you think will happen to it tomorrow?
Perceive relationships	A skill that requires the reader to identify the similarities among ideas in a selection and to relate or classify the ideas.	How are plants and animals similar in terms of basic needs?
Identify an implied sequence of events	A skill requiring the reader to infer from given information the order of the ideas or information.	From the given information, decide the order of the events that led to the Civil War.
Select implied cause-effect relationships	The skill of interpreting from given information the implied relationships in an event.	The floods devastated the country. Why were the floods a surprise to the people?
Interpret figurative language	A skill in which the reader must interpret words or phrases which are used in a nonliteral or unusual way to add force or style.	What is meant by the statement, "The girls were like two peas in a pod"?
Understand mood and emotional reactions	A skill requiring that the reader respond to the imagery or feeling conveyed by the author.	How did the general react when he received the cable from the President?
Summarize information	A skill used especially in preparing reports and projects. It requires the student to condense the information read.	Read the article and the section in the text on molecules. Then use the ideas to prepare a report for the science fair.

TABLE 3.5 (continued)

Skill	Meaning	Sample Question/Statement
Synthesize data	A skill requiring the student to combine ideas to form a general concept.	After reviewing the information and relating it to your ideas, tell why the United Nations has not solved the world's problems.
Tell the implied main idea	A skill in which the reader must determine what a paragraph or selection is about and tell in his/her own words.	After reading the article about the space flight, tell in one sentence what the article is about.

In reading social studies materials, students are frequently required to make generalizations about them. Making valid generalizations depends to a great extent on being able to support them with details. When students cannot support a generalization with factual information, they may reach an incorrect conclusion. Generalizing is also used in reading science materials, especially when students are conducting an experiment and evaluating their summary data. Generalizations form the basis for drawing conclusions or suggesting that the interaction among different variables could be expected to yield a given response. This problem-solving skill reflects the experimental nature of the science content, that is, to use given facts to explore an idea. As ideas are explored, students are continuously asked to predict outcomes based upon the information and relationships that are found. Similarly, in reading mathematics, students can predict the correctness of their estimated answers. Students must be encouraged to work with numbers in an easy, comfortable way, estimating approximate answers before doing the final calculations. Math has been taught as a one-correct-answer "exact" science for so long that many students have lost interest in using the data along with their judgments to make a prediction about the answer. Predicting outcomes to math problems adds interest to learning, and requires an understanding of the processes that may not be necessary when problems are literally computed in a rote manner.

As students remember details and understand the relationships expressed or implied, they continuously summarize information. Details are summarized in order to see relationships, and relationships are summarized in order to make generalizations, predict outcomes or draw conclusions. Thus, summarization helps students remember the many ideas presented in content materials.

As students summarize information from their mathematics and science materials, they must use these summaries to synthesize the data and solve the problem. Summarizing information requires that the students understand the details, paraphrase them into their own words, and then mentally outline the ideas in a summary way. This process is helpful in sorting the essential from the nonessential information. The necessary information can then be synthesized or combined to reach a solution.

Interpretive or inferential comprehension skills are closely interwoven as they are applied to content reading. In the preceding section, only a few examples are given, and in discussing them, other skills are mentioned because they depend on one another. Therefore, in identifying reading skills, content teachers should identify the most closely related skill needed for understanding the content information, and realize that successful application of this skill is associated to other interdependent skills.

ACTIVITIES

Comprehension: Biology

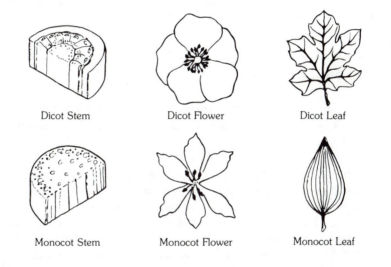

Dicot Stem   Dicot Flower   Dicot Leaf

Monocot Stem   Monocot Flower   Monocot Leaf

Class Angiospermae. About 70 percent of all plant species are flowering plants. When walking outdoors, you will probably notice that the flowering plants dominate the scenery. They are the trees, shrubs, hedges, flowers, vegetables, and grasses that you are most likely to see in any natural environment.

The angiosperms get their common name from the flower, which is the reproductive system for all members of this class. (However, some also reproduce asexually.) Generally, the plants that exhibit bright, colorful flowers rely on insects for pollination. Flowers that are small and seldom recognized as flowers (like the flowers on the grasses) are usually wind pollinated.

There are two subclasses of angiosperms. One is the subclass Monocotyledoneae. The members of this class are commonly called *monocots*. The other subclass is the Dicotyledoneae. Its members are called *dicots*. The primary difference between the two groups of flowering plants is in the number of cotyledons, or seed leaves, inside the seed. Monocots have one seed leaf, and dicots have two. More obvious differences between the two subclasses can usually be observed in the leaves and flowers. Monocot leaves are usually parallel-veined, and the organs of the flower are in fours or fives or multiples of these numbers. Cattails, grasses, lilys, and orchids are common examples of monocots. Roses, sunflowers, and dandelions are examples of dicots. Which flower on page 251 is a monocot and which is a dicot?

William L. Smallwood and Edna R. Green, *Biology* (Morristown, N.J.: Silver Burdett, 1974), p. 250.

Details:
1. What percent of all plant species are flowering plants?
2. What are angiosperms?
3. What are the two subclasses of angiosperms?

Comparison/Contrast:
Identify the similarities and differences of monocots and dicots.

Perceiving Relationships:
Using the descriptions of the two subclasses of angiosperms, categorize the plants provided at your lab table.

Comprehension: Music

Give the student a reading selection from a music book or a sheet containing the lyrics of a song. The questions may be used to guide reading and to direct a discussion after reading.

When *The Rite of Spring* by Igor Stravinsky was performed in Paris in 1913, many people believed that modern music had arrived. This beginning of the Impressionistic Period cannot actually be attributed to one composer or one work. However, since that time music has been characterized by barbaric rhythms, dissonant harmonies, and fragmentary motives. This music as compared to the Romantic Period was quite different. As this Period has developed, the United States has become a focal point of world music. This country is adopted as the homeland for many composers, either by birth or by choice. The computer age in the United States has also had a great impact as music has been composed and played via electronics.

Details:
1. The beginning of the Impressionistic Period began about when?
2. What is the name of the composer who is credited with marking this beginning? The work?
3. What country has become the focal point of world music?

Comparison/Contrast:
1. How do you think the music of the Impressionistic Period differs from the Romantic Period?
2. How is electronic music like and different from other types of music?

Generalizations:
We have listened to music by Aaron Copland. Characterize his music according to its period. Tell why you made this decision.

Comprehension: World History

The Nile

The Nile River flows north 4000 miles, or 6400 kilometers, from the mountains of central Africa to the Mediterranean Sea. The last 600 miles, or 960 kilometers, is in Egypt. There the river cuts a narrow, green valley through the desert. Shortly before the Nile reaches the sea, it branches to form a fan-shaped area of fertile land called a **delta**. Most ancient Egyptians lived in this delta area. For a long time they were protected from foreign invasions by the desert, the sea, and waterfalls called **cataracts**.

The Egyptians had an advantage over the people of the other river valley civilizations. They knew that every year, about the middle of July, the Nile would overflow its banks. By November the floodwaters would go down. But the waters left behind large amounts of rich soil good for growing crops.

The Egyptians learned to control the flood waters. To do this, they built a system of dams and ditches to drain the extra water from the land. They also dug out **basins**, or bowl-shaped holes. They used these to hold and store the extra water. A machine called a **shadoof** lifted the water from the river to the basins. To bring the water to the fields during the dry season, the Egyptians dug irrigation canals.

F. Kenneth Cox, Miriam Greenblatt, and Stanley S. Seaberg, *Human Heritage: A World History* (Columbus, Ohio: Charles E. Merrill, 1981), p. 55.

Purpose:
These paragraphs should be read to learn more about the Nile River. A second reading may be necessary to remember the impact of the Nile on the Egyptians.

Sequence:
What steps did the Egyptians follow to use the Nile River for growing crops?

Predicting Outcomes:
What may have happened to the Egyptian civilization had they not learned to use the Nile River to grow crops?

Cause-Effect Relationships:
What effect has the Nile River had on people who live in the delta area?

Making Generalizations:
How would you describe the ancient Egyptians based on this limited information?

Comprehension: Literature

Ask students to choose a character they have read about in literature and research this character. After obtaining as much information as possible, students will portray the character through dramatization or in a written passage. This portrayal will be presented to the class. It may be desirable to have several students research one character. Some suggested characters are Sherlock Holmes, Julius Caesar, Brutus, Scarlett O'Hara, Rhett Butler, and Daisy (the Great Gatsby).

1. What are some of the details of these people's lives that stand out?
2. How would you compare and/or contrast the characters of Rhett Butler and Scarlett O'Hara?
3. What was the relationship between Sherlock Holmes and his trusted friend, Dr. Watson?
4. Describe the shifts in mood before, during, and after the War Between the States in *Gone With the Wind*.

Adapted from Esther Tolbert, Baton Rouge Reading Clinic, Baton Rouge, Louisiana.

Comprehension: Art

Students are given prints of famous paintings from different schools of art such as the Realists or the Impressionists. After observing and noting the details in each print, the students are asked to look for the differences in the style of each painting. The teacher then asks the students to read a short description about one of the styles or schools of art presented. Using this information the student selects the painting that corresponds to the description in the passage.

Skills developed in this activity include:

Reading for details

Reading illustrations

Comparing and contrasting information

Vocabulary development

Making generalizations.

Adapted from an activity by Susan Beyer, East Baton Rouge Parish School, Louisiana.

Critical reading skills represent another level of comprehension skills. At this level, the reader analyzes and evaluates what is read. Questioning strategies should ensure that students locate the essential details and make a generalization about them; they must also evaluate the author's meaning and critically analyze the ideas. The development of skills at this level requires the application of the information previously learned in a practical way as well as the synthesis of ideas. An example of a questioning activity is: "After reading the book, *One Day in the Life of Ivan Denisovich* by Alexander Solzhenitsyn, what do you think the author's purpose was in writing this book?" Table 3.6 (p. 83) provides a listing of critical reading skills with a definition and sample question.

Critical reading skills are possibly the most important and least developed of the comprehension skills. Problem-solving skills relate not only to understanding content information, but they are also used in our daily lives as practical thinking skills. In reading math materials, as well as information in other content areas such as science and business education in which problems are to be

TABLE 3.6

Critical Reading Skills

Skill	Meaning	Sample Question
Interpret propaganda techniques	A skill which assists the reader in identifying and interpreting ideas or doctrines promoted by a special group.	Read the news cl... ing what the Soviet Ne.. Agency said about the U.S. intervention in the mid-east. What is meant by the statement "Russian armies were needed to protect the legitimate Afghanistan government from U.S. inspired rebel forces."
Differentiate facts and opinions	The skill which requires the reader to distinguish between statements which can be proven (facts) and ideas (opinions).	Review the two articles regarding the use of laetrile in treating cancer. Identify the two different opinions expressed, and list facts used to support these opinions.
Use problem-solving techniques	The skill which requires the reader to use all skills to analyze and reach a solution to problems.	The U.S. economic situation has been declining for about a decade. Read the folder of articles on past and current economic conditions. Then identify two ways you would suggest for solving the problem.
Recognize fallacies in reasoning	A skill which requires the reader to recognize the use of words to create an illusion which causes illogical or unsound ideas to be relayed.	All candidates for office continuously try to convince the voter that they are the best. Why does John Doe think he is the best candidate? How is he trying to convince you?
Identify relevant and irrelevant information	A skill which requires the reader to sort out information which is pertinent to the central thought being communicated	Read the article and select the information which is most relevant to understanding the solidarity movement in Poland.
Determine reliability of author	The skill which asks the reader to judge the background experiences and characteristics of the writer that determine his qualifications to report information on a certain subject.	For a report on the internal problems of the Iranian government, you have read information written by an American captive in Iran, the Iranian ambassador to France, and a professor of Iranian history at the state university. Identify each author's credentials and bias.

solved, students must know how to use a problem-solving strategy to reach a solution. Cooney, Davis, and Henderson support the use of guidelines for teachers to consider in helping students learn to solve problems.[26]

ACTIVITY

Math Word Problem

Problem:
Mr. and Mrs. Roberts were going on a vacation. They decided to go by plane because their time was short. The plane tickets cost $394.46 each. Their hotel room costs $75.00 a night and they estimate their meals to be $45.00 a day for both of them during their five-day trip. What is the minimum cost of this trip?

Situation:
A couple is taking a trip and needs to determine the minimum cost.

Details:
2 plane tickets at $394.46 each
hotel room at $75.00 for five days
meals at $45.00 for five days

Procedure:
Multiply to determine cost of plane tickets, total cost of room, and cost of meals. Then add the totals.

Prediction:
The trip will cost between $1200 and $1400.

Conclusion:

Plane tickets	788.92
Hotel	375.00
Motels	225.00
	$1388.92

In reading science materials, students must apply problem-solving skills when performing experiments, analyzing the results of experiments, understanding demonstrations or examples, or applying science knowledge to situations. The basic steps involved in the application of the problem-solving skill are,

Identify the problem

State hypotheses

Determine experiments to be performed to verify or discard the hypotheses

Perform the experiments

Evaluate the data

Form generalizations

In literature, such as essays and editorials, students are expected to differenti- ate between fact and opinion as they read. This is especially important when essays present facts and opinions. Likewise in reading social studies informa- tion, students must carefully analyze the material in order to differentiate facts and opinions. The details given in the material must be investigated for correct- ness in order to eliminate the possibility of arriving at the wrong conclusion. Some writers frequently state opinions using those facts that support their posi- tion, and deliberately delete those that would undermine their position. Other writers present all the facts, but may interpret this information differently from someone else. Students must also be aware of propaganda techniques as they read editorials or other social studies related materials.

LAGNIAPPE

A Guide for Developing Problem-Solving Skills

1. Make sure students understand the problem.
   a. Do the students understand the meanings of the the terms in the problem?
   b. Do the students take into consideration all the relevant information?
   c. Can the students show what the problem is asking them to find?
   d. Can the students state the problem in their own words? If appropri- ate, can students explain the problem in terms of a sketch?
2. Help students gather relevant thought material to assist in creating a plan.
   a. Assist the students in gathering information by having them analyze the given (and sometimes the assumed) solution.
   b. Help students obtain information by analyzing an analogous problem.
   c. When students have become discouraged by pursuing an unproduc- tive approach, help them view the problem from a different perspective.
3. Provide students with an atmosphere conducive to solving a problem.
4. Once students have obtained a solution, encourage them to reflect on the problem and the means of solution.
   a. If possible, have students verify solutions that have not been estab- lished deductively.
   b. Encourage students to seek and present alternate ways of solving a problem.
   c. Challenge students to investigate variations of the given problem.

H. Alan Robinson, *Teaching Reading and Study Strategies: The Content Areas,* 2nd ed. (Boston: Allyn and Bacon, 1978), p. 252.

In critically reading content information, students must learn to distinguish the relevant from the irrelevant. As a variety of materials are read for research projects in social studies or a word problem in math is studied, students must determine their purpose for reading and give close attention to the most rele- vant information. Articles, pamphlets, and other materials that are used to sup- plement content instruction too frequently are filled with information that is irrel- evant to the title of the material. Students must be encouraged to use their critical reading skills to recognize this form of misinformation.

As students interpret and evaluate information in content materials, they should note the credentials of the authors of the different materials. Various opinions are given due to the assorted backgrounds, degree of knowledge, and experiences of the writers. Students must be aware of these variances and consider them as materials are studied. For example, material written by a national economist would have a more diverse perspective on America's economic situation than material written by the president of a local savings institution. Similarly, an article or book on space travel would be more credible if written by a NASA employee than by a person who is just interested in space travel. Students should evaluate the authors' credentials to determi e their merit in writing the particular material.

LAGNIAPPE

In 1937 the Institute of Propaganda Analysis released a list of propaganda techniques that are used to influence a person's thoughts. These include

Name calling
Glittering generalities
Transfer
Plain folks
Testimonials
Bandwagon
Card stacking

Charlotte Agrast, "Teach Them to Read Between the Lines," *Grade Teacher* 85 (November 1967):72–74.

As content teachers use these different comprehension levels and sample questions to enhance the development skills, a word of caution is needed. The content teacher must be extremely familiar with materials before developing questions, in order to know if they are directly answered in the material, or if they are only implied. A "why" question on one selection may need only recall, while a "why" question on another requires critical reading. Content teachers must, therefore, develop greater sensitivity to the levels of comprehension, specific skills, and questions as they relate to the different content materials.

The application of comprehension skills is of extreme importance in content reading. Because this is an area in which students are often deficient, and because content information cannot be learned without the proper application of comprehension skills at all levels, content teachers must help in developing the comprehension skills. Table 3.7 presents a content passage with sample questions at different levels. Additional ideas on integrating comprehension into the content classroom, also different questioning strategies, are given in Chapter 5. More sample comprehension activities are provided in Appendix A.

TABLE 3.7

Sample Comprehension Questions at Different Levels

Missing a Beat in Washington:
The FDA Rejects the Artificial Heart—for Now

Heart transplants are sometimes the only hope for people dying of heart disease. But such operations are expensive, donors are scarce, and the recipient's body often rejects the new organ. Fewer than 50 transplants are done in the U.S. each year, and only 50% of patients survive five years. A more dazzling option seemed imminent when researchers from the University of Utah announced last month that they were ready to implant artificial hearts in humans. Only one hurdle remained: permission from the Food and Drug Administration. But last week the FDA rejected their application—for the time being at least.

The agency cited several problems with the proposal. First was concern over when and how doctors would decide to implant the plastic and aluminum device. The Utah team said it would try the procedure only as a last resort, when a patient's heart could not take over for the heart-lung pump used during surgery. But the FDA suggested that the doctors first consider using a less drastic mechanical aid, the so-called assist device. This piece of equipment leaves the natural heart intact but takes over the operation of one of the pumping chambers, usually the left ventricle, giving it a chance to recover and resume functioning. Says Cardiologist Melvin Cheitlin, who headed the FDA advisory panel that evaluated the device: "Once you've taken someone's heart out, you've really burnt the bridge."

The FDA also wondered whether the patient consent forms proposed by the Utah doctors fully spell out the kind of life the implant recipient should expect. The heart runs on compressed air and is electrically powered. That means the patient will be permanently tethered to air hoses and plugged into an electrical outlet, a sedentary, chair-to-bed existence.

Another issue is the difficulties posed by the bulky support equipment, including a refrigerator-size air compressor. Says Cheitlin: "There was discussion about the logistics of getting the power source into the operating room and eventually into the home. What about back-up systems for the home?" Some implant recipients may later be considered for heart transplants at Stanford University. "How," asks Cheitlin, "will they get them from Utah to California?"

Finally, the FDA believes the proposal does not go into enough detail on what, if any, information will be gathered after the implant. Will the researchers, for example, record the effect on the blood, measure exercise tolerance of the patient or monitor the new heart's pumping ability?

The FDA did not concern itself with some of the longer-range questions about the artificial heart, such as how to pick recipients or how to pay for implants (upwards of $50,000). William DeVries, the surgeon who hopes to do the first operation, and Robert Jarvik, who designed the device, hope that a revised application can be submitted within two months. Cheitlin was most encouraging about their chances: "They are going to come through with an acceptable proposal. I don't see any problem that it will eventually be granted."

---

1. What is this selection about? (Interpretive)
2. Why did the FDA reject the application? (Literal)

3. What effect would the artificial heart have on the life style of the recipient? (Interpretive)
4. "Once you've taken someone's heart out, you've really burnt the bridge." What is meant by this statement? (Interpretive)
5. Pretend that you are Dr. DeVries. You have performed a heart transplant on a person and when the heart-lung machine is removed after surgery the patient's heart could not take over. The patient will die without the heart-lung machine or an artificial heart. What would you do? (Critical)
6. One problem faced by the doctors in getting their artificial heart accepted is the bulky support equipment that would impede transport of the patient. How would you suggest that they solve this problem? (Critical)
7. Where was the artificial heart developed? (Literal)
8. If you had a serious heart disorder and the only way that you could be kept alive was with an artificial heart, would your choice be to live or die? State reasons for your decision. (Critical)

REFLECTION

Using a lesson in one content area, select three comprehension skills that you think are essential in learning that content information and tell why you think they are important.

PART C

STUDY SKILLS

Study skills are those skills that students use in organizing and assimilating information that must be learned. Study skills are probably the most important skills that students apply in content learning. Unfortunately, however, these skills frequently receive the least amount of attention in elementary school reading instruction and little, if any, emphasis in middle and secondary school instruction. To assist content teachers in developing a better understanding of these study skills it is first necessary to consider several notions about study and learning.

Four major variables involved in the complex act of studying have been identified. They include:

1. The nature of the criterion task or goal for which the student is preparing;
2. The nature of the material the student is studying;
3. The cognitive and affective characteristics of the student; and
4. The strategies the student uses to learn the material.[27]

These variables, of course, interact in ways that make teaching students how to study an even more complex task.

As in reading any material, students must hold some purpose for reading. This may be established by the teacher initially, but students must develop the skill on their own. Establishing purposes for reading are discussed in the previous section on "Comprehension," while more explicit techniques are presented in Chapter 5.

The second variable involved in studying relates to the materials. In content instruction, both textbooks and supplementary materials are used. These materials must be carefully selected (specific techniques are given in Chapter 8) and students must understand how the information in the material is organized. Many difficulties develop in studying content materials because students are unable to determine which comprehension skills to apply. This difficulty is usually due to a lack of understanding of the organizational patterns used by the authors in writing the material. Chapter 6 provides a detailed explanation of organizational patterns.

Content teachers know that each student is different, but frequently they are unable to identify the different cognitive and affective characteristics. Rita Dunn and Kenneth Dunn have written extensively about the learning styles of students. They have identified eighteen elements that influence how a student learns. Simply stated, these eighteen elements are organized into four categories of stimuli.

1. The Environmental Elements of Learning Style
   a. Sound: To what extend does background noise enhance or distract the learner?
   b. Light: Is study done best in a low or high lighting environment?
   c. Temperature: Is attention better focused in a warm or cool room?
   d. Design: Is a casual or structured environment preferred for study?

2. The Emotional Elements of Learning Style
   a. Motivation: To what extent do the students perceive a need to learn what they must study?
   b. Persistence: How long can the student work at a task before losing interest or giving up?
   c. Responsibility: How much direct supervision does the student need in order to complete a task?
   d. Structure: To what extent does the teacher have to organize, manage, and direct the students' learning experience?
3. The Sociological Elements of Learning Style
   Does the student learn best in an individual or group situation?
4. The Physical Elements of the Learning Styles
   a. Perceptual: Does the student learn best visually, auditorially, tactually, or through kinesthetic learning?
   b. Intake: Is learning enhanced if the student drinks or nibbles or do they learn better when slightly hungry?
   c. Time: At what time during the day does the student prefer to study?
   d. Mobility: How much movement does the student need as studying is done?[28]

Rita Dunn and Kenneth Dunn, TEACHING-STUDENTS THROUGH THEIR INDIVIDUAL LEARNING STYLES, 1978, pp. 5–17. Reprinted with permission of Reston Publishing Co., a Prentice-Hall Co., 11480 Sunset Hills Road, Reston, VA 22090

DIAGNOSING LEARNING STYLE

Stimuli	Elements					
Environmental	Sound	Light	Temperature	Design		
Emotional	Motivation	Persistence	Responsibility	Structure		
Sociological	Peers	Self	Pair	Team	Adult	Varied
Physical	Perceptual	Intake	Time	Mobility		

Rita Dunn and Kenneth Dunn, TEACHING STUDENTS THROUGH THEIR INDIVIDUAL LEARNING STYLES, 1978, pp. 5–17. Reprinted with permission of Reston Publishing Co., a Prentice-Hall Co., 11480 Sunset Hills Road, Reston, VA 22090

FIGURE 3.2

Elements of Learning Style

To determine the best study situation for students, content teachers should consider elements that vary for each student. Cognitive and affective characteristics of the learner have a tremendous impact on developing study skills.

In discussing study skills, the topic that is usually addressed first and only are the specific strategies that should be taught to help the student learn the material. Notetaking, outlining, summarizing, using book parts, and map reading are definitely important in the study process; however, research has failed to confirm the benefits of these techniques or to identify one technique as being superior to another. What is known about these various study techniques is that the use of the appropriate strategy with the right material does enable the student to process the information better; and that if students are to use study techniques they must be carefully taught to use the technique to advantage.[29] Additionally, research indicates that students who can already study effectively may find training in a new strategy to be more harmful than helpful.[30]

Thus, content teachers must know their students and provide instruction in the study skills only as needed. However, content teachers should realize, as discussed previously, that the application of various reading skills is different in each content area. Therefore, each content teacher must teach the study skills as appropriate to the areas of study.

LAGNIAPPE

In 1909, F. M. McMurray, Distinguished Professor of Education, Columbia University, published a book, *How to Study,* which presented seven steps for effective study:

1. Develop specific purposes or objectives as to why some things should be studied.
2. Try to supplement an author's ideas by going beyond what has been written.
3. Realize that "the sum of details does not equal the whole." In other words, read with the attitude that the meaning of a passage exists in the ideas that are built from examples.
4. Judge the worth of what an author writes. Simply because an idea appears in print does not make it true.
5. Knowing how to memorize is a valuable skill.
6. Try to apply the idea embodied in reading material to your own experiences.
7. Develop a flexible attitude toward knowledge. Learning is a growing process; not a fixation of information.

F. M. McMurray, *How to Study* (Boston: Houghton Mifflin, 1909), pp. 15–27.

While study skills are introduced in the elementary grades, the emphasis on using them becomes more intense as students begin to encounter content material in their middle and secondary classes. Many students who have been successful in reading, and who were able to use the other reading skills, experience difficulty in understanding and applying study skills. Study skills seem to be the last bridge that students must cross before becoming independent learners. Because students seem more removed from deciding when and how to use study skills, content teachers must not only provide instruction but should also be consistent in expecting students to apply the skills independently. Additionally, content teachers should help students realize that study skills must be applied to all content areas with material written at any level.

There are three basic categories of study skills: reference skills, organizational skills, and specialized study skills. In the following pages, each of these skill areas is briefly defined with an example of the skill. The specific skills in each area are summarized in Table 3.8 (pp. 93–95).

Skills that are concerned with locating information in various sources are referred to as *reference skills.* Such skills as using reference books and the library card catalog, and locating information in numerous sources are included in this category. Because emphasis is placed on using outside references and locating information in content assisgnments, learning to use these skills is essential in studying content materials. If students are asked to use reference materials, content teachers must be sure they know how to use them.

Organizational skills are perhaps even more difficult to apply than reference skills. Skills in this classification are outlining, underlining, and taking notes during reading. In using these skills, students must not only synthesize and evaluate the material read, they must also organize the information into a workable format. All of these organizational tasks require a higher level of cognition. Research, as well as classroom observation, shows that training in these skills is clearly lacking by many students in content classes. As students are taught these skills, their chances of success improve. Chapter 5 provides specific suggestions for teaching these organizational skills.

The third category of study skills is the *specialized study skills.* These skills are essential for obtaining and understanding information from books or other materials. Some of he skills in this area include using parts of a book; reading maps, graphs, tables, and charts; skimming and scanning; adjusting reading rate according to purpose; and the appropriate use of study techniques such as SQ3R. One of these specialized study skills, which is used differently in the various content areas, is that of reading different types of illustrations such as charts, tables, and diagrams. Charts and diagrams are used in reading physical education and health materials, while reading tables and graphs is important in reading math and science.

In reading art materials, however, students must not only read diagrams to understand directions, they must, more importantly, learn to read information from paintings and other works of art. Art illustrations can be interpreted to determine the style, medium, time period, the artist, and the mood. This interpretation of the illustration is a major objective in art instruction.

Science materials contain many illustrations; some serve to reinforce ideas found in the narrative, while others present new information that must be related. Regardless, this information should be read and put into perspective to aid in better understanding the concepts.

A major part of physical education learning is often done through the use of charts or diagrams. As teachers discuss concepts and directions, they usually draw diagrams to indicate court dimensions, for example, or to outline game strategy. If students experience difficulty in reading these diagrams, they will miss important information in the physical education class. Teachers frequently find that students need help in reading illustrations; thus, special instruction should be given before asking them to use diagrams or charts.

TABLE 3.8

Study Skills

Skill	Meaning	Activity
Reference	**Skills that require the use of outside reference materials:**	
Use dictionary	Skills needed to use the dictionary to pronounce words and obtain meanings.	As a selection in a content book is read, students should be told to check certain words in the dictionary for pronunciation and meaning.
Use encyclopedias and other reference materials such as the atlas and almanac	Skills needed to understand when and how to use the various reference materials for additional information.	Provide one group of students with a study guide and several reference materials that can be used to locate specified information. After showing students how to use the materials, tell them to use these sources for more information about the concepts being taught.
Use library card catalog	Skills needed to locate materials in the library.	Give each student an index card containing a key term about the concepts being taught. Have them use the card catalog for various sources that tell more about the term.
Organizational	**Skills needed to organize ideas for study:**	
Develop outlines	Skills used to organize ideas into a skeletal format or outline.	Provide students with a selection related to the concepts being studied and a series of questions that forms the basis of an outline as they are answered. For example: What is the first major topic discussed in this selection? What are three characteristics of a democratic government?

TABLE 3.8 (continued)

Study Skills

Skill	Meaning	Activity
Underline important points or key ideas	Skills needed to identify major ideas related to a topic and to note these ideas for future study.	Use a modification of the preceding activity and tell students to underline answers to questions. These questions should be carefully worded to reflect only the key ideas.
Take notes during reading	The skill of understanding the most important ideas to be written down for later recall.	Demonstrate to students how outlining can be used in notetaking to write the most important ideas for use in future study. Initially a teacher-made outline that corresponds to the material being read may be helpful.
Specialized Study Skills	**Skills necessary for using the content textbook and studying special parts of the text:**	
Using parts of the book	Skills needed to use the table of contents, index, glossary, etc. in the book to locate information.	Prior to using a text or other content material, show students the various parts of the material by using a scavenger hunt procedure in which questions are used to locate information in the different parts of the book.
Reading maps, graphs, tables, charts, and other graphics	Skills used to read pictorial representations of information within printed materials.	Provide the student with a graphic (picture, map, chart, etc.) and a series of questions that can be answered only by interpreting the illustration.
Skimming and scanning	Skills used to read content material hurriedly in order to locate specific information or to get a general impression of the content.	Give the student a specific question and direct him/her to scan the material to locate the answer. The teacher may also tell students to skim material to determine what it is about so that questions they want answers to can be asked.

TABLE 3.8 (continued)

Study Skills

Skill	Meaning	Activity
Adjusting rate according to purpose	The skill of reading information with appropriate speed for understanding the content.	Discuss with students the importance of reading information at varying rates according to their purpose for reading. Then before reading different materials ask them to say whether the information should be read quickly or slowly.
Using study techniques	The use of specialized study procedures such as SQ3R to obtain more information from the text.	Present a study technique to students and work through the various steps with them. As assignments are given, remind them of the steps in the study technique and encourage the application of the skill.
Developing test-taking skills	The ability to apply systematic procedures in studying for and taking exams.	Outline procedures that should be followed in studying for a test. Ask half of the class to use the procedure and the others to study as usual. Give a test (for no grade, of course) and see which group performs better.

A major part of mathematical reading involves the interpretation of graphs, diagrams, tables, and charts. The illustrations are often filled with symbols or notes that must be interpreted in order to get the meaning, or to relate the information to the narrative.

Many types of illustrations are used in content materials. Bar graphs, circle graphs, and line graphs are read differently, as are the various tables, diagrams, and charts. Students should be shown how to read these important parts of the content materials and encouraged to study them carefully as they read—illustrations should never be skipped in content reading.

Another specialized study skill that relates to all content areas is the use of study strategies. Many study strategies are presented in Chapter 5. Using these as a guide, content teachers may select the strategy that most closely relates to the content area and the needs of the students. For example, the English teacher may find the EVOKER strategy to be most helpful, while the science

As students read about art, they might view actual art objects, or pictures of them, as they make generalizations.

teacher may find SQ3R or PQRST more suitable. Regardless of the strategy selected, content teachers must be consistent in expecting students to apply the strategy.

Content teachers may find it necessary to help students develop skills in studying for and taking tests. In the current educational system, this skill is most crucial when one considers the number of tests that students must take and the importance placed on each—promotions, graduations, college entrance, etc. Because these skills are so essential to success in middle and secondary schools, a section in Chapter 5 is devoted to instructional procedures in developing these skills.

REFLECTION

Consider the types of materials that students must study in your content area and identify the study skills you think would be most helpful to them. Tell why you think these are the most necessary.

Suggestions for teaching study skills are given in Chapter 5, with more sample activities provided below and in Appendix A. Learning to use study skills properly is essential for functioning in content classes and in society in general. These are skills that must be mastered to assure success in learning. There are many daily activities that require the use of one or more of these skills; thus, content teachers should emphasize the importance of acquiring these skills.

ACTIVITIES

Notetaking and Outlining

To help students take notes, provide them with an outline like the one below. Then dictate notes that will aid them in completing the outline.

I.   Heating Matter
    A. Heating a gas
       1.
       2.
       3.
       4.
    B. Heating a liquid
       1.
       2.
       3.
       4.
       5.
    C. Heating a solid
       1.
       2.
       3.
II. Particles in Matter
    A.
    B.
    C.
    D.
    E.
    F.
III. Speed of Moving Particles
    A.
    B.
    C.

Reading Illustrations

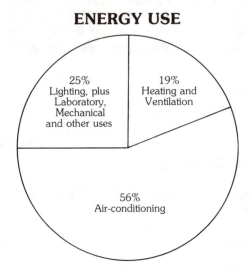

ENERGY USE

Energy consumption declines but cost is climbing

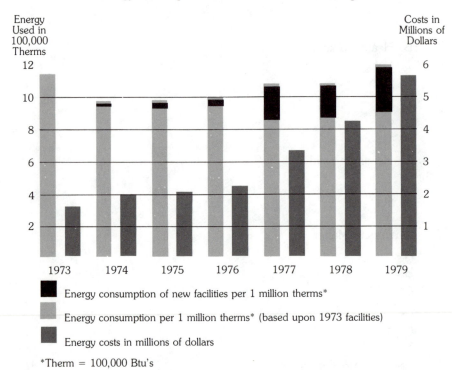

Energy consumption of new facilities per 1 million therms*

Energy consumption per 1 million therms* (based upon 1973 facilities)

Energy costs in millions of dollars

*Therm = 100,000 Btu's

Provide a graph or table and ask the students to calculate the answers to these problems.

1. If the cost of energy is $5.5 million dollars in 1979 and 19 percent of this amount is for heating and ventilation, how much does it cost for heating and ventilation?
2. What was the approximate cost of the energy consumption of new facilities in 1977?
3. What is the approximate amount of energy reduction in the facilities existing in 1973 between 1973 and 1979?
4. What is the approximate difference in energy costs between 1973 and 1979?
5. According to the circle graph, what is the largest consumer of energy?

Reading Maps

Using this map of Florida as a guide, ask students to answer the following questions about it.

1. What highway would you take to go from Jacksonville to Miami?
2. What is the Sunshine Parkway?
3. What is the southernmost city in Florida according to this map?
4. Which interstate highway passes the closest to Gainesville?
5. Which city is the westernmost city in Florida according to this map?

Book Parts

Tell students to use the textbook to answer these questions. They must read the information carefully in order to completely answer some of the questions. Advise them to take their time and get acquainted with the new textbook.

1. On what page does the glossary begin?
2. What is the title of the book?
3. What do the authors hope to accomplish in this book? (Read the foreword.)
4. How many authors are there? Who are they and where are they from?
5. How many chapters does the book contain?
6. What chapters deal with nonmetric and metric geometry?
7. Where can you find a table of mathematical symbols? What is the meaning of 41?
8. On what pages could you find information on isosceles triangles?
9. Does this book feature an answer key?
10. What is included in the "Chapter Supplement" at the end of each chapter?

Reading Diagrams

Using diagrams like this one, students can be guided in reading them through the use of questions like those below. This is a diagram of a flower.

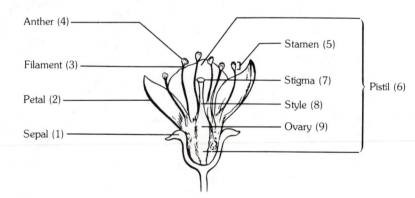

1. What part of the flower holds the petals together?
2. Identify the parts of the pistil.
3. What supports the anther?
4. What part of the flower collects pollen?

Understanding Charts and Tables

Give students a copy of the following financial statement. Tell them to analyze the data and then ask questions about the statement so that their depth of understanding can be determined.

Financial Statement

Assets	*June 30, 1983*	*June 30, 1982*
Cash	$ 67,419	$ 41,462
Short Term Investments	1,894,277	1,206,179
Inventory of Publications	148,652	176,827
Other Current Assets	60,913	12,964
Total Current Assets	2,171,261	1,437,432
Investment in Stocks and Bonds	279,045	202,315
Fixed Assets	709,396	729,737
Buildings	114,646	116,327
Furniture and Equipment	40,178	40,178
Total Fixed Assets	864,220	886,242
Other Assets		
Deferred Costs	20,644	10,607
Total Other Assets	20,644	10,607
Total Assets	$3,335,170	$2,536,596
Liabilities		
Current Liabilities:		
Accounts Payable	$ 101,986	$ 37,998
Memberships	1,012,523	730,417
Other Current Liabilities	54,030	64,687
Total Current Liabilities	1,168,559	833,102
Fund Balance	2,166,631	1,703,494
Total Liabilities and Fund Balance	$3,335,170	$2,536,596

1. What assets generated the most revenues in 1983?
2. Why were buildings and furniture and equipment valued at lesser amounts in 1983 than 1982?
3. Why is revenue generated by memberships listed as a liability?
4. What is the percentage of increase of total assets from 1982 to 1983?
5. What is the percentage of increase of total current liabilities from 1982 to 1983?

After the students have completed this activity, give them completely new data, and ask them to fill out a financial statement using this format.

FITTING CONCEPTS AND READING SKILLS TOGETHER

After the teacher has identified the concepts that must be taught in a specific content area (Chapter 2), the reading skill or skills that can most effectively help in learning these concepts must also be identified. At this point, the skills become the tools in the instructional process that enable students to learn the concept presented. Thus, to integrate reading instruction into content teaching, the teacher must decide what the students are to learn about the content information. These are the concepts. To enhance learning these concepts, the content teacher should also know which reading skills students must apply to understand the concepts. With this information, the teacher can proceed with instruction that includes concept and vocabulary development, as well as a review of the necessary reading skills. Although this initial planning to identify concepts and reading skills does require extra time, content teachers usually report that instruction is better organized, and that students seem more excited about content learning. Table 3.9 presents an example of concepts and reading skills that were identified for a unit on latitude and longitude. Added to this table is an explanation of why a skill was needed to develop a concept. This is given only for clarification and would not be necessary for teachers to follow.

To decide which reading skills relate to the concepts being taught, teachers may find the following procedure to be helpful:

1. Look at the concepts to be learned and the material to be used.
2. Decide if there are any words that the student must be taught to pronounce or for which the meaning may be unknown. If so, decide which word identification skills need to be reviewed.
3. Ask yourself what the student must understand from the material in order to learn the concepts that are identified. Using Tables 3.4, 3.5, and 3.6, identify the comprehension skills that are necessary.
4. If a large number of skills are identified, narrow them down to a manageable number that can be reviewed before the student reads the material. A manageable number would probably be three to five of the most essential skills.
5. Look at the list of study skills in Table 3.8 and decide if there are any study skills that need to be emphasized so that the student can learn the concepts.
6. List the skills, making sure that only the most important have been identified so that not too much content instructional time is taken, and yet enough review of the skills is provided to help students learn the content information.

Because the primary emphasis in content teaching is on concept development, the various reading skills must be integrated into the instructional process. Using reading skills as tools to teach the content concepts is not only effective, but efficient as well. Table 3.1 (pp. 47–49) provides a summary list of the different reading skills that relate to the various content areas. Content reading instruction enhances content learning as well as sharpens the reading skills essential to understanding content information.

REFLECTION

Using the concepts that you identified in Step I (Chapter 2), relate five reading skills that are necessary for understanding the concept. Follow the procedures outlined in this section.

TABLE 3.9

Concepts and Related Reading Skills

Concept	Skills and Why Needed

Longitude is a system for determining location on the earth's surface.

1. *Recall of important points:*
   a. Necessary for remembering that longitude is represented by vertical lines on a map called meridians.
   b. These are measured in degrees.
   c. Prime Meridian.
   d. East and West.
2. *Cause-effect:* Earth is a sphere; as we move closer to poles, degrees of longitude become smaller; as we move toward the equator, degrees of longtude become greater.
3. *Word meaning:* Longitude and Prime Meridian—give meaning rather than analysis of word parts or use of contextual analysis.
4. *Syllabication:* Longitude and meridian—alternative to word meaning, divide words into syllables.
5. *Problem solving and map reading:* Determine the location of a ship or plane using computation and a world map or globe.
6. *Using parts of a book or other material:* The student might wish to explore this concept of longitude in more detail in other sources.
7. *Relationship:* The student must see the relationship between longitude and latitude to find direction on a map.

Latitude is a system used in conjunction with longitude for determining location on the earth's surface.

1. *Recall of important points:*
   a. Equator divides earth into two equal parts.
   b. Lines of latitude are horizontal.
   c. Run North and South of equator.
   d. Measured in degrees.
2. *Cause-effect:* Circumference of earth is 24,900 miles and there are 360 degrees of latitude; results in a degree of latitude equaling 69 miles in length.
3. *Word meaning:* Latitude and circumference—emphasize meaning rather than analysis of word parts.
4. *Syllabication:* Latitude and circumference—alternative to word meaning, divide words into syllables.
5. *Problem solving and map reading:* Determine the location of a ship or plane using computation and a world map or globe.
6. *Using parts of a book or other material:* The student may wish to explore this concept of latitude in more detail in other sources.
7. *Relationship:* The student must see the relationship between latitude and longitude to find directions on a map.

SUMMARY

As students learn the information presented in content classes, it becomes apparent that many students are unable to deal with the materials and information. This is often caused by students not having been taught to relate their reading skill knowledge to their content reading. To help content teachers in aiding students with this dilemma, this chapter presents information on reading instruction as well as the various reading skill areas.

The reading skill areas that are essential to content reading include word identification, comprehension, and study skills. In word identification, emphasis is placed on contextual analysis and structural analysis skills to help in pronouncing words and determining meaning. In comprehension, the discussion includes information on the the three levels of comprehension — literal, interpretive, and critical reading skills. The third skill area, study skills, includes reference skills such as using the dictionary, organizational skills such as outlining and notetaking, and specialized study skills such as using book parts, adjusting reading rate, and applying study techniques.

The final part of the chapter presents a procedure for use in relating reading skills and concepts.

FOR DISCUSSION

1. What are the three levels of comprehension? Define each area and tell how it relates to your content teaching.
2. As a content teacher, how do you see reading skills relating to your classroom instruction? Which skills do you think will be most important in your content area?
3. Why is it necessary to identify concepts that are taught before deciding the reading skills to be used in your content instruction?
4. What is your opinion of teaching word identification skills in the content classroom? Which of the word identification skills do you think are most important? Why?

OTHER SUGGESTED READINGS

Aulls, Mark W. *Developmental and Remedial Reading in the Middle Grades.* Boston: Allyn and Bacon, 1978. Chapters 1, 4, 9.

Axelrod, Jerome. "Getting the Main Idea is Still the Main Idea," *Journal of Reading* 18 (February 1975):383–87.

Brown, A. L., and Smiley, S.S. "The Development of Strategies for Studying Tests." *Child Development* 49 (December 1978): 1076–88.

Clary, Linda Mixon. "How Well Do You Teach Critical Reading?" *The Reading Teacher* 31 (November 1977):142–46.

Cunningham, Patricia M. "Applying a Compare/Contrast Process to Identifying Polysyllabic Words." *Journal of Reading Behavior* 12 (Fall 1980):213–23.

Cunningham, Patricia M.; Cunningham, James W.; and Rystrom, Richard C. "A New Syllabication Strategy and Reading Achievement." *Reading World* 20 (March 1981):208–14.

Cushenbury, D.C. "Effective Procedures for Teaching Reference Study Skills." *Reading Horizons* 19 (Spring 1979):245–47.

Dauzat, JoAnn, and Dauzat, Sam V. *Reading: The Teacher and The Learner.* New York: John Wiley and Sons, 1981. Chapters 2–11.

Dean, J. "Study Skills—Learning How to Learn." *Education* 5 (October 1977):9–11.

Devine, Thomas G. *Teaching Study Skills.* Boston: Allyn and Bacon, 1981.

Dillner, Martha H., and Olson, Joanne P. *Personalizing Reading Instruction in Middle, Junior, and Senior High School.* New York: Macmillan, 1977. Chapters 1–4, 10.

DuBois, Diane, and Stice, Carole. "Comprehension Instruction: Let's Recall It for Repair." *Reading World* 20 (March 1981):173–84.

Dyer, J. W. "An Analysis of Three Study Skills: Notetaking, Summarizing and Rereading." *Journal of Educational Research* 73 (September/October 1979):3–7.

Ehri, Linnea C.; Barron, Roderick W.; and Feldman, Jeffrey M. *The Recognition of Words.* Newark, Del.: International Reading Association, 1978.

Forgan, Harry W., and Mangrum, Charles T. *Teaching Content Area Reading Skills,* 2nd ed. Columbus, Ohio: Charles E. Merrill, 1981. Modules 5–7.

Gagné, Ellen D., and Memory, David. "Instructional Events and Comprehension: Generalization Across Passages." *Journal of Reading Behavior* 10 (Winter 1978): 321–35.

Goodman, Yetta; Burke, Carolyn; and Sherman, Barry. *Reading Strategies: Focus on Comprehension.* New York: Holt, Rinehart, and Winston, 1980.

Harker, W. J. "Reading and Study Skills: An Overview for Teachers." *Reading* 12 (July 1978):2–9.

Harris, Larry A., and Smith, Carl B. *Reading Instruction,* 3rd ed. New York: Holt, Rinehart, and Winston, 1980. Chapters 5–9.

Heilman, Arthur; Blair, Timothy; and Rupley, William H. *Principles and Practices of Teaching Reading,* 5th ed. Columbus, Ohio: Charles E. Merrill, 1981. Chapters 7–9.

Ives, Josephine P.; Bursuk, Laura Z; and Ives, Summer A. *Word Identification Techniques.* Chicago: Rand McNally, 1979.

Kapinus, Barbara. "Miniclinics: Small Units of Reading Instruction Can Be a Big Help." *Journal of Reading* 24 (March 1981):469–74.

Krulee, Gilbert K.; Fairweather, Peter G.; and Bergquist, Sidney R. "Organizing Factors in the Comprehension and Recall of Connected Discourse." *Journal of Psycholinguistic Research* 8 (March 1979):141–63.

Lamberg, Walter J., and Lamb, Charles E. *Reading Instruction in the Content Areas.* Chicago: Rand McNally, 1980. Chapters 3–5.

Liebert, Burt, and Liebert, Marjorie. *A Schoolwide Secondary Reading Program: Here's How.* New York: John Wiley and Sons, 1979. Chapters 7–11.

Lindsey, Jimmy D.; Beck, Frances W.; and Bursor, Davele E. "An Analytical-Tutorial Method for Developing Adolescents' Sight Vocabulary." *Journal of Reading* 24 (April 1981):591–94.

Mangrum, Charles T., and Forgan, Harry W. *Developing Competencies in Teaching Reading.* Columbus, Ohio: Charles E. Merrill, 1979. Module 3–6.

Manzo, Anthony V., and Casale, Ula. "The Five C's: A Problem Solving Approach to Study Skills." *Reading Horizons* 20 (Summer 1980):281–84.

Marshak, D. "What's the Status of Study Skills in Your School?" *NASSP Bulletin* 6 (December 1979):105–10.

Mattleman, Marcience S., and Blake, Howard E. "Study Skills: Prescriptions for Survival." *Language Arts* 54 (November/December 1977):925–27.

Memory, David M., and Moore, David W. "Selecting Sources in Library Research: An Activity in Skimming and Critical Reading." *Journal of Reading* 24 (March 1981):469–74.

Pennock, Clifford, ed. *Reading Comprehension at Four Linguistic Levels.* Newark, Del.: International Reading Association, 1979.

Rehder, Lynne G. "Reading Skills in a Paperback Classroom." *Reading Horizons* 21 (Fall 1980):16–21.

Riley, J. D., and Dryer, J. "The Effects of Notetaking." *Reading World* 19 (October 1979):51–6.

Rodgers, Dennis. "Which Connection? Signals to Enhance Comprehension." *Journal of Reading* 17 (March 1974):462–66.

Roe, Betty D.; Stoodt, Barbara D.; and Burns, Paul C. *Reading Instruction in the Secondary School,* rev. ed. Chicago: Rand McNally, 1978. Chapters 4–7.

Ross, Elinor Parry. "Checking the Source: An Essential Component of Critical Reading." *Journal of Reading* 24 (January 1981):314–15.

Santz, Carol Minnick, and Hayes, Bernard L., eds. *Children's Prose Comprehension.* Newark, Del.: International Reading Association, 1981.

Schachter, Sumner W. "Developing Flexible Reading Habits." *Journal of Reading* 22 (November 1978):149–52.

Smith, Bonnie, ed. *Teachers, Tangibles, Techniques: Comprehension of Content in Reading.* Newark, Del.: International Reading Association, 1975.

Stoodt, Barbara D. *Reading Instruction.* Boston: Houghton Mifflin, 1981. Chapters 4–6.

Stoodt, B. D., and Balbo, E. "Integrating Study Skills Instruction with Content in a Secondary Classroom." *Reading World* 18 (March 1979):247–52.

Vacca, Richard T. "A Study of Holistic and Subskill Instructional Approaches to Reading Comprehension." *Journal of Reading* 23 (March 1980):512–18.

Weaver, Phyllis. *Research Within Reach.* Newark, Del.: International Reading Association, 1978.

Whimbey, Arthur; Carmichael, J.W.; Jones, Lester W.; Hunter, Jacqueline T.; and Vincent, Harold A. "Teaching Critical Reading and Analytical Reasoning in Project SOAR." *Journal of Reading* 24 (October 1980):5–10.

Zintz, Miles. *The Reading Process,* 3rd ed. Dubuque, Iowa: William C. Brown, 1980. Chapters 9–14.

NOTES

1. R. D. Boyd, "Growth of Phonic Skills in Reading," in *Clinical Studies in Reading III*, ed. Helen M. Robinson, Supplemental Educational Monographs, no. 97 (Chicago: University of Chicago Press, 1969), pp. 68–87.
2. Emma E. Plattor and Ellsworth S. Woestehoff, "Specific Reading Disabilities of Disadvantaged Children," in *Reading Difficulties: Diagnosis, Correction and Remediation*, ed. William Durr (Newark, Del.: International Reading Association, 1970), pp. 55–60.
3. Gerald G. Glass and Elizabeth H. Burton, "How Do They Decode? Verbalizations and Observed Behaviors of Successful Decoders," *Education* 94 (September/October 1973):58–64; George Marsh, Peter Desberg, and James Cooper, "Developmental Changes in Reading Strategies," *Journal of Reading Behavior* 9 (Winter 1977):391–94.
4. Walter J. Lamberg and Charles E. Lamb, *Reading Instruction in the Content Areas* (Chicago: Rand McNally, 1980), p. 265.
5. Ruth F. Waugh and K. W. Howell, "Teaching Modern Syllabication," *The Reading Teacher* 29 (October 1975):20–25.
6. Phyllis Weaver, *Research Within Reach* (Newark, Del.: International Reading Association, 1978), pp. 21–24.
7. Harold Herber, *Teaching Reading in Content Areas,* 2nd ed. (Englewood Cliffs, N.J.: Prentice-Hall, 1978), p. 146.
8. Leo M. Schell, "Teaching Structural Analysis," *The Reading Teacher* 21 (November 1968):133–37; Donald C. McFeely, "Syllabication Usefulness in a Basal and

Social Studies Vocabulary," *The Reading Teacher* 27 (May 1974):809–14; Robert J. Marzano et al., "Are Syllabication and Reading Ability Related?" *Journal of Reading* 19 (April 1976):545–47.

9. Kenneth J. Smith, "A Combination of Strategies for Decoding," in *Reading Between and Beyond the Lines*, ed. Malcolm P. Douglas, Claremont Reading Conference Thirty-seventh Yearbook, 1973, pp. 148–55.

10. S. Jay Samuels, Gerald Begy, and Chaur Ching Chen, "Comparison of Word Recognition Speed and Strategies of Less Skilled and More Highly Skilled Readers," *Reading Research Quarterly* 11 (1975–76):72–86; Helen Altman Klein, Gary A. Klein, and Christy Hopkins Vigoda, "The Utilization of Contextual Information by High School Students," in *Reading: Convention and Inquiry*, eds. George H. McNinch and Wallace D. Miller, Twenty-fourth Yearbook of the National Reading Conference, 1975, pp. 148–54.

11. George D. Spache, *Diagnosing and Correcting Reading Disabilities* (Boston: Allyn and Bacon, 1976), p. 404; Kenneth S. Goodman, "A Linguistic Study of Cues and Miscues in Reading," *Elementary English* 42 (1965):639–43.

12. Harold L. Herber, *Teaching Reading in Content Areas*, 2nd ed. (Englewood Cliffs, N.J.: Prentice-Hall, 1978), p. 40.

13. Carl B. Smith, Sharon L. Smith, and Larry Mikulecky, *Teaching Reading in Secondary School Content Subjects* (New York: Holt, Rinehart, and Winston, 1978), p. 233.

14. Walter J. Lamberg and Charles E. Lamb, *Reading Instruction in the Content Areas* (Chicago: Rand McNally, 1978) pp. 160–61.

15. P. David Pearson and Dale D. Johnson, *Teaching Reading Comprehension* (New York: Holt, Rinehart, and Winston, 1978), pp. 8–19.

16. Thomas H. Estes and Joseph L. Vaughan, Jr., "Reading Interests and Comprehension: Implications," *The Reading Teacher* 27 (November 1973):149–53.

17. Margaret S. Steffensen, Chitra Joag-Dev, and Richard C. Anderson, "A Cross-Cultural Perspective on Reading Comprehension," *Reading Research Quarterly* 15 (1979):10–29.

18. Hilda Taba, "The Teaching of Thinking," *Elementary English* 42 (May 1965):534.

19. Frank J. Guszak, "Teaching, Questioning and Reading," *The Reading Teacher* 21 (December 1968):227–34.

20. Dolores Durkin, "What Classroom Observations Reveal About Reading Comprehension Instruction," *Reading Research Quarterly* 14 (1978–79):521.

21. Richard C. Anderson, James W. Picher, and Larry L. Shirey, *Effects of the Reader's Schema at Different Points in Time*, Technical Report no. 119 (Cambridge, Mass.: Bolt, Beranek and Newman; Urbana, Ill.: Center for the Study of Reading, 1979).

22. E. Marcia Sheridan, "A Review of Research on Schema Theory and Its Implications for Reading Instruction in Secondary Reading" (South Bend, Ind.: Indiana University at South Bend, 1978). (ED 167 947).

23. Benjamin S. Bloom, et al., eds., *Taxonomy of Educational Objectives: Handbook I, Cognitive Domain* (New York: David McKay, 1956); Norris M. Sanders, *Classroom Questions—What Kinds?* (New York: Harper and Row, 1966); Thomas C. Barrett, "Taxonomy of Cognitive and Affective Dimensions of Reading Comprehension," in Theodore Clymer, "What is Reading? Some Current Concepts," *Innovation and Change in Reading Instruction*, Sixty-Seventh Yearbook, National Society for the Study of Education, Part II (Chicago: University of Chicago Press, 1968), pp. 19–23.

24. Ellen Lamar Thomas and H. Alan Robinson, *Improving Reading in Every Classroom* (Boston: Allyn and Bacon, 1972), p. 395.

25. Joan Baez, "If I Knew," *David's Album* (Vanguard, 1969).

26. Thomas J. Cooney, Edward J. Davis, and K. B. Henderson, *Dynamics of Teaching Secondary School Mathematics* (Boston: Houghton Mifflin, 1975), pp. 246–72.

27. Bonnie B. Armbruster and Thomas H. Anderson, "Research Synthesis on Study Skills," *Educational Leadership* 39 (November 1981): 154.
28. Rita Dunn and Kenneth Dunn, *Teaching Students Through Their Individual Learning Styles: A Practical Approach* (Reston, Va.: Reston, 1978), pp. 5–17.
29. Armbruster and Anderson, "Research Synthesis," p. 155.
30. B. Y. L. Wong and W. Jones, "Increasing Metacomprehension in Learning Disabled and Normally-Achieving Students Through Self-Questioning Training," mimeographed (Burnaby, B. C., Canada: Simon Fraser University, 1981).

STEP THREE

ASSESSING STUDENT NEEDS

The third step in successfully implementing reading instruction through content teaching involves assessing the student's needs. Obtaining diagnostic information about each student is essential to the development of appropriate instructional strategies. Diagnosis enables the teacher to determine the strengths and weaknesses of each student, thereby facilitating the instructional process. Formal and informal diagnostic procedures helpful to the content teacher are discussed in Chapter 4. Teachers should select procedures that can be used most easily in their classrooms. Other diagnostic ideas may be added as needed.

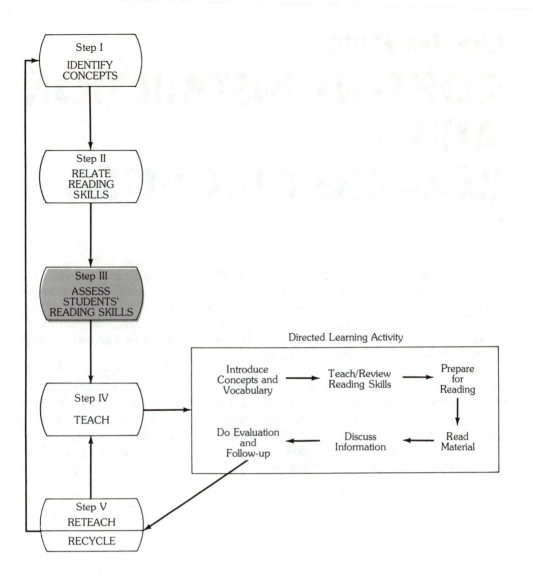

Step I
IDENTIFY CONCEPTS

Step II
RELATE READING SKILLS

Step III
ASSESS STUDENTS' READING SKILLS

Step IV
TEACH

Step V
RETEACH
RECYCLE

Directed Learning Activity

Introduce Concepts and Vocabulary → Teach/Review Reading Skills → Prepare for Reading

Do Evaluation and Follow-up ← Discuss Information ← Read Material

CHAPTER FOUR

CONTENT INSTRUCTION AND READING DIAGNOSIS

Reading diagnosis in the content classroom? "#@?/¢!" says the content teacher. This initial reaction is not unexpected because content teachers are now almost at the breaking point with overloaded classes, students on different levels, discipline problems, and the constraints of short class periods. Teachers find these and other problems difficult enough without adding another task—diagnosis. However, diagnosis is an essential step in implementing reading instruction through content teaching.

Teachers must use diagnosis as a basis for instruction since each student's strengths and weaknesses in various skills areas, instructional and independent reading levels, concept knowledge, and other diagnostic data will be helpful in implementing a content reading program. This step in the content reading process not only provides helpful information, but saves time by eliminating trial-and-error methods in teaching.

In this chapter various diagnostic procedures are discussed and examples given of the informal instruments that are most helpful.

STUDY QUESTIONS

1. How does diagnosis relate to content instruction?
2. What are some of the more appropriate diagnostic procedures?
3. Which diagnostic procedures can be used with groups in the total content class?
4. What information can be obtained from various diagnostic tests?

VOCABULARY

Cloze procedure
Criterion-referenced tests
Diagnostic tests
Formal diagnostic procedures
Frustration level
Group Reading Inventory

Independent level
Informal diagnosis
Informal Reading Inventory
Instructional level
Observation
Simplified Reading Inventory

DIAGNOSIS AND CONTENT INSTRUCTION

The emphasis in content teaching is on teaching students how to learn the information in each content area. Teachers are concerned with attaining optimum concept development; however, in a developmental program where heterogeneous grouping exists, many instructional reading levels also exist. The student's instructional reading level is the operational level for classroom instruction, while the student's independent level is that at which a student reads without assistance, usually lower than the instructional level. For example, in a seventh grade science class, the students' instructional reading levels may vary from low second grade to high tenth grade.

Not only do reading levels vary, but students also exhibit different strengths and weaknesses in reading skills that are used in content reading. For example, in a ninth grade social studies class a few students are able to determine the cause-effect relationship in a passage, while others are unable to do so at all.

Content teachers often do not recognize these skill weaknesses early in the school year and only discover them later through trial and error. Fortunately, this situation can be eased by using diagnostic procedures at the start of the school year or as each unit of study is introduced.

Although content teachers are usually unaccustomed to using diagnostic procedures, they can get much information through relatively simple techniques.[1] An obvious advantage to obtaining diagnostic information about each student is that instructional strategies can be planned to facilitate better learning. Guesswork is eliminated as alternative instructional procedures and materials are selected.

Information obtained early in the year also enables the teacher to avoid such difficulties as discovering nine weeks into the school year that one-third of the class is unable to read the textbook. With diagnostic information, the teacher can make instructional adjustments before problems develop.

Although early diagnosis is important in expediting content reading instruction, it must be continuous throughout the year. As the needs of the students change, so must instruction. As a result, continuous diagnosis helps maintain an effective learning environment in the content classroom. (Continuous diagnosis does not mean daily or even weekly formal testing, but simply implies the need for informal student review as the year progresses.)

Even though the benefits of diagnosis in the content classroom greatly outweigh the problems, a few comments about these difficulties would be in the best interest of the teacher. Perhaps the most formidable obstacle the teacher must overcome is time. This is especially true for teachers with up to one hundred and fifty students every day in five or more class periods. Teachers feel great pressure, whether real or perceived, to start instruction immediately in an effort to cover as much material as possible in a specific content course. As a result, many do not believe they have the time to diagnose even superficially. Thus, diagnosis is often deleted as part of content teaching.

Class size—usually thirty or more students in a single class—is especially acute in attending logistically to each student's diagnostic needs. These concerns are discussed later in this chapter.

The problems of time and class size and their adverse effect on using diagnostic procedures effectively must be acknowledged. Some good news, however, is that there are diagnostic procedures that require a relatively minimum amount of time and are administered to groups of students rather than to individuals. The individually administered instruments also require minimum time, although more than the group diagnostic procedures.

DIAGNOSTIC PROCEDURES FOR THE CONTENT TEACHER

In examining the various types of diagnostic procedures, content teachers find that there are a variety of tools at their disposal. Each diagnostic tool has a specific purpose. Some serve several purposes, and content teachers must know them and be able to determine which best meets their needs. In an effort to help teachers learn more about diagnostic procedures, this chapter is devoted to discussing the various types of diagnostic instruments that may be used in the content classroom.

Diagnostic procedures are separated into two major categories, formal and informal diagnostic tools. Each category is discussed along with tests and diagnostic techniques.

FORMAL DIAGNOSTIC PROCEDURES

Although there are some excellent formal instruments available for diagnosing the individual student's reading strengths and weaknesses, most are not suggested for use by the content teacher. These tests are more appropriately used by reading specialists, classroom teachers in self-contained classrooms with more time than the content teacher, and teachers of reading in middle schools, and junior and senior high schools. Thus, this discussion of formal diagnostic procedures will deal only with those instruments that can provide maximum information with minimum time and effort. In an effort to present usable formal procedures to content teachers, no individually administered instruments are discussed. The formal procedures discussed are strictly group-administered. This is in keeping with our philosophy that content teachers should not devote too much time to reading diagnosis.

Achievement Tests. Achievement tests, although not diagnostic tests, are discussed briefly because most content teachers participate in the administration and interpretation of these instruments every year. Therefore, the content teacher should critically evaluate the usefulness of achievement tests and their role in providing diagnostic information.

Achievement tests are designed to fulfill several functions in the testing hierarchy. They measure such things as the depth of a student's knowledge in various areas of the curriculum, the extent to which acquisition of specific information has occurred, and the extent to which certain skills have been mastered. Primarily, the purpose of these instruments is to determine the overall effectiveness of instruction in the broad areas of the curriculum.

These instruments are rigidly standardized using national norms developed from a large sampling of the appropriate school-age population. They are group-administered tests that *survey* various curriculum areas taught in the schools. The information obtained is not in-depth diagnostic information. Achievement tests are not diagnostic and provide general, rather than specific, information. Scores are reported in grade equivalents, stanines, or percentiles.

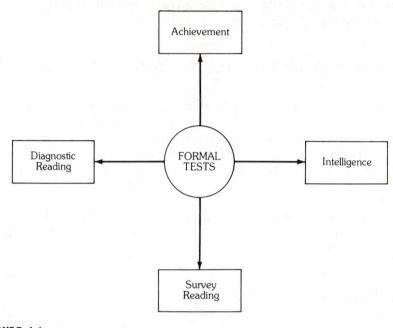

FIGURE 4.1

Formal Testing Procedures

Grade equivalents represent a derived score converted from the raw score on a standardized test, usually expressed in terms of a grade level divided into tenths. The grade equivalents in ninth grade, for example, range from 9.0 to 9.9 with 9.9 indicating nine years, nine months or the end of the ninth grade. In using this score, the content teacher should remember that it represents the students' frustrational levels or level at which they should not be taught, and must be viewed with caution in terms of students' actual reading levels.

Stanines are represented on a normal curve by a 9-point scale that is another form of a standard score with a mean of 5 and a standard deviation of about 2. The 9 stanines fit along the base of the normal curve with stanines 1, 2, and 3 considered below average, stanines 4, 5, and 6 average, and stanines 7, 8, and 9 above average. These scores are more usable for the content teacher in determining students' areas of strengths and weaknesses since they represent a wider range that better accommodates fluctuations in students' scores.

Percentiles are percentage scores that rate the student according to the percentage of others in a group who are below the score. A student at the 47th percentile has done better on the test than 47 percent of the others taking the test. Percentile scores may be reported in quartiles and deciles, in which case a 50th percentile is in the second quartile and the fifth decile. Percentiles, quartiles, and deciles cannot be averaged, added together, subtracted, or treated arithmetically in any manner.

Because school systems want to determine the effectiveness of their instruction, and to evaluate as many areas of instruction as possible, achievement tests are frequently used as the primary method of evaluation. Their popularity is further enhanced by their cost, since they represent the least expensive way to get this broad range of information. Various curriculum areas—language, mathematics, reading, science, and social studies—are measured by these instruments.

LAGNIAPPE

Misuse of Grade Equivalents

WHEREAS, standardized, norm-referenced tests can provide information useful to teachers, students, and parents, if the results of such tests are used properly, and

WHEREAS, proper use of any standardized test depends on a thorough understanding of the test's purpose, the way it was developed, and any limitations it has, and

WHEREAS, failure to fully understand these factors can lead to serious misuse of test results, and

WHEREAS, one of the most serious misuses of tests is the reliance on a grade equivalent as an indicator of absolute performance, when a grade equivalent should be interpreted as an indicator of a test-taker's performance in relation to the performance of other test-takers used to norm the test, and

WHEREAS, in reading education, the misuse of grade equivalents has led to such mistaken assumptions as: (1) a grade equivalent of 5.0, on a reading test means that the test-taker will be able to read fifth grade material, and (2) a grade equivalent of 10.0 by a fourth grade student means that student reads like a tenth grader even though the test may include only sixth grade material as its top level of difficulty, and

WHEREAS, the misuse of grade equivalents promotes misunderstanding of a student's reading ability and leads to underreliance on other norm-referenced scores which are much less susceptible to misinterpretation and misunderstanding, be it

RESOLVED, that the International Reading Association strongly advocates that those who administer standardized reading tests abandon the practice of using grade equivalents to report performance of either individuals or groups of test-takers and be it further

RESOLVED, that the president or executive director of the Association write to test publishers urging them to eliminate grade equivalents from their tests.

Resolution passed by the Delegates Assembly of the International Reading Association, April 1981

Four of the more widely used achievement tests and their subtest areas are outlined below:

California Achievement Test
CTB/McGraw-Hill, Monterey, California, 1977, 1978
(Grades K–12)
Measures reading, spelling, language, mathematics, and reference skills.

Comprehensive Test of Basic Skills
CTB/McGraw-Hill, Monterey, California, 1973, 1975, 1977 (Readiness), 1981
(Grades 0.1–13.6)
Measures reading, language, mathematics, reference skills, science, and social studies.

Metropolitan Achievement Test
The Psychological Corporation, New York, New York, 1977, 1978
(Grades K–12.9)
Measures reading comprehension, mathematics, and language.

Stanford Achievement Test
The Psychological Corporation, New York, New York, 1973
(Grades 1.5–9)
Measures reading comprehension, language skills, mathematics skills, science, social science, and auditory skills.

Achievement tests, like other instruments, have strengths and limitations, as shown in Table 4.1.

Properly used, achievement tests can provide useful information to the content teacher and to the school system in evaluating the effectiveness of their total curriculum; however, information on individual students must be used with great caution.

Intelligence Tests. Intelligence tests are instruments that are designed for prediction—predicting the level of proficiency that a student may attain on a specified activity. They measure not only past learning, but also learning that is

Achievement tests are often a primary method of evaluation.

TABLE 4.1

Strengths and Limitations of Achievement Tests

Strengths	Limitations
Scores for a wide range of curriculum areas are provided to school systems.	Ascertaining any in-depth diagnostic information necessitates an item analysis that some test companies are willing to provide for a fee.
These tests are easily administered by classroom teachers.	
These instruments follow strict norming procedures	Scores received are on the student's frustration level.
A student's progress can be evaluated over a period of time.	School systems must be careful of negating the effectiveness of the instruments through massing large groups of students together to take the tests.
	Silent reading skills are required, thus often reflecting poor reading ability rather than lack of knowledge of, for example, the math or social studies material being tested.
	Teachers may not receive test results promptly.
	Local norms may be unavailable.

unexpected or unplanned. Standardization for these instruments is similar to achievement tests in that strict norming procedures are followed. Group-administered intelligence tests attempt to evaluate a student's general aptitude in such areas as verbal concepts, mathematical capabilities, and following directions. Scores are provided in terms of stanines, percentiles, and standard scores, with the batteries providing an I.Q. and a mental age.

LAGNIAPPE

"We must recognize that testing students, especially with group tests, will not guarantee that we separate functionally literate from functionally illiterate students. We need to define functional literacy and create instruments that will more closely and holistically describe, diagnose, and measure the characteristics of the successfuly functioning literate adult."

Patricia Anders, "Tests of Functional Literacy," *Journal of Reading* (April 1981): 618.

Some of the more widely used group intelligence tests are given in the following section. Two of them are used in conjunction with achievement tests. These are the *California Short-Form Test of Mental Maturity* used with the *California Achievement Test,* and the *Otis-Lennon Mental Ability Test* used with the *Stanford Achievement Test*. Others include:

California Short-Form Test of Mental Maturity
CTB/McGraw-Hill, Monterey, Calif., 1963
(Grades K–Adult)

Measures logical reasoning, numerical reasoning, verbal concepts, and memory.

Otis-Lennon Mental Ability Test
The Psychological Corporation, New York, N. Y., 1967
(Grades K.5–12)
Measures the ability to classify through the use of pictures and geometric designs, following directions, and using quantitative reasoning, verbal concepts, and analogies.

Short Form Test of Academic Aptitude
CTB/McGraw-Hill, Monterey, Calif., 1970
(Grades 1.5–12)
Measures vocabulary, analogies, sequences, and memory. A Reference Scale Score is used in lieu of an I.Q. in evaluating language and nonlanguage capabilities; however, I.Q. scores are available upon request of the school system.

In examining group-administered intelligence test results, remember that even under optimum conditions, these results may be suspect. Scores should be carefully evaluated in relation to the student's cultural and socioeconomic background, experiential background, reading proficiency, and any other variables that can affect the test results.

Reading Tests. Although there are many good reading tests available for providing information about students' reading capabilities, only three are presented for the content teacher's consideration. These particular instruments were selected for their versatility and wide use. They are representative of the trend in reading to provide accurate and usable instruments to assist classroom teachers in evaluating students' reading performances in a group situation. Two of the instruments are classified as survey reading tests and one as a diagnostic reading test. All are group-administered instruments.

TABLE 4.2

Strengths and Limitations of I.Q. Scores

Strengths	Limitations
Information concerning the students' aptitude for achievement is received by the school system.	A performance variable is lacking. In many instances, reading ability, rather than aptitude, is measured.
These instruments can be administered by classroom teachers.	Frequently, the test items are culturally biased.
Strict norming procedures are followed.	Improper administration may result in inaccurate test results.
	The teacher's attitude toward the student may be adversely affected by a poor score.

Survey reading tests are used extensively in determining reading levels of students, partly because of the ease with which teachers can administer them. They are popular also because of the clear instructions, time factor, norms, and test construction. They can be administered quickly, easily, and also yield useful information. One disadvantage of survey tests is that they do not provide in-depth information; however, they are designed as screening devices, not diagnostic instruments.

The scores obtained are in the general areas of vocabulary, comprehension, and, depending upon the instrument, rate of reading. Scores are reported in grade equivalents, stanines, percentiles, or all three. Content teachers should note that scores represent students' frustration level, and do not indicate their independent or instructional levels. These scores, however, represent a starting point for the teacher and can be most helpful in use with the cloze test or informal reading inventory discussed later in this chapter. The two survey reading tests chosen for discussion are the *Gates-MacGinite Reading Tests* and the *Iowa Silent Reading Test*.

Gates-MacGinitie Reading Tests, 2nd ed.
Arthur I. Gates and Walter H. MacGinitie
Houghton Mifflin Company, Boston Mass., 1978
(Grades Readiness–12)

The *Gates-MacGinitie Reading Tests* exhibit all of the survey-test characteristics. A unique feature of this instrument is that an effort was made in the 1978 revision to relate the test to more current experiential patterns and to develop items that decreased cultural bias. This effort has resulted in an instrument that better measures the current reading performances of students.

There are seven levels of the *Gates-MacGinitie* Reading Tests, with two test forms at each level. Each level provides vocabulary, comprehension, and total reading scores. The levels are divided as follows:

Basic R, Grade 1
Level A, Grade 1
Level B, Grade 2
Level C, Grade 3
Level D, Grades 4, 5, and 6
Level E, Grades 7, 8, and 9
Level F, Grades 10, 11, and 12

Iowa Silent Reading Test (ISRT)
Roger Farr, Coordinating Editor
The Psychological Corporation, New York, N.Y., 1973
(Grades 6–12, College)

There are three levels in the latest revision of this test: Level 1, Grades 6–9; Level 2, Grades 9–Community College; and Level 3, above-average readers in the eleventh and twelfth grades. Areas tested in the *ISRT* are: vocabulary, reading comprehension, directed reading, and reading efficiency. Stress is also placed on applying skills and knowledge, thus mimimizing testing for literal information.

In the vocabulary section, for example, knowledge of words is measured with words that have been carefully selected as to level of difficulty and frequency of use. A feature of the comprehension section is the use of high-interest materials reflecting various reading styles and content. The directed reading section of the instrument evaluates proficiency in the use of the dictionary, as well as library skills and knowledge of other sources of information. Skimming and scanning skills are also assessed, using materials from encyclopedias. Reading efficiency measures a student's speed and accuracy using a modified cloze procedure.

The *ISRT* yields somewhat different data from that of the *Gates-MacGinitie*; so, it is important to choose the instrument that best fits the teacher's instructional objectives.

Group diagnostic reading tests are used quite extensively in many school systems. Like survey reading tests, they are easy to administer and interpret. The primary difference between the two is that the diagnostic instrument gives more in-depth information about a student's strengths and weaknesses. Several subtest scores provide help to determine these strengths and weaknesses. Other differences between the two instruments are that survey tests are generally less time-consuming and usually less expensive.

The group diagnostic reading instrument chosen for discussion is the *Stanford Diagnostic Reading Test.*

Stanford Diagnostic Reading Test (SDRT)
Bjorn Karlsen, Richard Madden, and Eric F. Gardner
The Psychological Corporation, New York, N.Y., 1976
(Grades 1.6–13)

The *SDRT* is one of the more extensively used group diagnostic reading tests. There are four levels with two forms (A and B) at each level. Each level measures specific areas:

Red Level (Grades 1.6–3.5): Auditory vocabulary, auditory discrimination, phonetic analysis, word reading (word recognition), and comprehension.

Green Level (Grades 2.6–5.5): Auditory vocabulary, auditory discrimination, phonetic analysis, structural analysis, and literal and inferential comprehension.

Brown Level (Grades 4.6–9.5): Auditory vocabulary, literal and inferential comprehension, phonetic analysis, structural analysis, and reading rate.

Blue Level (Grades 9–13): Literal and inferential comprehension, word meaning, word parts, phonetic analysis, structural analysis, scanning and skimming, and fast reading.

The *SDRT* is designed to diagnose specific strengths and weaknesses of students. Students are given the test that most closely approximates their reading level. If students are on the upper end of the level, they are given the next higher level test to prevent receiving inflated scores. Scores are reported in stanines, percentiles, and grade equivalents. *SDRT*'s excellent manual gives detailed information for administering the test, scoring and interpreting the results, and using the student profile.

Other assets of the *SDRT* include teacher time and ease of administration. Because it is a group test, the *SDRT* can be given in approximately two hours and yet provide much useful diagnostic information.

REFLECTION

Some educators feel that students are given too many formal tests like achievement tests, state assessment tests, etc. What is your reaction to this? Why do you feel as you do?

INFORMAL DIAGNOSTIC PROCEDURES

Because of the nonstandardized nature of informal tools, flexibility in diagnosis is enhanced, allowing content teachers to adapt specific instruments to their particular classroom situations. Some of the informal diagnostic procedures discussed require more time and interpretation than others. Instruments that are group-administered usually require less time than those that are individually administered; however, in some instances, the extra time required to administer an instrument may be necessary to learn more about the individual student.

Informal instruments discussed are observation, the Simplified Reading Inventory, Group Reading Inventory, cloze procedure, criterion-referenced tests, and Informal Reading Inventory. An advantage of informal diagnostic procedures is that they can be developed by the content teacher or the local school district to meet specific needs. In some instances, they may also be purchased from commercial sources.

Informal diagnostic procedures provide useful information to the content teacher such as:

1. Indicating the students' instructional and independent reading levels.
2. Giving clues as to each student's specific strengths and weaknesses in various reading skill areas.
3. Providing information on students' reading levels that aids in classroom organization such as grouping for instruction.
4. Facilitating the selection of materials and instructional techniques to meet the needs of each student's reading level, interests, and skill development.
5. Encouraging continuous diagnosis to evaluate each student's progress during the year.
6. Providing specific information about each student for use in parent conferences.

In using informal diagnostic procedures, remember that some are used with groups and some are individually administered. Also remember that certain procedures are more appropriate for some students than for others. Teachers must decide which procedures should be used in their own classrooms. With the important information derived from informal diagnosis, the content teacher is greatly helped in providing effective instruction.

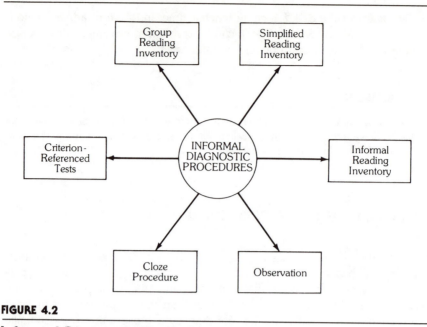

FIGURE 4.2

Informal Diagnostic Procedures

Observation. One of the teacher's most valuable and commonly used methods of diagnosis is observation of students in the content classroom. Activities like student interaction, participation in class discussions, attention to tasks, and independent work habits are important indicators of the student's capabilities and level of performance. Observation enables the teacher to see the beginning of a learning problem, changes in attitude, and variations in behavior that may affect content learning. The teacher can also observe students' reading performances and determine their skills in content reading.

When using observation as a diagnostic procedure, the technique should be used in combination with other procedures for diagnosing reading performances. Observations must be verified or refuted using other diagnostic strategies. Because students' performances are continously changing, any conclusions based on observation must be made from a recent evaluation. These evaluations should take place over several observation periods in order to determine if a consistent pattern of reading behavior is shown. Teachers must also remember that only facts should be noted about observations, with opinions being reserved until the conclusions can be examined following several observations.

For the content teacher, the most effective technique for structured observation is a *checklist*. Checklists are excellent for large classes. They do not require a great amount of time, and they are flexible. A checklist may be one page or several, and it can be used to evaluate several students or only one. The principal disadvantages of checklists are that they do not lend themselves to in-depth observations over a long period of time, and that they may be distracting to the teacher whose prime concern is to teach content information. A sample group checklist is provided in Figure 4.3 (pp. 127–28).

In developing a checklist form, certain criteria should be followed: (1) items should deal with specific behavior that can be observed; (2) space for additional observations and comments should be provided; and (3) items should be limited so that the checklist is easy to use. Items that may be included in a content reading checklist are:

Rate of reading assignments
Understanding material read
Participation in classroom discussions
Desire to read assigned or other material
Types of material read during leisure time
Skill in responding to various levels of questions
Ability to recognize new words, especially specialized and technical vocabulary
Variety of vocabulary used

In using a checklist, these specific steps should be followed:

1. Develop a checklist that meets the needs of the content classroom.
2. Have appropriate copies of the checklist available.
3. Be familiar with the checklist in order to record maximum information during a limited observation period.
4. Prepare the classroom instructional plan carefully to insure observation of the student(s) in a reading situation.
5. Designate one or two specific areas on the checklist to be observed at one time so that strengths and weaknesses in those areas can be carefully evaluated.
6. Note any additional problems experienced by the student(s) during this particular observation period.
7. Select other areas to be observed at different times.

Evaluating students' interaction with content materials through observation is a useful way to obtain initial diagnostic information about content reading. However, maximum benefit can be obtained only through careful examination of results. Teachers should remember that diagnosis based on one or two observations will be superficial at best. Teachers must also be aware of their students' various behaviors and learning patterns, and exercise caution in interpreting the information. Observations should indicate to the content teacher any further diagnosis that may be necessary, as well as adjustments that are needed in the instructional program.

Simplified Reading Inventory (SRI). The SRI represents an effort to "try material on for size" and shows the teacher at the beginning of the school year whether students are able to read the content textbook or other materials. Although this is an unrefined diagnostic tool, it does tell the teacher which materials are beyond the reading capabilities of some students, but too easy for others. Since this is a somewhat simplistic procedure, more refined diagnostic instruments should be used for a specific diagnosis of reading level and difficulties in reading.

Teachers need to observe a student's independent work habits.

Teachers' use of the SRI, however, does prevent student placement in material that is too difficult or too easy at the beginning of the school year. Motivation for content learning is much easier with material that students can read and assignments that challenge but do not go beyond students' capabilities. As a preliminary step, this diagnostic procedure gives the teacher general information about the students' reading capabilities—their ability to read a specific material and some idea of strengths and weaknesses in word identification and comprehension.

The SRI is, in effect, a screening device that shows where further informal testing must begin. In administering the SRI, each student is asked to read a short selection aloud from the content textbook. After the selection is read, the teacher asks the student one or two questions about the material. The student's oral reading and response to the question shows whatever difficulty he/she can be expected to experience in reading the textbook. Too many errors tell the teacher that the material is too difficult for the student. The teacher should consider an oral reading error to include the mispronunciation of a word or the pro-

FIGURE 4.3

Sample Observation Checklist

Content Area: World Geography   Date: 9–10–83   Teacher: Mrs. Smith

	Joe	Chris	Mary	Vicki	Sally	Bo	Pat	Jeri	Eric	Dave
General Behavior										
Reads tests satisfactorily										
Enjoys reading content text										
Attends to tasks well										
Motivated to learn content material										
Answers questions when called upon										
Volunteers answers to questions										
Holds text at appropriate distance when reading										
Responds well to oral directions										
Seeks help when needed										
Works well in group situation										
Organizes time efficiently										
Demonstrates good rapport with teacher										
Works well independently										
Reads in spare time										

128

FIGURE 4.3 (continued)

	Joe	Chris	Mary	Vicki	Sally	Bo	Pat	Jeri	Eric	Dave
Specific Behavior										
Uses structural analysis										
Uses contextual analysis										
Knows the meaning of symbols and abbreviations										
Comprehension Skills										
Locates details in the chapter										
Follows directions well										
Recognizes comparison/contrast relationship										
Reads for a purpose										
Identifies cause-effect relationships										
Identifies the main idea										
Draws conclusions from specific information										
Differentiates fact from opinion										
Study Skills										
Uses the various parts of a book										
Reads maps										
Adjusts reading rate according to purpose										
Outlines material adequately										
Uses notetaking skills										

nunciation of a word by the teacher. Technical terms or words that would be taught as a part of vocabulary development should not be considered as errors. Errors should be confined to words that students are expected to know from previous learning experiences.

The selection used for reading should be a part of the content textbook. The amount read varies from student to student, with poorer readers possibly reading only one or two sentences. A few sentences are still enough for the teacher to know how well they read the textbook. The SRI can be administered in one of two ways. The students may come individually to the teacher's desk and read, or the teacher may choose to go through the class and ask students to read aloud. A combination of the two is usually best. The teacher can allow volunteers to read aloud in a group situation and later call other students to the desk for individual oral reading. Regardless of the procedure used, it should not cause students to be embarrassed in front of their peers.

Group Reading Inventory. Another informal diagnostic procedure is the Group Reading Inventory (GRI). A Group Reading Inventory is a test used by content teachers to diagnose the specific skills needed to learn the concepts taught in a content lesson. The GRI also provides the content teacher with information about the students' understanding of the concepts being studied. Although the primary purpose of this inventory is to assess the students' ability to apply appropriate skills in reading content materials, additional information may be generalized as to their knowledge of the content concepts.

The first step in developing a GRI is for the teacher to identify the concepts or content to be taught during a specific time. Using the identified concepts, the teacher must then identify the reading skills necessary for understanding the content material. When these two aspects, concepts and reading skills, are identified, the GRI test items can be developed. Figure 4.4 is an example of concepts and reading skills that have been identified for use in developing a GRI.

Concepts	Related Reading Skills
1. The development of industries changed the way of life for the American people.	Cause-effect relationships Details Fact and opinions
2. Many inventions were made during the Industrial Revolution.	Details Vocabulary
3. Transcontinental transportation provided impetus to the development of industries in America.	Vocabulary Details Main idea Cause-effect relationships
4. Mass production began with the development of industries.	Cause-effect relationships Reading charts and graphs

FIGURE 4.4

Concepts and Skills Identified for the Group Reading Inventory

Using the reading skills that have been identified, three to five questions for each skill should be developed using content materials related to the identified concepts and written at an appropriate readability level for the students. Using materials provided by the teacher, the student answers the questions. An example of a GRI is presented in Figure 4.5.

Because the student is asked to read specific content materials and to give written responses to a series of questions before beginning the content unit, the teacher gathers considerable information about each student's strengths and weaknesses in the specific skill areas. This information enables the teacher to provide instruction and alternative activities for students to broaden the development of these skills and to learn the content material more easily.

Among the several advantages in using the GRI, the principal one is that it can be administered to a group of students. It can also be used frequently during the school year, since the ability to apply different skills to various concepts is assessed each time. This enables the teacher to note students' progress throughout the year. In using the GRI, it is important to remember that students read at different levels. Materials at various levels should be used, therefore, in order to assess skills knowledge accurately. When preparing the GRI, students reading at or above grade level can use the textbook; those two or three years below grade level need a lower level textbook; and those who are considerably below level need an elementary one. If an elementary textbook is used, the teacher must choose one that focuses on the same content and concepts being taught in the class. Without this distinction in reading levels, the teacher is unable to determine whether the student does not know the skill or just is unable to read the material.

Group reading inventories are viewed by some content teachers as pretests to determine skill knowledge, as well as understanding of the content information. While these two purposes cannot be clearly separated in developing and interpreting the GRI, the prime objective is to assess the students' ability to apply the reading skills in understanding content materials. Deficiencies should be noted and instruction provided to help students learn the concepts, and apply the reading skills. Concept learning is enhanced when teachers first diagnose, and then instruct students based on the diagnostic information.

Cloze Procedure. A widely recognized and versatile informal procedure for determining students' reading levels and for giving the content teacher insight into their analytical reading skills is the cloze procedure. Wilson Taylor developed the cloze in 1953 primarily as a tool for measuring readability;[2] however, additional research shows that the cloze procedure can also be used effectively as an alternative to the Informal Reading Inventory for determining students' reading levels.[3] This procedure is useful also as a quick assessment of the student's ability to understand the textbook.[4]

Because of the time factor and the size of content classes, this informal diagnostic tool is especially valuable to the content teacher by showing the student's independent, instructional, and frustration reading levels in a relatively quick and easy way.

The cloze may be the first diagnostic tool content teachers select for determining students' reading levels. This instrument is favored because it is easy to construct and administer, and it is a group test. In contrast to the Informal Reading Inventory (discussed later in the chapter), which is individiallly administered,

Word Meanings:
   Read pages 20–21 in your book. Then tell what these words mean:
1. interchangeable parts
2. mass production
3. specialization
4. distribution
5. transcontinental

Comprehension—Cause-Effect Relationships:
   Read page 23 in your book. Then answer the following questions:

1. Why did the industries grow so quickly?
2. Why did the life-styles of the people change during this time?
3. What caused the cities to grow so much in such a short period of time?
4. Why were the working conditions in mines and factories so poor?
5. What effect did the factory system have on family life?

   Details/Main Idea:

Remembering what you read on pages 20–21, answer these questions:

1. Identify two things that Eli Whitney developed.
2. What was used to transport goods before the railroad?
3. Tell in one sentence what these two pages are about.

   Fact and Opinion:

Read each of these sentences. Then tell if the sentence is a fact or an opinion.

1. *When people work together, they produce more goods than if each worked alone.*
2. *Horses are the safest means of transporting goods.*
3. *Government should not interfere with industry to try to control the working conditions.*
4. *From 1750 to 1850, the population in Britain tripled.*
5. *People work better when they have to work harder.*

Study Skills—Outlining/Notetaking:
   Read pages 17–18 in our book. Then complete the outline below to help you remember what was said. You may look back as you work.

I. Factories and Machines
   A. Inventions
      1.
      2.
      3.
      4.
   B. Usefulness of each invention
      1.
      2.
      3.
      4.
II. Industrial Revolution

FIGURE 4.5

Sample Group Reading Inventory

the cloze can usually be administered during one class period. For content teachers with little time and many students, the cloze is obviously the most expeditious procedure for ascertaining such basic diagnostic information as the reading levels of their students.

Additionally, developing a cloze test does not require a great deal of expertise in test construction. Any content teacher can quickly develop one by following a few basic guidelines. Teachers first select passages from content textbooks, or any other content related material deemed appropriate (the material must be unfamiliar to the students), and then follow these guidelines:

1. Select a passage of approximately 250–300 words on a level at which the student is or should be reading.
2. Check the readability level of the passage using the readability formula outlined in Chapter 8.
3. Retype the passage. Beginning with the second sentence, delete every fifth word. Replace each deleted word with a line, making sure that each line is of the same length. Do not delete words from the first or last sentences. There should be approximately fifty blank spaces in the selection.
4. Make copies of the selection for students to complete.
5. Tell students to fill in each blank with the words they think best complete the sentences.
6. Score the papers by counting as correct only those responses that *exactly* match the original selection; however, spelling errors should not be counted as incorrect responses. Using a percentage score of correct responses, determine the student's reading level:
   58%–100% correct = Independent Level
   44%– 57% correct = Instructional Level
   0%–43% correct = Frustration Level.[5]

Content teachers find this procedure useful in determining their students' reading levels. Students who are unfamiliar with completing passages should first be provided with activities in which they practice filling in incomplete sentences before using a cloze test for determining reading levels. Over a period of time, students may work individually or in groups to decide on words that can complete the passages. After checking the answers, discussions are helpful in determining why some words complete the blanks better than others. Practice exercises of this kind not only help students learn to take a cloze test to determine their reading level, but also assist in vocabulary improvement, develop skill in using context clues, and increase awareness of meaning in reading content materials.

Vocabulary development can be enhanced with the cloze procedure by providing exercises that ask students to list as many words as they can think of that could complete each blank. Difficulty in completing the assignment shows the need for further vocabulary development to help students understand the material.

Once students are familiar with the format of the cloze test the teacher may assemble a series of passages at the various readability levels for the students to work through as an assignment. Because the primary objective of the cloze procedure is to determine the estimated level at which the student can satisfactorily read, these passages at different levels can be evaluated to ascertain the students' reading levels.

Not only can this information be determined, but additional interpretation of the cloze can provide more in-depth diagnostic information about the students' comprehension skills. For example, if the student fills in the blanks with totally irrelevant words, the material is probably not understood. Further diagnostic information can be obtained from these passages by examining the types of words substituted in the blanks, and whether other words in the sentence were used in trying to figure out the omitted words. Failure to fully use these context clues shows a reading skill weakness. Additional diagnostic information obtainable from the cloze is the extent to which semantics, syntax, and reasoning processes are used by the student. Research shows that these factors play a major role in the student's ability to determine the word that has been deleted.[6]

Unquestionably, the cloze procedure is a valuable diagnostic tool for the content teacher and greatly helps make content reading instruction easier.

Figure 4.6 (p. 134) provides an example of cloze selection.

REFLECTION

As a content teacher, tell how you could use the cloze procedure in your classroom. What information would you get and what could be done with this information?

Criterion-referenced Tests. As relatively recent developments in testing, criterion-referenced tests are designed to measure what a learner knows or can do relative to a specific objective. The characteristics of a criterion-referenced test include a set of objectives containing conditions, outcomes, and criteria expected for the satisfactory completion of the task. Criterion-referenced tests can be used to diagnose content reading ability by assessing reading skill knowledge using content materials. As discussed in previous chapters, students may learn the reading skills in the elementary grades and experience reading difficulty when they are expected to read content materials at the middle and secondary levels.

This difficulty may be caused by not understanding how to apply reading skills to content materials. Content teachers should use criterion-referenced tests to determine if the students can use their reading skill knowledge to understand content information. For example, the content teacher may, using the following objective, assess students' ability to use the skill of recognizing cause-effect relationships in reading science materials.

> *Objective:* Given five selections from the ninth grade science book, students should be able to identify the cause-effect relationships in each paragraph.

Using this objective, the content teacher can determine the students' ability to transfer reading skill knowledge to content materials. This preassessment or diagnosis will help the teacher in knowing which students may have difficulty in understanding the content information due to their inability to apply the necessary reading skills. Instructional strategies can then be planned to help students see how to use their reading skills to obtain more meaning from the content materials.

Teachers can establish several objectives that relate to the reading skills needed for understanding content information. Test items can follow which measure each of the objectives, with the results used to plan for the teaching of vocabulary, concepts, and reading skills that are essential for understanding the content information. Criterion-referenced test items can be used in a way similar to the Group Reading Inventory previously discussed in this chapter. Both are easy to administer in a group situation and provide valuable diagnostic information needed for content reading instruction.

Informal Reading Iventory (IRI). This is a widely used informal diagnostic procedure whose findings are valuable to the teacher. The procedure is used frequently by elementary classroom teachers and reading specialists. Content teachers, however, do not use it often because it is an individually administered instrument for which the time factor may be prohibitive. Although fifteen to twenty minutes per student is needed to administer the IRI, the content

---

Readability Level: 9th (Fry Graph)

Silver is a soft metal that shines with a beautiful luster. It is by far the best known conductor of heat and electricity, but such an expensive metal is impractical for most electric wiring.

Most acids, and even strong bases cannot affect silver. This is not true, however, for concentrated nitric and sulfuric acids. Although silver does not oxidize in air, you have seen how silver tarnishes and turns brown or even black. Sulfur compounds present in such foods as mustard and eggs, and fumes of sulfur in polluted air, will cause silverware to tarnish. This tarnish is a coating of silver sulfide, produced by the reaction of silver with sulfur compounds.

Large quantities of silver are used in jewelry and other ornaments. Formerly, United States coins contained a high percentage of silver. Although the best table silver is solid sterling, a large amount of silverware is plated. Electrolysis is used to put a coating of silver on a cheaper metal.

Pure silver is too soft for most industrial and commercial purposes. To make it harder, it is mixed with copper. Sterling silver, for example, is 92.5 percent silver and 7.5 percent copper, a proportion fixed by law for this material.

Prior to 1965, our silver coins contained 90 percent silver and 10 percent copper. In an effort to get more silver into the commercial market, the Coinage Act of 1965 eliminated all silver from the dime and quarter and reduced the silver content of the half-dollar from 90 to 40 percent. The last time our silver dollar coins were minted was in 1935. Our dimes and quarters now have a copper base "sandwiched" between outside layers of copper-nickel alloy. This gives the coins a reddish-tinged edge. Such a combination of metals is called cladding. Clad-metal coins help stretch our silver resources.

George R. Tracy, Harry E. Tropp, and Alfred E. Friedl, *Modern Physical Science* (New York: Holt, Rinehart, and Winston, 1970), pp. 198–99. Copyright 1970. Reprinted by permission of Holt, Rinehart, and Winston.

FIGURE 4.6 A

Sample Cloze Selection (complete)

teacher's time is well spent when using it for at least some of the students in each class, preferably for those who score significantly above or below the level of the textbook as determined on the SRI or the cloze procedure. The IRI is an excellent follow-up for gaining more in-depth information about these students.

The IRI is a compilation of reading selections from different grade levels with comprehension questions to accompany each selection. The selections chosen for use by the teacher should be taken from content material.[7] This procedure enables the teacher to more accurately determine the student's capabilities for dealing with material from specific content areas. Using passages not specifically intended for a content area may provide an inaccurate picture of the student's reading capabilities in that students may understand more general types of material better than they comprehend ideas in a specific content area.

Since the IRI is administered individually, the teacher is able to examine specific word identification and comprehension difficulties while observing both oral and silent reading habits. Because of the nature of content teaching, the

---

Silver is a soft metal that shines with a beautiful luster. It is by far _____ best known conductor of _____ and electricity but such _____ expensive metal is impractical _____ most electric wiring.

Most _____ , and even strong bases _____ affect silver. This is _____ true, however, for concentrated _____ and sulfuric acids. Although _____ does not oxidize in _____ , you have seen how _____ tarnishes and turns brown _____ even black. Sulfur compounds _____ in such foods as _____ and eggs, and fumes _____ sulfur in polluted air, _____ cause silverware to tarnish. _____ tarnish is a coating _____ silver sulfide, produced by _____ reaction of silver with _____ compounds.

Large quantities of _____ are used in jewelry _____ other ornaments. Formerly, United _____ coins contained a high _____ of silver. Although the _____ table silver is solid _____ , a large amount of _____ is plated. Electrolysis is _____ to put a coating _____ silver on a cheaper _____ .

Pure silver is too _____ for most industrial and _____ purposes. To make it _____ , it is mixed with _____ . Sterling silver, for example, _____ 92.5 percent silver and _____ percent copper, a proportion _____ by law for this _____ .

Prior to 1965, our _____ coins contained 90 percent _____ and 10 percent copper. _____ an effort to get _____ silver into the commercial _____ , the Coinage Act of _____ eliminated all silver from _____ dime and quarter and _____ the silver content of _____ half-dollar from 90 to _____ percent. The last time _____ silver dollar coins were _____ was in 1935. Our _____ and quarters now have _____ copper base "sandwiched" between _____ layers of a copper-nickel _____ . This gives the coins _____ reddish-tinged edge. Such a _____ of metals is called _____ . Clad-metal coins help stretch our silver resources.

FIGURE 4.6 B

Sample Cloze Selection (as given to student)

teacher wants to be especially aware of comprehension skills as evidenced by the student's silent reading. In most content classrooms, there is a great need for silent reading comprehension skills. Thus, this phase of the IRI provides information that is a vital part of content instruction. The oral reading phase also yields such important clues as vocabulary knowledge, structural and contextual analysis skills, as well as oral reading comprehension. The IRI is also used to determine the student's independent, instructional, and frustration levels in reading. The levels are defined below.

1. *Independent level:* The level at which students read for recreational purposes. The material is easy enough to read quickly with maximum comprehension of the information.
2. *Instructional level:* The level at which instruction is provided. The student can read the material, but has some difficulty with the identification of words and comprehension to the extent specified in the criteria.
3. *Frustration level:* At this level, the student has extreme difficulty in pronouncing words and comprehending the material. This is the level at which the student should not be reading for instructional purposes and certainly not for leisure.

More specifically, the criteria used to determine these three levels is presented in Table 4.3.

TABLE 4.3

Criteria Used In Scoring Informal Reading Inventories

Book Level	Word Identification[8]	Comprehension[9]
Independent	99% or more	90% and above
Instructional	95% or more	70–80%
Frustration	90% or less	less than 70%

The IRI, to be used effectively, should be administered during the beginning weeks of school. Its distinct advantage is that the administration time decreases and the information gained increases as the teacher becomes more proficient in its use. The IRI is also helpful in providing continuous assessment of the students' individual strengths and weaknesses throughout the year.

In addition to school districts and individual schools that have developed their own IRI's, they are available from publishing companies. A word of caution to the content teacher: many of the published IRI's do not directly relate to content material and should, therefore, be examined carefully for their usefulness. Some of the IRI's available from publishers are listed in Appendix B. Because of the scarcity of published IRI's suitable for content areas, teachers may wish to work with the reading specialist in their school to construct an IRI. Information on constructing, administering and interpreting an IRI is presented in Appendix C. For more detailed information on constructing an IRI, content teachers should contact their reading specialist or a text on reading diagnosis. Such texts are identified at the end of the chapter.

An alternative to the IRI has been suggested by Vaughan and Gaus.[10] They proposed a Secondary Reading Inventory that can be used with groups of students to determine an approximate level of performance on different types of materials. This inventory consists of five reading selections on each of four reading levels: upper elementary (grades 5–6); intermediate (grades 7–8); secondary (grades 9–10); and advanced secondary (grades 11–12).

The five selections are based on a variety of materials—fiction, factual narration, social exposition, scientific description, and problematic exposition. The students' comprehension is assessed on independent reading and aided reading. An interest inventory composed of titles and brief descriptions of the selections is used in a discussion with the students, with selections ranked according to individual student interest.

Students read all five selections at each level and respond to the questions. The criteria for the IRI are used to score this inventory. Scores suggest to the content teacher not only the students' interest in an area, but also their performance in reading the different types of materials. For example, a student may score at the instructional level in reading science materials at all the various reading levels while scoring at the frustrational level in social studies at the upper elementary level. Additionally, the teacher may use part of each selection to determine the difference in scores when assistance, such as a discussion of the concepts, is given.

Because this alternative to the IRI may be administered to groups in the content classroom, the time factor which is such a problem in using the IRI is overcome. However, while this inventory saves time, it does not provide the same type of diagnostic information as the IRI. Thus, content teachers must decide which procedure provides the information needed most in their own classrooms.

Johns's *Advanced Reading Inventory* for grades seven through college is an informal reading inventory that provides two options for the content teacher—it can be administered individually or to groups of students.[11] As a result, testing time is minimized, and the gathering of data is made easier.

The IRI as well as the related alternatives and adaptations are helpful informal diagnostic strategies for the content teacher. While these procedures may not be used with every student in a classroom, the content teacher should make selective use of the IRI as needed. Figure 4.7 (p. 138) reviews the basic steps that should be followed in using an IRI.

Tips on Informal Testing. Using informal diagnostic procedures can provide much valuable information. In an effort to help the content teacher, the following suggestions are offered:

1. *Make testing situations as informal as possible.* Analyzing classroom work and using observation yields much diagnostic information.
2. *Check the readability levels of all materials used in informal testing.* It is important to know the readability levels of materials so that a student's success or failure can be accurately determined.
3. *Various instruments should be used in informal diagnosis.* As noted in the preceding pages, more than one instrument is needed to enhance diagnostic information.

4. *Limit the testing time according to an individual student's interests and atten-tion span.*

5. *Verify data from an instrument with information from another instrument or by using your opinion.* Conclusions should not be drawn immediately based upon information from one test or observation but should reflect a consensus of different evaluations.

6. *Ask for assistance from fellow teachers.* Compare results with that of other teachers. This provides a more accurate diagnosis, as well as gives more information about each student.

REFLECTION

Think about your middle and secondary school experiences in various content classes. What formal or informal tests were given to determine your reading ability? Would the use of tests such as those described in this chapter have been helpful? Why or why not?

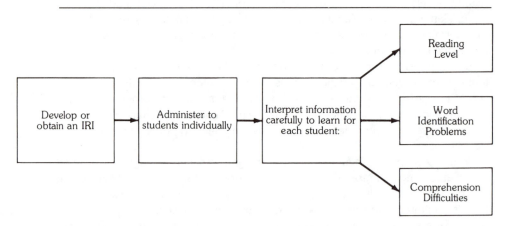

Martha Collins Cheek and Earl H. Cheek Jr., *Diagnostic-Prescriptive Reading Instruction: A Guide for Classroom Teachers* (Dubuque, Iowa: William C. Brown, 1980), p. 58.

FIGURE 4.7

Basic Steps in Using an Informal Reading Inventory

SUMMARY

In examining the relationship between diagnosis and content teaching, one must conclude that diagnostic information can be helpful to the instructional process. Knowing such information as the students' independent, instructional, and frustration reading levels facilitates instruction and enables the content teacher to adjust the instruction to each student's appropriate learning level. As pointed out in the chapter, content teachers enjoy a variety of diagnostic procedures at their disposal. Diagnostic procedures are separated into two main categories—formal and informal.

Formal instruments are achievement tests, intelligence tests, and specific reading tests. The three formal reading tests presented are the *Gates-MacGinitie Reading Tests*, the *Iowa Silent Reading Test* (ISRT), and the *Stanford Diagnostic Reading Test* (SDRT). All of these instruments are group-administered.

Informal diagnostic procedures available to the content teacher include such instruments as observation, the Simplified Reading Inventory (SRI), the Group Reading Inventory (GRI), the cloze procedure, criterion-referenced tests, and the Informal Reading Inventory (IRI).

Informal diagnostic procedures are considered more practical for use by the content teacher; however, there are some group formal diagnostic procedures that the content teacher may wish to examine for screening purposes or for some in-depth information such as that gained from the *Stanford Diagnostic Reading Test* (SDRT).

FOR DISCUSSION

1. Your principal asks that you use some type of instrument(s) to diagnose your students' strengths and weaknesses in reading. Identify three formal or informal instruments that you might select and tell why you chose each.
2. Discuss the pros and cons of asking content teachers to assess student performance in reading as related to their content area.
3. How would you use diagnostic techniques in your content classroom? Tell how you would begin and proceed to obtain initial information such as reading levels.
4. Differentiate between achievement tests and diagnostic tests. What are the advantages of each?

OTHER SUGGESTED READINGS

Bader, Lois A. *Reading Diagnosis and Remediation in Classroom and Clinic*. New York: Macmillan, 1980.

Blanton, William E.; Farr, Roger; and Tuinman, J. Jaap, eds. *Measuring Reading Performance*. Newark, Del.: International Reading Association, 1974.

Blanton, William; Farr, Roger; and Tuinman, J. Jaap. *Reading Tests for the Secondary Grades: A Review and Evaluation*. Newark, Del.: International Reading Association, 1972.

Bradley, John M.; Ackerman, Gary; and Ames, Wilbur S. "The Reliability of the Maze Procedure." *Journal of Reading Behavior* 10 (Fall 1978):291–96.

Brecht, Richard D. "Testing Format and Instructional Level with the Informal Reading Inventory." *The Reading Teacher* 31 (October 1977):57–59.

Cheek, Martha Collins, and Cheek, Earl H. *Diagnostic-Prescriptive Reading Instruction: A Guide for Classroom Teachers*. Dubuque, Iowa: William C. Brown, 1980.

Cunningham, James W., and Cunningham, Patricia M. "Validating a Limited-Cloze Procedure." *Journal of Reading Behavior* 10 (Summer 1978):211–13.

Davis, Carol A. "The Effectiveness of Informal Assessment Questions Constructed by Secondary Teachers." In *Reading: Disciplined Inquiry in Process and Practice*, ed. F. David Pearson and Jane Hansen. Twenty-seventh Yearbook of the National Reading Conference, 1978, pp. 13–15.

Dupuis, Mary M. "The Cloze Procedure: Can It Be Used with Literature?" *Reading Improvement* 13 (Winter 1976):199–203.

Ekwall, Eldon K. "Informal Reading Inventories: The Instructional Level." *The Reading Teacher* 29 (April 1976):662–65.

Ekwall, Eldon K. *Locating and Correcting Reading Difficulties*, 3rd ed. Columbus, Ohio: Charles E. Merrill, 1981.

Johns, Jerry L. et al. *Assessing Reading Behavior: Informal Reading Inventories*. Newark, Del.: International Reading Association, 1977.

Jongsma, Eugene A. *Cloze Instruction Research: A Second Look*. Newark, Del.: International Reading Association, 1980.

McKenna, Michael C., and Robinson, Richard D. *An Introduction to the Cloze Procedure: An Annotated Bibliography*. Newark, Del.: International *Reading Association*, 1980.

Marino, Jacqueline L. "Cloze Passages: Guidelines for Selection." *Journal of Reading* 24 (March 1981):479–83.

Meredith, Keith, and Vaughan, Joseph. "Stability of Cloze Scores Across Varying Deletion Patterns." In *Reading: Disciplined Inquiry in Process and Practice*, ed. P. David Pearson and Jane Hansen, Twenty-seventh Yearbook of the National Reading Conference, 1978, pp. 181–84.

Neville, Donald D., and Hoffman, Rudolph R. "The Effect of Personalized Stores on the Cloze Comprehension of Seventh Grade Retarded Readers." *Journal of Reading* 24 (March 1981):475–77.

O'Mara, Deborah A. "The Process of Reading Mathematics." *Journal of Reading* 25 (October 1981):22–30.

Pflaum, Susanna W. "Diagnosis of Oral Reading." *The Reading Teacher* 33 (December 1979):278–84.

Powell, William R. *Measuring Reading Performance*, November 1978 (ED 155 589).

Rakes, Thomas A. "A Group Instructional Inventory." *Journal of Reading* 18 (May 1975):595–98.

Rupley, William H., and Blair, Timothy R. *Reading Diagnosis and Remediation: A Primer for Classroom and Clinic*. Chicago: Rand McNally, 1979.

Schell, Leo M. "Criterion-Referenced Tests: Selected Cautionary Notes." *Reading World* 19 (October 1979):57–62.

Schell, Leo M., ed. *Diagnostic and Criterion-Referenced Reading Tests: Review and Evaluation*. Newark, Del.: International Reading Association, 1981.

Shannon, Albert J. "Effects of Methods of Standardized Reading Achievement Test Administration on Attitude toward Reading." *Journal of Reading* 23 (May 1980):684–86.

Vaughan, Joseph L., and Meredith, Keith E. "Reliability of the Cloze Procedure as Assessments of Various Language Elements." In *Reading: Disciplined Inquiry in Process and Practice*, ed. P. David Pearson and Jane Hansen. Twenty-seventh Yearbook of the National Reading Conference, 1978, pp. 175–80.

Wilson, Robert M. *Diagnostic and Remedial Reading for Classroom and Clinic*, 4th ed. Columbus, Ohio: Charles E. Merrill, 1981.

Zintz, Miles. *Corrective Reading*, 4th ed. Dubuque, Iowa: William C. Brown, 1981.

NOTES

1. Martha C. Cheek and Earl H. Cheek, "Diagnosis—A Part of Content Area Reading," *Reading Horizons* 19 (Summer 1979):308–13.
2. Wilson L. Taylor, "Cloze Procedure: A New Tool for Measuring Readability," *Journalism Quarterly* 39 (Fall 1953):415–33.
3. Eugene R. Jongsma, "The Cloze Procedure: A Survey of the Research" (Bloomington, Ind.: Indiana University, August, 1971). (ED050893)

4. Judith Thelen, *Improving Reading in Science: Reading Aid Series* (Newark, Del.: International Reading Association, 1976), p. 6.
5. John Bormuth, "The Cloze Readability Procedure," *Elementary English* 45 (April 1968):429–36.
6. Kenneth S. Goodman, "Behind the Eye: What Happens in Reading," in *Theoretical Models and Processes of Reading,* ed. Harry Singer and Robert Ruddell (Newark, Del.: International Reading Association, 1976), pp. 470–96; Robert Ruddell, "Language Acquisition and the Reading Process," in *Theoretical Models and Processes of Reading,* ed. Harry Singer and Robert Ruddell (Newark, Del.: International Reading Association, 1976), pp. 22–38; Frederick B. Davis, "Research in Comprehension in Reading," *Reading Research Quarterly* 3 (1968):499–545.
7. Edwin H. Smith, Billy M. Guice, and Martha C. Cheek, "Informal Reading Inventories for the Content Areas: Science and Mathematics," *Elementary English* 49 (May 1972):659–66.
8. Emmett A. Betts, *Foundations of Reading Instruction* (New York: American Book, 1957).
9. Jerry L. Johns, *Advanced Reading Inventory* (Dubuque, Iowa: William C. Brown, 1981).
10. Joseph L. Vaughan, Jr., and Paula J. Gaus, "Secondary Reading Inventory: A Modest Proposal," *Journal of Reading* 21 (May 1978):716–20.
11. Jerry L. Johns, *Advanced Reading Inventory,* pp. 7–23.

STEP FOUR

Instruction

As teachers consider ideas for incorporating the development of reading into the content classroom, the area of most importance is that of instruction. Because content teachers shoulder the responsibility of teaching content materials, their first thought is HOW? The previous steps leading to Step IV relate to the planning for instruction. In Step IV, the actual instructional process begins.

Within this step, many instructional strategies must be considered since there is no one way of incorporating reading into content instruction. Chapter 5 presents the basic framework for teaching content information while including the development of reading skills. In Chapter 6, information on the various organizational patterns found in content materials is presented along with ideas on using these patterns to enhance comprehension.

Chapters 7 and 8 give information on organizing content instruction and selecting materials. Examples of content lessons which incorporate the teaching of reading are presented in Chapter 9.

To assist the content teacher in teaching mainstreamed students, poor readers, language-varied and gifted students, Chapter 10 gives many helpful suggestions. Because motivation is such an important part of the instructional process, Chapter 11 offers special tips for teachers, parents, and students.

Although Step IV contains many suggestions, the successful implementation of these ideas in content instruction depends, to a great extent, on the use of the planning done in Steps, I, II, and III.

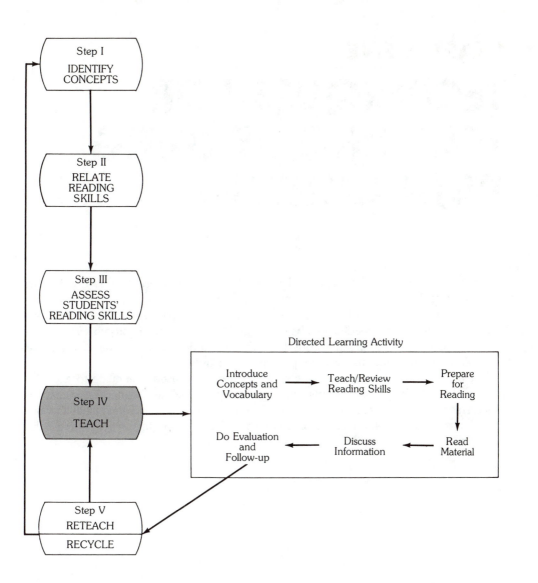

Step I
IDENTIFY CONCEPTS

Step II
RELATE READING SKILLS

Step III
ASSESS STUDENTS' READING SKILLS

Step IV
TEACH

Step V
RETEACH
RECYCLE

Directed Learning Activity

Introduce Concepts and Vocabulary → Teach/Review Reading Skills → Prepare for Reading

Do Evaluation and Follow-up ← Discuss Information ← Read Material

CHAPTER FIVE

TECHNIQUES FOR TEACHING READING WITH CONTENT

As content teachers read professional materials and hear presentations on content teaching, a feeling of confusion often creeps into their minds. To help overcome this uneasiness, an abundance of information is available on content reading instruction with numerous ideas on how reading can be developed in the content classroom. From these ideas, the teacher can confidently consider individual student needs as well as the entire curriculum and plan the instructional procedures accordingly.

In teaching content lessons, a basic structure should be used as a guide to expedite the direct teaching of the concepts and vocabulary, as well as the necessary reading skills. This structure must allow for the use of various techniques and great flexibility, but at the same time help the teacher organize and adjust content instruction to meet the many levels within the content classroom.

STUDY QUESTIONS

1. How does the identification of concepts, reading skills, and diagnosis relate to content reading instruction?
2. How can the content teacher teach content information as well as develop reading skills?
3. What ideas are helpful in introducing new concepts and vocabulary?
4. How are reading skills developed in a manner that uses minimum content teacher time?
5. What strategies can be used to help students prepare for reading content materials?
6. How does the content teacher accommodate the different reading levels in the content classroom?
7. Why are discussions important in implementing the concept of content reading?
8. How does the content teacher evaluate students when instructional procedures are varied to accommodate differences in reading levels?

VOCABULARY

Advance organizer
Cloze technique
Deductive teaching
Directed Learning Activity
EVOKER
General vocabulary
Guided Lecture Procedure
Inductive teaching
Instruction
PANORAMA
PARS
PQRST

PQ4R
REAP
Semantic context clues
Specialized vocabulary
SQRQCQ
SQ3R
Structured overview
Study guides
Study strategies
Syntactic context clues
Technical vocabulary
Vocabulary guide

RELATING CONCEPTS, SKILLS, AND DIAGNOSIS

As teachers begin to consider instructional procedures for content reading, the important information that has been compiled in Steps I, II, and III should be reviewed and related to instruction. Specifically, in preparing for teaching a unit or chapter, the teacher first identifies the concepts that are to be taught. These concepts may be listed as statements or questions. Regardless of the wording, the teacher specifies what the students are expected to know at the end of a certain period of time. Exact procedures for identifying concepts are discussed in Chapter 2.

Using these concepts, the teacher then determines what student reading skills are essential to learning the information. An emphasis should be placed on vocabulary. In order to understand the concepts and read related materials, students must recognize technical terms and know their meanings. Additionally, content teachers should teach comprehension skills so that students can understand what is read. These skills may be easily identified if the teacher decides what questions to ask after students have read the materials, and then determines which comprehension skills are included in the questions. A reading specialist may be helpful at this point as the teacher prepares the questions that determine the types of reading skills to be applied.

Another area of reading skills that is essential to reading content materials is that of study skills. Study skills involve not only reference skills, notetaking, and study strategies, but also the reading of charts, graphs, and maps. Just because students are often able to use these reading skills at an elementary level, teachers cannot assume that they can apply them in content reading. Therefore, as discussed in Chapter 3, the content teacher should plan to help students learn to apply the appropriate reading skills in their study of content information.

In order for the content teacher to know which students can apply the needed reading skills in the different content areas, some diagnostic information is helpful. While reading diagnosis is not the teacher's main consideration in incorporating reading into content teaching, instructional planning is enhanced when observation or the Group Reading Inventory procedure is used. Other diagnostic strategies such as the cloze procedure or an Informal Reading Inventory help the content teacher determine the students' reading levels.

With the basic planning for instruction being done in these first three steps, the content teacher is ready to begin to prepare the specific teaching procedures. As indicated earlier, instructional procedures that encourage the development of reading through content instruction follow a basic structure, a structure that has long been studied by researchers in reading. The result is the use of modifications of the Directed Reading Activity (DRA) or Guided Reading Lesson that is used in elementary school reading lessons. Several modifications of this procedure have been proposed for use in content instruction. Herber proposes a three-step procedure known as Instructional Framework,[1] while Burmeister discusses a five-step Directed Reading Activity.[2] Singer and Donlan present a slightly different Directed Reading Activity[3] which, like the others, is a modification of Stauffer's[4] reading-thinking plan. As a result of working with content teachers using these various plans for teaching a content lesson, we follow a teaching model that places greater focus on content information.

The Directed Learning Activity (DLA) lists six components outlined below. Each phase is discussed in greater depth in the following pages as techniques for instruction are suggested for each of the components.

1. *Introduce concepts and vocabulary:* Based on the students' background experiences, teachers must ready students for learning content information by introducing the concepts that are to be learned and by teaching the necessary vocabulary. Concepts and vocabulary introduction are grouped together because concepts that are definable are actually vocabulary words; therefore, the teaching of concepts enhances vocabulary development just as learning vocabulary words aids in understanding concepts. The time spent on this initial introduction of information is important to future learning because students must become familiar with new terms and ideas before studying additional content information.
2. *Teach or review reading skills:* When thinking of the skills needed to learn content materials, the content teacher must teach or review the necessary skills so that students can understand the content information.
3. *Prepare for reading:* In this phase, study strategies should be reviewed and used to help students in previewing the material before reading. At this time, purposes for reading are set initially by the teacher and later by the students.
4. *Read material:* Students are given materials at appropriate reading levels and that relate to the concepts to be learned. These materials are read silently to gain new information about the concepts and the purpose for reading.
5. *Discuss information:* Using questions generated by the teacher as well as those raised by students as they read, a total class or group discussion follows the reading of the materials.
6. *Do follow-up:* During the follow-up phase, the teacher may find that it is necessary to reteach some aspect(s) of the lesson or to extend an area of interest through various activities. A portion of this phase may also be used for evaluation purposes.

These six components represent another way of providing a content lesson that incorporates reading. The purpose of such a structured procedure is not for teaching reading skills, but rather to help students become more successful in

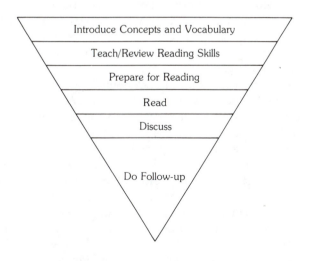

FIGURE 5.1

Directed Learning Activity

learning the content information they are expected to read. The use of the DLA in the content classroom requires that the teacher first plan for instruction by identifying concepts and relating the appropriate reading skills to the concepts. Additionally, some type of diagnosis is needed as the teacher enters the first and second components of the DLA. To facilitate a better understanding of this instructional procedure, a discussion of techniques that can be used in these six components of the DLA comprises the remainder of this chapter.

REFLECTION

As a content teacher or a student in a content classroom, how does the Directed Learning Activity parallel or differ from the instructional strategies with which you are familiar?

CONCEPT AND VOCABULARY INSTRUCTION

The first component in the DLA provides instruction to help students understand the concepts and vocabulary necessary to learn the content information. The instruction given in this initial instructional period is based on the students' background experiences. Some students need many different exposures to the new concepts and vocabulary due to their limited knowledge of the content information. Other students may offer a more extensive background of experiences and need only a brief introduction to bring the ideas into perspective. Content teachers must know their students and the concepts in order to provide the appropriate introduction of the information. This component may be called a structured overview or advance organizer by other authors. Ausubel suggests the use of advance organizers to help students establish a mental anticipation of the information to be read.[5] The advance organizer is actually a short reading selection that precedes the longer selection to be read later and requires a higher level of generality to be applied in order to comprehend the ideas. Structured overviews, another form of an advance organizer, are used to help students relate old information to new information or concepts. Because these techniques are effective ways to teach concepts, they are discussed in greater depth in the following pages.

Students are so diverse in terms of background experiences and past learning that the content teacher must assume the responsibility of developing concepts that help students to better understand the content information. As previous knowledge is related to new ideas, content teachers can arouse student interest in learning. An enthusiastic introduction to a content lesson instills a desire to learn more about the subject. For example, learning the abbreviations for various chemical elements can become a boring lesson for many students, but if the teacher introduces the lesson with an interesting experiment and writes the chemical equation on the board, the assignment takes on new meaning. Thus, content teachers must consider lively introductions of concepts and vocabulary to be a way of motivating students, as well as a time for bridging gaps between student experiences and content information.

As concepts are reviewed for instruction, the content teacher recognizes that the one aspect essential to concept learning is that of vocabulary. While concepts are abstract ideas, the terms needed to understand them are the technical and specialized vocabulary in the content area. At all levels, vocabulary understanding is the single most important predictor of comprehension. Forgan and Mangrum suggest that approximately sixty percent of comprehension is accounted for by vocabulary.[6] Thus, concepts cannot be understood without instruction in vocabulary; vocabulary becomes only memorization of definitions unless the words are related to the concepts to be learned, and comprehension is severely hampered without a knowledge of both. Therefore, content teachers should view this first component—concepts and vocabulary—as an essential part of their content instruction. To look more specifically at how this component can be implemented in the classroom, the following pages present specific techniques for teaching concepts and vocabulary. Although the teaching of concepts and vocabulary is interwoven, for organizational purposes the discussions will be separate, with the initial suggestions relating to the teaching of concepts.

Teaching Concepts

With identified concepts used to guide the teacher, instruction can begin. Consideration must be given to the students' basic understanding of the concepts—their past experiences, what they have been exposed to in previous chapters or courses, and even their interest in the information. This provides the content teacher with an idea of where to begin and how much time is needed for the introduction of concepts.

Concepts can be taught in different ways. The two basic procedures, however, are through either *inductive reasoning* or *deductive reasoning*. In deductive reasoning teaching moves from the general idea to the specific. Inductive reasoning proceeds from the specific to the general.[7] Deductive teaching is characterized by the teacher's giving information to the students, whereas in inductive teaching, examples are provided that encourage students to obtain the information through reasoning.

In presenting the inductive and deductive reasoning models, Eggen, Kauchak, and Harder note that deductive teaching is more highly structured and has a stronger content orientation, while the inductive model is less structured and has more emphasis on the affective goals of student involvement and enjoyment of learning.[8]

Teachers also feel that the inductive procedure is more time consuming as students discuss the ideas and the reasons behind them. Other teachers believe that the enthusiasm generated as students become more actively involved in the inductive procedure offsets the additional time factor. Which procedure is more effective depends largely on teacher preference, the concepts to be taught, and the students themselves. Before teachers can select the appropriate procedure, more information about each is needed.

Deductive Teaching. The deductive model for teaching is implemented by presenting concept information to students in a rather direct manner. The steps are:

The deductive approach to concept teaching is more structured and more content-oriented than the inductive approach.

1. Plan deductive teaching activities by identifying goals and preparing examples.
2. Implement the activities by presenting the abstraction (concept), clarifying terms (vocabulary), presenting the examples, and allowing students to develop examples.
3. Evaluate activities.[9]

Following these steps, deductive teaching can be used to introduce concepts and vocabulary in the content classroom as shown in the example below. In using this procedure, teachers must remember to begin with a concept definition and to follow it with examples. Additionally, the content teacher must realize that this procedure is dependent for success on the students' awareness of the concepts or abstractions and their ability to relate the examples to the concepts.

EXAMPLE

Deductive Teaching

Concepts
1. There are many kinds of one-celled animals.
2. Everything that happens in the systems of many-celled animals also goes on in this single cell.

To teach these concepts in a deductive manner the teacher could:

Concept 1:
1. State the concept or write it on the board.
2. Explain one-celled animals, showing a picture of a one-celled animal.
3. Give other examples of one-celled animals, using pictures or slides.
4. Ask the students to give some examples or describe one-celled animals.

Concept 2:
1. State the concept or write it on the board.
2. Explain the terms *systems* and *many-celled.*
3. Give examples of the things that happen in a many-celled animal and in a one-celled animal, such as absorption of food, etc.
4. Ask students to identify other examples of how many-celled and one-celled animals are alike.

Inductive teaching. A popular method for introducing concepts is known as inductive teaching. Some models classified under the general heading of inductive teaching are the Inquiry Method, Taba Model, and Concept Attainment Model. However, this discussion will focus on general inductive procedures. The basic steps are:

1. Plan inductive activities by identifying goals and preparing examples.
2. Implement activities by presenting examples, asking students to make observations about the data, and based on these observations, to form other observations or examples. From this, the student should be able to form an understanding of the concepts being taught.
3. Evaluate activities.[10]

This procedure promotes student interest by using discovery learning techniques in which examples of the concept are presented, and the student is encouraged to make observations in an effort to learn more about the concept. All responses are acceptable. This allows all students to become active participants in the observation activity.

Because the observations using teacher-prepared examples are such an important phase in the inductive procedure, careful teacher preparation is necessary. The examples must clearly broaden the understanding of the concepts and there should be enough examples for an accurate conclusion to be reached. A general example of how the concept of a "flatal" is presented in an inductive manner is given in Figure 5.2. A more specific example of the introduction of a content concept using an inductive procedure is found in the example on the following page.

EXAMPLE

Inductive Teaching

Concepts
1. There are many kinds of one-celled animals.

2. Everything that happens in the systems of many-celled animals also goes on in this single cell.

To teach these concepts in an inductive manner the teacher could:

Concept 1:
1. Call attention to the variety of protozoa shown in slides and pictures from the text.
2. Lead the students to generalize that all of these pictures represent one-celled animals and that there are many types of one-celled animals.
3. Ask them to locate information in the text to verify this idea.

Concept 2:
1. Show slides or an enlarged picture of a one-celled animal eating. Discuss the absorption of food in this animal.
2. Compare this to the eating and absorption of food in man.
3. Show also how a one-celled animal breathes and compare this to the breathing of a many-celled animal such as a dog.
4. Lead the students to the realization that the system of a one-celled and a many-celled animal do the same types of things but in different ways.
5. Ask the students to determine how the one-celled and many-celled animals are alike and different in other areas such as excretion and reproduction.

REFLECTION

Identify a concept that would be taught in your content area. Following the guidelines and examples in this chapter, tell how you would teach the concept through a deductive procedure. Then, using the same concept, tell how it could be taught inductively. Which procedure do you prefer? Why?

Another inductive strategy that may be used to introduce concepts and vocabulary is the *structured overview* or *graphic organizer*. This procedure, researched by Richard Barron, allows students to associate their prior knowledge to the new concepts and vocabulary through an active process in which the old and new information is interrelated using a verbal and visual presentation of the ideas.[11] More specifically a structured overview can be developed following these guidelines.

1. Analyze the concepts to determine those most important to learning the content information.
2. List the vocabulary words that the students must know in order to understand the information.
3. Arrange the vocabulary that you think the students do not know in a manner that shows the relationships among the concepts being studied. Put these into a diagram that reflects this relationship.
4. Use vocabulary terms that you think the students know and that can be used to discuss the basic ideas to be studied in the lesson.

5. Evaluate the graphic presentation and simplify when possible.
6. Develop guiding questions and introductory activities that help the students understand the terms and encourage them to contribute other ideas.
7. As new information is discussed, assist students in developing their own structured overviews.[12]

Example (shown to students):

All of these are flatals.

None of these are flatals.

Which of these are flatals?

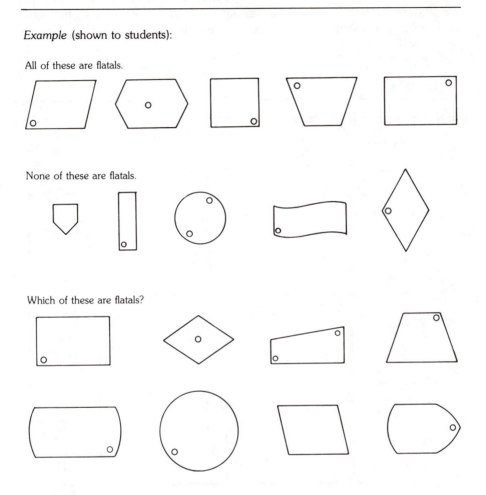

Discussion:
After the students observe the characteristics of a flatal by studying the shapes which are and are not flatals, they may then try to see if their observations are accurate by attempting to select the flatals from the last part of the example. As the flatal is identified, the students may give their definition as derived from the examples or provide other examples of the concept. In inductive teaching the student is led by example to understand the concept.

Note: Flatal is a nonsense word used in this example to mean a multisided figure that is of similar size as surrounding figures and has one small circle within the figure.

FIGURE 5.2

General Example for Inductive Teaching of Concepts

Examples of a structured overview are given in the following pages. Other examples are given in Appendix D. These examples reflect structured overviews that are complete. The teacher begins with the concept and selected vocabulary, then uses the questions to elicit more information from the students. This student interaction is essential to its success. For students with limited background knowledge, the content teacher may provide a complete structured overview including all the necessary vocabulary and use the questions to help the students better understand the various relationships. Regardless, the concept, related vocabulary, and questions are needed for every structured overview.

EXAMPLE

Structured Overview in History

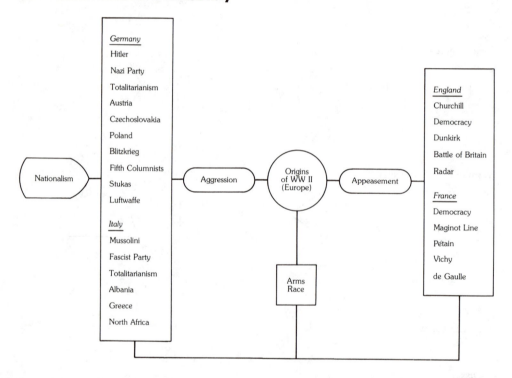

The teacher can guide the students in developing this structured overview by asking the following questions:

1. What were the primary factors that led to World War II?
2. What countries were characterized as aggressors? Why?
3. What countries were characterized as desiring peace at any cost? Why?
4. Why did appeasement fail?
5. How did the rise of nationalism in Germany and Italy influence these countries' behavior?
6. What countries participated in the arms race? Why?
7. What were some characteristics of Germany? Italy? England? France?

REFLECTION

Using the guidelines and examples provided, develop a structured overview that could be used in your content area to teach identified concepts. Identify the concept and related terms, then develop questions that would guide students to better understand the concept.

As content teachers consider the teaching of concepts, careful thought should be given to how the information will be presented. The deductive procedure is more teacher-directed and tends to give information to students in a straightforward way. Some students respond well to this procedure and prefer to learn what they are told. Likewise, some teachers feel more comfortable with deductive teaching strategies because the class is doing more listening than talking, thus cutting down on the opportunity for the students to get out of hand. Additionally, less teacher preparation time is usually required for deductive teaching because the examples clarifying the concepts are used for reinforcement rather than for observations.

EXAMPLE

Structured Overview in Science

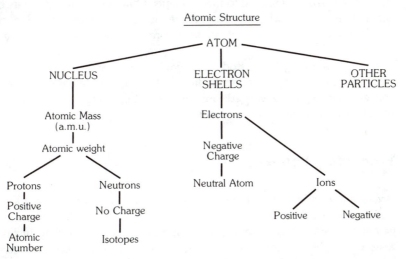

The following questions can be used to guide students in using the structured overview.

1. Of what basic components is an atom composed?
2. How were electrons discussed?
3. What type of charge do electrons possess?
4. What is a neutral atom?
5. Why is the term ions used in relationship to electrons?
6. Of what basic components is the nucleus of an atom composed?
7. What is the relationship between protons and neutrons?
8. Why does mass play a significant role in atomic theory?

Developed by Mary Hamilton, East Baton Rouge Parish School System, Louisiana.

REFLECTION

Use the concept that you chose to introduce in the previous activities and identify the vocabulary words that must be taught in order for the students to understand the concept. Follow the steps given in this section and try to limit the number of terms to five. Then tell how you would teach and reinforce these terms with your class.

In considering the use of inductive teaching strategies to develop concepts, the content teacher must carefully plan for instruction. When planning is done properly, the students become actively involved in the learning process. However, poor planning with inadequate examples allows students to become confused and possibly disruptive. This procedure also requires that the teacher tolerate student interaction in making observations about the examples and in formalizing an understanding of the concept being taught. As inductive procedures are used, teachers often find that students become more interested in content learning because they are involved in the learning process.

Regardless of the procedure used in concept instruction, the important consideration is that the concepts have been identified, and that the teacher tries to familiarize the students with the concepts before asking that content material be read. Special attention should be given to explaining concepts and giving the students experiences related to the concepts. Otherwise many students become either literal learners who try to memorize facts to pass a test or decide that content learning is irrelevant and try to ignore the course because they do not understand the concepts.

Concept learning helps students organize information according to categories, and aids not only in understanding, but also in remembering. Time spent in concept teaching is not wasted; only time spent in trying content teaching without first teaching concepts is wasted!

Vocabulary Instruction

Because the understanding of vocabulary is a major part of concept knowledge and comprehending content information, teachers must help students learn the words that are critical to content reading. Time for vocabulary instruction is always a problem. Herber suggests that "to teach one word adequately can take from two to five minutes."[13] Yet the need to develop vocabulary remains, for if students do not understand words, obviously they will not comprehend the content materials. What is the content teacher to do?

As concepts are taught, vocabulary is also developed. This assists in vocabulary understanding by giving students a background from which to generalize the meanings of unknown words. Thus, if all words cannot be taught, students should be familiar enough with the concepts to have an idea of related word meanings.

Another way to help students in vocabulary development in limited time is through word structure. This includes learning prefixes and suffixes that help determine the meanings of unknown words.

Context clues—using other words in a sentence or paragraph to learn the meaning of unknown words—also helps students build a vocabulary.

The easiest way to learn word meanings is by using the dictionary to locate words and determine appropriate definitions. Activities, both group and individual, may then be used to provide experiences with the dictionary. Content sentences may serve as the basis for a word-meaning scavenger hunt in which students locate the word and correct meaning and in turn give clues to other students to help them remember the new word. Students should *not* be given lists of words to locate in the dictionary because this method does not enable them to deal with the words in depth or as a part of direct learning experiences. Students should, however, be encouraged to use a dictionary to study word meanings as needed during their content study.

Although the use of context clues and the dictionary are considered necessary student aids, they should not be viewed as replacing vocabulary instruction. Vocabulary instruction should focus on understanding and meaning prior to reading. While some students experience difficulty pronouncing technical words, the more common problem is one of understanding. Because of the time factor, care must be taken to identify only essential words in the content materials while keeping in mind that some words are learned by using the procedures previously discussed. How then is the content teacher to decide which words are essential for teaching?

First it is necessary to consider the different types of vocabulary words that are found in content reading materials. Three types of vocabulary pertinent to content reading should be taught:

1. *General vocabulary:* Words in general communication that may be used in various content areas. Examples include *carat, luggage, rely.*
2. *Specialized vocabulary:* Words that have a precise meaning in one content area and change in another content. Examples are *squash*—to crush into a soft, flat mass (general); a game played on a walled court with rackets and a rubber ball (physical education); a vegetable (home economics), and *mold*—a hollow form (art); a fungus (science); loose, soft rich soil in decayed organic matter (vocational education).
3. *Technical vocabulary:* Words considered to belong to a specific content field. Examples include *adjective* (English); *plutonium* (science); *multiplicand* (mathematics).

General vocabulary development in initial reading instruction is sometimes referred to as teaching sight words or little words like "the," "of," "and," "in," and "at." Poor readers in the middle and secondary school have, and continue to experience, problems with these words that comprise a large percentage of all reading materials in every content area. In mathematics content reading these general vocabulary terms become specialized vocabulary that must be retaught in light of change in meaning and the mathematical actions required. For example, "and" in beginning reading indicates more than one, as in

Mary *and* John went to town.

In reading mathematics problems "and" indicates that the student is to perform more than one operation or that both things are to be done, as in

Estimate the diameter of a dime *and* a quarter.

Thus, these words that are thought of as general vocabulary may really be specialized vocabulary. Sullivan found that 50 of the "little" sight words comprised 51% of the words in elementary texts.[14] By teaching the mathematical meanings of these words to middle school students, she found the gains made in math to be significantly better than that of students who were not taught the words. Thus, vocabulary instruction with even little words is extremely important in content reading.

Considering the various types of vocabulary, their relative importance to content learning, and the interrelationships of vocabulary development and concept understanding, Herber suggests four criteria that can be used to identify the most important words to be taught.[15] Following this procedure, content teachers are able to narrow the list of words to a manageable number.

1. *Key concepts:* Teachers feel that terms crucial to the understanding of the *key* concepts must be taught. Therefore, the teacher should determine which concepts are most important and select corresponding terms.
2. *Relative value:* Because teachers often have a lengthy list when only the first criterion is used, further evaluation of the words to be taught is necessary. Given that there is probably not enough time to teach all the identified vocabulary words, the teacher must decide the contribution that each word will make to the overall understanding of the content information. Some words will be removed from the list at this point.
3. *Students' background:* Consider at this time the experiences that the students have had and which of the remaining words they should know based on these experiences. Using subjective judgment may be risky unless the teacher knows the class well. To support or refute what vocabulary the students understand, the teacher may wish to use an informal assessment like the criterion-referenced test or a section of the Group Reading Inventory.
4. *Ease of analysis:* With the remaining words identified for vocabulary instruction, the teacher should decide which may be analyzed using contextual or structural analysis. The remaining words must be taught in order for the students to understand the content information.

Considering the different types of words that students find in content reading, it becomes necessary to think next about how students learn word meanings. Words seem to be learned at three levels:

1. *Specific level of word meaning.* Students have a basic understanding of the word and can only relate the word to one definition or example.
2. *Functional level of word meaning.* Students are able to use the word in conversation. Their understanding of the word is greater than the literal recall of a single definition.
3. *Conceptual level of word meaning.* This is the highest level of understanding a word. At this level students recognize the different meanings and are able to use the word appropriately in the context of a situation.[16]

Students progress through these different levels when provided with learning experiences that encourage such development. New vocabulary words may be introduced at the specific level of understanding, but additional opportunities should be given to help students move to the higher levels. If vocabulary learning remains at the first level, the result is students who memorize words and their individual meanings and have a limited vocabulary for listening, speaking, reading, and writing.

LAGNIAPPE

Vocabulary Words and Their Meanings in Math

Word	Meaning
the	one specific thing
is	equals
a	any one thing
are	equals
can	able
on	on top of and under
page	one sheet in a book
who	question asking about someone
find	figure
one	idea in the head that stands for more than 0 and less than 2
ones	position; in a figure, the numeral to the far right
ten	idea in the head that stands for more than 9 and less than 11
tens	position; in a figure, the numeral to the left of the ones
hundred	idea in the head that stands for more than 99 and less than 101
hundreds	position; in a figure, the numeral to the left of the tens
and	something more, do both
or	either this or that but not both
number	idea in the head
numeral	sign or symbol used to stand for a number
how	question word asking for step or steps
many	amount, contrasted to few
how many	question asking for the number of something
what	question asking for things as opposed to persons
you	contrast to me, statement directed to you
your	contrast to mine, showing ownership
we	group including self, usually the subject of the sentence
it	contrast to he/she, in math refers to problem or thing
look	command to put eyes on and allow brain to react
write	put pencil in hand and make mark, symbol, etc., not write in cursive
each	every single one
numbers	ideas in the head
this	specific one in close location
that	contrast to this, specific but not in close location
set	group of things with something in common
us	group including self, usually the object of the sentence
there	contrast to here, not in close location
which	question that implies a choice
do	work or figure
same	alike, not different; equal in meaning
exercises	problems, not physical activities
these	contrast to those, more than one in close location
first	contrast to then, usually means spatial, e.g., first in line; in math has to do with time, e.g., do this first
have	contrast to have not or had, hold in one's possession
here	contrast to there, here is in close location

(continued)

LAGNIAPPE (continued)

Vocabulary Words and Their Meanings in Math

Word	Meaning
times	multiply; in "How many times" may mean the number of trials or performances
has	possession of, singular form
all	everything or everyone
equals	is, are, or the same amount on both sides

Kathryn Sullivan, "Vocabulary Instruction in Mathematics: Do the 'Little' Words Count?" Paper presented at American Reading Forum, December 10, 1981, Sarasota, Florida.

Before discussing specific activities that may be used to teach or reinforce vocabulary instruction, one additional look at vocabulary instruction research is necessary. Manzo and Sherk summarized the literature through 1970 regarding vocabulary learning. These selected findings may be used as guidelines for vocabulary instruction.

1. Vocabulary development must have the continued and systematic attention of all classroom teachers.
2. New words are learned best when taught as labels for direct experiences.
3. The study of Latin positively influences knowledge of morphemes, but does not seem to influence knowledge of vocabulary.
4. Almost any technique that draws attention to word parts and/or word meanings positively influences word acquisition when compared with the absence of such attention.
5. It is possible, but may be practically foolish, to teach words that are not a part of the verbal community in which students live. The lack of opportunity for use results in eventual atrophy.
6. The presentation of many new words and allusions in a game-like incidental learning fashion can often provide a major source of stimulation for, attention to, and consequent growth in vocabulary.
7. Many encounters with a word in various contexts are necessary before it can be learned.
8. Teachers' attitudes toward vocabulary improvement and the superiority of their own vocabulary are contagious and vital influences in improving student vocabulary.
9. The study of a limited number of words in depth is more productive than the superficial study of lists of words.
10. Successful learning of certain structured elements of words helps students unlock or partially unlock many words containing those elements.[17]

With these guidelines on vocabulary instruction and a list of priority words that must be taught before reading content information, the teacher is ready to present the new vocabulary. The initial step may be to put words on the chalkboard or overhead projector so that students can see the word and its spelling and hear its pronunciation. By putting the word in a sentence, students learn to recognize it in a more natural reading context. Additionally, by reading the word in context, a discussion can follow to help students decide the word's meaning.

LAGNIAPPE

The 76 Most Frequent Unfamiliar* Words in Selected U.S. Federal Application Forms

Rank Order	Word	T	I	S	Rank Order	Word	T	I	S
1.	benefits	93	22	71	27.	individuals	18	4	14
2.	insurance	92	31	61		programs	18	6	12
3.	application	85	11	74		premiums	18	—	18
4.	information	81	4	77		period(s)	18	9	9
5.	medical	69	9	60	28.	retirement	17	6	11
6.	assistance	61	19	42		request(ed)	17	1	16
7.	spouse(s)	55	6	49	29.	require(d, s, ing)	16	—	16
8.	applicant(s)	45	18	27		indicate(s, d)	16	5	11
9.	apply(ies, ied, ing)	43	8	35		compensation	16	10	6
10.	household	42	13	29	30.	supplemental	15	5	10
	section(s)	42	5	37		provide(s, d, ing)	15	1	14
11.	agency(ies	41	17	24		pension(er, s)	15	8	7
12.	administration	38	1	37	31.	wages	14	3	11
13.	disability	36	9	27		residence	14	2	12
14.	signature(s)	35	31	4		previous	14	5	9
15.	complete(d)	32	—	32	32.	self-employed	13	—	13
	employer(s)	32	13	19		notify(ied)	13	2	11
16.	support(ing)	31	26	5		permanent	13	9	4
17.	federal	30	3	27		eligible	13	2	11
	witness(es, ed)	30	16	14		arrangement(s)	13	3	10
18.	specify(ied)	29	22	7	33.	organization	12	6	6
	property	29	8	21		certification	12	7	5
19.	alien	28	28	—		authorize(d)	12	—	12
20.	initial(s)	26	26	—	34.	temporary	11	11	—
	relationship	26	20	6		widow(ed)	11	3	8
21.	expense(s)	25	16	9		obtain(ed, ing)	11	—	11
	resources	25	16	9		physician(s)	11	3	8
	statements	25	2	23		maiden	11	6	5
22.	disable(d, ing)	24	6	18		estate(s)	11	5	6
	remarks	24	9	15		additional	11	1	10
23.	zip	23	—	23	35.	union	10	9	1
24.	employment	22	9	13		veteran(s)	10	4	6
	mortgage	22	20	2		self-employment	10	1	9
25.	earnings	20	6	14		policy(ies)	10	5	5
	medicare	20	4	16		institution	10	7	3
26.	item(s)	19	7	12		furnish(ed)	10	5	5
	claim(s, ed)	19	10	9		enrolled	10	2	8
	include(ing, d, s)	19	5	14		certificate	10	7	3

T = Total frequency (basis for rank order)
I = Frequency in isolation
S = Frequency in sentences
*Not appearing on the Dale/Chall (1948) list

Peter P. Afflerbach, Richard L. Allington, and Sean A. Walmsley, "A Basic Vocabulary of U.S. Federal Social Program Applications and Forms," *Journal of Reading* 23 (January 1980):333. Reprinted with permission of Peter P. Afflerbach, Richard L. Allington, and Sean A. Walmsley and the International Reading Association.

Such a discussion should be structured in a way that helps students use the appropriate clues to determine meaning. For example, in teaching the word *trajectory* in a science lesson the teacher may do the following:

1. Include the word in a sentence on the board:
   The missile followed a trajectory path back to earth.
2. Initiate a discussion on clues for what the word means in these sentences:
   It has something to do with space.
   Trajectory deals with direction.
3. Using these observations, the word may then be divided into parts to look for more clues to the meaning. *Tra-* comes from the prefix *trans* meaning across, and *-jectory* comes from the Latin word *jacere* meaning to throw. Does the word mean *to throw across*?
4. Refer to the original sentence to see if this gives a complete idea of the word. In this example, the meaning is not complete; therefore, other clues are needed.
5. Give a second sentence clue or look at the word as used in the content material.
   Because the missile was launched at too low a speed, it followed a trajectory course. It could not overcome the force of gravity well enough to go straight.
   From this additional information, the student can see that trajectory means not straight, so the path traveled back to earth was curved. Thus, *trajectory* means "a curved path" or "crossing in space."

Teaching vocabulary words this way uses more time; however, reading skills are being developed that help students as they meet other unfamiliar terms in content materials. The skills of using context clues and word structure are demonstrated and reinforced as new words are introduced. Furthermore, in the discussion process, teachers are able to relate the students' experiences as well as previous knowledge as new words are taught.

Considerable attention is focused on the use of context clues or contextual analysis to determine word meanings and, in some cases, to pronounce unfamiliar words. Context clues include *syntactic context clues* that help determine meaning using the order or function of the word. For example, inflectional endings help in determining time through changes in verb tense. Signal words help readers know meanings of surrounding words by serving as markers. For example, words like *next, in addition*, or *furthermore* tell readers they should continue to read to obtain more information. Words such as *otherwise, however*, or *on the other hand* mean a change in direction in the materials or a comparison of information being made.

A second context clue is the *semantic context*. This commonly used clue depends upon the reading of surrounding words. In some cases, it defines the word or gives the entire meaning. Nine kinds of semantical context clues are shown below with examples.

Another procedure that may be used in vocabulary instruction is that of the *vocabulary guide*. This is an exercise designed by the teacher that identifies potentially troublesome words from the content to be read, and possibly gives their pronunciation and definition, as well as the page number on which the word appears. Some guides go further and ask that the student use the words to complete questions or other tasks.

A vocabulary guide may be used in a total class discussion situation prior to students' reading information. By using the guide this way, the class works together with teacher direction. The guide may also be used by students as they read the content materials. In this way, important terms are targeted. The content teacher must decide which procedure would prove most beneficial with individual students or classes. Slower students need the instruction given when the guide is used with teacher direction. Other students may need the guide only as a structure to help them recognize the more important terms. Regardless, the use of the guide not only helps students in remembering words, but also in aiding them to develop speaking and writing vocabularies. An example of a vocabulary guide is given below.

EXAMPLE

Types of Semantic Context Clues

Definition or direct explanation	Progressive income tax means that people pay a tax according to their incomes.
Description	A hurricane is a violent and destructive storm with winds reaching speeds of more than 150 miles per hour.
Restatement	Illiteracy, or the inability to read or write, is prevalent in many countries.
Comparison and contrast	In many Latin American countries, the standard of living is abysmal, while in North America it is high.
Reflection of mood	She took deep breaths of the dew-laden morning as she began at a trot and quickly moved her pace to a run. As she passed others, she felt extraordinarily hale.
Familiar expression	The people were poor and hungry with no home and only a doomsday ahead.
Example	The European farm may resemble a garden to an American. For example, the size of the European farm may be as small as five acres, whereas in the U.S., farms are hundreds of acres.
Summary	Different languages are spoken in Western Europe. Because the countries are small, people travel into the other countries often and are thereby required to speak the different languages. Thus, in most schools in Western Europe, it is compulsory to study a second language.
Association	The date palm is the bread of the desert just as grapes provide the drink for Mediterranean people.
Synonyms and antonyms	Deserts are known as flood areas because the hard land does not absorb the water quickly when rains occur.

EXAMPLE

Sample Vocabulary Guide for a Vocational Education Unit on Painting

I.   Match each word with the correct meaning. Place the letter of the correct meaning next to the word.

          _____ 1. solvent
          _____ 2. enamel
          _____ 3. whitewashing
          _____ 4. skin
          _____ 5. blistering

a. A mixture of lime and water used to give a white coat to surfaces.

b. A problem caused by putting paint on a wet surface or from heat.

c. A paint producing a hard glossy surface.

d. A scum-like covering on the top of an open container of paint.

e. The running or sagging of paint soon after application.

f. A substance that can dissolve another substance.

II.   Answer these questions.
1. What does *priming* mean in this sentence?
   More paint is required for the priming coat than for the succeeding coats.
2. What is a paint roller?
3. What does this sentence say you should do with your paint brush?
   To break in a new paint brush, immerse it in linseed oil at least 12 hours before it is to be used.

Vocabulary reinforcement is an important part of vocabulary instruction. As shown in the use of a vocabulary guide, reinforcement aids the student in remembering and using the newly learned words. Just as in the initial vocabulary instruction, there are many ways to provide vocabulary reinforcement. Teachers must remember that variety is needed to aid in motivation. The natural procedure in reinforcing the new words is through reading of content materials. This was the purpose of the initial instruction. *Reading of additional related topics*, however, also enhances learning these terms. Additionally, wide reading serves to expand continuously and reinforce the development of vocabulary.

Activities or games are another avenue for reinforcing vocabulary learning. These may be purchased or teacher-made. Teacher-made activities are more commonly used because they can be designed to relate directly to what has been taught. Crossword puzzles, worksheets, game boards, or class word files are examples. Each activity may be used to reinforce any type of vocabulary skill from a general review of all words taught during a specified time, to the use of context clues in determining meaning, the use of word structure to unlock meaning, or the definitions of words with multiple meanings. Examples of vocabulary reinforcement activities are given in the following pages, with more examples given in Appendix A.

ACTIVITIES

Building Vocabulary in Literature

Ask students to supply the names of Greek gods and goddesses to complete this cross-word puzzle. Students may use reference materials, but must work independently.

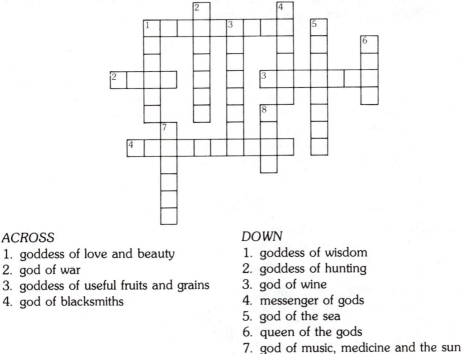

ACROSS
1. goddess of love and beauty
2. god of war
3. goddess of useful fruits and grains
4. god of blacksmiths

DOWN
1. goddess of wisdom
2. goddess of hunting
3. god of wine
4. messenger of gods
5. god of the sea
6. queen of the gods
7. god of music, medicine and the sun
8. king of gods

Betty Archambeault, Catholic High School, Baton Rouge, Louisiana.

Building Vocabulary in Mathematics

Provide hints such as those given below and ask students to complete the spelling of the words.

1. __ __   S __ __ __
2.   I __ __ __ __ __ __ __
3. __ __   N __ __ __ __ __
4. __ __   E __ __ __ __ __

1. To divide into two congruent parts or into two parts of equal value.
2. The set consisting of the natural numbers such as 1, 2, 3, . . .; the negatives of the natural numbers such as −1, −2, −3, . . .; and zero.
3. A five-sided polygon.
4. A statement to be proven true by means of basic assumptions.

What is the abbreviation for *sine*?
Tell how this term is used in mathematics.

Key: 1. bisect   3. pentagon
           2. integers   4. theorem

Building Vocabulary in Physical Education

How well do your remember the words we use in talking about different sports? Look at the words below and match them with a sport.

	Sport	*Meaning*
tackle	_____	_____
love	_____	_____
run	_____	_____
block	_____	_____
dribble	_____	_____
rebound	_____	_____
set	_____	_____
clip	_____	_____
foul	_____	_____
double	_____	_____

Now check your answers by finding the meanings under the correct sports. Put the correct letter of the meaning next to the word.

Baseball
a. A scoring point made by successfully moving around the bases.
b. A hit in which the runner goes as far as second base.

Basketball
c. To move a ball by bouncing.
d. Any infraction of the rules for which the penalty is either a free throw or giving the ball to the opponent.
e. A term usually applied when the ball bounces or bounds from the backboard or basket.

Football
f. Action of offensive linemen and backs in which they use their bodies to ward off defensive players from the ball carrier.
g. Action by player in which he throws his body across the back of the leg or legs of a player not carrying the ball.
h. When one player throws another player to the ground.

Tennis
i. No score.
j. A scoring unit between the game and the match.

Building Vocabulary in Home Economics

You are getting ready to follow some recipes to cook a meal for your friends. There are many abbreviations in the recipe. Test yourself to see if you know all of them.

lb.   _____
tbsp.   _____

tsp.   _____
pkg.   _____
c.   _____
doz.   _____
pt.   _____
oz.   _____
min.   _____
qt.   _____

Your recipes also have some directions which are not very clear. Can you tell what these
words mean?
baste the turkey   _____
cream the butter   _____
glaze the cake   _____
julienne carrots   _____
marinate the beans   _____

Building Vocabulary in Science

An antonym is a word that has the opposite meaning of another word. For example, *left*
and *right* are antonyms. A synonym is a word that means the same as another word.
Old and *antique* are synonyms. Using what you have studied in science, give the synonyms for these words.

germ   _____
dew   _____
decay   _____
surroundings   _____
poison   _____

Now give the antonyms for these words.

gas   _____
evaporation   _____
solar energy   _____
contraction   _____
inhale   _____

Use index cards to make a synonym/antonym game to test another student. Put the two
synonyms or antonyms on the card—one on the left end and the other on the right.
Then cut the card in half using an uneven cut.

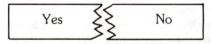

This makes a puzzle card for which the correct answer only will match. Use the
words from the lists above and add one synonym pair and one antonym pair to
your puzzle cards.

Building Vocabulary in Foreign Language

Give students a passage in which every seventh word is deleted. Also give them an alphabetical listing of words that are to be used to complete the passage. Ask them to put the appropriate words in the blanks.

Un día un perro entra en _____ tienda donde se vende carne, ej _____ hombre le tira un buen hueso. _____ perro le gustan mucho los huesos. _____ muy contento cuando sale. Va hacia _____ casa a través de unos campos, _____ pasa al lado de un peqeño _____ .

Hace buen tiempo, y el agua _____ rio está clara como un espejo. _____ perro se ve en el agua, _____ le parece que allí hay otro _____ .

Ese otro perro tambeín tiene un _____ en la boca. Y el otro _____ le parece mejor, y más grande _____ el hueso de él. Abre la _____ para tomar el hueso del otro _____ .

I. A. Richards, Ruth M. Romero, and Christine Gibson, passage taken from *Spanish Through Pictures, Book II and A Second Workbook of Spanish* (New York: Pocket Books, 1972), p. 206.

Al	Hueso	Río
Boca	Hueso	Su
Del	Perro	Un
El	Perro	Una
Está	Y	Y

Another procedure for vocabulary reinforcement is the use of the *cloze technique*. This procedure is described as a diagnostic technique in Chapter 4, but can also be used as an instructional tool to help students practice their contextual analysis skills for determining the meaning of an unknown word. In using the cloze procedure for instructional purposes, the teacher should:

1. Initiate the procedure with a multiple-choice format, deleting only nouns and verbs and giving only two choices for completing the blank. Be sure that the material is at or below the student's independent reading level. Gradually, give more items to select from to complete the blank, then require that students supply words on their own, and when they can do this, begin to delete other grammatical parts.
2. Instruct students to read the entire selection silently before completing any of the items.
3. Discuss the process used in completing the exercise. This may involve teaching students how to use other words in the context to aid in giving a sensible response.
4. Accept close guesses for answers. In using this procedure for diagnosis, however, the exact word is required.
5. Provide opportunity for self-checking of the answers.
6. Allow students to compare their responses with the original source.
7. Instruction should be systematic, long-term, and organized.[18]

Additional use of the cloze procedure may be made by encouraging students to work in teams to identify as many words as possible to fit the blanks. This allows students to learn vocabulary from one another. Not only are contextual analysis skills developed with this procedure, but students also learn synonyms, practice spelling skills, and better understand the various parts of speech.

A vocabulary reinforcement idea that motivates the entire class to learn new words is the development of a class word list or *word file*. Many ideas have been experimented with and adapted to classroom situations. In some classes, each student identifies one word a week that the whole class should know. The student must introduce the word, tell the class why they need to know it, use it in context, and insert it into the class word file. Then periodically, games are used in which the words are reviewed.

In introducing information prior to asking students to read content materials, the teacher should carefully determine the concepts and vocabulary that must be understood. Once identified, instruction must be provided to assist the students as they read the materials. Research[19] has shown that the use of any type of introductory overview of concepts and terms leads to superior comprehension. Therefore, content teachers must not overlook the importance of this first component.

TEACH READING SKILLS

The second component of the DLA involves the actual teaching of reading skills students must know in order to understand the content materials. In Step II, Chapter 3, suggestions are given for identifying reading skills needed to learn the content concepts. This section is based upon the identification of skills and discusses procedures involved in the actual teaching of these skills.

Content teachers are not expected to be reading specialists, nor are they asked to devote large amounts of classroom time to this component. They are, however, expected to help students adapt previously learned reading skills to content materials. For some students, this is almost automatic; for others, a more diligent effort must be made.

Using the results of the diagnostic instruments such as the Group Reading Inventory, the content teacher should know which students require assistance. With this information, the teacher may decide that reading skill instruction needs to be differentiated with several groups working on different skills. Ideas for grouping are discussed in Chapter 7. Teachers should note, however, that this is a component in which grouping procedures may be helpful.

Just as there is no one way of teaching concepts and vocabulary, there is no one way of teaching reading skills. There are, however, some basic guidelines that must be considered in skills teaching.

1. *The teacher should introduce the skill by telling and showing examples of the skill as used in content reading.*

   Example: The skill is implied cause-effect relationships. "Most events in our lives have a *cause* for happening. They also have a result or *effect*. This is true in many things that we read. In a science experiment, the reason we get a certain reaction is the *cause*. The result is the *effect*. Sometimes these *cause-effect* relationships are obvious, and may be explained in the materials we read. At other times the result or effect may be discussed and it is then up to the reader to determine the cause or why something happened. For example:

Lynn hurriedly pulled into the driveway, jumped out of the car, and ran into the house. The phone was ringing. As he talked on the phone, he looked out the window just in time to see the fence at the end of the driveway fall across the plants.

The cause of the fence falling on the plants is not directly stated. We can decide from the information given, however, that the car rolled into the fence. Thus, the *cause* is the car and the *result* is a knocked-down fence and broken plants.

   Now let's look at a cause-effect situation that we might find in reading our science book.''

2. *The teacher should show the students how to use the skill in reading their content materials.*

   Example: ''This is a selection taken from our science book. Let's see if we can find the cause-effect relationship.

To form a solution of lead nitrate, it is necessary to mix lead nitrate crystals with a liquid. The crystals dissolve in the liquid to form a solution. When a lead nitrate solution is formed, the crystals disappear, but the solution weighs the same as the crystals and liquid before they were mixed.

In this selection you are told what happened with the lead nitrate crystals and the liquid. This is the result. However, you were not told what caused this result to occur. Let's decide why a solution was formed and why it weighed the same as the crystals and the liquid. You are not given all the information in this selection, but use your ideas from what we've learned in the past to decide the cause. We'll do this together.''

3. *Provide opportunities for students, working together or individually, to demonstrate their use of the skill with content materials.*

   Example: ''Because you have to understand many cause-effect relationships as you read your lesson today, I would like you to get into groups of five to do some more exercises. In these exercises sometimes the cause and effect will be given and sometimes only one or the other. Work together to identify the cause or reason and write it on your paper under *cause*. Then try to find the effect or result and write it under *effect*.''

   In developing comprehension skills, direct instruction is important. Another strategy for use in comprehension development is the cloze procedure. This technique has been described previously as a means of identifying a student's reading level and a way of developing vocabulary. As a comprehension building strategy this technique has been researched at all levels through college.[20] Used as an instructional technique for comprehension, however, the format and procedures are the same as outlined in the ''Vocabulary'' section of this chapter. The passage may be shorter than needed for a diagnostic test, the deletions may be made selectively as needed, and discussion of the results is encouraged.

   As content teachers consider reading skills to be taught, emphasis should be placed on the development of comprehension as well as study skills. The understanding of the different skills in these two areas, along with the concept and vocabulary instruction, greatly enhances learning content information.

Students commonly have problems with study skills relating to organization of materials they are learning. These organizational skills affect the comprehension of information being read because students cannot remember information they cannot mentally organize. This affects their ability to use underlining, outlining, or notetaking strategies. Content teachers may find it necessary to teach these skills so that students clearly understand how the content material is organized.

To help develop these skills, the content teacher may begin by teaching *underlining* strategies. (As teachers know, some students tend to underline everything they read, feeling that every word is strategic, while others fail to highlight anything, because they cannot decide what is important to learn.) This skill may be developed by using questions to guide students in marking significant information. Content teachers should help students follow these five guidelines:

1. *Finish reading before marking.* Students tend to underline everything in a text which defeats the purpose of using this as a study strategy. Only the most important ideas should be marked for review. Students can better determine what is most important after reading the entire selection.
2. *Be selective by marking only what is important.* Underlining is done as an aid for review of the material at a later time—if everything is marked then complete rereading is necessary.
3. *Make notes in the margins to aid in review.* Rather than to underline entire sections, the students should be encouraged to make their own notes in the margin to highlight or summarize the idea.
4. *Underline quickly and reread only for an overview.* After reading and when underlining is done, the students should scan the material to locate the important ideas. Careful rereading will often result in the underlining of everything! Thus, scan and quickly mark the important information to be remembered.
5. *Be neat and don't clutter the page.* Underlining is done to aid the student in reviewing content material. If pages are overly marked and notes put in margins in a messy manner, the material becomes difficult to use as a review— so be neat![21]

Content teachers may find that underlining is not a feasible study strategy because students do not own the books, but it still may be taught using duplicated copies of the text or other materials such as the newspaper. A more practical, yet more time consuming, strategy that serves the same purpose, however, is that of outlining. Additionally, as outlining skills are developed, students should also improve their ability to underline.

Outlining skills help the student record, in abbreviated form, information that must be remembered. Outlining requires that the student understand the relationship between the main idea and supporting details. The main idea becomes the major heading in an outline with details as subheadings. Outlining skills become greater as students learn to use headings and subheadings within a chapter or table of contents as the principal topics in an outline. These outlines may be developed in sentence form, using complete sentences to record the information, or topic outlines that use key words or phrases.

Underlining of important ideas should be done after reading the entire selection.

In teaching students to outline content materials the traditional outlining format may be used in which the major heading is preceded by a Roman numeral and the subheading is indented and preceded by either a numeral or a letter.

EXAMPLE

Standard Outline

I.   Sioux Indians
   A. Life style
      1. Considered fearless by other tribes
      2. Also called Dakota
      3. Lived in the Great Plains of the Midwest
      4. Nomads who hunted
      5. Lived off bison
      6. Lived in tepees
   B. Work with other tribes
      1. Hunted with other tribes in summer
      2. Also a social time
      3. Stole food and horses from farmers
      4. Different clubs for young men
      5. Operated in a military manner
II. People of Rwanda
   A. Hutu
      1. Life in East Africa
      2. Farmers
   B. Watusi
      1. Live in East Africa
      2. Owned most of cattle
      3. Hired Hutu to do herding
      4. Ruled others in Rwanda

Another outlining procedure uses only numbers, as shown in the second sample. This outlining style is used almost exclusively with scientific or highly technical material.

EXAMPLE

Alternative Procedure for Outlining

1.0   Sioux Indians
1.1   Life style
1.1.1   Considered fearless by other tribes
1.1.2   Also called Dakota
1.1.3   Lived in the Great Plains of the Midwest
1.1.4   Nomads who hunted
1.1.5   Lived off bison
1.1.6   Lived in tepees
1.2   Work with other tribes
1.2.1   Hunted with other tribes in summer
1.2.2   Also a social time
1.2.3   Stole food and horses from farmers
1.2.4   Different clubs for young men
1.2.5   Operated in a military manner
2.0   People of Rwanda
2.1   Hutu
2.1.1   Live in East Africa
2.1.2   Farmers
2.2   Watusi
2.2.1   Live in East Africa
2.2.2   Owned most of cattle
2.2.3   Hired Hutu to do herding
2.2.4   Ruled others in Rwanda

Content teachers should be consistent in the outlining format used. Consistency of instruction improves learning as students develop expertise in applying specific study strategies. Teaching different outlining techniques is confusing and tends to result in the use of none. These procedures may be followed in teaching outlining:

1. Give students a short, complete outline and the passage from which the outline was made. An example is shown in the samples.
2. Show students how the information was selected to make the outline.
3. Give students a partially completed outline and the selection that may be used to complete the outline. Initially, the students may work in small groups and individually later.
4. Discuss how the final outline was developed.
5. Give students a basic frame for an outline and reading selection and ask them to develop the total outline.

Using these procedures over several weeks should not only help student readers develop outlining skills, but should also assist them in identifying important information necessary for underlining, summarizing ideas, and notetaking.

In studying for exams, in writing research papers, or as an aid in reading content materials, students are continuously faced with making notes. *Notetaking skills* are dependent upon summarization and outlining skills. Notes are made to enhance learning. This requires that information be put in the students' own words, and that ideas be organized regardless of whether lecture notes or reading notes are being developed.

Shepherd suggests the following procedures for teaching notetaking:

1. Read a chapter or section with the students and suggest the ideas which should be recorded in notes.
2. Discuss specific material with the students and evolve with them the most efficient form for their notes. This may be an outline, a list, a time line, or any form which is helpful to the student.
3. Guide the students to take notes in class by writing the main points on the board or on a transparency for use on an overhead projector as the lesson progresses.
4. With a newspaper article, instruct students to take notes to answer questions of Who? When? What? Where? Why? and How?[22]

Kelly and Holmes suggest the use of a Guided Lecture Procedure (GLP) to help students develop notetaking skills in a lecture situation. The basic components of this procedure are:

1. The students listen intensively during the lecture and take no notes.
2. Prior to the lecture the students are given a purpose for listening by reading and copying the lecture objectives. The objectives should be limited to four with new terminology listed next to the objectives.
3. The lecturer stops about halfway through the class period and asks students to write down in shortened form all recalled lecture information. About five minutes is given for this.
4. The students work in small groups to recapitulate the lecture. During this time the lecture notes are actually developed. If questions arise the lecturer serves as a guide to help students answer their questions.
5. Time is given for students to reflect on both the lecture content and the GLP activities. This helps build long-term memory.
6. After the reflections, the students write in their individual notebooks, in narrative form and without the previously developed notes, the major concepts, details, and conclusion from the lecture.[23]

This procedure motivates students. They listen and become involved in the lecture class. They become active learners.

Regardless of the notetaking strategy taught, content teachers should help students use basic guidelines like these:

1. Use an outline format that notes the main idea or key words and supporting details.
2. Include enough detail so that important information is not lost, but don't try to write everything.

3. Develop an abbreviation system for faster writing.
4. Reread notes as soon as possible so that gaps can be filled in and questions posed about unclear ideas.

Other suggestions for taking notes from written materials are:

1. Include complete bibliographical reference with notes from that source.
2. Use quotation marks for material taken directly from the source and note page number for each quote.
3. Summarize ideas from what is read but don't interpret them.
4. Use note cards or paper of the same size when taking notes for a research project. This helps to organize information when writing the report.
5. Organize notes according to ideas, time sequence or whatever system fits best with the subject, and add new notes to this collection after each reading.

Other study skills that must be taught include *reference skills* as well as the more general study skills—using book parts, reading graphics, and adjusting reading rate. Students are expected to use reference skills to write papers, learn additional ideas about concepts being discussed, and to locate information. The encyclopedia, library card catalog, atlas, and dictionary are common reference tools that secondary students are expected to use almost daily in their content studies. Many students shy away from using these tools, however, because they do not know how to use them. It is up to the content teacher, therefore, to instruct students in how to use these resources.

The school librarian can be helpful in introducing students to the library's reference books. Following this overview, the content teacher should then design activities in which students actually use reference materials to heighten their content learning. Once students are acquainted with the materials, their contents, and organizational format, teachers can expect them to refer regularly to these materials as they study concepts. Any new reference tool should be introduced and explained to students before expecting them to use it. Familiarity with reference materials furthers the application of reference skills to content concepts as well as advances organizational skills in writing reports and doing projects.

As students use content textbooks, reference materials, and other information sources, they are expected to apply *specialized study skills*. Those most frequently needed include learning when and how to skim or scan information, how to adjust rate of reading according to purpose, how to use various parts of the book to increase learning, and how to use appropriate study strategies. These are the content teacher's responsibility. Questions such as, "Where would you find the information about magnetic permeability?" would, for example, lead students into an exploration of the index and table of contents. Other questions posed by the teacher may help students locate and learn additional resources within the book such as a glossary, appendix, or bibliography. Students also learn how the book is organized and recognize the reason for the organizational format. For example, a text organized into sections according to a chronological sequence will be better understood if students already understand the format.

Additionally, students must be shown how to interpret graphic aids like illustrations, maps, charts, and diagrams related to the narrative information. Using an example from the text or other material, the content teacher must demonstrate this interpretive skill following the steps outlined previously for developing comprehension skills.

In teaching students to adjust their rate of reading, content teachers may begin by discussing when skimming and scanning should be used. Students may apply the scanning skill in sample activities as they try to find the answer to a specific question calling for the scanning technique. Skimming skills may be similarly developed as students practice quickly looking over a material to determine what the material is about and to formulate a list of questions to guide their more careful rereading. Students should also be taught that rates of reading depend on their purpose for reading.

LAGNIAPPE

The bulk of instructional materials used in classrooms is read at rather slow rates (100-250 words per minute); slowest rates . . . would probably be used with math and some science materials. The "lighter" the reading matter becomes and the less complex the purpose, the faster will be the rate normally . . . Light or easy fiction read purely for entertainment, not analysis, might be read anywhere up to 500 words or so per minute. Beyond 500-550 words per minute, skimming probably takes place where only partial ideas are gained in an attempt to get the general drift of the material. Scanning, or speeding through material until you locate a particular item, may be extremely fast—perhaps 1000 words per minute or more.

H. Alan Robinson, *Teaching Reading and Study Strategies* 2nd ed. (Boston: Allyn and Bacon, 1978), p. 285.

Study strategies are another specialized skill that students must learn to apply in reading content information. These strategies are discussed in the following section.

In teaching reading skills, the teacher is the crucial link. These skills must be discussed in relation to the content area in which they are to be used. Students do not improve in their ability to read content materials by merely completing isolated skills exercises. The teacher must instruct and show the use of the skills and devise exercises that relate directly to the content area. Reading skill development is not a separate component the teacher labels "reading instruction." Rather it is another means of readying students for reading content materials.

REFLECTION

Identify one reading skill that is important to your content area. Tell how you would teach this skill.

PREPARE FOR READING AND READ THE MATERIALS

The third and fourth components of the DLA involve the final part of the preparation for reading the content materials and the actual reading of the materials.

These two components are discussed together because many of the study strategies used in previewing materials also include the reading of the materials. Thus, although these are two components in the DLA, they are grouped together for discussion purposes. Different ways of preparing students for reading have been presented by various authors. Involved in all of these procedures, however, are the basic ideas of previewing the materials and establishing purposes for reading in an effort to make the reading component a successful experience.

Before discussing different study strategies, attention should be focused on the material to be read. As shown in preceding chapters, content teachers are faced with many students every day, each of whom reads differently. They read at different levels and have divergent skill needs, as well as various experiential backgrounds. Through concept and vocabulary instruction, the basic understandings needed to comprehend the materials, regardless of student background, should be developed and weaknesses overcome. But what about differences in reading levels?

Many content teachers find that more students are able to read the content textbook when time is spent in teaching before reading. Despite this strategy, some students cannot read the book. This difficulty can only be helped by providing materials other than the textbook for these students. Remember, the emphasis in content instruction is on the learning of concepts; therefore, any materials that relate to the understanding of concepts can be used—*not just the textbook*. For example, in studying the concept "space travel makes the universe smaller," some students may read news articles on the subject, others may study a text about the universe, while still others may look at TV tapes covering the travel of the spaceship *Columbia* and/or seek interviews with noted scientists. Thus, as students prepare to read or study materials, their preparation should relate directly to the materials. These components usually require a differentiation of assignments and group work within the content classroom.

Study Strategies

Study strategies are viewed as the major procedures followed in previewing and reading content materials. Although each procedure varies, all basically consider an initial review of the material, setting purposes for reading, reading the material, and a follow-up review of what is read. Some of the procedures lend themselves more to specific content areas, while others may be used in all areas. The general strategies will be discussed first, with the more specialized strategies mentioned toward the end of this section.

SQ3R. SQ3R, the oldest and most commonly used study strategy, was developed by Francis Robinson. The steps followed in the SQ3R procedure are:

1. *Survey:* The student should survey the introductory statement, headings, and summaries quickly to get the main idea and scope of the assignment. Attention should be given to graphic aids and questions at the end of the chapter.

2. *Question:* The student formulates his own questions that set the purpose for reading. He may use headings or a question that the survey may have prompted.
3. *Read:* The material is read by the student to answer the questions.
4. *Recite:* The student tries to answer the questions formulated without referring to the book or any notes he may have taken.
5. *Review:* The student rereads portions of the book or notes to verify if his answers to the questions are correct.[24]

Although students are often instructed in the use of this study strategy, few seem to use it as they read. The reasons given include the time taken to follow the procedure, the lack of understanding, and because students usually wait until the last minute to read assigned materials and do not have time to follow the procedures properly. With careful teacher guidance, however, students can learn to use and study with this strategy. The teacher may consider devoting several class periods to explain the procedure, to distribute copies of the strategy for student reference, to demonstrate the strategy, to allow practice with SQ3R, and finally to get the student into the content assignment using the strategy. An example of how this strategy may be used in studying a content textbook is presented in Figure 5.3.

PARS. A modified and simplified study strategy discussed by Carl Smith and Peggy Elliot is PARS. This strategy is recommended for use with younger students or students who have limited experience in using study strategies. The steps are:

1. *Preview* the material to get a general sense of movement and organization . . . its important headings or concepts.
2. *Ask questions* before reading to make sure that you are setting a purpose or purposes that satisfy you and your perception of what the teacher will emphasize.
3. *Read* with those purpose-setting questions in mind.
4. *Summarize* the reading by checking information gained against the pre-established questions.[25]

PQ4R. This strategy is another variation of the SQ3R developed by H. Alan Robinson and Ellen L. Thomas. PQ4R is designed to help students become more systematic and discriminating readers. The steps are:

1. *Preview* the material during teacher assigned time using general questions as a guide. This should become an automatic step with everything the student reads.
2. *Question* using interpretive as well as literal questions to guide reading. These should be questions that help the student know what to look for in reading.
3. *Read* the material using the questions as a guide.
4. *Reflection* occurs when the student looks back over the material and rereads sections that are unclear. This aids the student in organizing thoughts.
5. *Recite* to oneself to determine if the questions have been answered in the reading.
6. *Review* the material to be sure that all information was read and remembered.[26]

1 and 2. *Survey and Question:* Review the headings and terms and pose questions that
establish purposes for reading.

    a. Heading: *Relation Between Heat and Work*
        Question: What commonalities exist between heat and work?
    b. Heading: *First Law of Thermodynamics*
        Question: What is thermodynamics? What is the first law of thermodynamics?
    c. Heading: *Conversion of Heat into Work*
        Question: How is heat converted into work?
    d. Heading: *Work Done by a Gas*
        Question: How does a gas do work?
    e. Heading: *Specific Heats of Gases*
        Question: How do the specific heats of gases affect work?
    f. Heading: *Efficiency of Ideal Heat Engines*
        Question: What is an ideal heat engine?
    g. Heading: *The Second Law of Thermodynamics*
        Question: What is the second law of thermodynamics?
    h. Terms: Mechanical equivalent of heat
        Isothermal process
        Adiabatic process
        Joule's method
        Question: What do these terms mean and how do they relate to heat and work?
3. *Read:* Direct the students to read the selection using the identified questions to guide
   their reading.
4. *Recite:* Using each previously formulated question, attempt to answer it in your mind.
5. *Review:* Reread sections of the material to verify your answers and to study more
   carefully those questions which could not be answered.

Headings and terms from John E. Williams et al., *Modern Physics* (New York: Holt, Rinehart, and
Winston, 1972), pp. 209–21.

FIGURE 5.3

Application of SQ3R: "Heat and Work"

PQ4R is a step-by-step approach for studying content materials. Teachers
and students should, however, adjust the strategy to meet individual needs and
different reading materials.

REAP. One of the newer study strategies was developed by Marilyn Eanet and
Anthony Manzo for use in reading and content area classrooms. This strategy is
designed to develop independence in reading while strengthening thinking and
writing skills. REAP encourages students to demand meaning as they read,
because the strategy requires an overt response. The four steps are:

    1. *Read:* The student reads to find out what the writer is saying.
    2. *Encode:* The writer's message is translated by the student into his or her
       own language.
    3. *Annotate:* During this step, students write the message in notes for them-
       selves. Any one of several forms of annotations may be used: heuristic,

summary, thesis, question, critical, intention, and motivation annotations are all useful.

    4. *Ponder:* The student thinks about the author's message. Discussion with others may be a part of this step.[27]

    This study strategy differs from others in that students are not required to preview the material or establish questions to guide reading. Thus, there is no preparation for reading, but rather the emphasis is on reading the material and remembering what the author has said. This strategy requires that the student be skilled in summarizing and notetaking.

PANORAMA. Another general study strategy was developed by Peter Edwards. This strategy consists of eight steps that are divided into three stages with the third stage omitted as necessary. The strategy is outlined as follows:

    1. *Preparatory Stage:*
        a. *Purpose:* The reader decides why the materials are to be read.
        b. *Adapting Rate to Material:* The reader decides how fast the selection should be read.
        c. *Need to Pose Questions:* This step is similar to the "Question" step in the SQ3R. Headings of various types may be converted into questions. The student then reads to find the answer.
    2. *Intermediate Stage:*
        a. *Overview:* This step is similar to the "Survey" step in the SQ3R. The main parts of the material are surveyed to determine the organizational format of the author.
        b. *Read and Relate:* The material is read and answers to the formulated questions are sought during the reading.
        c. *Annotate:* Annotations can be made in the book if permitted, or on a piece of paper.
    3. *Concluding Stage:*
        a. *Memorize:* The student uses outlines and summaries as aids to memorization.
        b. *Assess:* Evaluation is determined in relation to the achievement of purposes stated and retention of the important parts of the material.[28]

    An awareness of these different study strategies helps content teachers in determining ways that students can be prepared for reading content materials. Although vocabulary, concepts, and necessary reading skills may be taught, it is still helpful if direct preparation for reading is also done. More specialized study strategies have been developed for use in reading English, mathematics, and science materials. Although general strategies may also be used in these three content areas, specialized strategies may fit the content material more easily.

EVOKER. This strategy was developed by Walter Pauk to assist in reading prose, poetry, and drama. The six steps in this strategy are:

    1. *Explore* by reading the selection to develop an idea of the overall message.
    2. *Vocabulary* study is needed to learn the key words.
    3. *Oral reading* should be done with good expression.
    4. *Key ideas* are located to understand what the author has said.

5. *Evaluation* is necessary to determine how the key words and sentences relate to the central theme.
6. *Recapitulation* means that rereading the selection is helpful.[29]

Because the EVOKER strategy is designed for reading specific types of materials, there is no provision for previewing the material. Thus, students use it only while reading the materials rather than as a complete study strategy.

SQRQCQ. Leo Fay developed this strategy to aid students in studying mathematics materials. The six steps are:

1. *Survey* the word problem to learn its general nature.
2. *Question* to decide what is being asked.
3. *Read* the problem again, more carefully than before, to note the details and relationships.
4. *Question* as to what processes should be used.
5. *Compute* based on the decision made on the previous question.
6. *Question* the answer to see if it is logical in regard to what is asked in the problem.[30]

This strategy greatly helps students in reading mathematics word problems.

PQRST. This is a study strategy developed by George Spache and Paul Berg that can be applied to social studies and science materials. The strategy is similar to SQ3R in the steps of *previewing*, *questioning* and *reading*. The fourth step is to *state the information* remembered after reading and serves to answer the question. The last step is *testing*. At this time the students ask themselves questions like those the teacher might ask.[31]

In each of these study strategies designed to help students prepare for reading, one step included was that of *question*. Each strategy suggests the need for questions to be established either by the teacher or student before reading. Herber and Nelson recommend that teachers consider the types of questions asked before reading to be sure that students possess the skills necessary to use the information to answer the questions. They further suggest the use of statements to guide reading. Statements serve as a stimulation activity and can lead to the use of questions. The six phases of development suggested to help students use statements and questions to guide reading are:

1. Teacher prepares statements for students' reaction with references to pages given.
2. Teacher prepares statements for students' reaction with no references given.
3. Teacher prepares questions for students to answer along with references to the text where students may find the necessary information.
4. Teacher prepares questions with no references given.
5. Students prepare and answer their own questions.
6. Students write statements of meanings, concepts, and ideas as they read.[32]

An example of statements and questions at three levels that may be used to guide content reading is presented below.

EXAMPLE

Three Levels of Statements and Questions to Establish Purposes for Reading

	Statement	Question
Literal Level	1. Failure to maintain vigilance in preventing wastes and other contaminants from reaching surface water results in water pollution.	1. What is the result of wastes and other contaminants reaching our surface water sources?
	2. Bacterial and viral pollution, chemical pollution, toxic pollution, thermal pollution, and spills are all forms of water pollution.	2. What are five examples of surface water pollution?
	3. In recent history, people have been the primary culprits in causing water pollution.	3. Who must assume primary responsibility for the pollution of our surface water?
Inferential Level	1. Bacterial and viral pollution of surface water from untreated sewage may result in illness and epidemics.	1. How can bacterial and viral pollution of surface water cause epidemics?
	2. Filtering and chlorinating water purifies waste water and greatly reduces waterborne epidemics.	2. Why does filtering and chlorinating waste water greatly reduce waterborne epidemics?
	3. Harmful pollutants such as nitrogen and phosphorus enter our surface water from such sources as industrial plants, irrigation waters, and some types of mines.	3. How can the chemical pollution of our surface water supply be contained?
Applied Level	1. Water pollution is extremely costly to our economy.	1. How does the problem of water pollution create economic hardships for industry and consumers?
	2. Water pollution can be costly to our health.	2. Why is water pollution hazardous to our health?
	3. Water pollution can be prevented.	3. In what ways can we protect ourselves from the vagaries of water pollution?

REFLECTION

Consider the different study strategies discussed in this section and select one that would best fit your classroom or study habits. Describe it and tell why this strategy was selected.

Study Guides. In addition to these different study strategies that help students prepare for and read content materials, special study guides are used in some content classes to help reading. Although study strategies and study guides are similar in structure, they differ in the method used to study materials. Study strategies are student-directed procedures students learn to use automatically when reading content materials. Study guides, on the other hand, are teacher-directed and usually written guides. They are developed by the teacher to help students through their reading of content information, and serve various purposes. They can be developed to help students learn to read content material, they may be designed to guide them through reading of the material, or they may be constructed to do both. Regardless of the study guide's design, students should always receive preliminary instruction in learning concepts and vocabulary, as well as become involved in follow-up discussions after using the guides.

Information on content reading classifies study guides according to several different types. Herber's three-level study guide is one of the more commonly used guides.[33] It is designed to help students in understanding content materials at different levels. The three levels specified by Herber are literal, interpretive, and applied. These guides are prepared by providing the students with statements at various levels to direct their reading. Following the reading, questions at the three levels are used for discussions and to check comprehension. Sample three-level study guides are given on the following pages and in Appendix D.

To develop the three-level study guide, the content teacher should follow these steps:

1. Review the information the students are to read and determine what content is to be remembered.
2. Develop statements or questions students can use to guide their reading of the information. These statements or questions should reflect three levels of understanding—literal, interpretive, and applied—and should be grouped accordingly.
3. The guide should be typed and should tell students to find the statement or its paraphrase as they read or to answer the questions from the materials. This reflects the literal level of understanding and forms Part I of the three-level study guide.
4. Directions for Part II, which requires interpretive thinking, should ask students to find supporting evidence in the material to determine the accuracy of the generalized statement or to answer questions requiring an interpretation of the material.
5. The last part of the three-level study guides necessitates the application of information. This requires that the reader relate information read to ideas from other sources including past experiences. Directions for Part III may ask students to locate supporting evidence for the application statements or require them to apply information learned to solve a problem.
6. Statements or questions generated by the teacher must reflect information from the passage to be read. Students' experiences as well as ideas from other sources, have an impact on responses. The study guide must, however, relate directly to the printed material.

Another type of study guide helpful in concept teaching is the concept guide, designed to help students focus on concepts to be learned and to organize their reading. Because the use of the concept guide is related to the awareness of organizational patterns, it is discussed further in Chapter 6.

A pattern guide, or organization guide, may be helpful in assisting students in understanding the four organizational patterns in the content textbook—

enumeration, relationships, persuasive, and problem-solving. If the materials that students are to read are written using one of these patterns and if the understanding of this pattern is helpful to students in reading the material, then the pattern guide is a helpful means of guiding content reading. More information on the pattern guide is given in Chapter 6 on the use of organizational patterns in content reading.

EXAMPLES

Three-Level Study Guide: Social Studies

Literal Level:
The Middle East and Northern Africa are lands of contrast. Decide which life-style each statement reflects. Use this letter code: N = Nomadic lifestyle, V = Village life, C = City life.

1. ____ Parents rejoice the birth of a son.
2. ____ Water comes on wheels to the camp.
3. ____ Bargaining may be heard.
4. ____ Many of the streets have roofs over them.
5. ____ Fellahins rent from landlords.
6. ____ Camels mean meat and a method of travel.
7. ____ Several clans make a tribe.
8. ____ Some areas are surrounded by walls.
9. ____ Two kinds of suburbs exist: middle class and poverty level.
10. ____ Providing hospitality is an honor and a sacred duty.

Inferential Level:
Check (✔) the statements that you feel are logical inferences about the Middle East and Northern Africa.

1. ____ Western ways have had a great influence on the woman's role.
2. ____ The geography of the Middle East affects where and how people make a living.
3. ____ Irrigation is the key solution to all dry areas of the Middle East.
4. ____ Land ownership is very important.
5. ____ A country does not have to have raw materials to be industrial.
6. ____ A Bedouin would make an excellent factory worker.
7. ____ Industrialization has made life easier for the Nomad.
8. ____ A traveler might find an antique for sale at a reasonable price in the bazaar.
9. ____ Job specification has not reached the Middle East.
10. ____ Areas of the cities would resemble Baton Rouge.

Applied Level:
1. Which one of the three life-styles would you prefer? Select one (Nomadic, Villager, City dweller) and write an account of your typical day.

2. Construct a drawing of a market place. Label the shops, stalls, and various people one might see.

3. Pretend you are a travel agent. A customer has asked you to develop a tour to the Middle East for her. Construct the tour, giving all destinations, methods of travel, important sights to visit, foods to try, and the possible expenses involved.

Developed by Beth Tope, Louisiana Department of Education, Baton Rouge, Louisiana

---

Three-Level Study Guide: Polynomials

Level I (Literal):
   1. Ascending order is the standard way of writing expressions. (True or False)
   2. What is the degree of $5X^4$?
   3. "Descending   order   is   the   _____   way   of   _____
      _____ ."

Level II (Interpretive):
   4. In $7X^9$, 7 is the _____ .
   5. X is the _____ .
   6. 9 is the _____ .

Level III (Application):
Given: $8X^4 + 9X^5 + 2X^2 + 5X^3$
   7. Arrange the expression in descending order.
   8. Arrange the expression in ascending order.
   9. Arrange the expression in descending order inserting the missing terms.
   10. How many terms does the expression have? What would you call it?

Developed by Sharon Linamen, Orange County Schools, Florida.

Because study guides have no exact format in terms of style or content, content teachers should be generally familiar with their development for use in supplementing content instruction. Tierney, Readence, and Dishner provide general procedures that may be used in making any kind of study guide.[34] The three parts include (1) development of the guide, (2) its construction, and (3) its use.

Developing the guide involves analysis of the material to determine what is to be emphasized and which skills are to be used in reading. The skills emphasis may need to be comprehension. For this, a three-level study guide would be helpful . . . or the organizational pattern guide . . . or the concept guide . . . or vocabulary guide. The teacher must determine what needs to be included in the guide based on the students' abilities and the content materials. At this time, the teacher may decide that a study guide procedure is not the best way to teach reading of the material.

If, however, the study guide is deemed the appropriate procedure, the teacher may then construct it, following the appropriate directions. In assembling the guide, the teacher may differentiate levels of difficulty to provide for student needs. This may be done by noting that students do only certain parts of the guide or by making guides at different levels. Regardless of the levels, the information must be interesting to the student and reflect the instructional decisions that were made initially.

Once the guides are constructed and ready for student use, the teacher must carefully explain this procedure for reading content materials. Students must always be teacher-prepared for reading materials—the study guide cannot replace the teacher's introduction of the concepts and vocabulary. Additionally, students must be "walked through" the guide during the initial use; after the guide is complete, a follow-up discussion is necessary to review and evaluate what was learned.

Study guides can be helpful tools to help in some aspects of content learning. They encourage students to become active learners, despite being time-consuming to develop and tending to place the responsibility of stimulating learning almost totally on the teacher. Study guides must be adapted solely to the needs of students and should be designed to fit the purposes of instruction.

In preparing students for reading materials the content teacher is responsible for helping the student become a successful learner of content information. Using ideas that have been presented in this section, content teachers should realize that they have choices in these procedures. Regardless of what techniques are used, the following suggestions should be kept in mind when asking students to read content materials:

1. Help students establish purposes for their reading by formulating thought-provoking questions.
2. Provide materials at the appropriate readability levels.
3. Teach concepts and vocabulary first.
4. Know how the material is organized and show the students.
5. Assist students in using an appropriate study strategy, and aids such as headings.
6. Discuss the various rates used in reading and decide the appropriate reading rate for this material.

LAGNIAPPE

"Physical education teachers and coaches can introduce more reading into the gym. When they do so, they will not only help develop more mature middle and secondary school readers, but will also add variety and reinforcement to physical education content."

Gerald H. Maring and Robert Ritson, "Reading Improvement in the Gymnasium," *Journal of Reading* (October 1980): 31.

DISCUSS INFORMATION

Following the silent reading component of the DLA, students and teacher must pull the ideas together. This is usually done through the use of a discussion strategy. As was noted in the information on silent reading, because of the students' different reading levels, various content materials relating to the concepts being taught should be used for silent reading. Therefore, all students are not reading the same materials and are not learning the same information. Because the content teacher initially identified specific concepts to be learned, these concepts should be understood by pooling knowledge gained from the different reading materials. Thus, discussion strategies may be used for encouraging students to share ideas from their reading.

An example of how students can be led into a discussion can be seen in Mr. Perez's junior high school social studies class. Using the components of the DLA, concepts for teaching were first identified, followed by the selection of key vocabulary words and related reading skills. Recognizing that the reading levels in this class ranged from about a mid-second grade level to a high tenth-grade level and that the chapter in the textbook was written at an eighth-grade level, instruction obviously had to be adjusted.

The class was instructed as a whole as the concepts and vocabulary were taught. The reading skill of understanding cause-effect relationships was also taught to the entire class. While this skill was reviewed using some reinforcement activities, Mr. Perez provided more instruction to the lower group on remembering facts to use in understanding cause-effect relationships. Additionally, the skills of outlining and notetaking were reviewed with the highest level group.

Students were prepared for reading with a brief review of what they were to consider as they read (concepts), and were told that because of the large amount of information, they were being asked to read different materials. The top group was given some reference materials and library books related to the concepts and asked to use their notetaking skills to record information to be shared with the class.

The middle group read a portion of the textbook, and the low group was given a filmstrip and tape that related to the concepts as well as some brochures that had numerous illustrations to further their understanding of the concepts. The students were also given some questions that could be used to guide their reading and were told that after reading, the class would come together to share information.

This preparation led to the discussion component of the DLA and allowed each student to participate fully throughout the lesson. In addition, all of the information necessary to understand or reinforce understanding of the concepts was read by one of the groups with each group sharing with others. Students felt that this procedure made better use of their time, and they liked being responsible for "teaching" certain information to their peers.

Why then are discussion strategies not used more often in content classrooms? There are many different answers to that question, but the predominant one is that some content teachers do not feel comfortable with discussions. Discussion is sometimes viewed as a talking time in which students can get out of control. This is a valid concern. Unless discussions are planned and all students can contribute, a discussion may become disruptive. If students have read, viewed, or heard information that pertains to the concepts to be discussed, however, and if the teacher is prepared, then a discussion is a motivating learning experience.

Orlich et al. suggest that, as content teachers consider the use of discussion strategies in the classroom, they first assess their own attitude. The following statements may be used:

Respond to the statements listed here. To what extent do you agree with them? Use this three-point scale: Agree (A), Disagree (D), or No Opinion (N).

_____ 1. A student's achievement is highly correlated to the teacher's expectation of the student.
_____ 2. One way to show trust toward your students is to allow them to make suggestions concerning their own learning activities.
_____ 3. Students can conduct their own discussions if provided with the necessary discussion skills.
_____ 4. Students can learn to express their ideas and feelings confidently.
_____ 5. Being supportive and providing positive reinforcement are more conducive to student participation and learning than listing a set of rules.[35]

Using these statements, content teachers can determine both attitude and atmosphere in their classrooms. Discussions flourish best with teachers who have a positive attitude toward students and whose classroom environment is open to student interaction. Teachers who answered each of the statements with an *A* will feel more successful in using discussion strategies. Teachers who feel less secure in using discussions should, nonetheless, strive to try this technique in order to develop better discussion strategies. These attitudinal changes must be made by the individual teacher. They occur more readily as the teacher becomes better acquainted with the alternatives that can be used in content teaching.

Discussion strategies are appropriate for use in any classroom regardless of the level or subject. Learning is increased through the use of more verbal interaction, provided, of course, the interaction has a meaningful purpose and students recognize the common topic or problem being discussed. Discussions that fail in a classroom may be the result of

Unprepared students
Unprepared teachers
Lack of student participation
Allowing a few students to dominate the discussions
Permitting the unprepared to depend on those who are prepared.

Any one or all of these problems may contribute to unsuccessful discussions. How, then, can teachers be prepared and also prepare students for a successful discussion?

Possibly the first task is to decide on the type of discussion that best fits the topic and the students. Four types of discussions have been identified.[36] The first of these, *free discussion*, is basically unstructured with minimum teacher control. The focus is general and the discussion may not reach a conclusion, answer a question, or really get anywhere. This is the type of discussion that some teachers get into when they really prefer a more structured one. This may not be the type of discussion that is tried initially with a content classroom, especially one in which the teacher needs to maintain control. However, the free discussion may be used as students become familiar with discussion techniques, and in situations where answering a question is not imperative.

The second type of discussion is the *semicontrolled discussion*. This has more structure than the free discussion in that it begins with a focus question which is broad enough to encourage interaction yet specific enough to concentrate on the discussion. The discussion is based on student contributions with the teacher having little control. This may be a good way to initiate a discussion in the content classroom since students are encouraged to gain control of the discussion with the teacher serving primarily to help in posing questions.

A third type of discussion is called the *discussion clusters*. In this, the class divides into groups with each group having a leader. A short time, possibly five minutes, is spent in each group determining the problem or question and discussing possible solutions. At the end of this time the solutions or answers to the questions are recorded for presentation or discussion with the entire class. These discussion clusters may also take on the format of panel discussions or even debates.

The fourth type of discussion is the *controlled discussion*. This discussion is carefully planned with the questions developed by the teacher and sequenced from easy to difficult questions with the answer to a question leading to the next question. The teacher maintains control of this discussion by posing the questions and allowing students to interact only in response to the questions. Using this procedure initially may help some teachers feel that they have control of the situation, but it may also stifle some students who do not feel they have *the* correct answer to a question. As shown, teachers shoulder the major responsibility in the controlled discussion. Thus, they must be able to:

Set the focus for discussion;
Refocus the discussion topic as necessary;
Change the focus of the discussion when needed;
Clarify confusing points;
Offer support;
Initiate exploration in new areas brought out in the discussion;
Recap and summarize; and
Move students to higher levels of thinking.

Content teachers should recognize that these are responsibilities that must be assumed by someone in a discussion situation—either the teacher or the students. When no one assumes these responsibilities, problems develop. Of paramount importance in successfully using discussion strategies is the asking of questions. Whether it is the initial focus question or the continuing questions used in the controlled discussion, the content teacher should be aware of the importance of employing good questioning strategies. The development of questions and the use of questioning strategies follows.

Questioning

In the content classroom, much summarization of information is done after the students read materials silently. This summarization may take the form of discussions, as suggested previously, or a more direct question-answer class period. Regardless of the procedure used, the teacher's skills in questioning are crucial. As suggested earlier, students cannot be expected to respond to questions unless they have been taught the necessary comprehension skills. Teachers are not able to identify the necessary skills, however, until they determine the types of questions to ask.

In considering the various types and levels of questions, teachers may become so overwhelmed with terminology that the learning process becomes ineffective. To remove confusion, and before proceeding with the discussion on questioning, some parallel terms are considered.

In Chapter 3 in the discussion on identifying reading skills, the terms used to note the three levels of comprehension are literal, interpretive, and critical. Literal comprehension skills relate to basic recall or recognition of information, interpretive skills involve inferring information from what is given, and critical skills include the evaluation and judgment of ideas. These are terms used by reading specialists, and they appear also in materials that promote the ideas of content reading. In more general curriculum materials, however, the terms describing levels of thinking are convergent, divergent, and evaluative. Convergent thinking focuses on narrow objectives, lower levels of thinking, and short responses. This seems to coincide with literal comprehension. Divergent thinking has a broader focus, is a higher level of thinking, and seems to relate to interpretive comprehension. The third and highest level of thinking is evaluation. This relates to critical reading.

The three levels of thinking and three levels of comprehension are also discussed in conjunction with the taxonomies of learning. These comparisons are shown in Figure 5.4.

Questioning relates directly to these levels and taxonomies in that questions determine the level of thinking sought and become the teacher's major tool for encouraging thought in the content classroom. To further emphasize the importance of questioning, research shows that teachers ask large numbers of questions at low levels, but do little preteaching of skills necessary to answer questions. Melnik found that some teachers ask as many as 150 questions per class hour.[38] This large number of questions is reinforced in a study by Clegg in which a sample of high school teachers asked an average of 395 questions a day.[39] In order to understand how so many questions can be asked, the findings of Rowe's research should be noted.[40] She found that teachers are very impatient when asking questions, allowing only fractions of seconds for an answer before calling on another student. To see the types of questions that can be answered in this time frame, Guszak's research on levels of questioning should be mentioned again.[41] He found that questioning techniques at the lower grades were mainly at the literal level, with 57.8 percent of all questions at the sixth grade level of the literal type. This overuse of low level questioning may relate to Durkin's study of comprehension instruction in reading and social studies in grades 3−6.[42] She found practically no comprehension instruction—just questions. These research findings may lead to the conclusion that low level questions are used predominately because students can answer them with little additional instruction. However, questioning strategies and teaching techniques must be expanded to develop the higher level skills necessary for maximum content learning.

In order to break this cycle, which leads to the continuous asking of only low level questions that do not promote thought, the content teacher should learn more about questioning strategies. The first idea to consider is that students may not need to remember all of the facts in order to move on to higher level questions. This misconception causes teachers to dwell on low level questions, believing that higher level questions cannot be understood without all the facts. Donlan suggests that teachers may want to begin with questions at the highest level working back to the literal level.[43] Using this strategy, students can understand how the facts are used at higher levels.

A second suggestion is that teachers should spend more time in advance preparation of questions. After reviewing information that students are asked to read, the teacher should list questions that serve to help students remember information and understand concepts. Once this list of questions is formulated, the teacher should identify the level of each question to make sure there is variety. Questions at different levels allow all students to participate in the questioning sessions. Additionally, listing questions makes it easy to evaluate the quality of the questions as well as the level. Well-designed questions are more important than the level of the question. Well-designed questions, however, usually reflect various levels of thought.

After the quality and levels of questions are studied, the teacher may select several questions that serve as stimulus types for use as students read and in initiating the discussion after reading. As questions are asked, teachers should be aware of practices that cause students to "turn off" or "turn on" the questions.

Turn-offs

1. The use of yes-no questions requires little thought and does not promote discussions.
2. Teachers who answer their own questions make students feel that their answer is not necessary or wanted.
3. Teacher opinion on every question is unwelcomed. This takes time away from students.
4. When students have difficulty answering a question, the teacher should not move immediately to another student, but instead should redirect the question and help the student answer by asking other questions.
5. Repeating questions before students are allowed to answer may be distracting.

Turn-ons

1. Allow students to give their personal feelings about a question—this tends to get students involved and promotes discussion.
2. Encourage students to ask questions and use these questions to promote discussions.
3. Ask questions that require forethought; tell students to think about the answer before raising their hands.
4. Listen carefully to students' answers. The student who perceives that the teacher does not listen will quickly let others know, and the class will decide that the teacher is not concerned about their answers.

Questioning is an important aspect of content teaching. The types and levels of questions used are the major procedures that determine the information that is remembered. Literal questions lead to remembering of facts, whereas critical or evaluative questions result in students becoming more analytical in their reading.

During this discussion component of the DLA the content teacher helps students organize ideas so that they understand the important concepts. At the conclusion of this component, the teacher should know if the concepts have been learned and if not, be able to decide where further instruction is needed. In order for teachers to know this, students must be encouraged to participate in the discussions. For teachers having difficulty getting students involved in this activity, consideration may be given to reviewing the questioning strategies used to guide the discussions. Sincere trial and error with careful planning before each trial is one of the best ways to improve questioning strategies and to increase student participation.

		Taxonomies	
Levels of Comprehension	Levels of Learning	Bloom	Barrett
Literal	Convergent	Knowledge Comprehension	Recognition Recall
Interpretive	Divergent	Application Analysis Synthesis	Inference
Critical	Evaluation	Evaluation	Evaluation Appreciation

From J. P. Guilford, "Three Faces of Intellect," *American Psychologist* 14 (1959):469–79; Benjamin Bloom et. al., *Taxonomy of Educational Objectives—Handbook I: The Cognitive Domain* (New York: David McKay, 1956); Thomas C. Barrett and R. Smith, *Teaching Reading in the Middle Grades* (Reading, Mass.: Addison-Wesley, 1976).

FIGURE 5.4

Relating Levels of Comprehension, Levels of Learning, and Taxonomies

FOLLOW-UP

As the instructional step draws to a conclusion the content teacher must consider one last component in order to complete the instructional process. This component is called "follow-up" because at this stage all previous instruction is reviewed and reinforced as necessary, further enrichment activities are provided, and evaluation is completed. Throughout the instructional components, the classroom teacher observes which students are doing well and what needs reinforcement with other students. If the problem is severe, the teacher must provide additional instruction immediately, prior to this step. If the difficulty is not major, however, then further teaching may be done during the follow-up component.

This is not just a time for dealing with concepts, vocabulary, or skills that need reteaching. It is also an enrichment time for students who have become interested in a concept and wish to pursue it further. Reference activities, films, or resource persons may be used to help students continue their learning in the area.

Using this follow-up portion of the lesson to review and extend learning helps to reach closure. At this time, the teacher must decide if the concepts have been learned and what needs further emphasis before the final evaluation of students' understanding of the concepts. When the teacher decides that students are ready for the evaluation, a test is usually given.

Again, further teaching of test-taking skills may be necessary in order to determine just what the students have learned. Teachers sometimes feel that students are ready for an exam only to realize later that while they seemed to know the information, they did not know how to take the exam. Thus, productive time may be spent in teaching test-taking skills.

In preparing for an exam, the student should:

1. Have a thorough, systematic grasp of the content including an understanding of the various concepts and the interrelationships among the concepts.
2. Anticipate the form of the exam as well as some of the questions. This can be done by considering the type of information and the topics which have been emphasized.
3. Write a practice exam. As the student studies notes or the text, the information can be turned into questions which help in checking understanding of the information.
4. Know the meanings of the various terms used in essay exams. To *discuss* indicates that a basic definition along with all supporting information is needed. To *compare* or *contrast* asks for likenesses and differences, while *trace* implies that a sequence or chronological order is necessary for an answer.
5. Know several basic strategies to use in writing exams. Before answering essay questions, all questions should be read. A time schedule should be set for writing which allows a few extra minutes at the end for rereading to check spelling and grammar. Then the response should then be outlined before the final answer is written. In writing the final answer, be as explicit as possible.[44]

Further tips that the content teacher may pass along to the student are:

1. Use study strategies for reading material.
2. Have review sessions with a few friends to discuss notes. (This should not be the night before the exam.)
3. Do not discuss ideas about the exam before taking it—this causes panic.
4. Read objective test items carefully. One word may change the answer.
5. All parts of a true-false item must be true in order for it to be marked as a true statement.
6. Answer items that are most familiar first. Then go back and answer the other items, placing a mark beside them to indicate a questionable response. Later read them again to see if the same answer seems correct.
7. On multiple choice items, a foil that is longer or shorter than the others is often the correct answer.
8. Correct choices may be noted through the use of words such as usually, sometimes, or often. Incorrect choices may be noted in terms such as never, always, or all.
9. Learn important definitions. These are helpful in essay and objective questions.
10. Organize answers to essay questions before writing and respond in an organized way. This often has a positive influence on the grader.

11. Proofread the exam to be sure that the original answer still seems appropriate and to check for spelling and grammatical errors.

While these test-taking tips do not enable a poor student to do well on an exam, they help those students who know the information to get good scores. Teachers must be cautious about exams. For many students, passing an exam is the most important part of education. For them, evaluation becomes more important than instruction. This encourages cheating. Thus, the content teacher should use an exam as only one part of an evaluation scheme and emphasize learning rather than class marks.

When the evaluation is complete, the teacher then has a more objective report of what the students have learned. For concepts that were not learned to a degree allowing students to move ahead, then reteaching must occur. When the identified concepts have been learned, a new set of concepts must be identified and Steps I, II, III, and IV begun again.

REFLECTION

Using a content book of your choice and the DLA procedure, outline the components of a complete lesson beginning with the introduction of concepts and vocabulary and going through the follow-up. How does this procedure differ from what you have used or seen used in content classes? What is your reaction to trying the DLA procedure in a content class? How will you begin?

SUMMARY

Instruction is the most important part of content learning. To enhance the learning of content information, the teacher must realize the importance of helping students read the material. Additionally, instruction is helped through the use of a planned teaching procedure. The procedure discussed in this chapter is the Directed Learning Activity (DLA).

Six components make up the DLA:

1. *Introduce concepts and vocabulary:* This involves direct instruction of concepts and vocabulary necessary for understanding content materials.
2. *Teach reading skills:* Skills necessary for reading content materials should be taught or reviewed before reading. These are usually comprehension and study skills.
3. *Prepare for reading:* Using study strategies or study guides, the student prepares for reading the materials. Purposes for reading are set at this time.
4. *Read materials:* Students read silently materials that relate to the concepts being taught and that are written at the students' appropriate levels. Different materials may be used to allow for various reading levels.
5. *Discuss information:* To summarize ideas from the readings, a class discussion helps students learn from one another.
6. *Do Follow-up:* The final component serves as a time for review, reinforcement, enrichment, and evaluation.

FOR DISCUSSION

1. Identify two teaching strategies that may be used to incorporate reading instruction into content teaching. Describe each strategy and tell why you selected it.
2. What are the three steps that should always be followed in teaching reading skills? Discuss each of them.
3. How can a content teacher provide reading instruction in the content class without lessening the content instructional time?
4. In introducing concepts and vocabulary, what specific techniques may be used? How would you go about teaching concepts and vocabulary deductively? Inductively?
5. Content classes are composed of many students, each of whom has various skill needs in reading at different levels. How can the content teacher accommodate these differences and still teach the content information?

OTHER SUGGESTED READINGS

Bean, Thomas W., and Pardi, Rick. "A Field Test of a Guided Reading Strategy." *Journal of Reading* 23 (November 1979):144–49.

Castallo, Richard. "Listening Guide—A First Step Toward Notetaking and Listening Skills." *Journal of Reading* 19 (January 1976):289–90.

Coles, Peter, and Foster, Jeremy. "Typographic Cueing as an Aid to Learning from Typewritten Text." *Journal of Applied Programmed Learning and Education Technology* 12 (March 1975):102–8.

Duffelmeyer, Frederick A. "The Influence of Experience-Based Vocabulary Instruction on Learning Word Meanings." *Journal of Reading* 24 (October 1980):35–40.

Eeds, Maryann. "What To Do When They Don't Understand What They Read— Research Based Strategies for Teaching Reading Comprehension." *The Reading Teacher* 34 (February 1981):565–75.

Hansell, T. Stevenson. "Stepping Up to Outlining." *Journal of Reading* 22 (December 1978):248–52.

Ignoffo, Matthew F. "The Thread of Thought: Analogies as a Vocabulary Building Method." *Journal of Reading* 23 (March 1980):519–21.

Johns, Jerry L., and McNamara, Lawrence P. "The SQ3R Study Technique: A Forgotten Research Target." *Journal of Reading* 23 (May 1980):705–8.

Kaplan, Elaine M., and Tuchman, Anita. "Vocabulary Strategies Belong in the Hands of Learners." *Journal of Reading* 24 (October 1980):32–34.

Karahalios, S. M. "Using Advance Organizers to Improve Comprehension of a Content Text." *Journal of Reading* 22 (May 1979):706–8.

Kaufman, Maurice. *Reading in Content Areas.* West Lafayette, Ind.: Kappa Delta Pi, 1980.

McClain, Leslie J. "Study Guides: Potential Assets in Content Classrooms." *Journal of Reading* 24 (January 1981):321–25.

Manzo, Anthony V. "Three 'Universal' Strategies in Content Area Reading and Language." *Journal of Reading* 24 (November 1980):146–49.

Moore, David W., and Readence, John E. "Processing Main Ideas through Parallel Lesson Transfer." *Journal of Reading* 23 (April 1980):589–93.

Moore, Mary A. "C2R: Concentrate, Read, Remember." *Journal of Reading* 24 (January 1981):337–39.

Ribovick, Jerilyn K. "Developing Comprehension of Content Material through Strategies Other Than Questioning." Paper presented at the International Reading Association annual convention, May 1977, Miami Beach, Florida. (ED 141 786)

Richards, John P. "Notetaking, Underlining, Insertial Questions, and Organizers in Text: Research Conclusions and Educational Implications." *Educational Technology* 20 (June 1980):5–11.

Richards, John P., and McCormick, Christine B. "Whole versus Part Presentation of Advance Organizers in Text." *Journal of Educational Research* 70 (January/February 1977): 147–49.

Riley, James D. "Statement-Based Reading Guides and Quality of Teacher Response." *Journal of Reading* 23 (May 1980):715–20.

Smith, Ellen R., and Standal, Timothy C. "Learning Styles and Study Techniques." *Journal of Reading* 24 (April 1981):599–602.

Starks, Gretchen A. "New Approaches to Teaching Study Skills in High School and College." *Journal of Reading* 23 (February 1980):401–3.

Tadlock, Dolores Fadness. "SQ3R—Why It Works, Based on an Information Processing Theory of Learning." *Journal of Reading* 22 (November 1978):110–12.

Thomas, Keith J. "Modified Cloze: The Intralocking Guide." *Reading World* 19 (October 1979):19–27.

Thomas, Keith J., and Cummings, Charles C. "The Efficacy of Listening Guides: Some Preliminary Findings with Tenth and Eleventh Graders." *Journal of Reading* 21 (May 1978):705–9.

Vacca, Richard T. *Content Area Reading.* Boston: Little, Brown, 1981. Chapters 5–9.

Winne, Phillip H. "Experiments Relating Teachers' Use of Higher Cognitive Questions to Student Achievement." *Review of Educational Research* 49 (Winter 1979):13–49.

Wolfe, Ronald E. "Using Subject-Matter Areas to Raise Reading Achievement Scores." *Reading Improvement* 15 (Winter 1978):242–45.

NOTES

1. Harold L. Herber, *Teaching Reading in Content Areas,* 2nd ed. (Englewood Cliffs, N.J.: Prentice-Hall, 1978), pp. 226–27.

2. Lou E. Burmeister, *Reading Strategies for Secondary School Teachers* (Reading, Mass.: Addison-Wesley, 1978), pp. 94–100.

3. Harry Singer and Dan Donlan, *Reading and Learning from Text* (Boston: Little, Brown, 1980), pp. 52–53.

4. Russell G. Stauffer, *Teaching Reading as a Thinking Process* (New York: Harper and Row, 1969), pp. 14–15.

5. David Ausubel, "The Use of Advance Organizers in the Learning and Retention of Meaningful Verbal Material," *Journal of Educational Psychology* 51 (1960): 267–72.

6. Harry W. Forgan and Charles T. Mangrum II, *Teaching Content Area Reading Skills,* 2nd ed. (Columbus, Ohio: Charles E. Merrill, 1981), p. 124.

7. Paul D. Eggen, Donald P. Kauchak, and Robert J. Harder, *Strategies for Teachers* (Englewood Cliffs, N.J.: Prentice-Hall, 1979), pp. 106, 110.

8. Eggen, Kauchak, Harder, *Strategies for Teachers,* pp. 115–38.

9. Eggen, Kauchak, Harder, *Strategies for Teachers,* pp. 129–38.

10. Eggen, Kauchak, Harder, *Strategies for Teachers,* pp. 115–28.

11. Richard F. Barron, "The Effects of Advance Organizers and Grade Level Upon the Reception, Learning, and Retention of General Science Content," in *Investigations Relating to Mature Reading,* ed. Frank P. Greene, Twenty-first Yearbook of the National Reading Conference (Milwaukee, Wis.: National Reading Conference, 1972), pp. 8–15.

12. Thomas H. Estes and Joseph L. Vaughan, *Reading and Learning in the Content Classroom*, abr. ed. (Boston: Allyn and Bacon, 1978), pp. 148–49; Betty D. Roe, Barbara D. Stoodt, and Paul C. Burns, *Reading Instruction in the Secondary School*, rev. ed. (Chicago: Rand McNally, 1978), p. 59.

13. Harold Herber, *Teaching Reading in Content Areas*, p. 131.

14. Kathryn Sullivan, "Vocabulary Instruction in Mathematics: Do the 'Little' Words Count?" Paper presented at American Reading Forum, December 10, 1981, Sarasota, Florida.

15. Harold Herber, *Teaching Reading in Content Areas*, pp. 138–42.

16. Harry Forgan and Charles Mangrum, *Teaching Content Area Reading Skills*, p. 129.

17. Anthony V. Manzo and John K. Sherk, "Some Generalizations and Strategies for Guiding Vocabulary Learning," *Journal of Reading Behavior* 4 (Winter 1971–72): 81–82.

18. Patricia L. Grant, "The Cloze Procedure as an Instructional Device," *Journal of Reading* 22 (May 1979):699–705.

19. Richard A. Earle, "Use of the Structured Overview in Mathematics Classes," *Research in Reading in the Content Areas: First Year Report*, eds. Harold L. Herber and Peter L. Sanders (Syracuse, N.Y.: Reading and Language Arts Center, Syracuse University, 1969); Thomas H. Estes, Daniel C. Mills, and Richard F. Barron, "Three Methods of Introducing Students to a Reading-Learning Task in Two Content Subjects," *Research in Reading in the Content Areas: First Year Report*, eds. Harold L. Herber and Peter L. Sanders (Syracuse, N.Y.: Reading and Language Arts Center, Syracuse University, 1969); Sue M. Karahalios, Marian J. Tonjes, and John C. Towner, "Using Advance Organizers to Improve Comprehension of a Content Text," *Journal of Reading* 22 (May 1979): 706–8.

20. Billy M. Guice, "The Use of the Cloze Procedure for Improving Reading Comprehension of College Students," *Journal of Reading Behavior* 1 (Summer 1969):81–92.

21. Walter Pauk, *How to Study in College* (Boston: Houghton Mifflin, 1974):153–54.

22. David L. Shepherd, *Comprehensive High School Reading Methods,* 3rd ed. (Columbus, Ohio: Charles E. Merrill, 1982), p. 105.

23. Brenda Wright Kelly and Janis Holmes, "The Guided Lecture Procedure," *Journal of Reading* 22 (April 1979):602–4.

24. Francis P. Robinson, *Effective Study*, rev. ed. (New York: Harper and Row, 1961).

25. Carl B. Smith and Peggy G. Elliot, *Reading Activities for Middle and Secondary Schools* (New York: Holt, Rinehart, and Winston, 1979), pp. 194–95.

26. Ellen Lamar Thomas and H. Alan Robinson, *Improving Reading in Every Class* (Boston: Allyn and Bacon, 1972), pp. 115–27.

27. Marilyn G. Eanet and Anthony V. Manzo, "REAP—A Strategy for Improving Reading/Writing/Study Skills," *Journal of Reading* 19 (May 1976):647–52.

28. Peter Edwards, "Panaroma: A Study Technique," *Journal of Reading* 17 (November 1973):132–35.

29. Walter Pauk, "On Scholarship: Advice to High School Students," *The Reading Teacher* 17 (November 1963):73–78.

30. Leo Fay, "Reading Study Skills: Math and Science," *Reading and Inquiry*, ed. J. Allen Figurel (Newark, Del.: International Reading Association, 1965), pp. 93–94.

31. George D. Spache and Paul C. Berg, *The Art of Efficient Reading* (New York: Macmillan, 1966).

32. Harold L. Herber and Joan B. Nelson, "Questioning is Not the Answer," *Journal of Reading* 18 (April 1975):512–17.

33. Harold Herber, *Teaching Reading in Content Areas*, pp. 37–68.

34. Robert J. Tierney, John E. Readence, and Ernest K. Dishner, *Reading Strategies and Practices* (Boston: Allyn and Bacon, 1980), pp. 64–68.

35. Donald C. Orlich et al., *Teaching Strategies: A Guide to Better Instruction* (Lexington, Mass.: D. C. Heath, 1980), p. 236.
36. Harry Singer and Dan Donlan, *Reading and Learning from Text*, pp. 111–24.
37. Harry Singer and Dan Donlan, *Reading and Learning from Text*, p. 114.
38. Amelia Melnik, "Questions: An Instructional-Diagnostic Tool," *Journal of Reading* 11 (April 1968): 509–12, 578–81.
39. Ambrose A. Clegg, Jr., "Classroom Questions," in *The Encyclopedia of Education*, vol. 2 (New York: Macmillan, 1971), p. 2, 183–90.
40. Mary Budd Rowe, "Wait-Time and Rewords as Instructional Variables, Their Influence on Language, Logic and Fate Control: Part I, Fate Control," *Journal of Research in Science Teaching* 11 (1974): 81–94.
41. Frank J. Guszak, "Teaching, Questioning and Reading," *The Reading Teacher* 21 (December 1968):227–34.
42. Dolores Durkin, "What Classroom Observations Reveal About Reading Comprehension Instruction," *Reading Research Quarterly* 14, no. 4 (1978–79):521.
43. Dan Donlan, "How to Play 29 Questions," *Journal of Reading* 21 (March 1978):535–41.
44. Lawrence E. Hafner, *Developmental Reading in Middle and Secondary Schools: Foundations, Strategies, and Skills for Teaching*, (New York: Macmillan, 1977), p. 175.

Chapter Six

ORGANIZATIONAL PATTERNS FOR CONTENT LEARNING

"I never know what I'm supposed to remember," says one student. Another chimes in, "In one class you have to try to remember why things happen, and in another you learn how they happen."

As the study hall teacher listened to the endless complaints of the students while they prepared assignments and studied for tests, he became concerned about the confusion that students had experienced in studying the various content areas. He knew there are many conditions existing that enhance or deter content learning: various levels of students, differences in students' reading levels and text materials, the abundance of technical vocabulary, the need to use more advanced study skills and to apply different reading skills—all came to mind as Mr. McDaniel thought about the students.

He also realized that content materials are sometimes difficult to read because they have so many concepts presented in limited space, and sometimes because the students are asked to read from different sources. This triggered a question—What about the variety of organizational patterns used in content materials? Could this be a student problem in the different content areas? As Mr. McDaniel pondered this question, more came to mind. He jotted them on a card to discuss at the next team meeting (see "Study Questions").

STUDY QUESTIONS

1. Do different organizational patterns exist in content materials?
2. What are the different organizational patterns?
3. How do organizational patterns affect the understanding of content information?

4. How can content teachers help students learn to use organizational patterns to enhance their study in the different content areas?

VOCABULARY

Concept guide
Enumeration pattern
Organizational patterns
Pattern guide

Persuasive pattern
Problem-solving pattern
Relationship pattern

ORGANIZATIONAL PATTERNS

Textbooks, newspapers, magazines, brochures, books, and other printed materials are written in a variety of styles. Some use a narrative descriptive style of presentation, while others may use many examples or illustrations to help impart information to readers. Still other materials are filled with problems to be solved or ideas that must be related in order to remember the content. These different means of presenting information are known as organizational patterns, and are important to understanding content materials. They are a form of comprehension skill essential in content learning. As early as 1917, Thorndike reported that one reason for reading failure is the student's inability to organize and understand organizational relationships in written materials.[1]

In 1964, Nila Banton Smith and James McCallister suggested that different patterns of writing existed in various content areas and served as aids to understanding.[2] Smith's hypothesis was made based on the awareness of different patterns of writing in literature; therefore, she believed that patterns also existed in science, social studies, and mathematics. She found that, while different patterns do exist in these content materials, in many content materials a variety of patterns exist within a chapter. Thus, students must recognize changes in patterns in order to adjust their reading to understand the information. Although this research was based only on an analysis of textbooks used in Grades 7 through 12, others agreed that patterns could be identified by students, and that the idea had relevance for all content instruction. Writers such as Dechant, McGuire and Bumpus and Niles encouraged teachers to help students learn to look for the author's organization in a text in order to increase their retention.[3] While these recommendations were based more on common sense accompanied by the limited research of Smith, they seem even more feasible now in light of current research in the area of comprehension.

As mentioned in Chapter 3 in the discussion of comprehension skills, new research in this area suggests that comprehending text material is a holistic process based on the identification of the schema, or organization of the material.[4] Using known comprehension skills, a reader can identify a particular pattern from a sentence, word, paragraph, or complete text, or a particular pattern could impress different meanings on individuals reading the same information because of differences in the way they organize the information in their minds.[5] Thus, schema theory research by Anderson et al., Rumelhart and others emphasize that students comprehend information based on their ability to organize new ideas around existing knowledge.[6] Major schemata have been identified by different researchers as they investigate the organization of text materials using a procedure known as discourse analysis. Meyer identified five basic patterns: response, comparison, antecedent/consequent, description, and collections.[7] These patterns can be related to organizational patterns suggested by McCallister, Smith, Niles, Shepherd, Roe, Stoodt, and Burns, and Robinson.[8] From past and present research related to understanding the organization of content information, and a review of current middle and secondary school content materials, the authors have identified four organizational patterns that are commonly used in content writing. The patterns are presented in this section with a sample passage given to clarify the definition. Instructional strategies for helping students use organizational patterns to enhance their content learning are given in a later section of the chapter.

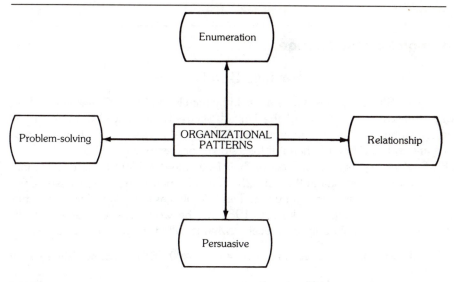

FIGURE 6.1

Organizational Patterns in Content Reading

The organizational pattern found most frequently in content textbooks is that of *enumeration*. This pattern can occur in a variety of ways in different content areas, but all have the same basic structure—an idea is presented with supporting information given to heighten the understanding of the concept or idea. The pattern involves the introduction of a topic immediately followed by additional information to expand the topic. This information may be within the paragraph or developed over a series of consecutive paragraphs. The enumeration pattern may occur in the form of:

an explanation,

a main idea with supporting details,

an example or illustration to clarify a narrative description,

a question/answer format in which the question represents the basic idea and the answer serves to enumerate or explain the information, or

a generalization followed by subtopics or supporting information that enhances the generalization.

Because many content materials are organized using this pattern, content teachers must be sure that students can recognize the pattern and use it to remember content information. Difficulty in reading materials that follow the enumeration pattern is usually due to a lack of understanding or identification of the basic idea being discussed. Once students learn to identify this idea, they seldom have problems reading materials using the pattern. Teachers may help students recognize the enumeration pattern by teaching them to identify when a paragraph, or series of paragraphs, provides information through descriptions, details, or characteristics about an idea. Definitions, along with functions or other examples, may be included to further enumerate on the topic. An example of an enumeration pattern is given below.

EXAMPLE

Enumeration Pattern Passage

Savings Bonds

Series EE United States Savings Bonds are sold by the United States Government. They are a way to invest in the future of the United States. Bonds pay 9% interest compounded semiannually if purchased after May 1, 1981. Along with a good interest rate, the bonds are replaced free of charge if lost, stolen, or destroyed.

The EE Savings Bonds cost one-half of their face value. A $50 EE bond has a face value of $50. It would cost half of that, or $25. The $25 price is known as its issue price. A bond reaches its face value in eight years. This is known as *maturing*. This means that a $50 bond that was bought on June 1, 1981 will be worth $50 on June 1, 1989. Whenever the bond is cashed in, you receive what is called the *redemption price*.

> Find the issue price and redemption price of a $200 EE U.S. Savings Bond held to maturity.
>
> $1/2 \times \$200 = \$100$
>
> face value   The issue price of a $200 bond is $100 and the face value is $200.

The savings bonds can be cashed in anytime after six months. The difference between the issue price and the redemption price is the interest that is earned.

> Find the amount of interest that is earned on a $200 EE bond that has reached maturity.
>
> $200   redemption price at maturity
> − 100   issue price
> $100

A $200 EE bond will earn $100 of interest if kept until maturity.

From Jack Price et al., *Mathematics for Today's Consumer* (Columbus, Ohio: Charles E. Merrill, 1982), p. 280.

A second organizational pattern found in content materials is the *relationship pattern*. It is used as frequently in content materials as the enumeration pattern. Likewise, the relationship pattern occurs in a variety of ways such as through the use of cause-effect or comparison-contrast styles of writing, the use of a classification scheme, or directions and the sequencing of ideas that can be remembered best by relating one task or event to another. Students may learn to recognize the relationship pattern by noting when similarities and differences of ideas are presented, or when the understanding of ideas depends on establishing a link with other information in the passage. These relationships are critical in the understanding of social studies, science, and literature materials. An example of a relationship pattern is given below.

The third organizational pattern is the *persuasive pattern* that uses various propaganda techniques to sway students to believe or disbelieve certain ideas. Students must learn to recognize this pattern, and learn how to read it critically, since it is written to influence the reader's thinking or behavior. The information is usually harmless to the reader, but material written in this style does attempt to influence decisions. Students must learn to evaluate everything they read, and make decisions based on their assessment of the facts. There are seven basic propaganda techniques used in persuasive pattern writing:

1. Glad words or glittering generalities
2. Unpleasant words
3. Transfer
4. Testimonials
5. Plain folks
6. Bandwagon
7. Card stacking

XAMPLE
_____

Relationship Pattern Passage

Air Circulation

\ir in the troposphere is constantly in motion. Horizontal movements of air are called *\inds*. Vertical movements of air are called *currents*. Winds and currents together carry eat from the equator to the poles. This heat comes directly from the earth but indirectly `om the sun. Winds and currents determine the major circulation pattern of the air as 1ey move air from high pressure areas to low pressure areas. High pressure is associ-ted with cold air. Low pressure generally is associated with warm air. The density of air ; determined by its temperature and the amount of water vapor per unit volume. A iven volume of water vapor has less mass than the gases it displaces. Thus, moist air is 2ss dense than dry air.

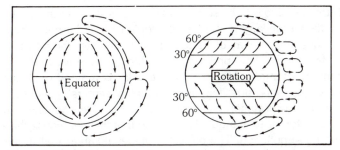

Figure 1–18. Major north-south convection currents in the atmosphere are broken into eddies by the earth's rotation, forming the wind patterns of the globe.

The portion of the earth between latitudes 23.5° north and south of the equator 2ceives the most radiant energy. Therefore, air at the equator is warmer and less dense 1an air at other latitudes. Cool surface air flows toward the equator and forces currents ¶ warm air to rise. In the upper atmosphere, warm air flows toward the poles.

This air gradually cools and at the poles it is cold, dry air. Cold air sinks to the earth's 1rface in the polar region. From the poles, the air flows toward the equator. This circu--tion of air carries heat from the equatorial region to the rest of the earth. But air circula--on is not a simple north-south movement. Circulation is complicated because Earth >tates on its axis and areas of land and sea are unequal.

_____

`om Margaret S. Bishop, Phyllis G. Lewis, and Berry Sutherland, *Focus on Earth Science* (Columbus, Ohio: harles E. Merrill, 1976), p. 352.

Persuasive patterns are used to a great extent in social studies materials to convince readers of the rightness or wrongness of a governmental philosophy, political view, or issues related to morality. They are also used in literature and music through poetry and lyrics in songs. An example of a persuasive pattern found in a social studies textbook is presented below.

EXAMPLE

Persuasive Pattern Passage

Land as a Resource

If you owned one of the 50 states in the United States, what would you do with it? Would you build cities on faults or on unstable slopes? Would you plant crops in a desert and then use vast amounts of water to irrigate them? Would you drink water polluted by industrial and sewage wastes? Would you cut down all your forests and lay bare large areas of land to erosion? Would you use up all your mineral resources to meet immediate need? Overpopulate your cities and create urban slums? Or would you develop and carry out long range plans for the best use of the land and natural resources within your state?

Land is probably the most valuable single natural resource that we have. There are about 9,363,474 km^2 of land area in the 50 states. We, as tenants, use it for agriculture, mining, industry, transportation, building homes, and recreation. Right now there is approximately 0.045 km^2 of land for every person living in the United States. This isn't really a large amount of space. We must plan to make the best use of it. Good *land-use planning* can prevent environmental problems before they develop.

The purpose of land-use planning is to be sure we make the best use of the land. This will yield long range benefits for the largest number of people without harming the environment. Each of us will have a better way of life from this planning for the future. Presently, a number of city, state, and federal projects are under way to study and develop plans for the most efficient use of our land. These projects will recommend the best possible areas for new homes, schools, hospitals, and shopping centers. They also will design streets, roads, and transportation systems that will cause the least traffic problems. Plans will be made for locating industrial areas so that they will cause the least amount of air, water, and noise pollution. The projects will identify areas that should be used for agriculture, mining, recreation, and other essential uses. The results of these long range planning projects should yield a more healthful, beautiful, and productive nation. Does your local community have a similar project in operation? If so, what type of plans are being made?

From Margaret S. Bishop, Phyllis G. Lewis, and Berry Sutherland, *Focus on Earth Science* (Columbus, Ohio: Charles E. Merrill, 1976), pp. 473–74.

The *problem-solving pattern* is another organizational pattern students use in mathematics, science, business education, and vocational education to understand a concept. In mathematics, the understanding of word problems is often the most difficult part of mathematics. This lack of understanding may be attributed to the students' inability to read the words in a problem. The more common reason for the frustration, however, is a lack of student knowledge of the process to be used in reading this pattern.

In scientific writing, the problem-solving pattern may consist of a problem with the solution given, implied, or left up to the reader to give. If the answer is given or implied, students must then apply their skills in identifying an enumeration pattern in which examples or illustrations are used as an explanation, or a relationship pattern in which they must interrelate the solution to the problem to determine if they understand the solution. When the solution is not given, the students must then use their skill in reading the problem-solving pattern in order to analyze the problem and provide a solution. An example of the problem-solving pattern is given below.

EXAMPLE

Problem-Solving Pattern Passage

Find the solution set of each of the following systems by using Cramer's Rule. If the system contains dependent or inconsistent equations, so state.

1. $x + y + z = 4$
    $2x - y + 2z = 5$
    $x - 2y - z = -3$

2. $2x - y - z = -6$
    $x + 3y - z = 0$
    $2x + y + z = -2$

3. $4x - y + 2z = 5$
    $2x + y - 3z = 7$
    $10x - y + z = -2$

From Robert H. Sorgenfrey, William Wooton, and Mary Dolciani, *Modern Algebra and Trigonometry,* Book 2 (Boston: Houghton Mifflin, 1973), p. 627.

As implied in the presentation of these four organizational patterns, one pattern may be identified in a part of a content material, and another one or two patterns used in the following pages. Therefore, there is no neat, absolute way of relating any one of these patterns directly to a content area, because many of the patterns are used at some point in most subjects. There are, however, some patterns that are used more frequently in certain content materials. Table 6.1 provides a summary of the four organizational patterns related to the different content areas.

Using the definitions and related information on each of these organizational patterns, the remainder of this chapter presents instructional techniques that can be used to help students use organizational patterns to strengthen their comprehension of content information.

REFLECTION

Select two textbooks in the content areas of your choice. Randomly select three passages in each of the books and decide which organizational pattern is used.

TEACHING ORGANIZATIONAL PATTERNS

The importance of helping students learn to use the organization of content materials as an aid in understanding has been clearly shown regardless of whether the organization was referred to as patterns,[9] textual schema,[10] schematic structures,[11] super structures,[12] or writing paradigms.[13] Researchers in psy-

TABLE 6.1

Summary of Organizational Patterns as Related to Different Content Areas

Content Area	Enumera- tion	Relationship	Persuasive	Problem- solving
Art	X	X		
Business Education	X	X		X
Foreign Language	X	X		
Health	X	X		
English	X	X	X	
Mathematics	X	X		X
Music	X	X	X	
Physical Education	X	X		
Science	X	X		X
Social Studies	X	X	X	
Vocational Education	X	X		X

chology and education continue to find that students who understand the organization of a material remember more information for longer periods of time than those who use no organization scheme.[14] Because of the importance of this knowledge to content learning, this section presents different techniques that can be used in teaching students to identify and process the information contained in the different organizational patterns. In addition to ideas for understanding individual patterns, information on using pattern guides and concept guides is given. Because instruction in organizational patterns can occur at several points within the Directed Learning Activity presented in Chapter 5, further discussion of these components of the DLA is provided.

As the teacher identifies the reading skills that students must apply to learn the selected concepts, consideration should also be given to the organizational

Students who understand the organizational pattern of the content material retain more of what they read.

patterns used in the material. Understanding how to apply a specific skill is heightened if students know how to identify the organizational pattern. Comprehension skills such as cause-and-effect, main idea, details, problem-solving, etc., are closely interrelated with the different organizational patterns. Thus, content teachers should consider this relationship as the necessary comprehension skills are identified.

Content teachers may also consider the different organizational patterns as they assess student knowledge of the reading skills. Included in a Group Reading Inventory may be questions that require students to identify different organizational patterns used in materials to be read. This diagnostic information can then be used by the teacher to provide instruction prior to reading the materials.

When instruction begins, organizational patterns can be taught and discussed at several points. The teacher may give a review of the organizational patterns, or ask students to identify the pattern or patterns used in a passage as other reading skills are taught or reviewed. Following this review, and as students are prepared for reading, the teacher may remind students to consider the patterns as they read. If students are relatively astute at pattern identification, teachers may simply ask that they use a study strategy and survey or preview the material before reading in order to determine the materials' patterns. For students who have just been taught how to identify patterns, this step in preparation for reading allows them to check their ability to apply the new knowledge before actually reading.

To help students apply their knowledge of the different organizational patterns, content teachers may provide pattern guides or concept guides to aid their understanding. Following reading of the information, the class discussion should serve to identify those students who do not understand the information. Their lack of understanding may well show a lack of ability to use organizational patterns to help their comprehension. If this is the problem, additional instruction may be given during the follow-up phase of the lesson. Should more instruction be needed, the content teacher would have to recycle the lesson.

Teaching Enumeration Patterns

The enumeration pattern can be identified when a central idea or concept is presented with supporting information given through narration, illustrations, or examples. In reading passages using this pattern, Robinson suggests that students follow three basic steps for succesful reading.[15] The first involves the recognition of the topic—what does the passage explain or what will be enumerated in the passage. The topic should be noted in the opening statement. Also included in the opening statement is an indication or signal word alerting the student to the subtopics or descriptions to be discussed in the enumeration. Signal words used in an enumeration pattern include:

to begin with	most important
first	also
secondly	in fact
next	for instance
then	for example[16]
finally	

Using the signal word as a clue, students should proceed by looking for sub-topics or enumerated information and how they relate to the topic. Comprehension of enumeration depends upon the perception of these connections.

In noting enumeration passages, the content teacher must help students identify the important concepts, understand the meaning of related words, and see the association between the topic and the expanded information. In content reading, the materials contain so many concepts presented in such a compact manner, that often concepts are hidden within explanations. Students thereby experience difficulty understanding the linkage. The problem can be solved only if teachers carefully identify and introduce the necessary vocabulary, and give appropriate introductory instruction about the new concepts.

To show how enumeration patterns can be demonstrated to students, see the following examples. Two selections from content textbooks have been analyzed with the enumeration pattern and signal words identified.

In these examples, the central topic or idea is first identified. To help the reader in following the enumeration pattern, the first example contains two signal words that guide the reader to focus on the two persons discussed in the selection. These signal words are used to show that two ideas will be elaborated on within the selection. In the second example there are no signal words. The first three sentences, however, identify the topic with boldface and italicized print used to note the different ideas being enumerated. In addition, an illustration is shown to further clarify the narrative.

The content teacher may point out signal words that commonly appear in reading materials.

EXAMPLES

Enumeration Pattern from a Social Studies Textbook

Disraeli and Gladstone

The period between 1866 and 1884 was dominated by two men who were entirely different in character and outlook. One was Benjamin Disraeli, a leader of the Conservative Party, who served twice as prime minister. He was witty, shrewd, and greatly interested in British foreign affairs and the enlargement of the empire. The other was William Gladstone, who, as leader of the Liberal Party, was prime minister four times. He was most concerned with British domestic and financial matters. Devout and cautious, he was a great contrast to Disraeli. He was so pompous and formal that Queen Victoria once complained: "Mr. Gladstone addresses me as if I were a public meeting."

Disraeli's first term as prime minister, in 1868, was short; but during his second ministry, from 1874 to 1880, Britain gained control of the Suez Canal and Queen Victoria became Empress of India. These were major concerns of the Conservative Party.

The Liberal Party was more occupied with the "Irish Question." In 1801, Ireland and Great Britain had been joined by the Act of Union into the United Kingdom of Great Britain and Ireland. The Irish were poorly represented in the British Parliament, however, and the people—most of them Roman Catholics—resented having to pay taxes to help support the Anglican Church.

The Irish hated British rule, especially the absentee landlords who owned much of the land.

From MEN AND NATIONS: A WORLD HISTORY, Third Edition, by Anatole G. Mazour and John M. Peoples, copyright © 1975 by Harcourt Brace Jovanovich, Inc. Reprinted by permission of the publisher.

Enumeration Pattern from a Science Textbook

In studying topographic maps, the first thing to examine is the stream pattern. Even arid regions have many features that are the result of erosion by runoff. Thus, stream patterns are important in all areas. If all the rock exposed in an area has about the same

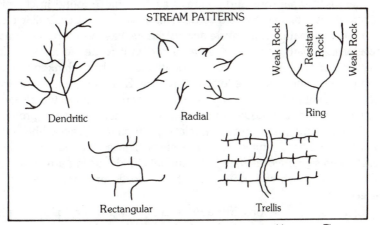

Figure 4-9. Stream patterns are clearly shown on topographic maps. They may be dendritic, radial, ring, rectangular or trellis.

resistance, the stream pattern will be *dendritic*. **Dendritic** means treelike. A map of a dendritic stream pattern resembles a branching tree. Tributaries enter the main stream at acute, or V-shaped angles.

Trellis patterns are somewhat like the rectangular pattern that follows joint systems. Tributaries enter the mainstream at right angles, but the mainstream does not make right angle turns. The trellis pattern usually has tributary streams that are parallel to each other. The tributary streams flow over weak rock. The mainstream is older and well established. It cuts across resistant rock. This pattern is another clue to the presence of alternating resistant and weak layers of tilted sedimentary rock.

Radial patterns are streams that flow outward from a central location. Usually such streams develop on the slopes of volcanoes. Sometimes they may form on intrusive domes such as laccoliths.

Rivers may erode an area in any of these patterns. The dendritic pattern, however, is most common. This pattern tells you only that the underlying rock resistance is about the same throughout the area of the map. It does not tell you what kind of rock is present.

From Margaret S. Bishop, Phyllis G. Lewis, and Berry Sutherland, *Focus on Earth Science* (Columbus, Ohio: Charles E. Merrill, 1976), p. 237.

Because the enumeration pattern exists so commonly in all content materials, teachers can help students identify the pattern by using as many clues as possible, i.e., signal words, type variations, illustrations, examples, and listings. As students become familiar with this organizational pattern, details become easier to remember since they fit into an overall organizational plan. Explanations also become more logical because they are related to a central idea interrelated to the other ideas within the selection.

Teaching Relationship Patterns

Many types of relationships are used in content materials. Social studies materials are loaded with cause-effect relationships, and science materials contain numerous comparisons and contrasts such as those found in chemistry, when different reactions are related to determine similar and dissimilar responses.

Historical materials in music and art, as well as in history, have a sequential relationship, with one event remembered as it relates to another. In studying this type of relationship pattern, students must learn to think in terms of associating events with dates in a logical sequence. Relationship patterns are more difficult to identify than the enumeration pattern, because the relationships are usually implied and require the reader to use interpretive comprehension skills.

To help students determine a relationship pattern, Vacca[17] has related signal words with different types of relationships. These words are included in Figure 6.2. Using signal words may help students in identifying a relationship pattern, although they should note that these words are not used in all pattern selections.

Examples of relationship patterns are given on the following pages. Both examples contain signal words with the first example containing a sequence as

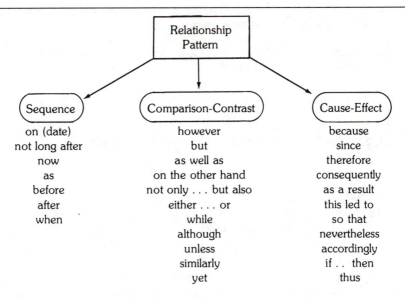

Richard T. Vacca, *Content Area Reading*, p. 143.

FIGURE 6.2

Signal Words for a Relationship Pattern

well as a cause-effect situation. The signal words help the reader follow the sequence of events in which there is an implied cause-effect event. In the second example, three rulers of Mexico are compared. The signal words obviously provide clues identifying the pattern used in the example.

Because there are many types of relationships that occur in this pattern, students must use their comprehension skills to help recognize the pattern. If they do not have this knowledge, they should be shown that in a relationship pattern the reader identifies the topic, and then determines if information about it is associated with other ideas. In the relationship pattern, there is an interconnection among the information that must be recognized in order to understand the ideas or concepts.

EXAMPLES

Relationship Pattern from a Science Textbook

Autotrophs include green plants and some protists. They appear to be green (because) chlorophyll blocks mostly the green portion of the spectrum. The other wavelengths of light are absorbed or transmitted. A spectrum of chlorophyll is obtained by passing white light through a solution of chlorophyll and then through a prism. When this spectrum is compared to the spectrum of white light, differences are seen (Figure 5-16). (Because) certain wavelengths are either reduced or absent in the chlorophyll spectrum it is called an **absorption** (uhb SORP shuhn) **spectrum.** Violet, blue, orange, and red wavelengths are almost totally absorbed by chlorophyll. When light energy is absorbed, it is transformed. (Thus,) chlorophyll absorbs violet, blue, red, and orange wavelengths and transforms them into chemical energy.

From Raymond Oram, Paul J. Hummer, Jr., and Robert C. Smoot, *Biology: Living Systems*, 3rd ed. (Columbus, Ohio: Charles E. Merrill, 1979), pp. 102–3.

Relationship Pattern from a History Textbook

Corruption and Reform

Comparison/Contrast

Most caudillos ruled as dictators. They did not care about improving the lot of the people or the country. (One) such caudillo was Juan Manuel de Rosas, who ruled Argentina from 1835 until 1852. He was ruthless and crushed anyone who did not agree with him. During his rule, Argentina was divided into two groups that threatened to split the country. One was the people of the city of Buenos Aires. The other was the ranchers of the ***pampas,*** or plains. Only the strong control kept by Rosas held the country together.

(Another) example is Antonio López de Santa Anna. He led his troops into Mexico City in 1833 and had himself elected president. Between 1833 and 1855, he ruled Mexico six times. Under his rule, Mexico lost half of its land to the United States.

(A different type) of caudillo took Santa Anna's place. He proved that a caudillo could care about other people's needs. His name was Benito Juárez. He was the first Indian to rule Mexico since the fall of the Aztec Empire. Juárez cared deeply about the people of Mexico. He wanted to put an end to the special privileges enjoyed by the rich. He made laws to restrict the power of the Catholic Church. The laws also provided for the sale of church property not used for worship. Juárez also worked to give the poor people of Mexico land of their own. This led to three years of civil war. When it looked like Juárez was gaining ground, his enemies brought in the French. They made a European prince named Maximilian emperor. Juárez and his followers finally won out over the French.

In 1867 Juárez became president of Mexico. He served as president until his death in 1872. During his presidency, Juárez worked to hold free and democratic elections. He started schools to educate Indian children. He reduced the size of the army. In Mexico today, Juárez is still remembered as a great hero.

From F. Kenneth Cox, Miriam Greenblatt, and Stanley Seaberg, *Human Heritage: A World History* (Columbus, Ohio: Charles E. Merrill, 1981), pp. 552–53.

Teaching the Persuasive Pattern

Of all reading patterns, the persuasive pattern is given the least attention in the middle and secondary content classrooms. This may be due to the belief that school textbooks do not contain information written according to a persuasive pattern. In part, this is an incorrect assumption. Textbook selection committees do, however, prevent extreme propaganda from reaching the classroom. Nonetheless, since teachers use a variety of materials to teach different concepts, students encounter material that assumes a contrasting or novel posture on certain issues. But the persuasive pattern does not just occur in supplementary reading done in the content classroom. It also occurs in subtle ways in some content textbooks. For example, in one social studies textbook, a section is devoted to the availability of resources in the world. The subject tries to persuade readers that people in the United States use too many resources, and that they are using more than their share. Factual information is presented in an opinionated way.

Persuasive patterns exist in social studies materials as well as in literature and music. Lyrics in songs contain persuasive patterns that try to sway the listener or reader through emotions, generalizations, or testimonials. In the following example, the lyrics to the song "Old Smoky" are given. In this song, the writer is trying to use persuasion to show the hurt felt by a woman when a relationship is one-sided. Other verses, such as those found in poetry, use figurative language and implied meanings to play on emotion in order to encourage the readers to believe whatever is being told.

EXAMPLE

Persuasive Pattern from a Music Textbook

Old Smoky

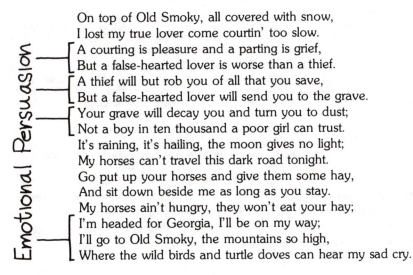

On top of Old Smoky, all covered with snow,
I lost my true lover come courtin' too slow.
A courting is pleasure and a parting is grief,
But a false-hearted lover is worse than a thief.
A thief will but rob you of all that you save,
But a false-hearted lover will send you to the grave.
Your grave will decay you and turn you to dust;
Not a boy in ten thousand a poor girl can trust.
It's raining, it's hailing, the moon gives no light;
My horses can't travel this dark road tonight.
Go put up your horses and give them some hay,
And sit down beside me as long as you stay.
My horses ain't hungry, they won't eat your hay;
I'm headed for Georgia, I'll be on my way;
I'll go to Old Smoky, the mountains so high,
Where the wild birds and turtle doves can hear my sad cry.

The second example presents a table that outlines the predictions of Karl Marx and what happened according to the American perspective. If these perceptions were analyzed by a communist, they would be unlike those presented in this social studies text. Thus, social studies materials use many subtle, persuasive techniques to further democratic ideals and the American way of life. Although this certainly should not be changed, students must learn to analyze all materials they read to determine the beliefs of the authors, and decide why they present the information as they do.

EXAMPLE

Persuasive Pattern from a Social Studies Textbook

Predictions of Karl Marx

Karl Marx, as you read in Chapter 21, made several predictions about the future. He based these on history as he saw it and on the industrialized societies of the late 1800's. Events have not worked out as Marx thought they would, and neither communism nor capitalism developed as he foresaw. The column on the left, below, summarizes some of Marx's predictions. The column on the right, based on today's vantage point, shows what happened.

Marx predicted	*What happened*
Capitalist society would undergo increasingly severe depressions until wealth would be concentrated in the hands of a few capitalists, with a vast mass of suffering proletarians.	Capitalism has been more flexible than Marx predicted. Although there have been depressions, the rich have not grown richer and the poor poorer. In capitalist nations—the United States and most of Western Europe—wealth has been distributed more and more equitably, with workers receiving an increasingly larger share of the profits and standards of living constantly rising.
The proletarians in industrially advanced nations would unite and seize power by force in a revolution.	Communist revolutions have occurred in industrially backward nations, such as the Soviet Union and China. And they have been carried out by small groups of highly trained and disciplined revolutionists, not by the masses.
After a period characterized by a "dictatorship of the proletariat," the state would "wither away."	In such communist countries as Russia and China, there is no "dictatorship of the proletariat," but rather a dictatorship tightly controlled by a small minority of the Communist Party. The state shows little sign of "withering away."
Under communism, a truly classless society would come into existence. People would contribute what they could, and receive what they needed.	In communist countries, important party members, scientists, engineers, and other professionals enjoy higher incomes, better housing, and more privileges than other citizens. The children of these privileged people have a better chance for higher education.

From MEN AND NATIONS: A WORLD HISTORY, Third Edition, by Anatole G. Mazour and John M. Peoples, copyright © 1975 by Harcourt Brace Jovanovich, Inc. Reprinted by permission of the publishers.

As students learn to recognize the different patterns in content reading, the persuasive pattern must not be overlooked. Supplemental content materials such as newspapers, magazines, and brochures offer a variety of information from many different perspectives. Students must read these materials carefully and critically in order to determine the philosophy being presented.

Teaching the Problem-Solving Pattern

The problem-solving pattern is used extensively in content materials covering mathematics, science, and business and vocational education. These materials are often difficult for the students, because they are frequently unfamiliar with, or unable to apply, the necessary problem-solving skills to reach a solution. The inability to solve word problems in mathematics causes frustration for students and teachers alike.

Word problems contain three parts that need to be recognized separately and then integrated to reach a solution. Initially, students should note the situation or condition under which the problem took place. Second, they must determine what is being asked—what operation is to be performed. Third, they must note numbers and other math values. These three elements are then interrelated to solve the problem. An example of this process is given below.

Students also experience difficulty in reading word problems, because many of them are poorly written. Information may be vague, implied, or totally missing. Thus, math teachers should carefully evaluate all word problems before they are assigned.

EXAMPLE
_____

Reading a Word Problem

Problem:
Two cars, A and B, are traveling on the same road in the same direction. Car A leaves later than Car B and is driving 60 miles per hour. Car B is traveling at a rate of 50 miles per hour and is 250 miles ahead of Car A. How long will it take Car A to catch Car B? How many miles will it take for Car A to reach Car B?

1st reading:
Situation
2 cars going in same direction, one ahead of the other.

2nd reading:
What is asked?
1. How long for Car A to catch up?
2. How many miles for Car A to catch up?

3rd reading:
Car A—60 mph   Car B—50 mph
                     250 miles ahead of A

Solution
1. x = how long to catch up
    60 mph − 50 mph = 10 mph (difference in speed)   2. x = how many miles
    250 mile lead ÷ 10 mph = x 25 hrs. • 60 mph = x
    x = 25 hrs   1500 miles = x

LAGNIAPPE
_____

Steps in Problem Solving

1. *Read through the problem quickly.* Try to get a general grasp of the situation and visualize the problem as a whole. Don't be concerned with actual names, numerals, or values.
2. *Examine the problem again.* Try to understand exactly what you are asked to find. This may be stated in a question or a command. Although it often comes at the end of the problem, it may appear anywhere in the problem.

3. *Read the problem again to note what information is given.* At this point you are looking for exact numbers and values.
4. *Analyze the problem carefully* to note the relationship of information given to what you are asked to find. Note information that seems to be missing as well as surplus information.
5. *Translate the relationships into mathematical terms.* Indicate both values and operations. This almost always involves planning a sequence of steps that correspond to the operations. The end result will be one or more mathematical sentences or equations.
6. *Perform the necessary computation.*
7. *Examine the solution carefully.* Label it to correspond to what the problem asks you to find. Finally, check the value against your grasp of the problem situation to judge whether it seems sensible.

Richard A. Earle, *Teaching Reading and Mathematics*, pp. 49–50.

In another example, a physics problem is given, followed by the solution. With this format, students must read the information carefully, taking time to reread as necessary, in order to understand fully how the solution was reached. Students should even try to cover the solution and work through the problem to demonstrate an understanding of the concepts used.

EXAMPLE

Problem-Solving Pattern in a Science Textbook

Example:
Sound energy is radiated uniformly in all directions from a small source at a rate of 1.2 watts. (a) What is the intensity of the sound at a point 25 m from the source? (b) What is the intensity level at this reception point?

Read to determine what is to be done and then reread to be sure!

Solution:
Assuming no absorption of sound energy by the transmitting medium, the 1.2 watts of sound power flows through a spherical area having a radius of 25 m.

Relate back to example; cover solution and work through independently... then check!

(a) $I = \dfrac{P}{A} = \dfrac{1.2 \text{ w}}{4\pi \ (2500 \text{ cm}^2)} = 1.5 \times 10^{-8} \text{ w/cm}^2$

(b) $\beta = 10 \log \dfrac{I}{I_o} = 10 \log \dfrac{1.5 \times 10^{-8} \text{ w/cm}^2}{10^{-16} \text{ w/cm}^2} = 10 \log (1.5 \times 10^8)$

$= 82 \text{ db}$

From *John E. Williams, Frederick E. Trinklein, H. Clark Metcalfe, and Ralph W. Lefler, Modern Physics* (New York: Holt, Rinehart, and Winston, 1972), p. 255.

The problem-solving pattern can be easily recognized in content materials, although students may have difficulty understanding it. This may result from their inability to identify the relevant information, or failure to take enough time to work through the problem. Instruction in problem solving, as outlined in this section, increases student ability to work logically through information given in problem-solving patterns.

Concept Guides

The first step in identifying any organizational pattern requires students to recognize the principal concepts or ideas, and then to associate other ideas with these concepts. Concept guides can be developed by the content teacher to help in this regard. Concept guides are designed around the premise that students must first identify the important concept to be learned, and second, to associate the concept with information already known. By grouping new ideas with those that have previously been learned, students can better retain the information. Thus, the theory of "chunking" of information is applied to content learning. Ausubel defines chunking as the "process for rearranging the stimulus input into a more efficiently organized 'sequence of chunks.' "[18] The concept guide therefore serves two functions in enhancing content learning:

1. Students are helped in their recognition of major concepts within a selection, and
2. Students learn to associate the new information with ideas already known.

Meyer has suggested through her research that students must learn to recognize top level ideas and subordinate other ideas in order to understand organizational patterns in textual materials.[19] The research of Anderson et al. shows that students remember more information when their existing knowledge is used in relation to the new ideas being learned.[20] Therefore, concept guides seem to be another valuable tool for use in the content classroom. The following steps should be followed in developing a concept guide:

1. Determine the major concepts that the students are expected to learn. List each in a word or phrase. According to the model for content reading instruction presented in this book, concept identification is Step I. Specific procedures for identifying concepts are presented in Chapter 2. The identified concepts form Part II of the concept guide.
2. Reread the materials and select statements that underlie the major concepts chosen for presentation. For each of the major concepts, statements are selected which expand the concepts. These statements can be reworded or used as taken from the book. These statements form Part I of the concept guide.
3. Arrange the guide so that statements from the selection become Part I of the guide, and the major concept categories or associations become Part II.[21]

Examples of two concept guides are shown on the following pages.

Concept guides are best used as students prepare to read their content materials. After the concepts and vocabulary have been introduced, and materials are previewed or surveyed, students are ready to use the guides in identifying the most important concepts and classifying them. The concept guide in the first example is designed for use in a seventh grade vocal music class in which the students are learning about time signature. Part I of the guide uses statements made in relation to the various time signatures to be studied. A listing of terms and definitions may be given as the technical vocabulary is introduced. The listing helps students remember the various terms. Part II of the guide requires students to associate the definitions with a line of music.

ACTIVITY

Concept Guide in Music

Topic: Time Signature

Part 1:

As you review the pages to be read in your text and look at the different examples of pieces of music, complete the sentences below. Knowing this information will help you remember what you read.

1. In order to connect notes in music of the same pitch we use the _____ .
2. A _____ and a _____ are made alike, but the _____ connects notes of the same pitch and the _____ notes of different pitch.
3. Pitch and duration are represented by symbols on a _____ .
4. The distance between two bar lines is called a _____ .
5. The speed of a song is referred to as the _____ of the song.
6. When the conductor holds a note longer than its written value, he is using the _____ .
7. In 4/4 time, two _____ will equal one half note.
8. In 3/4 time, we may not have a _____ note since it has four beats.
9. The 8th rest will get one-quarter count just like the _____ note.
10. In music, silence is represented by the _____ .

measure	fermata	half note
bar line	staff	whole note
slur	tempo	8th note
tie	quarter note	rest

Part 2:

Study the piece of music below. Note the numbers next to the different signatures. Then look at the term and associate the terms with the numbered example. Put the number on the line next to the term.

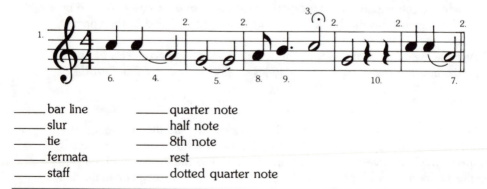

_____ bar line   _____ quarter note
_____ slur   _____ half note
_____ tie   _____ 8th note
_____ fermata   _____ rest
_____ staff   _____ dotted quarter note

Adapted from a guide developed by E. Tyrrell Owen, Conway Junior High School, Orange County Schools, Florida.

The second example is a concept guide designed for a life science class. It helps students identify the organizational pattern used in learning the concept that a food chain includes producers, consumers, and decomposers. Part I requires that students note information about the different categories to be learned. Part II uses concept categories to help students relate other information to them.

EXAMPLE

Concept Guide in Science

Topic: Food Chain

Part 1:
As you preview pages 444-450 in your text, complete these statements.
1. Organisms containing chlorophyll are _____ .
2. Microorganisms that cause the decay of dead plants and animals are

_____ .

3. _____ are animals that eat other animals and plants.

Part 2:
Put the words in the list below into their proper group based on their method of obtaining food. (Use Appexdix D to help identify any unfamiliar organisms.)

azalea bush	rabbit	grass
mushroom	man	bread mold
dandelion	eagle	seaweed
kangaroo	gardenia	spider
trout	fern	cedar tree
palm tree	roach	bacillus bacteria
horse	coccus bacteria	poinsettia
cactus	fly	bass
spirillum bacteria	slime mold	penicillium
fungus	mold	E. coli

Producer	Consumer	Decomposer
1. _____	_____	_____
2. _____	_____	_____
3. _____	_____	_____
4. _____	_____	_____
5. _____	_____	_____
6. _____	_____	_____
7. _____	_____	_____
8. _____	_____	_____
9. _____	_____	_____
10. _____	_____	_____

Adapted form a guide developed by Cliff McInturff, Oconee Junior High School, Orange County Schools, Florida.

Concept guides provide content teachers with another way to assist students who have difficulty identifying the basic concepts used in the different organizational patterns. Content teachers may also find that concept guides are helpful in teaching concepts and vocabulary in the beginning step of the Directed

Learning Activity. Regardless of where this type of guide is used in content instruction it should be viewed as another way of helping students learn to read content information. Additional examples of concept guides are provided in Appendix D.

REFLECTION

Following the guidelines and examples presented in this discussion of concept guides, develop a concept guide that could be used in a content classroom of your choice.

Pattern Guides

As students are learning to identify the different organizational patterns in content material, they need practice in determining how patterns are used in content writing. To this end, teachers may develop a pattern guide. Pattern guides help students use the organizational pattern within the material for information. Actually, the guide tends to dissect content material and then encourages students to put it back together as they use the organizational pattern.

Identifying relationships, explanations, and other organizational patterns, and then interrelating the ideas to determine the pattern, requires that students frequently work with pattern guides in group situations. This encourages discussion and helps students realize why and how the organizational pattern enhances understanding. The content teacher should consider the following in developing a pattern guide:

1. Read through the text selection, identifying a predominant pattern.
2. Develop an exercise in which students can react to the structure of the relationships represented by the pattern.
3. Decide on how much you want to provide in the pattern guide. If it suits your purposes you may develop sections of the guide for interpretive and applied levels. Or you may decide that these levels can be handled adequately through questioning and discussion once students have sensed the author's organization through the guided reading activity.[22]

Using these steps, two pattern guides are presented in the following pages. The first example is a pattern guide developed for a science material that has a relationship pattern, specifically a cause-effect relationship. In Part I, students are given statements of causes for which they are to identify the effects as they read. Following this procedure, the students are learning how to recognize a relationship pattern by being guided through the relationships that exist in the selection. Part II of this pattern guide helps students use the isolated causes and effects identified in Part I to interpret the content information in light of other specific facts within the passage. Part II moves the student from examining isolated relationships to an awareness of how the information is interrelated and can be identified as a relationship pattern of organization.

The second example is a pattern guide for use in a Spanish class. The textbook follows a generalization and example format that represents the enumeration pattern of organization. This guide has only one part, and is designed to help students associate the generalization with the Spanish example. Following the use of this guide, the content teacher should have a discussion to allow students to apply these generalizations to other examples. Additional examples of pattern guides are in Appendix D.

EXAMPLES

Pattern Guide for Relationship Pattern

Topic: Water Pollution

Part 1: Cause-Effect Relationships
In the chapter on "Water Pollution" in the text, find the effects of the following causes. Write your answer in the space provided.

1. Cause: Bacterial and viral pollution
   Effect: _____
2. Cause: Chemical pollution
   Effect: _____
3. Cause: Eutrophication
   Effect: _____
4. Cause: Toxic pollution
   Effect: _____
5. Cause: Thermal pollution
   Effect: _____
6. Cause: Spills
   Effect: _____
7. Cause: Septic tanks
   Effect: _____
8. Cause: Deicing of roads and highways
   Effect: _____
9. Cause: Salt water intrusion
   Effect: _____

Part 2:
What do you think the author was trying to say? Write your answer in the space below each question.

1. Why has water pollution become a problem in many areas of the world?

2. How does it affect the quality of life that we have come to expect?

3. Why has the need to stockpile oil in our country greatly increased the likelihood of water pollution?

4. As our underground water becomes more and more threatened by pollution, how does this affect those people who depend on this source for most of their water?

Pattern Guide for Enumeration Pattern

Match the following generalizations from your text to the correct examples at the bottom of the page.

_____ 1. Spanish subjects and verbs agree in person and number.

_____ 2. A compound subject requires a plural verb ending.

_____ 3. All Spanish nouns belong to one of two gender classes: masculine or feminine. Find the feminine noun.

_____ 4. Nouns whose singular ends in a vowel, add _s_ to form the plural.

_____ 5. The definite article _los_ is used with masculine plural nouns.

_____ 6. An adjective agrees in gender and number with the noun it modifies.

_____ 7. When the direct object of a verb is a noun or an indefinite pronoun which refers to a person, it is usually preceded by _a_.

_____ 8. The verb _estar_ is used to refer to the location of something or someone.

_____ 9. The verb _ser_ is used to link two noun phrases.

_____ 10. Only _ser_ is used to refer to the time and place of events.

a. Yo soy Christina.

b. El senor es prentencioso.

c. los maestros

d. la puerta

e. Busco a alguien

f. La reunion es a las ocho.

g. Juan y ella llegan hoy.

h. ellas practican

i. regalos

j. Aqui estoy

Pattern guides can greatly help students in learning the different organizational patterns and to use them to increase their understanding of content information. Teachers should consider including these guides as another effective instructional strategy for their classes.

REFLECTION

Use the examples and guidelines for pattern guides and develop guides for two different organizational patterns. The task will be easier if you first carefully study all the examples in the chapter and the appendix.

SUMMARY

This chapter discusses the importance of organizational patterns found in content materials. Research shows that students who are aware of organizational patterns as they read remember more about what they have read. Four organizational patterns are identified and examples given for each pattern. The patterns include: enumeration pattern, relationship pattern, persuasive pattern, and problem-solving pattern.

Instructional strategies useful in presenting each pattern are given. Examples are used to help the content teacher identify and understand how each pattern can be demonstrated to students. Two additional techniques, concept guides and pattern guides, are also discussed. Steps for developing these guides are outlined along with examples of each guide.

FOR DISCUSSION

1. Identify the four organizational patterns discussed in this chapter and tell how each could be identified in the various content materials.
2. How are organizational patterns related to the comprehension skills and understanding of content materials?
3. What can content teachers do to help students learn to identify the different organizational patterns?

OTHER SUGGESTED READINGS

Aulls, Mark W. *Developmental and Remedial Reading in the Middle Grades.* Boston: Allyn and Bacon, 1978. Chapters 3–6.

Black, John B., and Bower, Gordon H. "Episodes as Chunks in Narrative Memory." *Journal of Verbal Learning and Verbal Behavior* 18 (June 1979):309–18.

Dee-Lucas, Diana, and DiVesta, Francis J. "Learner-Generated Organizational Aids: Effects on Learning from Text." *Journal of Educational Psychology* 72 (June 1980):304–11.

Elliott, Stephen N. "Children's Knowledge and Use of Organizational Patterns of Prose in Recalling What They Read." *Journal of Reading Behavior* 11 (Fall 1980):203–12.

Friedman, Myles I., and Rowls, Michael D. *Teaching Reading and Thinking Skills.* New York: Longman, 1980. Chapter 16.

Herber, Harold. *Teaching Reading in Content Areas,* 2nd ed. Englewood Cliffs, N.J.: Prentice-Hall, 1978. Chapter 4.

Herber, Harold, and Vacca, Richard, eds. *Research in Reading in Content Areas: Third Report.* Syracuse, N.Y.: Syracuse University Reading and Language Arts Center, 1977.

Lamberg, Walter J., and Lamb, Charles E. *Reading Instruction in the Content Areas.* Chicago: Rand McNally, 1980.

Meyer, Bonnie J. F. "The Structure of Prose: Effects on Learning and Memory and Implications for Educational Practice." In *Schooling and the Acquisition of Knowledge,* ed. Richard C. Anderson, Rand J. Spiro, and William E. Montague. Hillsdale, N.J.: Lawrence Erlbaum Associates, 1977. 179–200.

Shimmerlik, Susan M. "Organizational Theory and Memory for Prose: A Review of the Literature." *Review of Educational Research* 48 (Winter 1978):103–20.

Taylor, Barbara M. "Children's Memory for Expository Text After Reading." *Reading Research Quarterly* 15 (1980):399–411.

Thomas, Ellen Lamar, and Robinson, H. Alan. *Improving Reading in Every Class.* Boston: Allyn and Bacon, 1972.

Van Blaricom, Ginger. "The Effect of Passage Organization on Main Idea Comprehension at Three Response Levels." In *Reading Comprehension at Four Linguistic Levels,* ed. Clifford Pennock. Newark, Del.: International Reading Association, 1979.

NOTES

1. Edward Thorndike, "Reading and Reasoning: A Study of Mistakes in Paragraph Reading," *Journal of Educational Psychology* 8 (1917):323–32.
2. Nila Banton Smith, "Patterns of Writing in Different Subject Areas," *Journal of Reading* 8 (October 1964):31–37; James M. McCallister, "Using Paragraph Clues as Aids to Understanding," *Journal of Reading* 8 (October 1964):11–16.

3. Emerald Dechant, *Improving the Teaching of Reading* (Englewood Cliffs, N.J.: Prentice-Hall, 1970); Marian McGuire and Mary Bumpus, *The Croft Inservice Program: Reading Comprehension Skills* (New London, Conn.: Croft Educational Services, 1971); Olive S. Niles, "Organization Perceived," in *Perspectives in Reading: Developing Study Skills in Secondary Schools,* ed. Harold H. Herber (Newark, Del.: International Reading Association, 1974).

4. E. Marcia Sheridan, *A Review of Research on Schema Theory and Its Implications for Reading Instruction in Secondary Reading* (South Bend, Ind.: Indiana University at South Bend, 1978). (ED 167 947)

5. Asghar Iran-Nejad, *The Schema: A Structural or Functional Pattern,* Technical Report no. 159. (Cambridge, Mass.: Bolt, Beranek and Newman; Urbana, Ill.: Center for the Study of Reading, 1980).

6. David Rumelhart, *Schemata: The Building Blocks of Cognition,* Technical Report no. 79 (San Diego: Calif.: Center for Human Information Processing, University of California, 1978); Richard Anderson, Rand Spiro, and Mark Anderson, *Schemata as Scaffolding for the Representation of Information in Connected Discourse,* Technical Report no. 24 (Urbana-Champaign, Ill.: Center for the Study of Reading, University of Illinois, 1977).

7. Bonnie J. F. Meyer, "Structure of Prose: Implications for Teachers of Reading," Research Report no. 3 (Tempe, Ariz.: Department of Educational Psychology, Arizona State University, 1979), p. 2.

8. James McCallister, "Using Paragraph Clues as Aids to Understanding," pp. 11–16; Nila Banton Smith, "Patterns of Writing in Different Subject Areas," part 1, *Journal of Reading* 8 (October 1964): 31–37, and "Patterns of Writing in Different Subject Areas," part 2, *Journal of Reading* 8 (November 1964): 97–102; Olive Niles, "Organization Perceived," 1974; H. Alan Robinson, *Teaching Reading and Study Strategies: The Content Areas,* 2nd ed. (Boston: Allyn and Bacon, 1978), pp. 136–56; David L. Shepherd, *Comprehensive High School Reading Methods,* 2nd ed. (Columbus, Ohio: Charles E. Merrill, 1978), pp. 91–100, 214–19; Betty D. Roe, Barbara D. Stoodt, and Paul C. Burns, *Reading Instruction in the Secondary School,* rev. ed. (Chicago: Rand McNally, 1978), pp. 240–47, 254–62, 266–69, 272–74, 285, 308–10.

9. Olive S. Niles, *"Organization Perceived,"* 1974.

10. Bonnie J. F. Meyer, David M. Brandt, and George J. Bluth, "Use of Top-Level Structure in Text: Key for Reading Comprehension of Ninth-Grade Students," *Reading Research Quarterly* 16 (1980):72–103.

11. W. Kinstch and T.A. Van Dijk, "Toward a Model of Text Comprehension and Production," *Psychological Review* 85 (1978):363–94.

12. T. A. Van Dijk, "Relevance Assignment in Discourse Comprehension," *Discourse Processes* 2 (1979):113–26.

13. F. J. D'Angelo, "Paradigms as Structural Counterparts of Topoi," in *Linguistics, Stylistics, and the Teaching of Composition,* ed. D. McQuade (Akron, Ohio: University of Akron Press, 1979), pp. 41–51.

14. Bonnie J. F. Meyer, "Structure of Prose: Implications for Teachers of Reading," 1979.

15. H. Alan Robinson, *Teaching Reading and Study Strategies,* pp. 168–69.

16. Richard T. Vacca, *Content Area Reading* (Boston: Little, Brown, 1981), p. 143.

17. Richard T. Vacca, *Content Area Reading,* p.143.

18. David P. Ausubel, *Educational Psychology: A Cognitive View* (New York: Holt, Rinehart, and Winston, 1968), p. 59.

19. Bonnie J. F. Meyer, "Organizational Patterns in Prose and Their Use in Reading," in *Reading Research: Studies and Application,* ed. Michael Kamil and Alden Moe, Twenty-eighth Yearbook of the National Reading Conference (Clemson, S.C.: National Reading Conference, 1979), pp.109–17.

20. Richard C. Anderson, James W. Picher, and Larry L. Shirley, *Effect of the Reader's Schema at Different Points in Time,* Technical Report no. 119 (Cambridge, Mass.: Bolt, Beranek and Newman; Urbana, Ill.: Center for the Study of Reading, 1979).
21. Thomas H. Estes and Joseph L. Vaughan, *Reading and Learning in the Content Classroom,* abr. ed. (Boston: Allyn and Bacon, 1978), p. 170.
22. Richard T. Vacca, *Content Area Reading,* p. 151.

CHAPTER SEVEN

ORGANIZING AND MANAGING CONTENT INSTRUCTION

The usual mental picture of a content classroom is one of rows of desks for thirty to forty students who sit and listen to a teacher. This concept is probably more accurate for content areas of English and social studies than for areas having lab experiences. In far too many content classes, however, students are compelled to become passive learners.

Learning is an active process and students are active people. Passive learning turns them off. This in turn often creates disruptive behavior caused by frustration, boredom, and possibly fatigue. The content teacher will probably react adversely, feeling that students are being disrespectful and do not appreciate their learning opportunities. The proper approach to the problem is for the teacher to analyze what is happening to cause ineffective teaching and learning experiences and make necessary adjustments such as changing the classroom environment.

Using instructional techniques such as those discussed in Chapters 5 and 6 are only part of what is needed to strengthen learning. A classroom environment that is well organized and managed produces active student participants in the learning process and is effective in integrating reading and content instruction. This chapter focuses on techniques for organizing and managing content reading instruction.

STUDY QUESTIONS

1. What is meant by classroom organization and management?
2. Why is this important in content instruction?
3. How can a content teacher be concerned about organizing and managing instruction with so many students?
4. What is grouping?
5. What are the different types of groups?
6. How is grouping used in the content classroom?
7. How does grouping relate to the Directed Learning Activity?
8. How can the content teacher arrange the classroom to facilitate more active instruction?

VOCABULARY

Achievement groups
Classroom organization
Heterogeneous
Homogeneous
Individualization

Interest groups
Management
Peer grouping
Skills groups
Total class instruction

CLASSROOM ORGANIZATION

The first day of school has arrived. For weeks Ms. Smith has thought about how to organize the classroom. This year she is teaching ninth grade general science and biology. Past experiences have shown her that biology students can work on their own, but that general science students must be controlled. Last year was frustrating for Ms. Smith and seemingly for the students, too. They dragged into class and stumbled into their desks. No matter how hard she tried to teach, Ms. Smith felt the students did not really care about learning science. The thought of another year like that caused Ms. Smith to read up on other ways to teach her science classes. She considered different ideas, but now that school was about to start, she was not sure of her approach.

In pondering the different ideas, Ms. Smith tried first to find out why she felt changes in classroom organization would improve student learning, and what she actually hoped to accomplish. As she thought about her past students, she realized that in the heterogeneously grouped classes, the range in levels was tremendous. In checking reading levels in one class she found a range from a high second grade level to a low twelfth grade level. Analyzing the class more specifically, the breakdown looked something like this:

Reading Level	No. of Students
12th grade level	1
11th grade level	2
10th grade level	4
9th grade level	6
8th grade level	9
7th grade level	4
6th grade level	1
5th grade level	2
4th grade level	0
3rd grade level	0
2nd grade level	1

With such a diverse range, changes in classroom organization were necessary to help meet the different students' needs. The textbook used was written at about tenth grade level, and many students could not read and understand it.

By adjusting instruction to better meet the various levels in the class, Ms. Smith realized that efficient classroom organization becomes important. What would she do to help students at so many different levels? How could she involve them more in the learning process? When would she have time to work with individual students? What about noise and confusion? The more she thought about the needed change, the more questions came to mind, but she felt she had to take one step at a time.

Mangieri identified six characteristics of an effectively organized classroom in which reading instruction is to occur. They are:

1. The recognition and accommodation of individual differences in students.
2. Continuous diagnosis of reading strengths and weaknesses.
3. Planning for reading instruction on a regular basis.
4. The effective use of the available resources.

5. Using effective instructional procedures for individual students.
6. Continuous evaluation.[1]

These characteristics Ms. Smith agreed with, although she had to learn more about how to teach reading through science. She realized her students had to read science materials and that they needed help with reading. She believed changes in her classroom organization along with teaching concepts rather than the textbook would provide that help.

To start with, effective classroom organization calls for the curriculum to be student-centered. This does not mean student dictated, but it means that students must become active and get involved in the learning process.

Effective classroom organization techniques view the student as both a consumer and a resource. The individual needs of the student must be met. Likewise, students can learn from one another and should be used as a resource in activities and in teaching situations. Additionally, students become active participants in the learning process as they get involved in learning experiences that meet their individual needs.

As changes are made to improve classroom organization, teachers must make adjustments. They cannot prepare for and teach 150 or more individual students each day. They must use the students as resources and train them to work independently and in groups. Lessons should have a maximum amount of student activity with the teacher not only taking an active role as a manager of learning, but as an active participant in the learning process as well. Students should know what they are expected to do and where the needed materials are located. Directions should be written for reference by the student. In other words, as a classroom becomes efficiently organized, the teacher serves to plan, coordinate, and provide initial instruction, with the students functioning more independently as reinforcement and enrichment activities are used to increase learning.

How can the teacher get problem students to work in this type of classroom situation? There is no magic answer. Content teachers usually find, however, that several things help to change the behavior of problem students:

1. Provide reading materials at the student's level or use audiotapes of the information to be learned. Remember, the focus is on learning content information rather than reading the book.
2. Involve the students in classroom activities. Many times slower students or disruptive students are never given responsibilities or are seldom involved in group activities. They begin to feel like the failures teachers have labeled them. Students usually respond as they feel they are expected to respond.
3. Use heterogeneous groups that include the better and poorer students — they learn from one another.
4. Give praise for completing tasks and good work. Try using only positive comments and throw away negative words for a few weeks.

If the content teacher believes that change is needed in the classroom, these ideas serve as beginning points. Implementing these organizational changes requires the use of various grouping strategies, management ideas, and some adjustments in the physical arrangement of the classroom. As adjustments are made, teachers may wish to use Smith's checklist for an organized secondary classroom as a measuring stick:

1. Nobody seems to be obviously in charge and everybody seems to know where things are.
2. Directions are written out and posted in an easily accessible place.
3. Everybody seems to be involved with something, though not necessarily the same thing.
4. The teacher can leave the room or concentrate on an individual while group learning continues uninterrupted.[2]

REFLECTION

Think about your content classes — how you visualize the room and the amount of student involvement. Sketch the room arrangement on a piece of paper and tell how the students were involved in learning. Save this and compare it to the information given in this chapter.

STRATEGIES FOR ORGANIZING STUDENTS

Several strategies are available in organizing students for instruction. Each has an important place in the total instructional process. In the following pages, the more widely used strategies for classroom organization are discussed. These strategies include total class instruction, individualized instruction, and grouping.

Total Class Instruction

Total class instruction is unquestionably the most frequently used strategy for implementing instruction in the content classroom. Unfortunately, it is also probably the least effective, if used alone on a daily basis. Teaching the entire class as if all the students were on the same level, using the same material for each student, and giving the same assignments for everyone in the class may be somewhat effective although boring in a homogeneously grouped class, but, for a heterogeneously grouped class this approach is unlikely to succeed. In realistic terms, the strategy does not meet the needs of individual students. Using this strategy every day in a content class is not only ineffective, but often results in students that are unmotivated, disruptive, and perhaps even turns off those students capable of learning at a higher level. In a total class environment, each student's needs cannot be accommodated; thus, variety in instruction is essential. Individualize instruction, break into groups, use listening stations and other activities to motivate the students and give them an opportunity to learn.

In defense of the total class strategy, there are instances when it should be fully used. When introducing a unit, the teacher must meet with the entire class to indicate what is going to occur over a specific period of time. Introducing vocabulary and concepts may be done with the whole class. Setting a purpose for a specific activity or series of activities may require the presence of the entire class. Other activities such as showing films, reading poetry, and presenting plays are oriented toward the total class. Two of the more important purposes of total class instruction in content areas revolve around the discussion of information read and the use of the teacher's questioning strategies. These activities allow the teacher to observe the progress students are making toward learning content information.

In summarizing the effectiveness of the total class instructional strategy, teachers must recognize that it is mostly ineffective if used on a daily basis. Used in conjunction with grouping and other types of individualized instruction, however, total class instruction plays an important role.

Individualization

Individualized instruction is a topic that has been discussed a great deal in recent years. Many educators have debated what this term implies and what actually constitutes individualized instruction. Formerly, some educators believed it was strictly one-to-one instruction with each student in the class working on a different assignment. In recent years, however, the term has evolved to mean that instruction is individualized when students are given assignments on their instructional level (this may or may not correspond to their actual grade placement), and that they are capable of completing at a satisfactory level. Furthermore, these assignments do not necessarily have to be different from others in the class, as long as each student is engaged in a task designed to meet his or her individual needs. As a result, individualized instruction can be provided to each student through independent work or through the use of grouping techniques, since it is likely that there are other students in the class working at approximately the same levels or on the same skills.

In order to determine which students need instruction either in groups or separately, some basic diagnostic information is necessary. This information can be obtained through the use of the appropriate diagnostic procedures discussed in Chapter 4. After getting this information, students can then be placed in the appropriate instructional setting.

Shepherd suggests seven considerations for individualizing instruction. These are:.

1. Establish goals that are to be accomplished with the students.
2. Know your students, their interests, strengths and weaknesses, and as much related information as possible.
3. Diagnostic information is essential for providing appropriate individualized instruction.
4. Several methods of individualizing the class should be used.
5. The teacher must be flexible in regard to instructional methods. Because students change over the course of a year, so should methods of instruction.
6. It is important for the student to be able to work independently to some extent, since the teacher is unable to respond to all students in the class at the same time.
7. Extensive planning by the teacher is essential to the effective implementation of individualized instruction. This planning should incorporate student suggestions, as well as encourage self-direction and independence on the part of the students.[3]

Perhaps the most widely used technique for individualizing instruction is through grouping. Grouping usually occurs in a class as a result of diagnostic information indicating that several students in the class need work on the same skill, or that they are reading on the same level. This technique is discussed in greater detail in the following section.

Often individualized instruction is implemented by allowing periods of independent reading. In these cases, students do not have to be alone and separate from the class, but it does permit them to make some independent decisions about what they would like to read. Participation in independent activities should be encouraged and the students allowed some flexibility in expressing themselves in activities that originate from independent reading. Such activities might be writing poetry, short stories, role-playing, presenting a play, making a pretend movie with real cameras, or perhaps even a real movie, or developing a series of short stories for publication on the school duplicating machine. Activities of this type promote growth, enhance decision-making abilities, and invigorate the learning environment.

Another interesting technique for individualizing instruction is contracts. The theory behind the use of contracts is that teacher and student arrive together at a logical starting point for instruction. Goals are agreed upon and the completion of specific objectives determined. Student and teacher also agree upon the time for completion of the task as well as the specific task to be finished. In this arrangement, both parties are more or less bound to conform to their part of the contract. In some instances, the contract is actually signed by the student and teacher to create an atmosphere of responsibility and purpose. An interesting aspect of this agreement is that students may contract for the grade they wish to receive for their work; the actual grade received, however, depends upon the quality of the work.

Contracts can be used to some extent with poor readers, but there are limitations to consider. The student's ability to work independently, the reading skills needed by the student, and the availability of appropriate materials and activities must be considered when using contracts. Short-term contracts are recommended for poor readers, and when used wisely, can be quite effective. They are also highly motivating for above-average readers.

Techniques for implementing individualized instruction are numerous. For the content teacher, however, grouping is perhaps the key to facilitating good classroom organizational and management procedures and to implementation of effective instruction.

Grouping

Although grouping within classrooms is more widespread in elementary schools than in secondary schools, the need to use this instructional management procedure in content teaching is becoming more apparent. Grouping is a management tool that facilitates instruction and offers several advantages over total class instruction. For example, teachers are allowed more flexibility in instruction, and students who are above average can move along at a pace more conducive to their level of performance.

Many enrichment activities as well as independent projects and advanced reading can be better accommodated in this management procedure. Students with reading problems are also allowed to progress at their own rate. The emphasis in instruction changes from trying to keep everyone together each day at the same point in the textbook, to more emphasis on the needs of individual students. One important aspect of the added flexibility in the classroom is that individualized instruction in the content class improves. Teachers find themselves with more time to devote to individuals than they ordinarily would in a total-class format.

One of the more unique aspects of grouping is that it allows for more social interaction among students. Since one of the responsibilities of schools is to assist students in improving their social skills, various types of grouping patterns tend to encourage this. Greater independence among students is also fostered by grouping. Often this results in higher levels of performance when students are given the chance to make some of the decisions in the instructional process.

Many types of grouping procedures are used in classrooms. Two of the primary types are homogeneous and heterogeneous. Until recently, homogeneous grouping was commonly used in secondary schools, where students were ability-grouped or tracked, whereas heterogeneous grouping was usually found in elementary schools. In recent years, however, many secondary schools are turning to heterogeneous grouping and dropping the homogeneous type. As a result, content teachers are concerned because they are often unaccustomed to dealing with wide ranges of reading levels in one class. In actual practice, however, the distribution of reading levels in homogeneously grouped classes is usually diverse. Thus, the perception that homogeneous grouping alleviates the need for smaller groups within content classrooms is erroneous. Further grouping is almost always essential, whether a classroom is homogeneously or heterogeneously grouped according to a school management design. It is unlikely that every student will perform on the same level as every other student in that class, and that each student will need exactly the same instruction.

Since there are various ways that students can be grouped for instructional purposes, each of the specific techniques is discussed in more detail in the following pages. The basic grouping formats identified are achievement groups, skill groups, interest groups, and peer groups.

Achievement Grouping. This format is probably the most widely used grouping technique of the four. Students are selected for this format based on their demonstrated achievement. After obtaining the necessary data to determine each student's level of reading proficiency, the teacher divides the class into several groups. Those operating on the highest level are grouped together, and those operating on the lowest level are grouped together, with one or more groups between highest and lowest.

Although many teachers may try to form as few groups as possible, three groups, for example, may be inadequate to meet the different levels in a content class. Those teachers, however, who are inexperienced in using grouping procedures may want to begin with only two or three groups and extend the number later on. It is essential for teachers to note that in a typical ninth grade class that is heterogeneously grouped, the reading levels of the students may range from low second grade level to college level. The range, of course, depends upon the socioeconomic, experiential, and cultural background of the students in a particular school system. In some systems, the range between low

Name: _Max Crowden_   Grade: _9 – World Geography_

Starting Date: _Oct. 1, 19 _ _ _   Ending Date: _Oct. 5, 19 _ _ _

Objectives:

1. To differentiate north from south and east from west.
2. To understand the meaning of latitude and longitude.
3. To demonstrate the use of latitude and longitude on a map or globe.
4. To follow directions independently in completing this contract.

Assignments:

Objective #1:
- Works with the teacher in a total class discussion.
- After meeting with the total class, works with Group 3 on the activity, reviewing the directions north, south, east, and west.
- Select 1 of the following tasks. Complete and give your works to the teacher.
  (a) Take a U.S. map and indicate the part of the country in which the cities of New York, Omaha, Key West, and Portland are located. On your paper write the name of the city and tell whether

FIGURE 7.1
_____

Sample Contract

it is in the north, south, east,
or west section of the country.
Note also the state in which each
of the cities is located.
(b) Using a map of Europe, indicate
the direction of the following
countries in relation to Switzerland:
France, Sweden, Italy, and Bulgaria.
Write your response on your paper.
-Complete Activity 2 in your textbook, p.48
-Complete the activities at Learning
Station C.

Objectives #2 and #3:
-Work with the teacher in Group 2 to
discuss longitude and latitude.
- Select 1 of the following tasks.
Complete and give it to the teacher.
(a) Using the globe, determine the
longitude and latitude of
Washington D.C.. Write your
findings on a sheet of paper.
(b) Complete Activity 5 in your
textbook, p. 48.
(c) Complete the activities at
Learning Station A.
Objective #4
- Check your work to be sure that
you followed directions!

Max Crowden
Student

Mrs. Charlesworth
Teacher

FIGURE 7.1 (continued)

Sample Contract

and high students may be narrow, while in others, wide. Because of these diverse reading levels, several groups are needed to ensure effective instruction.

Caution should be used in designating student placement in achievement groups. Try to avoid a situation in which students are labeled as poor readers and are not given an opportunity to improve their position. Continuous student evaluation is necessary to prevent such an occurrence. Hence, flexibility in grouping techniques is essential in order to ensure that students are encouraged to perform at their highest possible level, and that they are able to move from one group to another to meet their needs.

Because correct placement of students is so important to achievement grouping, the teacher should be cautious as to what instruments are used in the placement process. As mentioned in Chapter 4, achievement tests often do not reflect the student's knowledge or skill. Thus, using these tests as a basis for grouping is risky. If achievement test results are the basis for determining student placement in groups, the teacher should consider other diagnostic tools for use with them. For example, the content teacher may wish to use a cloze procedure or an informal reading inventory (discussed in Chapter 4) to more accurately determine the student's reading level. Because it is the more widely used grouping procedure, achievement grouping is the key to successful content instruction; therefore, the integrity of this grouping format must be maintained through the use of reliable and accurate diagnostic measures. Remember, however, to avoid relying upon only one instrument for achievement grouping.

Skills Grouping. The placement of students in this format depends upon their reading skill knowledge. This is an area that should not be overlooked by the content teacher, since many students lack reading skills necessary for content learning. Perhaps the most effective means of determining the student's reading strengths and weaknesses is through the use of the Group Reading Inventory. Becoming proficient in the application of reading skills is essential if students are to absorb and understand content materials. Learning them depends upon the ability to locate the main idea, differentiate fact from fallacy, and to better use other significant reading skills.

Skills grouping is used to place students in specific groups for instruction on a given skill; it is usually different from achievement grouping. It is not unusual for a student in a high reading group to have difficulty with a reading skill that others in the group may have learned. Skills groups actually may be composed of students from several achievement groups who experience difficulty with the skill. In these groups, students not only develop their skills, but are enabled to enjoy some variety in the grouping process. In this type of management procedure, the primary method of implementation is to group students based upon their strengths and weaknesses in a specific reading skill.

Providing appropriate instruction for students lacking in specific skills is an essential component of the instructional process. The content class can handle this more efficiently through the skills grouping format. Teachers should again remember that skills should not be taught in isolation, but as an integral part of the class using content materials. Skills grouping is flexible and is used most effectively over a short period of time, since the primary purpose is to strengthen a skill deficiency. When the skill is learned, the student leaves the skill group and moves to another part of the instructional program as needed.

LAGNIAPPE

Lecturing is by far the most frequently used teaching technique in today's high schools. Eighty percent of both males and females report often or frequent exposure to lectures. Less than half of the 1980 seniors frequently worked on projects or in a laboratory and only about 25% of the seniors noted frequent use of individualized instruction.

Theodore C. Wagenaar, "High School Seniors' Views of Themselves and Their Schools: A Trend Analysis," *Phi Delta Kappan* 63 (September 1981): 31.

Interest Grouping. This is another grouping format that many teachers use effectively. It enables students with similar interests to work together to more fully explore those interests. Without question, the most positive aspect of interest grouping is the interaction among students from all achievement levels to work together on various interests without regard to reading level. This interaction helps students develop both academically and socially. Those students who rarely work together are enabled to learn about one another as well as from one another.

Unfortunately, one of the weaknesses of achievement grouping is this lack of opportunity for students from different levels to interact and discuss things of interest to themselves. Interest grouping, on the other hand, provides opportunities of this type especially to students who have become disenchanted with the learning process. Often, content material does prove uninviting. It is then that students need special-interest activities to pull them out of the doldrums. Since there is no need for every classroom assignment to be a chore, interest grouping can help motivate students to become enthusiastic over all their studies.

Interest grouping helps to motivate students and promotes social interaction.

An advantage of interest grouping is that students from deprived backgrounds interact with students from more diversified experiential backgrounds, enabling both groups to learn about each other. Used interchangeably with achievement and skills groups this type of grouping format should prove to be highly successful, since it motivates students to want to learn and to work together. Interest grouping is a proven technique that teachers should use as often as possible to motivate their content classes.

Peer Grouping. A fourth type of grouping used successfully in content classrooms is that of student or peer tutoring. This is characterized by students working together who are on the same grade level, but not the same reading levels. Often teachers find that a student may be able to help another understand a difficult concept or skill better than they can. Peer tutoring can work successfully through discussion groups, individual students working together, brainstorming sessions, and any other peer interaction that facilitates learning.

Experiences with peer tutoring have convinced many content teachers that it is a highly successful way to motivate poor readers, increase their interest, and improve their performance in the content classroom. Moreover, it helps students develop a more positive self-concept.

In organizing the classroom learning environment, the teacher should use some or all of the different grouping formats. As organizers of the instructional program, content teachers must use a variety of grouping procedures in order to provide the most effective instruction for each student.

REFLECTION

Of the four grouping procedures discussed in this section, which have you used or seen used in a content classroom? If you have used or observed one or more of these procedures, how did it work? What could have been done to improve on the use of this procedure?

MANAGING CONTENT INSTRUCTION

In managing the content classroom, the teacher should plan to integrate all of the instructional strategies in a way that ensures the integrity of the process. The plan must be structured and well organized and based on the three strategies for organizing instruction—total class instruction, individualized instruction, and grouping. Since the Directed Learning Activity affords an excellent format for implementing instruction, it is the logical choice to use initially in incorporating the various management strategies into the instructional format. Figure 7.2 presents the basic design for managing reading and content instruction in the content classroom.

The actual management of groups is a task that often creates considerable apprehension among content teachers. This is an area that should not be treated lightly, since the mechanics of grouping are essential to providing effective instruction. Therefore, the following suggestions are offered for the content teacher's consideration:

1. *Time the activities* so that one group does not finish its assignment long before the other groups.

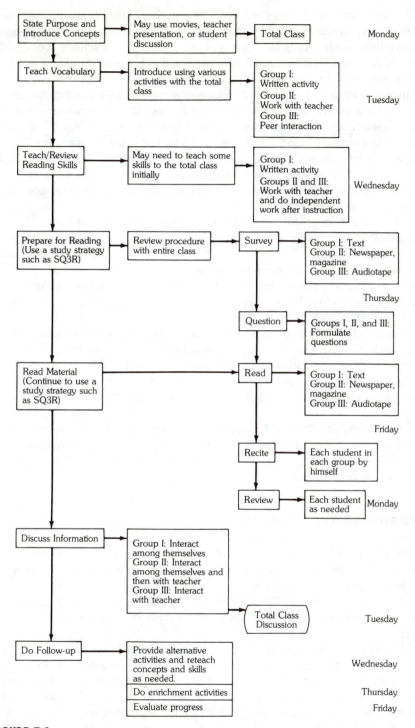

FIGURE 7.2

Organizational Format for Incorporating Reading Instruction and Grouping in a Content Class (using a two-week unit plan)

2. *Provide alternatives,* however, for those students who finish their assignments first. Students should be told what their alternatives are before beginning their assignments in order not to disturb the teacher's work with
another group, or others in the class. Alternative activities should be relevant
activities, not just busywork.

3. *Appoint a leader* for each group. Students should be able to direct questions
to a group leader without disturbing other groups or the teacher. If neither
the leader nor the group is able to answer the question, the leader may then
ask the teacher. A good group leader is a valuable contribution to effective
management of grouping. Not only does this procedure control students
who constantly seek the teacher's attention or choose not to listen to directions, it also enables students to develop a sense of responsibility and independence as well as problem-solving skills.

4. *Provide a variety of interesting activities.* Students should not be required to
complete paper-pencil tasks every minute of every class period. Assignments
and activities should vary so that students remain motivated and enthusiastic
about learning the content information.

5. *Use some time for total class activities.* This was discussed in an earlier section of this chapter. Remember that total class instruction is just one strategy
for organizing instruction.

6. *Provide activities that are appropriate* to the student's level and needs. Each
group is different and the activities provided must meet the individual levels
and needs of each student in that group. This is the primary purpose for
using grouping as a strategy for organizing students for instruction. Without
adhering to this basic principle, there is little reason to group.

Content teachers find that students learn more quickly and show greater
enthusiasm for the instructional process when teaching is adjusted to their reading levels and interests. As a result, organizing and managing the classroom
becomes an easier task.

ARRANGING THE FACILITIES

As teachers use various ideas in organizing and managing their classrooms, they
will need to consider how the classroom facilities may be arranged to assist the
program. The particular management ideas of each teacher will determine the
types of facilities needed. When considering physical arrangements, there are
various physical limitations that must be recognized; however, this must not
deter changes in instruction.

Although there are always some limitations in classroom arrangement, the
teacher must get as much as possible from the facilitates available. In content
classrooms, the teacher will likely have thirty or so desks with which to contend.
This is sometimes a difficult problem to work around, but is possible. The
teacher can compensate for this problem, and implement some grouped and
individualized instructional ideas, by arranging desks so that more flexible
instruction can be carried out.

In teaching high school social studies, Mr. Geczy found himself limited by the
existing physical facilities—thirty-seven desks and one table. The desks were in
straight rows, and the table, obviously rarely used by previous teachers, was in

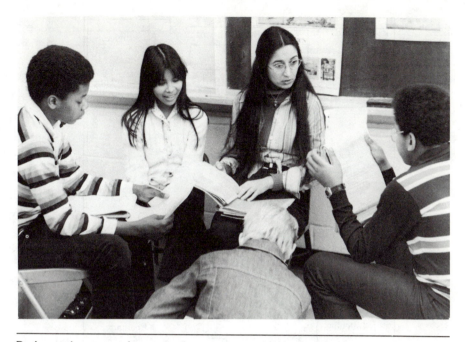

Desks can be arranged in circles for grouping and individualizing.

the back of the room. After the decision was made to group and individualize instruction, the desks were arranged in circles. Three to seven groups were taught each day, with individual students working independently when necessary. The table was converted into a listening station that became a key part of the instructional program. This example is an indication of what can be accomplished in an average content classroom when organizational strategies are varied to accommodate the students' individual needs.

To help the content teacher in arranging facilities, two diagrams showing arrangements that stress grouping and individualization procedures are provided in Figures 7.3 and 7.4. One of these designs is a typical content area classroom; the other is a vocational education classroom that shows a laboratory arrangement. These designs should not be considered the only appropriate arrangement of facilities. They are simply two of many ways to arrange the classroom for optimum instruction.

In addition to physical arrangement, the teacher must be concerned with the attractiveness of the classroom. A clean, attractive room helps to motivate students to learn. Bulletin boards, displays, and a convenient arrangement of materials also heighten student interest in content learning. Improving the classroom environment makes coming to school an enjoyable experience for both teacher and student.

REFLECTION

Your principal has asked that you design the ideal classroom for teaching in your content area. What would you include? Draw a floor plan to give to the principal.

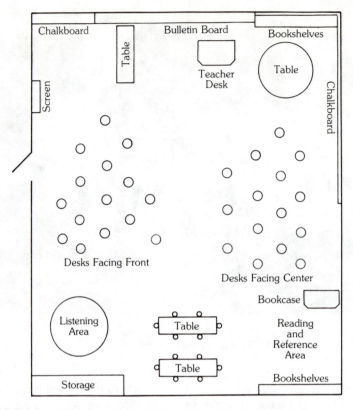

FIGURE 7.3

Content Classroom Arrangement (Nonlaboratory)

SUMMARY

In this chapter, the importance of classroom organization and management procedures in the content classroom is stressed. Properly used classroom management procedures not only enhance the learning environment, but improve the quality of teaching as well.

Strategies for organizing students for instruction are discussed. These include total class instruction, individualized instruction, and grouping. Grouping occupies a major role in effective classroom organization and management. Various grouping arrangements and their appropriate implementation are discussed at length. Four types of grouping procedures available to the content teacher are achievement, skills, interest, and peer grouping.

Techniques for effective management of instruction are mentioned, with tips that assist the content teacher in managing groups more effectively. A design for incorporating reading instruction and grouping in the content class is provided for the content teacher's perusal.

A section on arranging the facilities is also included, with two diagrams indicating possible arrangements for grouping and individualization procedures in the content classroom.

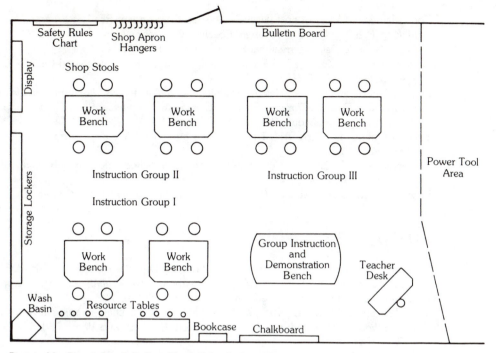

Designed by Ronnie Land, DeSoto Parish Schools, Louisiana.

FIGURE 7.4

Content Classroom Arrangement (Laboratory)

FOR DISCUSSION

1. You, like Ms. Smith, have decided to make some changes in the way your classroom, or a content classroom in which you have observed, is organized and managed. What changes would you make?
2. Consider the various grouping procedures discussed in this chapter. Tell how each procedure could be used in a classroom of your choice.
3. Discuss the pros and cons of using grouping procedures in the content classroom. Which procedure(s) would be best used in your classroom or a room in which you have observed?

OTHER SUGGESTED READINGS

Cassidy, Jack. "Cross-Age Tutoring and the Sacrosanct Reading Period." *Reading Horizons* 17 (Spring 1977):178–80.

Colwell, Clyde G. "Humor as a Motivational and Remedial Technique." *Journal of Reading* 24 (March 1981):484–86.

Deeds, Bonnie. "Motivating Children to Read through Improved Self-Concept." In *Motivating Reluctant Readers*, ed. Alfred J. Ciani. Newark, Del.: International Reading Association, 1981, pp. 78–89.

Doyle, Walter. *Classroom Management*. West Lafayette, Ind.: Kappa Delta Pi, 1980.

Flood, James. "A View of an Effectively Organized Secondary Reading Program." In *Making Reading Possible Through Effective Classroom Management*, ed. Diane Lapp. Newark, Del.: International Reading Association, 1980.

Herber, Harold L. *Teaching Reading in Content Areas,* 2nd ed. Englewood Cliffs, N.J.: Prentice-Hall, 1978. Chapters 4, 8.

Intile, JoAnn K., and Conrad, Helen. "Planning the Well Managed Classroom." In *Making Reading Possible Through Effective Classroom Management*, ed. Diane Lapp. Newark, Del.: International Reading Association, 1980.

Smith, Lawrence L. "Cross-Age Tutoring Using the 4 T's." *Reading Horizons* 21 (Fall 1980):44–49.

Stewer, Stephen J. "Learning Centers in the Secondary School." *Journal of Reading* 22 (November 1978):134–39.

Vacca, Richard T. *Content Area Reading*. Boston: Little, Brown, 1981. Chapter 2.

NOTES

1. John N. Mangieri, "Characteristics of an Effectively Organized Classroom," in *Making Reading Possible Through Effective Classroom Management,* ed. Diane Lapp (Newark, Del.: International Reading Association, 1980), p. 11.
2. Carl B. Smith, Sharon L. Smith, and Larry Mikulecky, *Teaching Reading in Secondary School Content Subjects* (New York: Holt, Rinehart, and Winston, 1978), p. 393.
3. David L. Shepherd, *Comprehensive High School Reading Methods,* 3rd ed. (Columbus, Ohio: Charles E. Merrill, 1982), pp. 192-93.

CHAPTER EIGHT

USING MATERIALS FOR CONTENT INSTRUCTION

Selecting materials, using the content textbook, adjusting materials, readability—why should the content teacher be concerned about these essentials to instruction plus the adjustments suggested in previous chapters? Although the actual instructional process is highly important, the selection and appropriate use of materials with which to implement it is equally important.

Following the teacher's choice of appropriate instructional strategies, the next logical steps are to determine the best classroom organizational procedures and to choose materials that elicit maximum effort from the students. Selecting or adjusting materials to student levels plays a key role in initiating a solid instructional program. Thus, the focus of this chapter is on selecting, adjusting, and using materials to enhance content reading instruction.

STUDY QUESTIONS

1. What is the importance of materials to content instruction?
2. What criteria should the teacher use in selecting materials for the various content areas?
3. What is readability? What role does it have in selecting materials and content reading instruction?
4. How does concept load affect the accuracy of readability formulas?
5. How does the teacher adjust materials to various levels?
6. How can teachers use a variety of materials to enhance content instruction?
7. What is undercutting and how is it used?
8. How can assignments be differentiated to accommodate various reading levels in a content classroom?

VOCABULARY

FOG
Fry Readability Graph
Material evaluation
Raygor Readability Estimate

Readability
SMOG
Undercutting

IMPORTANCE OF MATERIALS TO CONTENT INSTRUCTION

Content teachers are sometimes asked to teach classes with a limited amount of content related materials. The materials often consist of one textbook for each student and the teacher's notes. Unfortunately, this lack of materials forces the content teacher to rely heavily on lecture and classroom discussion methods of instruction. As a result, students who are good readers and listeners perform satisfactorily and average readers get by. It's the below-average readers who suffer, although many of them do absorb limited information from the teacher's lecture. In using only single textbooks and classroom lectures, good readers are insufficiently challenged, average readers learn only essential information, and below-average readers drag behind and become frustrated.

Today, some content teachers are being asked to teach more heterogeneously grouped classes with a single textbook, but definite changes are occurring. For example, teachers are recognizing the need to diversify teaching strategies, use classroom organizational and management procedures that facilitate instruction, and to develop materials that can accommodate the reading levels in a classroom.

Teachers are realizing, too, that materials must be matched with students' instructional reading levels. This necessitates having a variety of materials available whether they are teacher-developed or found in the library or elsewhere. Students given materials for their own instructional reading levels are less frustrated and actually become more actively involved in the learning process. Additionally, they cause fewer discipline problems. Materials written on a variety of reading levels, integrated with appropriate instructional strategies and good classroom organizational and management techniques, definitely improve content learning.

CRITERIA FOR SELECTING MATERIAL

When selecting material for use in the content classroom, specific steps should be followed to ensure that the materials are appropriate. Since students in a content classroom read on different levels, a first consideration should be that of supplying students with materials that enhance the instructional process. The following steps may be helpful.

First, the *needs of the students* must be identified. Using some type of diagnostic testing procedure, either formal or informal, the content teacher can obtain this information. For example, learning the instructional reading level of each student is essential. As discussed in Chapter 4, this information may be obtained from a variety of sources. Other important information that the content teacher should know is the reading skill knowledge of the students in the class. This assists in determining to what extent students are proficient in applying the skills necessary for understanding content material. Thus, in selecting materials, the teacher should consider which skills are important to students' levels of understanding as related to the skills they know. Materials should be used that encourage a continuation of growth and enhance the application of reading skills necessary for content learning.

Without this information there is no way, other than through trial and error, that students can be matched with appropriate reading materials. Likewise, in order to provide correct materials, the *level of the materials* must be determined. Techniques for determining these levels have been available to teachers for some time. These techniques are referred to as readability formulas or, in some instances, readability estimates or graphs. Readability procedures are discussed in greater depth later in this chapter.

LAGNIAPPE

Student reading level and the estimated readability level of a material do not have to match for a student to understand the material. A student reading at a seventh grade level may be able to read a material written at a ninth grade level, *but* his comprehension will not be as good as that of a student reading at a ninth grade level.

After the students' needs are ascertained and the level of materials determined, the next step in the selection process is to know the *interests of the students*. Although much of the material used in the content classroom does not allow for great flexibility of student interest, content teachers can allow some flexibility so that students can read concept-related materials of their choice. Materials should, of course, relate to the topic being taught; however, they may consist of any type of related material that increases student interest in content learning. Good readers are challenged through supplementary material, average readers learn adequately about the topic being studied, and below-average readers are given the opportunity to expand their knowledge of content information as well as to contribute to the class. The latter improves their self-esteem and enhances their prestige in the eyes of classmates.

The final step in selecting materials for the content classroom involves an *evaluation of the materials*. Content teachers should have the primary responsibility for choosing their instructional materials. This is often not the case. Content supervisors, principals, or a selection committee more commonly select both textbooks and supplementary materials. Often neither student nor teacher needs are considered, resulting in an unfortunate choice of materials.

As a means of alleviating this problem, or that of poor choices made by teachers themselves, some specific evaluation criteria must be followed. The teacher may develop or use an existing evaluation form[1] that states specifically the criteria to use in selecting materials or seek evaluation procedures or guides from state departments of education and local school districts. Two sample evaluation guides are presented below.

EXAMPLES

Criteria for Evaluating and Selecting Materials

1. Does the material include sufficient directions to the user so that it does not require students to have the very skills and understanding it purports to develop?
2. If a teachers' edition or manual accompanies the material, does it provide sufficient examples and suggestions for instruction?

3. Do the skills to which the material is directed relate to problems confronted in more realistic reading tasks?
4. Is the material appropriate to students' abilities, interests, and needs?
5. Does the material seem to lend itself to flexible, individual application in the class-room setting?
6. Will the content and format of the material promote interaction among pupils and between pupils and teachers?
7. Is the purpose of the material apparent to students, and will they be able to use it independently, given sufficient reading and study skills?
8. Is the appearance of the material attractive?
9. Does the material include a bibliography or additional resource material?
10. Is the material conducive to divergent, creative thinking, or is it convergent and dogmatic?

From Thomas H. Estes and Joseph L. Vaughan, Jr., *Reading and Learning in the Content Classroom* (Boston: Allyn and Bacon, 1978), p. 34.

Guidelines for Use in Evaluating Instructional Materials

Title of material: _____
Author(s): _____
Publisher: _____ Copyright Date: _____

	Yes	No
Content		
1. Meets needs and interest of the intended population	____	____
2. Is up-to-date and relevant to the times	____	____
3. Has a clear, concise style	____	____
Scope		
1. Is compatible with other materials and techniques being used	____	____
2. Coordinates well with other subjects	____	____
3. Complements objectives of district program	____	____
4. Is adaptable for varying types of teaching	____	____
Readability		
1. Vocabulary load is appropriate for level	____	____
2. Is strengthened by concepts	____	____
3. Is aided by language structure and length of sentences	____	____
4. Is appropriate for intended class	____	____
Format		
1. Includes appropriate type size and spacing	____	____
2. Has quality binding	____	____
3. Has adequate margins	____	____
4. Has quality illustrations	____	____
5. Provides for individual replacement of consumable parts	____	____
Teacher's Edition		
1. Provides sufficient direction	____	____

2. Provides adequate lesson plans   ____ ____
3. Identifies concepts to be taught   ____ ____
4. Provides suggestions for integrating reading skills in content materials   ____ ____
5. Defines terms   ____ ____

Evaluation
1. Provides individual or group assessment instruments   ____ ____
2. Provides suggestions for reteaching concepts and/or vocabulary   ____ ____

General Rating:
____ Recommend without reservation
____ Recommend with reservation
____ Not recommended

In reviewing or developing guides for use in evaluating content materials, the content teacher may use the following questions as criteria which must be considered.

1. Does the content of the material meet the needs and interests of the intended student population?
2. Is the style clear and concise?
3. Are these materials comparable with other materials already in use?
4. Is the material up-to-date and relevant to the times?
5. Is the readability level and concept level appropriate for the intended population?
6. Is the readability level compatible with the concept load?
7. Is the teacher's guide useful in presenting suggestions for teaching specific concepts to the students?
8. Are there suggestions as to how one can adapt instruction for the various reading levels in the classroom?
9. Do the materials enhance the learning of the identified concepts?
10. Is the information presented in an interesting or understandable manner?
11. Does the format of the material enhance its understanding and usefulness?

Using this criteria and a specific evaluation guide either adapted or developed for the content area, teachers should review different content materials to determine their usefulness in relation to the concepts being taught and student needs. Without careful evaluation, teachers may find that even with numerous materials, students' needs cannot be met due to inadequacies of the content presentation or levels of difficulty. Thus, content teachers should evaluate all materials in order to have the best possible tools to strengthen content learning.

REFLECTION

Select a content textbook and use one of the evaluation forms included in this chapter to determine the appropriateness of the book for a content class of your choice. What did you find? Is this text a good choice?

DETERMINING READABILITY

When content materials are being evaluated for possible use in the classroom, one consideration is the readability level of the materials. Readability involves the determination of the approximate grade level at which materials are written. Information provided from a determination of the readability level of materials used in the content classroom is helpful in assisting the teacher in matching materials with students' reading levels. Although publishing companies usually

Average number of syllables per 100 words

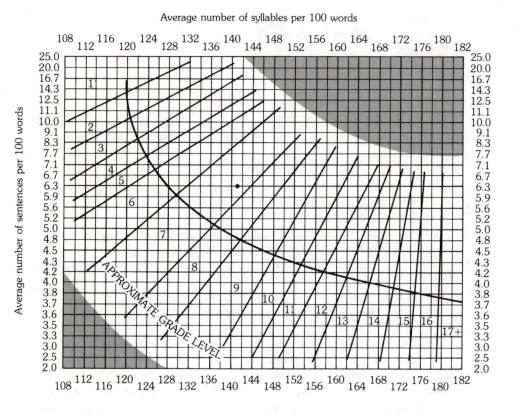

Directions: Randomly select 3 one hundred word passages from a book or an article. Plot average number of syllables and average number of sentences per 100 words on graph to determine the grade level of the material. Choose more passages per book if great variability is observed and conclude that the book has uneven readability. Few books will fall in gray area but when they do grade level scores are invalid

Count proper nouns, numerals and initializations as words. Count a syllable for each symbol. For example, "1945" is 1 word and 4 syllables and "IRA" is 1 word and 3 syllables.

	Syllables	*Sentences*
Example:		
1st Hundred Words	124	6.6
2nd Hundred Words	141	5.5
3rd Hundred Words	158	6.8
Average	141	6.3

Readability—7th grade (see dot plotted on graph)

FIGURE 8.1

The Fry Readability Graph

1. Count 10 consecutive sentences near the beginning of the text to be assessed, 10 in the middle and 10 near the end.
2. In the 30 selected sentences, count every word of three or more syllables. If a polysyllabic word is repeated, count each repetition.
3. Estimate the square root of the number of polysyllabic words counted. This is done by taking the square root of the nearest perfect square. For example, if the count is 95, the nearest perfect square is 100, which yields a square root of 10. If the count lies roughly between two perfect squares, choose the lower number. For instance, if the count is 110, take the square root of 100 rather than that of 121.
4. Add 3 to the approximate square root. This yields the SMOG grade, which is the reading grade that a person must have reached if he is to understand fully the text assessed.

G. Harry McLaughlin, "SMOG Grading—A New Readability Formula," *Journal of Reading* 12 (May 1969):639–46.

FIGURE 8.2

SMOG Readability Formula

provide a readability level for their materials, these levels may reflect an average for the entire set of materials, or a level determined in some unknown manner. Therefore, content teachers should be knowledgeable about ways of evaluating the readability levels of materials under review.

Four readability formulas appropriate for use by content area teachers are the Fry Readability Graph, McLaughlin's SMOG Readability Formula, Gunning's Fog Index, and Raygor's Readability Estimate.[2] These formulas are presented in Figures 8.1, 8.2, 8.3, and 8.4.

As compared to the Fry Graph, which is based on length of sentences and number of syllables in a selection, the SMOG is predicated on the theory that the difficulty of a selection can be determined by the number of polysyllabic words.

1. Take three 100-word passages; one from the beginning, one from the middle, and one from the end of the chapter or book.
2. Count the number of words in each passage that has three or more syllables. Do not count proper names, compound words or verb forms that become three syllables by adding ed or es.
3. Determine the average length of each passage, for example, 18 words per sentence. For a partial sentence, estimate the percentage that is included in the 100-word passage, for instance .6 of a sentence.
4. Total factors 2 and 3, and multiply the sum by 0.4. The result is the Fog Index for that passage. The score represents the approximate level of education needed to read the passage.

Robert Gunning, "The Fog Index After Twenty Years," *Journal of Business Communication* 6 (Winter 1968):3–13.

FIGURE 8.3

Gunning's Fog Index

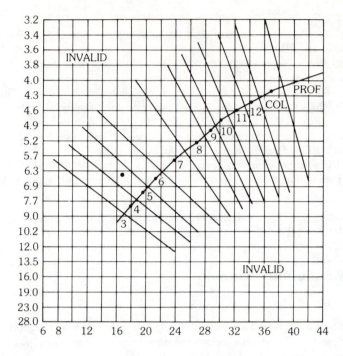

Directions: Count out three 100-word passages at the beginning, middle, and end of a selection or book. Count proper nouns, but not numerals.

1. Count sentences in each passage, estimating to nearest tenth.
2. Count words with six or more letters.
3. Average the sentence length and word length over the three samples and plot the average on the graph.

Example:	Sentences	6 + Words
A	6.0	15
B	6.8	19
C	6.4	17
Total	19.2	51
Average	6.4	17

Note dot on graph. Grade level is about 5.

FIGURE 8.4

Raygor Readability Estimate

The Fog Index differs somewhat from both the Fry Graph and the SMOG. In this formula, the primary components used for determining the reading level of a selection are sentence length and words with three or more syllables.

The Raygor Readability Estimate is a graph that is somewhat similar to the Fry Graph; however, there are two major differences in the formulas. In contrast to the Fry Graph, which covers grade levels one to seventeen plus, the Raygor Readability Estimate begins at the third-grade level and extends into an area designated as the professional level. The other major difference regards the procedures used in determining the readability level. Raygor uses sentence length and long words, those with six or more letters; the Fry Graph relies upon sentence length and the number of syllables in the selection.

An interesting alternative to readability formulas is proposed by Irwin and Davis.[3] They suggest the use of a readability checklist that analyzes the difficulty level of materials in terms of understandability and learnability for particular groups of students in content classrooms. The checklist is comprehensive and contains thirty-six items. Textbooks are rated on a scale from one to five, with one being the lowest rating and five the highest. The checklist follows the premise that after the content materials have been thoroughly analyzed, the resulting information assists content teachers in choosing the appropriate instructional strategies for their students. The checklist is presented in Figure 8.5.

Content teachers must also recognize the limitations of readability formulas. Readability formulas are helpful as a resource tool; however, teachers must remember that these formulas yield estimated reading levels and are not absolute measures of a material's readability level.

LAGNIAPPE

Remember that readability formulas consider but two elements in determining the level of a material—vocabulary and sentence length. Others to be considered are:

Prior student experiences
Teacher-introduction of information
Format of materials
Student involvement in learning
Awareness of purpose for reading
Organization of information
Interest in content

One element that must be considered when using readability formulas involves the theoretical basis from which readability formulas are developed. Readability formulas are based either on word difficulty and sentence length or number of syllables and sentence length in a selection. As a result, no consideration is given to the complexity of the concepts in the selection. The complexity of concepts, or *concept load*, in a selection increases the difficulty level of the materials being used for instruction. Often, content teachers rewrite materials to reduce the readability level, believing that a lower readability level should result in easier reading. However, because there is no formula available for measuring concepts, little can be done to alleviate this problem.

Because concept load cannot be measured, content teachers must rely on their judgment, even after reducing the readability level of the material. According to Nelson and Hittlemen,[4] this is a major consideration in questioning the effectiveness of readability formulas.

Difficulties in adjusting the concept load in math and science, for example, often result in frustration. Although many content teachers are aware of readability formulas and use them to determine the approximate levels of their materials, they sometimes find that the adjustment of readability levels does little to help students understand. The concept load simply remains too difficult.

A second element influencing readability formulas relates to the *different ways formulas are calculated*. One of these differences is tied to varying comprehension levels. For example, the Fry Readability Graph is based on 50-75% comprehension, which is roughly equivalent to the instructional reading level; the SMOG Readability Formula is based on 90-100% comprehension, which is equivalent to the independent reading level. Thus, the SMOG Readability

This checklist is designed to help you evaluate the readability of your classroom texts. It can best be used if you rate your text while you are thinking of a specific class. Be sure to compare the textbook to a fictional ideal rather than to another text. Your goal is to find out what aspects of the text are or are not less than ideal. Finally, consider supplementary workbooks as part of the textbook and rate them together. Have fun!

Rate the questions below using the following rating system:

5—Excellent
4—Good
3—Adequate
2—Poor
1—Unacceptable
NA—Not applicable

Further comments may be written in the space provided.

Textbook title: _____

Publisher: _____

Copyright date: _____

Understandability

A. _____ Are the assumptions about students' vocabulary knowledge appropriate?
B. _____ Are the assumptions about students' prior knowledge of this content area appropriate?
C. _____ Are the assumptions about students' general experiential backgrounds appropriate?
D. _____ Does the teacher's manual provide the teacher with ways to develop and review the students' conceptual and experiential backgrounds?
E. _____ Are new concepts explicitly linked to the students' prior knowledge or to their experiential backgrounds?
F. _____ Does the text introduce abstract concepts by accompanying them with many concrete examples?
G. _____ Does the text introduce new concepts one at a time with a sufficient number of examples for each one?
H. _____ Are definitions understandable and at a lower level of abstraction than the concept being defined?
I. _____ Is the level of sentence complexity appropriate for the students?
J. _____ Are the main ideas of paragraphs, chapters, and subsections clearly stated?
K. _____ Does the text avoid irrelevant details?
L. _____ Does the text explicitly state important complex relationships (e.g., causality, conditionality, etc.) rather than always expecting the reader to infer them from the context?
M. _____ Does the teacher's manual provide lists of accessible resources containing alternative readings for the very poor or very advanced readers?
N. _____ Is the readability level appropriate (according to a readability formula)?

Learnability

Organization

A. _____ Is an introduction provided for in each chapter?
B. _____ Is there a clear and simple organizational pattern relating the chapters to each other?

FIGURE 8.5

Readability Checklist

C. _____ Does each chapter have a clear, explicit, and simple organizational structure?

D. _____ Does the text include resources such as an index, glossary, and table of contents?

E. _____ Do questions and activities draw attention to the organizational pattern of the material (e.g., chronological, cause and effect, spatial, topical, etc.)?

F. _____ Do consumable materials interrelate well with the textbook?

Reinforcement

A. _____ Does the text provide opportunities for students to practice using new concepts?

B. _____ Are there summaries at appropriate intervals in the text?

C. _____ Does the text provide adequate iconic aids such as maps, graphs, illustrations, etc. to reinforce concepts?

D. _____ Are there adequate suggestions for usable supplementary activities?

E. _____ Do these activities provide for a broad range of ability levels?

F. _____ Are there literal recall questions provided for the students' self-review?

G. _____ Do some of the questions encourage the students to draw inferences?

H. _____ Are there discussion questions which encourage creative thinking?

I. _____ Are questions clearly worded?

Motivation

A. _____ Does the teacher's manual provide introductory activities that will capture students' interest?

B. _____ Are chapter titles and subheadings concrete, meaningful, or interesting?

C. _____ Is the writing style of the text appealing to the students?

D. _____ Are the activities motivating? Will they make the student want to pursue the topic further?

E. _____ Does the book clearly show how the knowledge being learned might be used by the learner in the future?

F. _____ Are the cover, format, print size, and pictures appealing to the students?

G. _____ Does the text provide positive and motivating models for both sexes as well as for other racial, ethnic, and socioeconomic groups?

Readability analysis

Weaknesses
1. On which items was the book rated the lowest?
2. Did these items tend to fall in certain categories?
3. Summarize the weaknesses of this text.
4. What can you do in class to compensate for the weaknesses of this text?

Assets
1. On which items was the book rated the highest?
2. Did these items fall in certain categories?
3. Summarize the assets of this text.
4. What can you do in class to take advantage of the assets of this text?

From Judith Westphal Irwin and Carol A. Davis, "Assessing Readability: The Checklist Approach," *Journal of Reading* 24 (November 1980):124–30. Reprinted with permission of the International Reading Association and Judith Westphal Irwin and Carol A. Davis.

FIGURE 8.5 (continued)

Readability Checklist

Formula may yield a score about two years higher than the Fry Readability Graph. No material, therefore, has an exact level according to the readability formulas.

This lack of exactness in readability levels is further noted as content teachers examine various textbook passages. It is not unusual for the readability level to vary from section to section or even on consecutive pages. Instances are reported of the readability varying as much as five or six grade levels within the same text. Obviously, this variance creates problems for the content teacher in attempting to match student reading levels with the appropriate level of materials. Because of the inconsistency, the readability level is usually reported by averaging or giving the range of levels. This is a method teachers can use more effectively.

A third element that must be considered in using readability formulas to evaluate content materials is *vocabulary*. The technical and specialized vocabulary in content materials increases the readability level; however, the concepts are often made more difficult by the multiple meanings of these words. This creates confusion. Students often find difficulty learning the meaning of vocabulary, especially when it is unfamiliar and does not relate to their prior reading experiences. In these instances, the actual readability level of the word may match a student's reading level, but the meaning the student associates with the word may not be correct in the context or content area.

This lack of understanding of content vocabulary or multiple-meaning words is critical in content reading and is not measurable by a readability formula. Campbell states that "subject-specific jargon" used in various content areas creates a significant problem when attempting to match material to reader.[5] Students must not only add new words to their vocabularies, they must also understand that the meaning of the same word may change from one content area to another. For example, the specialized word "base" changes meanings depend-

The average readability level of a newspaper is tenth grade.

ing on the content area. It has one meaning in mathematics, another in science, and yet another in language arts.

Efforts to lower the readability level of a selection becomes quite a task when specialized and technical vocabulary is involved. Because these terms are needed in the content reading selection, and because of the near impossibility of replacing these words with synonyms, readability formulas may not accurately reflect the difficulty level of the material. In these instances, content teachers should teach vocabulary rather than attempt to simplify the book.

LAGNIAPPE

The mean readability level of wire service articles in metropolitan newspapers is eleventh grade and nonwire articles average ninth to tenth grade. The average readability level of a newspaper is tenth grade.

See Wheat, Lindberg, and Nauman, *Illinois Reading Council Journal* (March 1977): 4–7.

Because of the *syntactical structure and semantic style* of some materials, another caution in accepting readability levels at face value occurs when evaluating materials composed of figurative and poetic language. Although readability formulas may indicate a specific level for this type of material, content teachers would be wise to view the results with reservation. Poetry does not follow the same kind of pattern as prose; thus, the rules for determining the readability level are not always applicable. Even if the readability level of poetry could be determined accurately, the problem of figurative language becomes a variable for consideration. This is also true of prose and plays that rely heavily on figurative language. English teachers or others using these types of materials must, therefore, use their judgment in conjunction with readability formulas.

Characteristics of the reader is a fourth element that influences the accurateness of the readability formula. Students' background experiences, interests, language, environment, and concept knowledge as well as other cognitive and affective areas that influence the reading act cannot be measured by a readability formula. Material that is readable by one student with a tenth grade instructional reading level may not be appropriate for another student with different characteristics who is reading at the same level. These individual reader differences should be weighed by the content teacher along with the level indicated by a readability formula. As Hittleman suggests:

> "Readability" is a "moment" at which time the reader's emotional, cognitive, and linguistic backgrounds interact with each other, with the topic, and with the proposed purposes for doing the reading, and with the author's choice of semantic and syntactic structures all within a particular setting. At such a "moment," the material is a constant on which two main sets of forces are being exerted: one, the characteristics of the reader; the other, the elements of the situation—actual and perceived."[6]

After examining all the factors that may affect the reliability of readability formulas, teachers may wonder why they are used at all. As stated previously, readability formulas are used primarily to provide an estimate of the reading level of the content materials the teacher may use. This level can be used in conjunction with the teacher's judgment to determine if specific stories, chapters, or passages in a material are suitable for use in the content classroom.

REFLECTION

Use all four of the readability formulas included in this chapter to check the level of a content textbook. Compare the results from the different formulas. Then compare the results from the readability formulas to the results from the Readability Checklist. Why do you think the results differ?

ADJUSTING MATERIALS

The availability of more easily used readability formulas such as those previously mentioned has encouraged some teachers to assume they should attempt to rewrite content materials to provide for the various reading levels in a heterogeneously grouped content classroom. Recent research, however, clearly indicates that there are difficulties inherent in shortening compound, complex sentences and substituting more easily understood words for polysyllabic words. Implications from Pearson's research suggest that reducing the sentence length or grammatical complexity may in fact increase the difficulty of understanding.[7] A series of shorter sentences requires the reader to infer an intersentence relationship in order to arrive at the meaning of passages.[8] Thus, shortening sentences without changing concept load may even interfere with, rather than enhance, comprehension.[9]

Klare suggests that words are more consistently predictable than the sentence variable when each is considered separately;[10] therefore, the content teacher might assume that by using synonyms and higher frequency words in lieu of polysyllabic words to adjust the readability level of materials, the student's ability to comprehend this material would be enhanced. Although the readability level is adjusted to a specific reading level, compensating for concept load and specialized and technical vocabulary becomes a problem.[11]

Teachers must exercise caution when rewriting materials and substituting high frequency words for the purpose of lowering the level of the material, because word frequency counts do not include all aspects of word difficulty. For example, the word *light* undergoes changes in meaning depending on its position in a sentence. It may be a verb, as in the sentence *"Please light the fire"* or an adjective, *"The light bulb is blown"* or as a noun, *"The light is turned on."* As this word changes in usage, the meaning also changes. Used as one part of speech, the word may be a high frequency word. However, when the usage changes, the meaning may become more complex, with the word actually no longer being a high frequency word, since high frequency word lists do not consider changes in meaning.

Although current research does not support rewriting materials, many content teachers may find themselves in situations with no materials available other than the textbook, which may be too difficult for some students in the class to use. In these instances, teachers may wish to rewrite *limited* sections of the textbook in order to accommodate as many students as possible. If teachers do any rewriting of their materials, they should remember all of the concerns expressed in the preceding paragraphs. Teachers must remember that rewriting content materials is time-consuming and tedious. However, when caution is followed in rewriting or undercutting,[12] the procedure is helpful in providing instructional materials to a more diverse group of students. As stated, undercutting requires shortening the length of sentences and reducing the number of polysyllabic words in a selection. Caution must be exercised to maintain the integrity of technical and specialized vocabulary as well as concept information.

For content teachers wishing to rewrite materials, the following guidelines may be helpful:

> List the general and specific objectives you wish the materials to meet.
> Keep in mind the experiential background of the target population.
> Consider the objectives of the students.
> Write in a natural style and edit when the selection is completed.
> Vary the length of sentences and paragraphs.
> Use concrete illustrations.
> Where appropriate, use a narrative style and contractions.
> Try the materials on students reading at the level indicated by the readability formula.
> Revise the material in accordance with the results.[13]

REFLECTION

Select several paragraphs from a content text. Check the readability level of the selection using the formula of your choice. Then, following the guidelines given in this section, rewrite the paragraphs aiming at a lower level. When complete, use the same readability formula to check the readability level again. Did you succeed in lowering the level? Is the passage easier to read? What kinds of difficulties did you experience with this activity?

OBTAINING MATERIALS FOR CONTENT INSTRUCTION

In following the content reading model presented in this text, the teacher's instructional emphasis is on concept development rather than textbook teaching. Thus, a variety of materials may be used to implement instruction. Some of the following suggestions are readily available to the content teacher, while others may require additional effort to prepare or obtain.

Because of the heavy reliance on textbooks, the teacher should obtain a variety of related textbooks at different grade levels. For example, the teacher with an eighth-grade American history class may wish to use textbooks designed not only for eighth-grade students, but also textbooks originally written for students in the upper elementary grades. Since the readability level of these books is lower, more students have an opportunity to use a textbook that is comprehensible. Teachers may locate textbooks at different levels by perusing book rooms in the school or by visiting the old textbook warehouse in the school district.

Of further assistance in textbook teaching are the books designed for a specific grade level, but written on differentiated readability levels. These books look exactly alike and contain similar information written at different readability levels. They are most effective in strengthening instruction in the content class; however, they are not readily available for all content areas at this time.

Another source of content materials that teachers may wish to consider are supplementary materials. These may be paperbacks, skill development material specifically designed for various content areas, newspaper and magazine stories that relate to the content topic, or related pamphlets and brochures. Many government agencies and commercial businesses provide free materials that can be used to enhance content teaching. A catalog specifying available sources for such materials is in all public libraries. Such materials not only provide additional content material, they also add interest to content learning through the use of current information presented in a more realistic format.

In addition to using supplementary materials, teachers should investigate fully the library facilities. Usually, there are numerous books written on content area topics paralleling classroom instruction; also books and encyclopedias that supplement the content area and develop personal reading skills. The librarian is a valuable resource in helping content teachers locate appropriate books on different reading levels for their classes.

Other materials that assist content teachers in providing effective instruction in the classroom are films, filmstrips, slides, pictures, and photographs. Photographs are effective in teaching comprehension to secondary school students as well as in significantly improving their morale.[14]

Another valuable resource for content teachers is the audiotape. The teacher may establish a learning station where one or several students can listen to cassette recordings on topics related to the content material. These recordings may

The audiotape is a valuable resource for content teachers.

be teacher-made and may involve any materials pertinent to the topic. Additionally, parts of the textbook may be recorded for those students who seem to learn better through auditory means. Research studies have shown that using taped information along with corresponding printed material improves student reading.[15] As a further note, some publishing companies are beginning to publish taped programs that cover an entire textbook. These should prove useful in many content classes.

REFLECTION

Make a list of five materials that you could obtain at no charge to provide additional materials to enhance a unit of your choice.

DIFFERENTIATED ASSIGNMENTS

Differentiating assignments in the content class is important because all students do not read on the same level or conceptualize information at the same rate. Content teachers, therefore, need to accommodate the different learning and reading levels in making assignments, the same as in instruction. Some of the following suggestions for differentiating assignments should be most helpful to content teachers in dealing with this problem area. These suggestions should widen each student's opportunity for satisfactorily completing the assigned task and improving concept learning.

One technique suggested for differentiating assignments is referred to as "slicing."[16] To use this process in the content classroom, the following steps should be followed:

> Differentiate concepts by assigning more concepts to better readers and fewer to less able readers, thus allowing the less able reader to focus on fewer topics, so that conceptualization is less difficult.
>
> Reduce the amount of material that the students are expected to read according to the reading proficiency, with poorer readers given the least amount.
>
> Divide technical and specialized vocabulary into categories that enable students to work at different levels.
>
> Vary the level of understanding by simplifying questions. This does not mean that some students deal with less important concepts, but rather, that the concepts are approached in a different way.[17]

Other suggestions for differentiating assignments include: varying the levels of understanding through questioning strategies, allowing students to choose the level of assignments they wish to complete; giving basic assignments with various possibilities for extension and enrichment; providing guidance by giving a purpose for an assignment; and ensuring the appropriate selection of materials to enable students to complete their assignments.

Because of the variety of student levels in the content classroom, teachers must differentiate assignments to encourage all students to become successful learners. Allowing everyone to learn the content concepts and contribute to class discussions creates an atmosphere in which content learning is interesting.

This, in turn, motivates both the teacher and the students to become readers of content information as well as content readers for enjoyment.

SUMMARY

Appropriate use of materials for content instruction is important in successfully implementing a content reading program. Although the amount of materials available may be limited, this does not prohibit the content teacher from getting maximum use of whatever material is available. Because of the diverse reading levels in content classrooms, teachers must provide materials to students on their levels to better facilitate instruction. Reliance on one textbook with little or no adjustment for various student levels is rarely successful; thus, it is important to provide a variety of materials to increase the probability of student success.

When selecting materials, it is important to follow specific criteria to assist in making practical choices: students' needs must be identified, their reading levels determined, and their interests ascertained. A final step in selecting materials for the content classroom involves an evaluation of the materials being considered. Evaluation procedures with specific criteria are presented in this chapter.

Another important part of selecting materials is readability. Determining the readability level of content materials is a useful tool for the teacher as long as the following considerations are remembered:

1. The determination of readability levels is based on sentence length and syllable count in a selection; concept complexity, or load, is not regarded.
2. Various readability formulas may be calculated differently, resulting in contradictory reading levels obtained for the same passage.
3. Technical and specialized vocabulary increase the difficulty level of selections. As a result, the readability level of those selections may indicate the correct reading level, but not accurately reflect the difficulty level.
4. Because of their syntactical structure and style, the results obtained from evaluating readability levels with figurative and poetic language should be viewed with caution.
5. Such reader characteristics as background experiences, language, environment, and concept knowledge are all elements that affect the accuracy of readability formulas.

Readability formulas that may prove useful to the content teacher are the Fry Graph, the SMOG, the FOG Index, and the Raygor Readability Estimate. An alternative to the readability formulas, the Irwin and Davis Readability Checklist, is also presented.

Current research shows that adjusting materials is an ineffective means of providing appropriate materials for students. Teachers may find, however, that their situations are so devoid of the right kind of materials that rewriting is the only corrective means of instructing their students at the appropriate levels. If limited rewriting is done, the teacher should follow the specific guidelines discussed in this chapter.

Content classroom materials may be obtained from many sources. Textbooks covering readability levels are useful. Supplementary materials like paperbacks, magazines, and brochures can be effective. The library is a source that can provide not only printed materials, but also films, filmstrips, slides, pictures, photographs, and audiotapes.

After all the materials are assembled, teachers must use differentiated assignments to accommodate the different learning and reading levels in content classes. Such techniques as "slicing," varying the levels of understanding through questioning strategies, allowing students to choose the level of assignment they wish to complete, and other suggestions discussed in this chapter are ways of differentiating assignments in a content class.

FOR DISCUSSION

1. Why do readability formulas give only an indication of the readability level of a material? Are there more accurate means of determining readability?
2. Why are materials so important in content instructions? How can content teachers better match materials with student needs?
3. Identify five criteria that should be considered in evaluating content materials. Tell why each is important.
4. With many different reading levels represented in every content class, how can the teacher differentiate assignments to better meet student needs?

OTHER SUGGESTED READINGS

Allington, Richard L., and Strange, Michael. "The Problem with Reading Games." *The Reading Teacher* 31 (December 1977):272–74.

Baldwin, R. Scott, and Kaufman, Rhonda K. "A Concurrent Validity Study of the Raygor Readability Estimate." *Journal of Reading* 23 (November 1979):148–53.

Cardinell, C.F. "Rewriting Social Studies Materials to Lower Reading Levels." *The Reading Teacher* 30 (November 1976):168–72.

Elkins, John, and Davies, Graeme. "Logical Connectives and Readability of Textbooks." *Reading Education* 3 (Spring 1978):15–23.

Fitzgerald, Gisela G. "How Many Samples Give A Good Readability Estimate?—The Fry Graph." *Journal of Reading* 24 (February 1981):404–10.

Forgan, Harry W., and Mangrum, Charles T. *Teaching Content Area Reading Skills*, 2nd ed. Columbus, Ohio: Charles E. Merrill, 1981. Modules 1-3.

Gilliam, Bettye; Peña, Sylvia C.; and Mountain, Lee. "The Fry Graph Applied to Spanish Readability." *The Reading Teacher* 33 (January 1980):426–30.

Harker, W. John. "Materials for Problem Readers: Why Aren't They Working?" *Journal of Reading* 18 (March 1975):451–54.

Harris, Albert J., and Jacobson, Milton D. "A Framework for Readability: Moving Beyond Herbert Spencer." *Journal of Reading* 22 (February 1979):390–98.

Irwin, Judith Westphal. "Implicit Connectives and Comprehension." *The Reading Teacher* 33 (February 1980):527–29.

Lamberg, Walter J., and Lamb, Charles E. *Reading Instruction in the Content Areas*. Chicago: Rand McNally, 1980. Chapter 7.

Layton, James R. "A Chart for Computing the Dale-Chall Readability Formula Above Fourth Grade Level." *Journal of Reading* 24 (December 1980):239–44.

Lowery, Lawrence F., and Leonard, William H. "Development and Method for Use of an Instrument Designed to Assess Textbook Questioning Style." *School Science and Mathematics* 78 (May/June 1978):393–400.

Manzo, Anthony V. "Imbedded Aids to Readers: Alternatives to Traditional Textual Material." *New England Reading Association Journal* 14 (1979):13–18.

Morrow, Lesley Mandel. "Manipulative Learning Materials: Merging Reading Skills with Content Area Objectives." *Journal of Reading* 25 (February 1982):448–53.

Roe, Betty D.; Stoodt, Barbara D.; and Burns, Paul C. *Reading Instruction in the Secondary School*, Rev. Ed. Chicago: Rand McNally, 1978. Chapter 7.

Singer, Harry, and Donlan, Dan. *Reading and Learning From Text*. Boston: Little, Brown, 1980. Chapter 8–9.

Smith, Carl B.; Smith, Sharon L.; and Mikulecky, Larry. *Teaching Reading in Secondary School Content Subjects*. New York: Holt, Rinehart, and Winston, 1978. Chapter 12.

Standal, Timothy C. "Readability Formulas: What's Out, What's In?" *The Reading Teacher* 31 (March 1978):642–46.

Trapini, Fred, and Walmsley, Sean. "Five Readability Estimates: Differential Effects of Simplifying a Document." *Journal of Reading* 24 (February 1981):398–403.

Troy, Anne. "Literature for Content Area Learning." *The Reading Teacher* 30 (February 1977):470–74.

Vacca, Richard T. *Content Area Reading*. Boston: Little, Brown, 1981. Chapters 10–11.

NOTES

1. Thomas H. Estes and Joseph L. Vaughan, Jr., *Reading and Learning in the Content Classroom* (Boston: Allyn and Bacon, 1978), p. 34.

2. Edward Fry, "Fry's Readability Graph: Clarifications, Validity, and Extension to Level 17," *Journal of Reading* 21 (December 1977):242–52; Robert Gunning, "The Fog Index After Twenty Years," *Journal of Business Communication* 6 (Winter 1968):3–13; G. Harry McLaughlin, "SMOG Grading—A New Readability Formula," *Journal of Reading* 12 (May 1969):639–46; Alton L. Raygor, "The Raygor Readability Estimate: A Quick and Easy Way to Determine Difficulty," in *Reading: Theory, Research and Practice*, ed. P. David Pearson, Twenty-sixth Yearbook of the National Reading Conference (Clemson, S.C.: National Reading Conference, 1977), pp. 259–63.

3. Judith Westphal Irwin and Carol A. Davis, "Assessing Readability: The Checklist Approach," *Journal of Reading* 24 (November 1980):124–30.

4. Joan Nelson, "Readability: Some Cautions for the Content Area Teacher," *Journal of Reading* 21 (April 1978):620–25; Daniel R. Hittleman, "Readability, Readability Formulas, and Cloze: Selecting Instructional Materials," *Journal of Reading* 22 (November 1978):117–21.

5. Anne Campbell, "How Readability Formulae Fall Short in Matching Student to Text in the Content Areas," *Journal of Reading* 22 (May 1979):683–89.

6. Daniel R. Hittleman, "Seeking a Psycholinguistic Definition of Readability," *The Reading Teacher* 26 (May 1973):783–89.

7. P. David Pearson, "The Effects of Grammatical Complexity on Children's Comprehension, Recall, and Conception of Certain Semantic Relations," *Reading Research Quarterly* 10 (1975/76): 155–92.

8. George Klare, "Assessing Readability," *Reading Research Quarterly* 10 (1975/76):62–102; J. Dawkins, *Syntax and Readability* (Newark, Del.: International Reading Association, 1975).

9. Joan Nelson, "Readability: Some Cautions for the Content Area Teacher," pp. 620–25.

10. George Klare, "Assessing Readability," p. 96.

11. Joan Nelson, "Readability: Some Cautions," p. 623.

12. Edwin H. Smith, *Literacy Education for Adolescents and Adults* (San Francisco: Boyd and Fraser, 1970), p. 120.
13. Edwin H. Smith, *Literacy Education for Adolescents and Adults*, pp. 121–22.
14. Marilyn J. Taylor, "Using Photos to Teach Comprehension Skills," *Journal of Reading* 21 (March 1978):514–17.
15. Mary H. Neville and A. K. Pugh, "Reading While Listening: The Value of Teacher Involvement," *English Language Teaching* 33 (October 1978):45–50; Helen Schneeberg, "Listening While Reading: A Four Year Study," *The Reading Teacher* 30 (March 1977):629–35.
16. P. David Pearson and Dale D. Johnson, *Teaching Reading Comprehension* (New York: Holt, Rinehart, and Winston, 1978), pp. 184–89.
17. John F. Readence and David Moore, "Differentiating Text Assignments in Content Areas: Slicing the Task," *Reading Horizons* 20 (Winter 1980):112–17.

CHAPTER NINE

LESSONS FOR TEACHING CONTENT READING

Content area teachers in the local school district discussed, studied, and reviewed different teaching ideas given for incorporating reading into their content classes. They recognized that the Directed Learning Activity provided an organizational structure for their instruction, but they were not confident of their skills in applying the strategies in their classes. The lead teachers in each school, therefore, met with their faculties and proposed that teachers in each content area work together to develop lessons that followed the Directed Learning Activity format. The steps in the model for content instruction were reviewed with emphasis placed on the instructional component. As an integral part of this review, each teacher was provided with a copy of the model, as shown opposite.

This chapter presents sample lesson plans developed in the content areas of social studies, mathematics, English, science, vocational education, physical education, music, and business education.

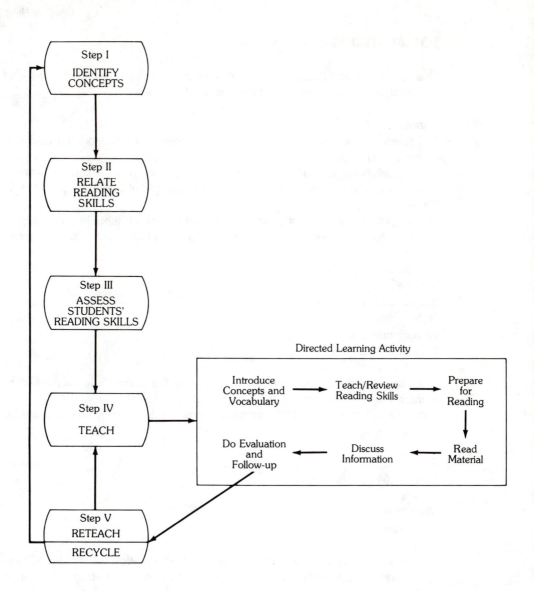

Step I
IDENTIFY
CONCEPTS

Step II
RELATE
READING
SKILLS

Step III
ASSESS
STUDENTS'
READING SKILLS

Step IV
TEACH

Step V
RETEACH
RECYCLE

Directed Learning Activity

Introduce
Concepts and
Vocabulary → Teach/Review
Reading Skills → Prepare
for
Reading

Do Evaluation
and
Follow-up ← Discuss
Information ← Read
Material

SOCIAL STUDIES

One group of social studies teachers designed a lesson for a tenth grade world history class. The concepts identified for teaching were:

Concepts
1. Imperialism represents the desire of one country to expand outward into another country or territory.
2. Imperialistic expansion is a policy to gain a foothold in a country without regard to the wishes of the government or people of that country.

In discussing these concepts, the teachers noted that students had to comprehend the following vocabulary words to help them understand the concepts:

Vocabulary
Imperialism
Surplus capital
Nationalism
Protectorate
Sphere of influence

As the teachers considered the concepts and the materials to be read, they realized also that students had to use several reading skills in order to understand the information. The following skills were identified as being important for review.

Reading Skills
Cause-effect relationships
Details
Main idea
Sequence

The teachers also realized that the textbook information was written following an enumeration pattern and a relationship pattern. This pattern information had to be reviewed prior to asking the students to read the materials.

Having identified the concepts and vocabulary, as well as the reading skills and organizational patterns, the social studies teachers felt ready to begin their instruction. However, according to the model for content instruction, they first had to have some assessment of students' various levels and skill needs. The teacher, whose class for which this lesson was designed, provided the following information and suggestions for further assessment:

Assessment
1. Using a cloze procedure, the range of reading levels within this tenth grade class was from a second grade to beyond high school level. With the results, the teacher placed the students into four groups:

   Group I (tenth grade reading level and above)—9 students
   Group II (seventh to ninth grade reading level)—12 students
   Group III (fifth to seventh grade reading level)—7 students

Group IV (second to fourth grade reading level)—3 students
2. A Group Reading Inventory was needed to assess the students' skills in understanding cause-effect relationships, noting sequence, and identifying enumeration and relationship patterns in a text. The assessment would be administered to students in Groups I, II, and III. During this time, the teacher could provide additional instruction to the students in Group IV.

With the diagnostic information of reading levels compiled, the teachers proceeded with their plans for instruction.

Using the results of the test, the social studies teacher must decide whether the concepts have been learned at an acceptable level. If most of the students adequately understand the concepts, then the class progresses to a new group of concepts. If most have not mastered this information, however, the teacher must reteach those concepts not learned. When only a few students do not understand some of the concepts, the social studies teacher should proceed to the new concepts, which in this example would be other events leading to World War I, and reteach those students by providing additional materials to read or by asking questions that help them clarify the concepts that were not developed.

Social Studies Lesson Plan

Introduce Concepts and Vocabulary

1. Use a structured overview procedure.
2. List these terms on board: imperialism, industrial revolution, surplus capital, nationalism, protectorate, condominium, concession, sphere of influence, missionary zeal.
3. Guide students into defining terms through questions and context clues.
4. As students define terms, list key words characteristic of imperialism.
5. Ask students if the United States could be called imperialistic.
6. Ask students to use a map and identify countries these characteristics describe.

Teach/Review Reading Skills

Main idea and details
1. Define skills for class and demonstrate how main ideas and details are identified in a selection. Read the selection while showing it to the class with an overhead transparency. After reading ask:

   What is the selection about? (main idea)

   What are you told about missionaries in this selection? (details)

   Underline the details as they are identified.
2. Give students two selections on an overhead transparency. Ask them to select the main idea or tell what each selection is about. Ask different students to underline the details that tell more about the main idea.
3. Show students how the details enumerate on the main idea. This is an enumeration pattern and is used in the text material.
4. Divide the class into groups to apply these skills as needed according to the results of the Group Reading Inventory.

Groups I and II: Read page 537 in the text and identify the pattern by noting the main idea and supporting details. Outline the information.

Group III: Read a worksheet passage on imperialism and identify the main idea and details.

Group IV: Work with the teacher using the worksheet passage on imperialism to identify the main idea and details.

Cause-effect Relationships

1. Introduce the skill by defining it for the class using a realistic situation such as "Your dad gives you the car with a warning not to drive over 55. However, you meet some friends, forget your dad's advice, and get a ticket (cause). What will happen (effect)?"
2. Use a passage related to the topic on an overhead transparency. Ask students to identify cause and effect in each passage. They should realize that some cause-effect situations are stated, while others are implied.
3. Provide students with selections from which they can identify cause-effect relationships.

Groups I and II: Use a selection from the text, pages 539–540. Ask students to read the selection and decide how the information is organized. Is it an enumeration pattern or does it use cause-effect relationships? Once the pattern is noted, ask them to identify the different cause-effect relationships.

Groups III and IV: The teacher should work with these students using an easier selection taken from a library book. They need to be guided in identifying the relationships and led to develop their own cause-effect relationships by the end of the discussion.

Sequence

1. Discuss with the class that history material is often organized in chronological order. Use the section of the chapter, pages 541–544, in which German imperialism is discussed. Outline on the board the order of events that occurred.
2. Ask students to work in groups of five, using the illustration on page 546 to outline the significant imperialistic movements after 1870.

Note: During skill development the social studies teacher should allow all students to participate in skill activities; also have more involvement with students who appeared deficient in a certain skill on the Group Reading Inventory.

Prepare for Reading and Read Materials

1. Review the SQ3R study strategy with the class.
2. Divide the class into four groups according to their reading levels. Provide each group with materials on their level and ask them to use the SQ3R study strategy.

Group I: Library materials including books and reference materials.

Group II: History textbook, Chapter 20.

Group III. Easier library materials and some pamphlets from the Department of Defense.

Group IV: Filmstrip and accompanying tape on imperialism and a rewritten section of the text that has been duplicated.

3. Ask students to SURVEY the materials and form QUESTIONS that they wish to have answered as they read. To guide their survey of the material, the teacher may provide a concept guide.
4. Direct the students to READ the materials after their questions are formed.
5. Ask the students to refer individually to the questions and RECITE the answers to themselves after their reading is complete.

6. REVIEW materials to check all answers or to locate any answers of which the individual is unsure.

Discuss Information

1. Initiate a discussion by grouping the students as follows:

   Groups I and II: Have them interact using a free discussion format guided by the initial questions formulated by both groups.

   Groups III and IV: Have them interact using a teacher-directed discussion format guided by questions posed by both groups as well as teacher-generated questions.

2. Pull all groups together for a total class-controlled discussion. The teacher uses a prepared list of questions relating to the identified concepts. Questions such as the following could be used:

   What is imperialism?

   Why do countries become known as imperialistic countries?

   Identify three imperialistic countries prior to the 1900s and tell why each is considered to be imperialistic.

   In the future, how will imperialism affect the course of history?

Do Follow-up

1. Involve Group I in an enrichment activity in which they design a plan of expansion for the United States and China.
2. Ask Group II to develop a map of German expansion between 1870 and 1914.
3. Let Groups III and IV make a time line of British expansion until 1914.
4. Evaluate the students' knowledge of the concepts using a written test. Students have an option of taking the test on their own or listening to a tape of the exam and writing their answers. Group IV will take the same exam, but will receive teacher assistance in spelling words, etc., or will give oral responses.

MATHEMATICS

The mathematics teachers designed a lesson for an eighth grade class. The concepts identified for teaching were:

Concepts
1. Decimal notation can be used to represent rational numbers.
2. Numbers can be written in expanded notation form.
3. Fractions have decimal equivalents.

In order to teach these concepts, the math teachers decided that the following vocabulary words must be introduced to help students understand the concepts.

Vocabulary
Expanded notation
Decimal
Exponent
Rational number
Decimal notation

As math teachers considered the concepts that had been identified, they realized that students must use several reading skills in order to understand the information. The following skill was identified as being important for review.

Reading Skill
Reading tables, examples and illustrations

The teachers also realized that the textbook was written following an enumeration pattern. Therefore, techniques for reading this pattern had to be reviewed prior to assigning work with the text.

Because math is a skill area for which there is often little correlation with reading levels, the math class for which this lesson is designed was diagnosed through a math skills checklist, obtained through observation and standardized test data. Additional information on students' skills in interpreting tables and examples, as well as on following a problem-solving procedure in working word problems in math, can be determined by using a Group Reading Inventory.

Assessment
1. The math skills checklist indicated that 15 students were ready to learn all 3 concepts, 10 students could learn concepts 1 and 2, and 5 students could learn only concept 1
2. A Group Reading Inventory was needed to determine how well students could read examples and tables related to decimals and to what extent they could understand word problems using decimals.

Using this diagnostic information, the math teachers continued to develop their plans for teaching these concepts.

From the results of the test, the teacher can regroup students for reteaching, if necessary. To assist in reteaching concepts, the math teacher may use additional peer-grouping procedures to allow students who learn quickly to work with slower students.

Mathematics Lesson Plan

Introduce Concepts and Vocabulary

1. Use an inductive procedure for introducing the concepts.
2. Put the following items on the board: $1/2$, $.50$, 10^1, 10^{-1}, $1/4$, $.25$.
3. Ask these questions.
   If $3/4$ is a fraction, identify the other fractions on the board.
   If $.30$ is a decimal notation, identify the other decimal notations on the board.
   If 21^1 has an exponent, what is an exponent? Find another example of a positive exponent on the board. A negative exponent.
   If $3/25$ is a rational number, identify another rational number on the board. How is a rational number different from a fraction?
4. Put this example on the board:

   $427 = (4 \cdot 100) + (2 \cdot 10) + (7 \cdot 1)$ or
   $\qquad (4 \cdot 10^2) + (2 \cdot 10^1) + (7 + 10^0)$

How could 32 be said in another way? 986? 2.96? 36.28? These changes are called expanded notation. Why do you think the procedure is called expanded notation?

5. Show students how a decimal notation can be used to represent a rational number. Ask students to develop an example.

6. Give students a fraction and show them how it can be changed into a decimal equivalent.

Teach/Review Reading Skills

1. Put a mathematical table on an overhead transparency to show how place value is used in decimal notation. After showing the table to students, ask them the following questions:

   What do the numbers 10^6, 10^5, etc., on the bottom line of the chart represent? Use the chart to find out what 10^1 means; 10^2; 10^0; 10^{-2}.

2. Give students the numerals 561.7 and ask them to use the table to put the number in an expanded notation form. Try other examples such as 34.3, 36.102, 5.1, 10.6.

3. Put a definition on the board such as: An expanded notation is a representation of a whole number as a sum of powers of ten.

4. Write this example following the definition:

   $$5243 = (5 \cdot 10^3) + (2 \cdot 10^2) + (4 \cdot 10^1) + (3 \cdot 10^0)$$

   Show students how the example expands and clarifies information in the definition.

5. Give students the following diagram and example to study prior to solving the problem.

1-place decimals	2-place decimals	3-place decimals
↓	↓	↓
21.6	21.65	21.651

   3.46 is a _____ place decimal.
   .659 is a _____ place decimal.

6. Show students how to look for a concept or idea followed by expanded information used in the text example on page 194. Point out that this is an enumeration pattern.

Prepare for Reading and Read Materials

1. Review the SQRQCQ study strategy with the class.

2. Divide the class into three groups according to their skill knowledge and provide each group with problems to work related to their skill level.

3. Ask students to SURVEY the first problem in their assignment to decide what it is about.

4. Direct students to QUESTION themselves about what is being asked.

5. Ask students to READ the problem again carefully to determine what they are being asked to do.

6. QUESTION students or let them question themselves on what processes should be used.

7. Direct students to COMPUTE the problem based on the answer of the previous question.

8. Ask students to QUESTION their answer to determine if it logically follows what the problem asked.

9. Suggest that students follow this procedure to complete the assigned problems.

Discuss Information

1. Assemble the class according to the three groups so that they can discuss the answers and solutions to the problems.
2. Put the class together as a total group, and, using problems representing the different concepts being taught, let them discuss the solution as they compute the problems. Students can learn from one another in this type of group discussion.

Do Follow-up

1. Pair off students, give them a worksheet of problems, and let them work together to reach a solution. Students should be selected from different skill groups when this form of peer-tutoring is used.
2. Evaluate students using a three-part written exam. Each part should relate to one of the concepts.
3. Ask students to complete the entire exam.
4. Score students on the part(s) related to the concepts they were to learn and use the other exam parts as diagnostic data for reteaching.

ENGLISH

The language arts teachers designed a lesson for a lower group of ninth graders. The concept identified for teaching was

Concept
Figures of speech give variety, ambience, and an added dimension in communication.

In order to understand this concept, the teachers identified the following vocabulary words to help the students understand the concepts:

Vocabulary
Metaphor
Simile
Personification
Hyperbole
Figurative language

As the language arts teachers considered the concept to be taught, they realized that students must not only learn to identify figurative language, but they needed several other reading skills. Thus, the following skills were identified as being important for review.

Reading Skills
Perceiving relationships
Comparison/contrast

With the concepts and needed reading skills identified, the language arts teachers then attended to assessing student ability to apply the necessary skills in identifying figures of speech. The class for whom this lesson was designed read on varying levels from a low second grade to low sixth grade level. With such low reading levels, students read very few materials containing figures of speech. The language arts teacher, therefore, needed other diagnostic information to determine how well students understood figures of speech.

Assessment
1. Using a modified cloze procedure, the teacher gave students five incomplete sentences containing incomplete figures of speech.
2. A group Reading Inventory was needed to assess the students' skills in technical vocabulary knowledge, perceiving relationships, and comparison/contrast.

Realizing that students had little experience in recognizing figures of speech and knowing from observation that they seldom used them in their conversations, the language arts teachers outlined their lesson plan.

As students begin to use figures of speech in their writing and receive positive feedback from the language arts teacher, their writing shows more excitement. Students who overlook these figures of speech should be reminded regularly to include them in their writing activities.

Additionally, as a review, the teacher may provide these students with samples of the various figures of speech to encourage their use. For students who show no understanding of this concept, the teacher should provide individual instruction as time permits. The concept is not one that must be mastered before moving on to another; reteaching can occur at the discretion of the teacher.

English Lesson Plan

Introduce Concepts and Vocabulary

1. Follow an inductive procedure to introduce the concepts. Using a cartoon-type chart, let students read examples of the different figures of speech.
2. Read students a poem, "Daffodils," by Wordsworth.
3. Ask students what is different about the sentences in the cartoon, the lines in the poem, and the way materials are usually written. Guide them to note that in these examples things are compared to something else.
4. Use a structured overview to help students relate the characteristics of the four figures of speech. Write the terms metaphor, simile, personification, and hyperbole on the board. Then read examples of each figure of speech. Ask questions that help lead students to identify each figure of speech.
5. Use a transparency that shows the vocabulary word, its pronunciation, and definition. For example: metaphor (met-a-4): An expression taken from one field of experience and used to say something about another. Do this for all four figures of speech.
6. Read sentences that contain different figures of speech and ask students to categorize them.

Teach/Review Reading Skills

Perceiving relationships
1. Use a sentence like, "Don't make a pig of yourself." Show students that the two ideas

expressed are a *pig* and *yourself.* Explain that in a metaphor, one idea is related to another in a figurative way.

2. Ask students to explain why *pig* is used in this sentence rather than *cat* or *dog.*
3. Discuss what is needed for a relationship.
4. Give students other examples on an overhead transparency and guide them as they locate the relationships.

Comparison/contrast

1. Put an example of a simile on the board: "He is as mad as a hornet today."
2. Show students that in this sentence the person is being compared to a hornet.
3. Give students a list of similes on the board and ask them to take turns telling what is being compared in the sentences.
4. Ask students to complete a worksheet on which they are to identify the ideas being related in the metaphors and mark the comparisons in the similes. When the worksheet is complete, students form groups of two or three to go over their answers.

Prepare for Reading and Read Materials

1. Review the four figures of speech and ask students to give an example of each.
2. Read from the book *Amelia Bedelia,* by Peggy Parish, to show them how figures of speech must be interpreted in order to be understood, but how much more interesting the story is because of the use of this language.
3. Provide each student with a poem or passage written at their level that contains figures of speech.
4. Review the PARS study strategy to guide students as they read to determine what the selection is about and what figures of speech are used.
5. Ask students to first PREVIEW the selection to decide what it is about.
6. Guide students in ASKING QUESTIONS to guide their reading. Such general questions as, "What figures of speech are used?" and, "How do figures of speech affect the information?" should be used by all students.
7. Ask students to READ the selections with their questions in mind.
8. Guide students in SUMMARIZING what they have read by checking their knowledge with questions generated prior to reading.

Discuss Information

1. Use randomly selected discussion clusters for students to review their selections and to choose at least one example of each figure of speech to share with the class.
2. Put all groups together to share their findings and to discuss again the characteristics of the four figures of speech.

Do Follow-up

1. Direct each student to develop an example of one of the figures of speech. Write a sentence using the figure of speech and do an illustration that literally interprets the sentence.
2. Ask the students to write several paragraphs about a topic of their choice. Students must include at least one figure of speech in each paragraph.
3. Evaluate students based on their use of figures of speech in language and in their weekly writing activities.

Science

The science teachers chose a tenth grade earth science course to use for their lesson plan. The concepts identified for teaching included:

Concepts
1. The bodies within the solar system have a specific pattern of movement.
2. Each of the planets have certain physical properties.
3. The sun holds members of the solar system in orbit.
4. There are inner planets and distant planets in the solar system.

In discussing these concepts and reviewing the science textbook, teachers noted that students had to comprehend the following vocabulary words in order to understand the concepts.

Vocabulary

Nebular	Density
Centrifugal force	Specific gravity
Perihelion	Photosphere
Aphelion	Chromosphere
Inertia	Axis

As the teachers considered the concepts to be learned, they identified several reading skills that needed to be reviewed with students prior to asking them to read the science materials.

Reading skills
Main ideas and details
Comparison/contrast
Structural analyses

The teachers also realized that the textbook was written using an enumeration pattern and a relationship pattern. Students needed a review of these patterns before reading.

With the identification of concepts and reading skills, the science teachers had to determine the students' reading needs. The earth science teacher had an idea of student reading levels, but other information was needed.

Assessment
1. Using a Simplified Reading Inventory, the teacher divided the class into three groups based on their ability to read the textbook. The three groups were:

    Group I: Could read the text as well as outside materials.

    Group II: Could read the text with only minimum difficulties; these problems were solved when concepts and vocabulary were introduced.

    Group III: Could not read the text.

2. A Group Reading Inventory was needed to assess the students' skills in sci-

entific vocabulary, main idea and details, and comparison-contrast. This assessment should be administered to the students in Groups I and II. As these groups complete the inventory, the science teacher can either reteach or begin to develop the new concepts for students in Group III.

Using diagnostic data along with general information on students' reading levels, the teacher proceeded with instructional plans.

Using the results of the test, the science teacher must determine if any of the concepts should be retaught before going on to another group of concepts that are an expansion of these ideas. If reteaching for a few students is necessary, a class period should be taken to do so, while involving the other students in related research projects.

Science Lesson Plan

Introduce Concepts and Vocabulary

1. Use a deductive strategy to introduce the concepts.
2. Tell students they will be studying about the solar system. As they study and discuss the information, attention should be given to several concepts: how the bodies within the solar system move, the physical properties of each planet, the effect of the sun on the planets, and the differences in the planets.
3. Give students a list of vocabulary words they should know when reading about the solar system. Two lists may be used, one for Groups I and II and another for Group III. The words for Group III may include names of planets, and the words asteroids, meteoroids, and comets.
4. Work with the class as a whole, and go over the meanings of words that Groups I and II must know. Through discussion of these words, Group III should absorb more about the concepts to be learned. As these terms are taught, note the word parts in *peri-helion* and *aph-elion* and *photo-sphere* and *chromo-sphere*. Use these parts to help determine the meanings of the words.
5. Provide a vocabulary guide to Groups I and II. Ask that they use their text and any other material to complete the guide.
6. Work with Group III to introduce their vocabulary. Use several vocabulary activities to help these students become familiar with recognizing as well as knowing the meanings of these terms.

Teach/Review Reading Skills

Skill instruction and review should be scheduled based on student needs from the Group Reading Inventory information. Those students not involved in the review of different skills should be working in small groups using a pattern guide to prepare for reading their materials.

Main idea and details
1. Define skills for class and demonstrate how main ideas and details are identified in a related selection. Show the selection to the group with an overhead transparency. After reading the selection ask:

   What is this selection about? (main idea)
   What are you told about the sun in this selection? (details)

2. Give students a selection on an overhead transparency and ask them to tell what the selection is about. Then ask different students to underline the details that tell more about the main idea.
3. Outline the information to show students how the details enumerate on the main idea. Use a passage from the text to show the enumeration pattern.
4. Give students two additional selections for which they should identify the main idea and details.

Comparison-contrast
1. Introduce the skill by telling students that when two or more items or ideas are alike, they can be compared; when they are different, they can be contrasted.
2. Provide an example of a selection that compares gravity on the different planets. Go through the selection with the class and list the comparisons.
3. Follow the same procedure with a selection that compares and contrasts Earth with another planet.
4. Point out the relationships that exist in such a passage. For example, the relationship of weight to the force of gravity on each planet is discussed in the selection.
5. Ask students to work through three examples on their own to identify the comparisons or contrasts and the relationships within the selection.
6. Provide time for students to discuss their answers and show them how the selection is written in a relationship pattern.

Prepare for Reading and Read Materials

1. Preview the PQRST study strategy with the class.
2. Divide the class into three groups according to their reading levels. Provide each group with materials they can read and that relate to one or more of the concepts.

   Group I: Article (that includes new discoveries about the planets) from a science journal.
   Group II: Earth science textbook.
   Group III: Issue of a science newspaper written on a lower reading level, and several library books on the solar system.
3. Ask students to PREVIEW their materials and form QUESTIONS they want to answer as they read. These questions give students a purpose for reading.
4. Provide time for students to READ the materials to answer their questions.
5. Ask students to TEST themselves when they complete the reading to see if they can answer the questions originally asked.
6. Provide other activities for students to extend their learning of the solar system as they complete their reading. A filmstrip on the solar system, supplemental books, and pictures may be available to further their understanding of the concepts.

Discuss Information

1. Use a semicontrolled discussion procedure with students randomly chosen to form four groups.
2. Provide several leading questions to initiate the discussion, letting the students know that the purpose of the discussion is to learn as much as possible from one another.
3. Organize students as a total class for a controlled discussion directed by the teacher using questions that expand on information from different materials.

Do Follow-up

1. Involve Group I in a research project to learn how astronauts deal with weightlessness in space.
2. Involve Group II in a research project to find out what astronauts learned about formation of the solar system on their last trip.
3. Ask Group III to develop a mural of the nine planets revolving around the sun using information from materials, discussions, or any other sources to make it as accurate as possible.
4. Evaluate students on a written exam over all concepts. For students who wish to use it, an audiotape of the exam is available if they cannot read the questions.

VOCATIONAL EDUCATION

The vocational education teachers decided that a lesson for a home economics class in which students were learning to cook would provide a basic plan that others could duplicate. The lesson was designed for an eighth grade junior high school class. The concept was:

Concept
Successful cooks read and carefully follow the recipe.

In considering this concept, teachers noted that students must be introduced to certain vocabulary words in their first experience with cooking. The following vocabulary words were identified:

Vocabulary

Recipe	Grater	Brown
Preheat	Wire rack	Spatula
Yield	Drain	Beat
Utensils	Simmer	Grease and flour
Liquid measuring cup	Dry measuring cup	

As the vocational teachers considered the concept and tasks that students were to be involved with, they realized that several reading skills had to be reviewed. Therefore, the following skills were identified:

Reading Skills
Abbreviations and symbols
Following directions and sequence
Details

After identifying the concept and vocabulary as well as reading skills, plans had to be made for assessing students' reading levels and reading skill knowledge. Because the home economics teacher did not know the students' reading levels, the following diagnostic procedures were outlined.

Assessment

1. The teacher checked the students' school records for achievement test reading scores.
2. The teacher also checked with the reading teacher who had instructed some of the students in the special reading class. From the Informal Reading Inventory that had been administered, the instructional reading level for these students was determined.
3. The language arts teachers had previously administered a cloze test to all eighth graders. Hence, the home economics teacher checked their lists of student reading levels.
4. To assess the students' skills in applying skill knowledge to reading recipes, the home economics teacher designed a Group Reading Inventory to measure the skills of interpreting abbreviations and symbols, following directions and sequence, and noting details. The assessment instrument would be administered to all students in the class to determine their skill knowledge.

With the approximate reading levels of the students determined and a design for a Group Reading Inventory, the vocational teachers proceeded with their lesson plans.

Based on teacher observation, the students are evaluated on their skills in reading and following recipes. Because the new concepts to be taught relate to more complex recipes, the teacher must group the class according to those who must learn more about following simple recipes and those who are ready to move to more difficult recipes. Using this procedure, some students are retaught while others move ahead.

Vocational Education (Home Economics) Lesson Plan

Introduce Concepts and Vocabulary

1. Use an inductive strategy to introduce the importance of following a recipe.
2. Write a recipe on the board and go through it, continuously talking to the class, not paying attention to the recipe, and not following the directions. The purpose is to demonstrate without telling the students that recipes must be followed carefully in order to have a successful product.
3. Give each of eight tables an identical set of cards containing vocabulary words and abbreviations. Ask students to group similar words together. Students must pool their knowledge on the task. Unknown words should be put aside.
4. Go over the vocabulary words in free discussion and ask students to match words with objects.
5. Give students a vocabulary sheet with each term defined for reference.
6. Review the parts of a recipe including ingredients and steps to be followed.
7. Use a practice recipe and ask students to identify the ingredients and name the utensils needed.

Teach/Review Reading Skills

Understanding abbreviations
1. Use an overhead transparency to show students a list of recipe abbreviations and the words for which they stand.
2. Discuss the meaning of words used in recipes.
3. Give students a vocabulary guide to review vocabulary words and abbreviations. Use pictures, scrambled words, matching, and completion activities.

Noting details
1. Put a recipe for making pizza cups on an overhead transparency and read it to the class. Then ask questions such as

   How much ground beef do you need?
   How hot should the oven be?
   What do you add to the ground beef when it is browned and drained?

2. Help students find the information in the recipe, and underline the answers.
3. Explain that these are details and that recipes have many details that must be read carefully.
4. Give students another recipe and a series of questions that must be answered with details.
5. Provide extra assistance to students who demonstrated a poor understanding of this skill on the Group Reading Inventory. Form a skills group with these students and work with them while the other students work independently.
6. Put the students together as a total class to discuss their answers.

Following directions and sequence
1. Use the pizza cup recipe again. Ask students questions like

   What do you put in the skillet first?
   When do you separate the biscuit dough?
   Do you put the biscuit dough or meat mixture into the muffin cups first?
   When do you sprinkle the pizza cups with cheese—before or after baking?

2. As students answer the questions, show them how they are putting details in sequence for following directions.
3. List the steps of the pizza cup recipe in sequence using a $1-2-3$ format. (This should help students see the sequence.)
4. Remind students of the mess the teacher made the day the recipe was demonstrated and directions not followed. Discuss the importance of following recipe directions in a specific order.
5. Provide students with two additional recipes along with a list of questions that require the use of their skills in following directions.
6. Work separately with those students who had difficulty with this skill on the Group Reading Inventory. The other students should work independently.
7. Put the students together as a total class to discuss their answers and review the steps in following a recipe.

Prepare for Reading and Read Materials

1. Use a study guide to help students note and remember important details as they read.
2. Ask students to read pages $71-76$ in their textbooks and to complete the study guide as they read. Go over the study guide to help students understand what they are looking for as they read.
3. Direct the eight students whose reading level is too low for reading the text to work

with the teacher in a corner of the class. The teacher can read the information to the students while they follow along and complete their study guides.

Discuss Information

1. Initiate a class discussion using several of the study guide questions as a beginning. Then use a list of prepared questions to stimulate using this information for application in the kitchen.
2. Divide the class into discussion groups with one group per table. Give each group a recipe. Ask students to discuss ingredients and utensils needed, the order in which the recipe is to be followed, and the estimated amount of time needed to prepare this recipe.

Do Follow-up

1. Give students a simple recipe for making fudge cake. Ask them to review the recipe, prepare their grocery order, and check their kitchen for utensils because they are going to work in groups to bake the cake.
2. Go over time schedules and job tasks.
3. Prepare cake and put in refrigerator; clean up.
4. Ice cakes, taste, and clean up.
5. Evaluate students' abilities to follow the recipe as well as teacher-directions.

PHYSICAL EDUCATION

The physical education teachers decided that their lesson plan should relate to tennis, which is taught in both junior and senior high school physical education programs. The specific concepts were related to learning to keep score in tennis.

Concepts
1. 0 points is called "love."
2. 1 point is called "15."
3. 2 points is called "30."
4. 3 points is called "40."
5. 4 points is called "game."
6. A score of 40 to 40 is called "deuce."
7. The score following "deuce" is called "advantage."
8. A game must be won by two points.
9. Six games is a set.
10. A player must win two sets to win the match.

To understand these concepts, the physical education teachers selected the following terms as being of most importance:

Vocabulary	Match
Game	40
Love	Deuce
Advantage	15
30	Set

In addition to learning this specialized vocabulary, the physical education teachers also realized that students had to apply reading skills in order to fully understand the concepts. The following reading skills were selected for review:

Reading Skills
Following directions
Notetaking

Because the lesson required little reading, the physical education teachers did not attempt to determine the reading level of each student. However, they were interested in knowing how well students followed directions and took notes.

Assessment
1. The teachers developed an observation checklist for each class. One skill listed was following directions. During several preceding class periods, teachers observed the students who had difficulty following directions. Observation sheets were marked so that teachers could provide special help to these students.
2. To determine the students' ability to take notes, teachers collected students' physical education notebooks. They were reviewed and individual weaknesses were noted on the observation form.

With the assessment procedures outlined, concepts and vocabulary identified, and reading skills noted, the teachers proceeded to develop their lesson plans.

As students are evaluated, the physical education teacher may find that some continue to have difficulty in keeping score. For these students, the teacher may form a special group and reteach the information while others practice.

Introduce Concepts and Vocabulary

1. Use a deductive strategy to introduce concepts.
2. Set up a bulletin board that shows how tennis is scored.
3. Put the different points and their technical names on an overhead transparency.
4. Show one line at a time and discuss what it means in a tennis game.
5. Outline the information so that students can copy it from the screen. (Most students are poor notetakers.)
6. Use a videotape of a game between Chris Evert-Lloyd and Tracy Austin. Ask students to listen to the way the game is scored.
7. Discuss the scoring procedure.
8. Use several vocabulary exercises to reinforce the terminology.

Teach/Review Reading Skills

Because some students do not need additional work in following directions, they should be given a scoring card, asked to view another videotape, and score the game.

Following directions

1. Use the rules to demonstrate the importance of listening and following directions.
2. Select two students, one the server and one the receiver, and read them specific directions. They are to demonstrate the action as it is read.
3. Discuss the importance of listening to every word in a direction. If one word is not followed, the direction often becomes confused.
4. Put students in groups of three. One gives the directions while the others follow. The teacher provides each group with a sheet of directions. When a student does not follow a direction, that student becomes the directions giver.
5. Use this procedure for several weeks as a five-minute class warm-up.

Notetaking

1. Call the entire class back together.
2. Discuss the importance of taking good notes. Students must learn to identify the most important parts of information and write them down, rather than every word the teacher or book says.
3. Show students a selection about tennis on an overhead transparency.
4. Use a marking pen to highlight the most important concepts in the selection. Explain that these are the major areas discussed in the selection.
5. Underline information important to remember about each of these areas.
6. Show students an outline of this information as it should appear in their notes.
7. Give a brief lecture on the history of tennis, providing the students with an outline to follow and expand in their notes.
8. Divide the class into groups to compare notes and ask questions about ideas that were missed.
9. Use visuals to help guide lectures and also as an aid to students in their notetaking. Include a brief lecture in every other class period. Slowly remove the visuals and help students listen and study independently.

Prepare for Reading and Read Materials

1. Use a one-page duplicated sheet that discusses scoring procedures for tennis and a three-level study guide to help students understand the important ideas.
2. Go over the questions in the three-level study guide so that the students will know what to look for as they read.
3. Ask students to read the materials and answer questions in the study guide. If help is needed, the teacher is available or the selection has been prerecorded to accommodate each student's needs.

Discuss Information

1. Ask students to work in groups of six to eight to discuss their answers on the study guide.
2. Assemble the class as a total group and give scoring situations to discuss.

Do Follow-up

1. Divide the class into tennis teams for doubles and assign an extra student to keep score. The scorekeeper position should rotate so that everyone has an opportunity to practice keeping score.
2. Evaluate students' skills during the next two weeks in which they are practicing.

MUSIC AND ART

The music and art teachers decided that a lesson plan for secondary music students that related to creating music would provide a basic lesson plan that could be tied to both areas. The concepts identified were:

Concepts
1. A word, rhythm, or harmonic approach can be used to create music.
2. Poetic meter and mood influence the choice of time signatures used in creating music.
3. Cadences indicate the ends of phrases of music.
4. A musical sentence is a complete musical idea consisting of two or more phrases.

To understand these concepts, the teachers identified the following vocabulary words as important for study:

Vocabulary

Cadence	Forephase
Afterphase	Nonharmonic tones
Neighboring tones	Passing tones
Binary form	Ternary form

As the music teachers considered the concepts that had been identified and the materials to be used, they realized that students must use several reading skills in order to understand the information. The following skills, therefore, were identified as being important for review.

Students must use a number of reading skills in understanding musical concepts.

Reading Skills
Contextual analysis
Following directions
Understanding examples or illustrations

Because music is a performing art for which there is often little correlation with reading levels, the music class for whom this lesson was designed was diagnosed for their musical abilities using an observation checklist. The use of this checklist began early in the school year; the teacher, therefore, reviewed it only to determine the students' readiness to learn these concepts. Additional information about the students' abilities in applying reading skills in music can be determined by using a Group Reading Inventory.

Assessment
1. The music observation checklist showed that sixteen students could learn the concepts as well as apply them in creating music. However, six students would have difficulty once they reached the application stage.
2. A Group Reading Inventory was needed to determine how well students could associate the new vocabulary in content and use examples or illustrations to further understand the text.

Using this diagnostic plan, the music teachers continued to develop their lesson for teaching these concepts.

For students who do not learn the concepts taught in this lesson, the music teacher may reteach as the class progresses to new information. These concepts are not necessary in order to move on the next lesson, so an immediate reteaching is not essential. The teacher may also use peer grouping and, as a change of pace during the semester, ask students to work together to create music for a special event or a person. Having students who have learned the concepts and enjoy creating music work with other students who do not know the information helps spread enthusiasm throughout the class.

Music Lesson Plan

Introduce Concepts and Vocabulary

1. Use an inductive teaching strategy to introduce the concepts.
2. Put a short written verse on an overhead transparency. Ask students if they could write a song from this. Lead them to recognize that some song writers begin with a verse and then add music.
3. Put a nursery rhyme showing an accented pattern on an overhead transparency. Ask if this nursery rhyme could be made into a song using the accent pattern. Lead students to understand that songs must have verses with a rhythm.
4. Discuss the rhythm approach to creating music. Include how the mood of the rhythm and the meter of a poem influence the creation of music.
5. Provide students with verses and a time signature for each. Put students in groups to count out the rhythm for each verse.
6. Put a line of music on an overhead transparency. The notes should consist of only one chord per measure and should be limited to a choice of I, IV, and V7 chords. Ask students if this could be made into a creative piece of music. Lead them to recognize that harmony may serve as a beginning to music.

7. Show students how notes from the chord may be repeated and set with a rhythm of the composer's choice.

8. Summarize the presentation by telling students that they have discussed three ways that music can be created—the word approach, the rhythm approach, or the harmonic approach. Explain that musicians have different preferences and sometimes combine these approaches to develop their own style.

9. Tell students that they are going to learn how to create music using each of the three approaches. They must first become familiar with words that composers use.

10. Introduce the identified vocabulary words by listing them on the board. On a duplicated sheet, give the students an example of each term, but do not put the term on the page. As the teacher gives the definition of a term in the context of a sentence, ask students to work in groups of two or three to locate the correct example. Then discuss why it is an example of the term. This will remind students that context clues must be used as they learn the meanings of new terms.

11. When all terms have been discussed, give students a vocabulary guide to use as they review the terms.

Teach/Review Reading Skills

Following directions
1. Use an example of a verse that needs to be written with an appropriate rhythm. Give these directions on an overhead transparency: Use 2/4 time with this verse. Write the time signature at the beginning and draw in bar lines as required.
2. Tell students the important parts of these directions that must be followed. Underline them on the transparency.
3. Give students another example along with a set of directions that asks that they clap a specified rhythm and add an appropriate conclusion. Ask students to underline the most important parts in the directions that they must remember.
4. Provide several examples with the directions. Ask students to underline the most important parts in the directions that they must remember.
5. Work with the six slowest students in a group if they seem to have difficulty.

Understanding examples or illustrations
1. Put a narrative explanation followed by an example on an overhead transparency. Show students how the example helps them visualize what the narrative says. Help them understand that examples cannot be skipped, but should be carefully studied.
2. Give another explanation followed by two examples, one that relates and another that does not. Ask students to study the information and decide which example goes with the narrative. Discuss how they made the decision and how the example expands the narrative information.
3. Ask students to look in their activity book, page 154. On the first page of their material there is an example of the word approach to writing music. Read the narrative and the example to show how the example extends the narrative information. Discuss students' comments.

Prepare for Reading and Read Materials

1. Use a concept guide to help students follow the information related to each of the approaches to creating music. They can complete the guide as they read.
2. Ask students to read the materials by sections, i.e., they should read the word approach first; after applying this information, they move to the rhythm approach, etc.

3. Assign pages 154-157 to be read to learn how to create music using the word approach. When students finish, put them in groups of two, being sure that the six slowest students are not paired together, and ask them to use this approach to create a verse. Share the verses when they are complete.
4. Ask students to read pages 158-161 to learn how to create music using the word approach. Follow the same procedure as outlined in #3 to allow them to apply their reading.
5. Read and apply information on the harmonic approach as outlined in the previous steps.

Discuss Information

1. Initiate a class discussion by asking students which approach they preferred and why.
2. Put those who preferred the word approach together in a group, the rhythm approach in a group, and the harmony approach in a group. Ask each group to identify specific reasons why they preferred their approach, how they carried out the approach, and to try to persuade others that their way was best.
3. Reassemble the class as a whole and ask students to use their persuasive skills as they discuss each approach.

Do Follow-up

1. Allow students to work alone or with another person to create a new piece of music.
2. Pair the six slowest students together in groups of three and work with them.
3. Evaluate the product of each student as the "musical masterpiece" is presented to the class.

BUSINESS EDUCATION

The business education teachers selected for their lesson a portion of an advanced typing course. The concepts related to preparing a student to type in a medical office.

Concepts
1. Typing an abstract of a medical research report requires skill in typing multiple copies and careful attention to medical terms.
2. A medical secretary must be able to compose brief office memos for general correspondence.
3. Forms such as Medicare and other insurance forms as well as patient identification cards must be typed by the medical secretary.
4. Medical secretaries must type reports of surgery and medical letters.

In learning these concepts, students come in contact with numerous medical terms and abbreviations. These must only be typed, however, and the understanding of each is not essential. No new vocabulary words are needed.

The business education teachers, however, realized that students had to apply several reading skills in order to be efficient medical secretaries. The following reading skills were identified:

Reading Skills
Adjusting rate of reading according to purpose.
Reading charts and tables
Following directions

To assess students' skills in applying these skills in their typing, the teachers administered a Group Reading Inventory.

Assessment
A Group Reading Inventory following a slightly different format was needed. The inventory should be administered through typing, with students being given several paragraphs in a technical medical report to type. Their skill in adjusting rate should be assessed in this manner. To determine their skill in reading charts and following directions, the students should be given a Medicare form to complete, along with directions.

Using information from this inventory, the typing teacher can adjust instruction within the lesson. Figure 9.8 presents the business education teachers' lesson.

Students who seriously desire to pursue this occupation but are unable to develop these basic skills to become a medical secretary, may practice independently. The teacher should note their progress and, if they do not show marked improvement, encourage them to consider other opportunities as a typist.

REFLECTION

Select a content area of your choice and develop a lesson. Be sure to:

Identify concepts and vocabulary
Select necessary reading skills
Plan for assessing the students
Outline instruction using the Directed Learning Activity format
Consider reteaching alternatives

Business Education (Typing) Lesson Plan

Introduce Concepts

1. Use a deductive strategy for introducing the concepts.
2. List the following tasks that must be performed by a medical secretary on an overhead transparency:

   Type a medical research report
   Compose brief office memos
   Complete insurance forms and other necessary forms
   Type reports of surgery or other treatments

3. Discuss the tasks and what kinds of typing skills are needed for each.
4. Ask students to type a selection for their speed and control test for the day. The selection describes the responsibilities of the medical secretary.

5. Discuss the pros and cons of being a medical secretary as compared to those of a legal secretary, which has previously been studied.

Teach/Review Reading Skills

Adjusting rate according to purpose
1. Give the students their rate score on the inventory. Ask them to compare that score with their score on the previous speed test.
2. Discuss the differences in the scores and reasons for these differences.
3. Point out that medical secretaries must be careful to type exactly what the doctor gives, and that familiarity of terms, as well as rate, increases with experience.

Read charts and following directions
1. Give each student a sample insurance form and the directions. Also put sample data that could be used to complete the form on the board. As a class, review each step in the directions and decide first how the information should be put on the form. Then type in the information before continuing with the directions.
2. Give students other insurance forms along with appropriate data for completion. Ask them to type the forms.
3. Discuss the forms when they are complete, first allowing the students to discuss their work with one another, and then talking as a class about common problems.

Prepare for Reading and Read Materials

1. Review the need for adjusting rate according to the student's purpose and ability to follow directions.
2. Assign the students lessons 292–295 in their typing books.
3. Review each assignment as it is turned in.
4. Work with individual students as problems come up.

Discuss Information

1. Talk about some of the problems noted in typing medical information.
2. Ask students how they can solve those problems if they want to become a more efficient medical secretary.

Do Follow-up

1. Give students other examples of medical information to type.
2. Compare their initial rate with their current speed in typing medical information.
3. Evaluate the students on an exam consisting of the different types of medical typing.

SUMMARY

This chapter provides examples of lesson plans that follow the model for content instruction outlined in this text. Eight different content area lessons are presented for review by teachers who wish to implement reading instruction in their content classroom. Health teachers should use the science lesson as an example, and foreign language teachers should find the English lesson helpful.

In each lesson, specific concepts and vocabulary are identified. Reading skills needed to learn these concepts are also specified. Various informal assessment procedures are discussed to identify the reading strengths and weaknesses of the students. Using this information, a Directed Learning Activity format is applied to each of the content areas to provide an outline of lessons that incorporate reading instruction into content teaching.

FOR DISCUSSION

1. How do the identification of concepts and vocabulary, selection of related reading skills, and assessment relate to what the teacher plans in the DLA? Could a DLA be implemented appropriately without this information? How?
2. In what ways do these lessons differ from the usual content lessons? What features of these lessons do you like most? Least?

CHAPTER TEN

CONTENT INSTRUCTION FOR STUDENTS WITH SPECIAL NEEDS

As the content teachers in the Leon School District met to discuss their progress in incorporating reading into their classes, a concern of many seemed to be just how to teach students with special needs. Mr. Murphy had four students who were mainstreamed into his science class from the EMR room; Mrs. Estaras had many students in her eighth grade English classes who were poor readers; Ms. Johnson and several other teachers had students for whom English was a second language; and each teacher had at least one student who could be considered gifted. Additionally, there were several Chapter I schools with a major portion of the students from low-income families and extremely limited experiential backgrounds. What could be done to provide better content instruction to the students?

Realizing there are no simple solutions to this complex issue, the teachers decided to give some time to the problem, in hopes that ideas would emerge to help them expand their content reading program. As a first step they identified several questions (see Study Questions) that could serve as a guide for their discussions and future inservice sessions.

Using these questions as their guide, the content teachers sought suggestions from reading teachers, special education teachers, central office staff, and administrators, as well as from professional materials. The following pages provide a summary of what these teachers learned.

STUDY QUESTIONS

1. Who are the students with special needs?
2. What strategies can be used to help poor readers improve reading skills and learn content information?
3. What can be done to include the mainstreamed student in learning activities?
4. How can content teachers deal with the special needs of bilingual students or students who are learning English as a second language?
5. How can instruction be adjusted to better meet the needs of gifted students in the content class?

VOCABULARY

Bilingual
Dialectical differences
Educable mentally retarded
Gifted
Language-varied
Learning disabled

Mainstreamed
Monolingual
Multicultural
Physically handicapped
Poor reader

STUDENTS WITH SPECIAL NEEDS

With compulsory school attendance laws, legislation that provides education for the handicapped at all ages, and a society in which a high school diploma is essential, secondary schools have a higher enrollment of students now than ever before. Among these students is a large enrollment of "special" students or students whose needs are different from the typical middle or high school student. Although they appear to be typical middle and secondary school students, they have special learning needs that necessitate additional instructional adjustments in the content classroom. These students are grouped into four categories: poor reader, mainstreamed, language-varied, and gifted.

Poor readers are the students that content teachers discuss most frequently. These students do not read at the grade levels to which they are assigned; thus, they are often unable to read the textbook or other materials. Poor readers in a content class may be reading anywhere from one year to five or more years below their grade placement. They are often not motivated to learn because they cannot read, and usually believe they cannot learn. Poor readers are students who benefit most from the motivation provided by teachers, especially the physical education, art, and music teachers. These students have the ability to learn, they just need an extra boost to help them along.

A relatively new category of "special" students—mainstreamed—has resulted from the implementation of P.L. 94-142. Mainstreamed students are

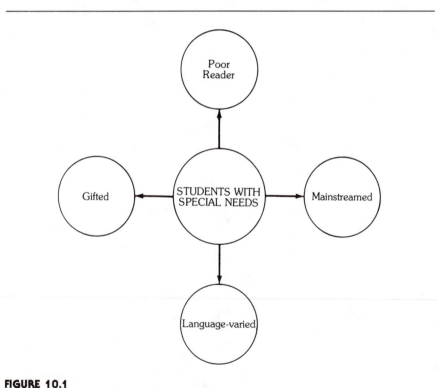

FIGURE 10.1

Categories of Students with Special Needs

those who attend the regular classroom part time and are with a special resource teacher part time. These students may be classified as learning disabled, educable mentally retarded (EMR), or physically handicapped. Gifted students may also fit into this category. Because of their different needs, however, they will be discussed separately. The learning disabled and EMR students seem to concern content teachers the most, with the physically handicapped being a special instructional concern only if they have severe visual or auditory impairments that may impede content learning. Moreover, these students do not present major instructional problems, because they are usually not mainstreamed until they learn to function independently.

LAGNIAPPE

General Provisions of Public Law 94-142

PART X—EDUCATION AND TRAINING OF THE HANDICAPPED

EDUCATION OF THE HANDICAPPED ACT

Part A—General Provisions
Short Title; Statement of Findings & Purpose Definitions

Sec. 601.

(a) This title may be cited as the "Education of the Handicapped Act".

"(b) The Congress finds that—

"(1) there are more than eight million handicapped children in the United States today;

"(2) the special educational needs of such children are not being fully met;

"(3) more than half of the handicapped children in the United States do not receive appropriate educational services which would enable them to have full equality of opportunity;

"(4) one million of the handicapped children in the United States are excluded entirely from the public school system and will not go through the educational process with their peers;

"(5) there are many handicapped children throughout the United States participating in regular school programs whose handicaps prevent them from having a successful educational experience because their handicaps are undetected;

"(6) because of the lack of adequate services within the public school systems, families are often forced to find services outside the public school system, often at great distance from their residence and at their own expense;

"(7) developments in the training of teachers and in diagnostic and instructional procedures and methods have advanced to the point that, given appropriate funding, State and local educational agencies can and will provide effective special education and related services to meet the needs of handicapped children;

"(8) State and local educational agencies have a responsibility to provide education for all handicapped children, but present financial resources are inadequate to meet the special educational needs of handicapped children; and

"(9) it is in the national interest that the Federal Government assist State and local efforts to provide programs to meet the educational needs of handicapped children in order to assure equal protection of the law.

"(c) It is the purpose of this Act to assure that all handicapped children have available to them, within the time periods specified in section 612(2) (B), a free appropriate public education which emphasizes special education and related services designed to meet their unique needs, to assure that the rights of hand-

icapped children and their parents or guardians are protected, to assist States
and localities to provide for the education of all handicapped children, and to
assess the effectiveness of efforts to educate handicapped children".

On November 19, 1975, Congress passed Public Law 94-142. The law
mandates significant changes regarding the education of children with
special needs. The most significant change is the requirement that handicapped children be educated with their nonhandicapped peers as much as
possible.

Mainstreaming these students, as mandated in P.L. 94-142, provides them
opportunities to associate with other students their age. The law does not
require students to stay with their peers for the entire day, however. It does
require that a special education resource teacher be available to give help to the
regular classroom teacher in handling mainstreamed students. There are, however, some students who may be learning disabled or EMR, but who have not
been identified because their parents will not allow them to be tested. These
students are in the regular content classes and do not get special help from a
resource teacher. As a result, content teachers are frustrated in teaching these
students.

The language-varied student in the content classroom is usually the bilingual
student, the student for whom English is a second language, or the non-English
speaking student. Some content teachers, especially English teachers, also
become greatly concerned with students whose dialect impairs their communication skills. The multicultural segment of the middle and secondary school
population comprises students who do not use American English as their primary language. Included are Hispanics (Mexican-American, Cuban, Puerto
Rican), Vietnamese, Europeans, Asians, and others. For these students, language causes difficulty in reading content materials. Another problem is the different background of experiences that often places an even greater barrier
between the student and content learning.

Content teachers must have special assistance in instructing some of these
students. Guidelines have been developed by the U.S. Education Department
in an effort to ensure the right of these students to an appropriate education and
to prevent any type of language discrimination. Using these guidelines, many
school districts have received special funds to provide teachers with additional
training and assistance in teaching these language-varied students.

Gifted students represent another group with special needs. Their special
needs may not be acknowledged as quickly as students in the other categories
because they are able to complete assignments successfully, they can read the
textbooks with no difficulty, and they often express a unique curiosity to learn
more. Content teachers sometimes wish for a classroom full of these students
because of the feeling that gifted students are easier to teach. They are often
neglected in the content classroom, however, because they seem quite capable
of taking care of themselves. The gifted students, as described by Marland, are:

> Those identified by professionally qualified persons, who, by virtue of out-
> standing abilities, are capable of high performance. These are children who
> require differentiated educational programs and services beyond those nor-
> mally provided by the regular program in order to realize their contribution to
> self and society.[1]

Gifted students may comprise as much as five percent of the school population. Terman and Oden suggest that these students are from two to four years beyond the average level in school work, they have a wide range of interests, and contrary to popular belief, they interact well with peers and tend to be very successful adults.[2]

Because content classes contain such a variety of students, teachers always have students with special needs. Instructing such a diverse population is no easy task. To assist the content teacher, the following sections provide ideas for instructing students in each of the four categories previously discussed.

POOR READERS

Many of the special needs of poor readers in the content classroom can be met as teachers follow the model for content instruction suggested in this book. Poor readers cannot be ignored in the content class. Teachers must provide the appropriate materials and encouragement needed for content learning. As concepts are taught, a variety of materials must be used in order to provide poor readers with related materials they can handle. The time spent introducing concepts and vocabulary enhances content learning, especially for the poor reader. Smith et al. state the role of the content teacher in working with poor readers extremely well. They suggest:

> There are many things that the content teacher cannot do for a student who has serious reading deficiencies and at least one very important thing that the teacher can do . . . what the content teacher can do is help to reverse the trend set in the student's former classes, which has given him every reason to believe that reading is not necessary or important or perhaps not possible in his life. The teacher can do this by making reading part of the students' classroom experiences.[3]

Teacher expectation and attitude are critical factors in instructing poor readers. Content teachers must reflect a positive attitude toward the content area and toward students. Much encouragement is needed as the students are provided with an adjusted work load that allows them to function within the group by participating in discussions and projects. Poor readers must be challenged to think maturely, but not overstimulated to the extent they become frustrated.

Content teachers should determine, through the use of some informal diagnostic techniques discussed in Chapter 4, the level at which students are reading. Using this information along with knowledge of the readability level of the content materials, content teachers can better match students with materials.

Along with positive attitudes and appropriate materials, there are other ideas that content teachers may use to strengthen content learning. Nichols[4] suggests the use of paragraph frames to assist poor readers with written assignments. This technique resembles a cloze procedure, but is designed by the teacher to elicit desired responses. Using the incomplete frame, students complete the blanks after reading the materials. Figure 10.2 provides an example. Newspapers are excellent materials for instruction.

Many resources are available that give suggestions for using the newspaper in all content classrooms. Content teachers should contact their local newspaper

FIGURE 10.2

Paragraph Frames

Completed Frames

Sample 1

Content Area: English   Topic: Cyrano De Bergerac
Grade Level: Senior   Assignment: Book Review
                                                          (Character Analysis)

In the story *Cyrano De Bergerac* by *Edmond Rostand* the major character is *Cyrano who is a hot-tempered swordsman with a huge nose who is also a clever poet.* Another main character is *Roxane, a beautiful young woman with whom Cyrano is in love. Christian DeNeuvillette, a clumsy young soldier who eventually marries Roxane* is also important in the story.

The problem which the major character faces is that *Cyrano has fallen in love with Roxane, but would never hope to win her because of his ugliness. He then assists Christian in winning the hand of Roxane by providing him with tender, poetic words which make Roxane fall in love with Christian.*

The problem is finally resolved when *fifteen years after Christian's death Roxane realizes that Cyrano had written her the love letters she thought had come from her husband.*

The story ends with *Roxane confessing her love for Cyrano on his deathbed. Cyrano dies happily knowing this.*

The lesson I learned from reading this story was *that beauty is not the most important factor for falling in love or choosing friends. I will remember this lesson in dealing with people in the future.*

Sample 2

Content Area: American History   Topic: World War I
Grade Level: Sophomore/Junior   Assignment: Essay (Summary: Time
                                                         Order Pattern)

At the end of *World War I* what happened was that *the various treaties, such as the Treaty of Versailles, radically changed the face of Europe and began many social, political and economic changes.*

Previous to this *German resources had been exhausted and German morale had collapsed. This had resulted in Germany surrendering and the war ending without a single truly decisive battle having been fought.*

Before this the *"Great War" had raged from 1914-1918 chiefly in Europe among most of the great Western powers.*

The entire chain of events had begun for a number of reasons including *imperialistic, territorial, and economic rivalries which had been growing since the late nineteenth century.*

Some prominent incidents which helped trigger the conflict were *the assassination of the Archduke Francis Ferdinand of Austria-Hungary in 1914 and the sinking of the Lusitania in 1915.*

Sample 3

Content Area: Biology   Topic: Cold and Warm-blooded Animals
Grade Level: Freshman   Assignment: Essay (Summary: Compari-
                                                         son-Contrast Pattern)

Mammals are different from *reptiles* in several ways. First of all *mammals are warm-blooded which means that they maintain a relatively constant body temperature independent of surrounding temperature* while reptiles are cold-blooded which means that their body temperature depends on their surroundings.

In addition, *mammals are more adaptable and are found all over the earth* while reptiles are generally limited. Reptiles are usually not found in the coldest regions and hibernate in cool winter areas.

Finally, *mammals generally have their young develop within the female's body. The young are born live* while reptiles lay eggs.

So it should be evident that *although reptiles millions of years ago were the ancestors of mammals that they are very different today.*

Incomplete Frames

Sample 1 (Character Analysis)

In the story _____ by _____ the major character is
_____ who is _____ . Another main character is
_____ . _____ who _____ is also important in the
story.
The problem which the major character faces is that _____ .
The problem is finally resolved when _____ .
The story ends with _____ .
The lesson I learned from reading this story was that _____ .
_____ .

Sample 2 (Essay: Time Order)

At the end of _____ what happened was that _____ .
Previous to this _____
_____ .
Before this _____
_____ .
The entire chain of events had begun for a number of reasons including_____
_____
Some prominent incidents which helped to trigger the conflict were _____
_____ .

Sample 3 (Essay: Comparison-Contrast)

_____ are different from _____ in several ways. First of all
_____
while _____ .
Secondly, _____
while _____ .
In addition, _____
while _____ .
Finally _____
while _____ .
So it should be evident that _____
_____
_____ .

James N. Nichols, "Using Paragraph Frames to Help Remedial High School Students with Written Assignments," *Journal of Reading* 24 (December 1980):229–30. Reprinted with permission of the International Reading Association and James N. Nichols.

or that of a nearby city for more information on the *Newspaper In Education* program for use in motivating students to read.

LAGNIAPPE

American parents discuss the newspaper more with their daughters than with their sons.

See "Confirming the Newspaper Habit," by Gerald Stone and Roger Wetherington, *Journalism Quarterly* 23 (1979):554–66.

Content teachers may find that the understanding of different organizational patterns used in content materials is most helpful to poor readers. Because these students may become confused in learning the many different patterns, however, content teachers should teach only the two major patterns—enumeration and relationships. Easier materials use these basic patterns and through an awareness of writing styles, the poor reader's comprehension should be improved.

A major difficulty poor readers experience in studying content materials is that they do not understand how reading skills must be applied. They tend to focus entirely on content, failing to apply their word identification, comprehension, and study skills. Thus, Step II as discussed in Chapter 3, is extremely important in helping students recognize which skills should be used as they study materials. Content teachers must assist poor readers in this transfer of learning, for the task cannot be done by one teacher or by a reading teacher. Only content teachers have the information to which reading skills must be applied for content learning.

Another suggestion that content teachers may wish to try to help poor readers is the use of study guides (discussed in Chapters 5 and 6). Additionally, the use of class discussions encourages poor readers to contribute ideas generated from their materials. The materials should be written at levels appropriate to poor readers' abilities.

For students who can read, but are functioning at a level below their grade placement, content teachers can usually find ways to adjust instruction. Teachers sometimes find themselves faced with nonreaders, however, or perhaps students who read at such a low level that the teacher cannot locate materials that interest a fifteen-year-old and are written at a first grade level. This dilemma cannot be solved by suggesting the use of alternative books or high interest/low vocabulary materials.

Materials for the severely disabled reader do not exist in great abundance. Content teachers must attempt to use nonprint forms to communicate concepts. These materials may include television, pictures, movies, tapes, records, and sometimes newspapers and magazines. The content teacher or other students can tape a chapter in the textbook and ask the disabled reader to follow along in the book as the tape is played. These tapes should be shared among the teachers and reused each year as needed. This procedure should only be used as a last resort and must not become the only instruction that the students receive, since this indicates to them that the teacher has given up and feels they can never learn to read. These extremely poor readers need opportunities to interact with print in a successful manner.

Because content teachers do not have time or specialized expertise to teach these severely disabled students to read, they should not hesitate to ask for assistance from the school reading teacher or from the central office staff's reading specialist. These specialists can administer in-depth diagnostic reading tests and design an instructional program appropriate to the student. Some schools have developed programs that provide reading instruction to students for the major portion of the day and allow them to participate in nonacademic classes with their peers. Such programs closely resemble those designed for the mainstreamed learning disabled or EMR students. Content teachers should ascertain whether extremely poor readers have been evaluated for such programs and, if they qualify, make use of the special education resource teacher.

Ideas for assisting the poor reader are many and their success depends on the student and the teacher—good rapport is essential. As content teachers work with these students, other ideas may come to mind. Try them—there is no magic formula for teaching poor readers how to read content materials. There are, however, some basic guides to keep in mind:

1. *Follow the Directed Learning Activity format in teaching content lessons.* This provides some structure in the lesson, encourages the use of a variety of materials, and class discussions. Using this procedure, all students regardless of their reading level have an opportunity to participate successfully.
2. *Teach students how to apply the skills they know in reading content materials.* This transfer of learning can be done only in the content classroom.
3. *Show students how to identify the organizational patterns used in content materials.* Comprehension is broadened as these styles are understood.
4. *Prepare students for reading the content materials and learning concepts.* Introduce the concepts, teach the vocabulary, review and teach as needed the reading skills that must be used, and help students set purposes for reading. Readiness for reading cannot be overlooked.
5. *Provide materials written at a level on which students can experience success.* Print and nonprint materials should be used to provide variety and to take advantage of the different learning styles of students. Such materials would include books written at lower readability levels that could be obtained at the school library or central resource centers in the district, as well as tapes, films, and miscellaneous pamphlets and brochures. The newspaper is an additional material that may be considered as a resource.
6. *Work with students to set immediate, achievable goals which will assist in building self-confidence as well as an understanding of the content.* When students understand why they are asked to study certain information that may be different from the text that other students are using, they usually respond positively. They tend to appreciate the special efforts of the content teacher. Their attitudes, self-concept, and interest in the content information is heightened.
7. *Reward students verbally or with other clear signs that seem important to them.*
8. *Help students learn to apply study techniques as they read.* This increases their understanding and helps them realize that they can learn.
9. *Provide motivational activities to reinforce instruction.* Poor readers who are encouraged to learn content information through an enthusiastic

teacher, interesting instruction, and materials with which they can experience success not only increase their content knowledge but also develop an enjoyment for learning.

10. *Give short reading assignments.* Poor readers are usually slow readers. If they are expected to read long selections, they tend to skim the material and comprehend little. Requiring that they read only a few pages per assignment encourages the completion of the task and motivates the student to participate more actively in the content class.

These guides can be used with different instructional activities to help poor readers feel successful in the content classroom. Teachers should remember that in order to assist poor readers they must spend time preteaching concepts and vocabulary, relate reading skills to content reading, and provide easier content reading materials. With preliminary instruction on concepts and content vocabulary, poor readers are often able to read a book that otherwise would be beyond their grasp. Poor readers in the content classroom require special help; with only minimum instructional adjustment, however, poor readers can become successful content learners.

REFLECTION

Think about your content class or a class that you have recently observed. What was done to provide special help to the poor reader? What other techniques could you now suggest?

MAINSTREAMED STUDENTS

With the implementation of P.L. 94–142, content teachers are finding students who have been placed in special programs being moved into the regular classroom for designated periods of time in order to interact with their peers. These students are most often mainstreamed into nonacademic classes such as physical education, music, and vocational education; however, English, social studies, science, and mathematics teachers may also have mainstreamed students in their classes.

Students who have been identified as learning disabled or educable mentally retarded are most frequently mainstreamed, although visually and auditorily impaired students may also be included. Content teachers should remember that when a student is mainstreamed, the special education resource teacher *must* provide assistance to the student and the classroom teacher in order to make this a successful experience. Resource teachers cannot stay in the classroom and teach, but in accordance with P.L. 94-142, they can and must help the content teacher in planning for students as well as assisting them in being successful in the class. Although many suggestions given for poor readers are also useful in teaching mainstreamed students, content teachers should be aware of their special needs.

Learning Disabled

Learning disabled students represent a large percentage of the mainstreamed population. These students are best described and identified by the characteristics suggested by Gilliland. These characteristics include

> Students are usually much better in math than reading.
> Word identification skills are poorly developed in comparison to other reading skills.
> Many students are hyperactive, experiencing difficulty sitting still while working on a task.
> Concentration on interesting tasks is interrupted because of sound or movement around them.
> There are difficulties in recognizing likenesses and differences in similar spoken or printed words.
> Students have difficulty in drawing simple shapes.
> Reversals of letters or changes of the order of sounds in a word are symptoms of specific learning disabilities.
> There is some lack of coordination in writing or walking.
> The student tends to repeat the same errors over and over.
> Many students have great difficulty in following directions.
> There is quite a lot of variance in performance in different areas.
> Students experience difficulty in organizing their work.
> Many students are very slow in finishing their work.[5]

Hallahan and Kauffman identify several categories of learning disabilities including (1) perceptual disabilities related to visual or auditory perception; (2) attentional disabilities that involve student distractibility in learning situations; (3) language production disabilities; and (4) socioemotional disabilities.[6] Students with any one of these disabilities demonstrate difficulty in content learning and must receive instruction that helps to compensate for the disability.

Students with visual perceptual disabilities tend to confuse words and letters, have difficulty remembering sequences of letters or other information, have poor sight vocabularies, often have problems remembering information, and demonstrate poor visual motor skills when writing or drawing. Auditory perception disabilities are evident in some students who have difficulty distinguishing sounds of letters, thereby demonstrating problems in phonetically decoding words. Additionally, these students have difficulty remembering information given auditorily, and they prefer visual activities over auditory tasks.

Attentional disabilities are noted through symptoms of distractibility in the classroom such as hyperactive behavior, inattentiveness, perseveration or inability to change from one activity to another, and hypoactivity or extreme lethargy. Obviously, any of these symptoms would cause learning problems in the content classroom. Even the slightest distractions cause these students to lose their concentration and get off task. To help students with this disorder, content teachers must remove as many distractions as possible, keep tasks short, and use materials that hold students' attention. Separate these students from the distractions of the total class for brief periods of time, and keep classroom activity to a minimum. Students with attentional disabilities often prefer to work in a quiet, isolated area in the content classroom and should be provided with such an area if possible. If classroom size prohibits this, the content teacher may locate a space elsewhere in the school, such as the library or a corner in a quiet hallway, for these students to occupy.

Learning disabled students with language difficulties have a severe problem in learning content information. These students are troubled in using syntax appropriately when speaking, they have difficulty in remembering and applying word identification strategies to words in their reading, they cannot retrieve vocabulary from their memory for spontaneous usage in reading and speaking, and they have problems in expressing their ideas with words they know. Content teachers can help these students by introducing new words and concepts gradually and explicitly, emphasizing comprehension over expressive skills, providing meaningful and relevant materials, and giving much repetition on concepts, vocabulary, and content information. Language disabled students have difficulty communicating. Their weak speaking and writing skills also cause problems in reading as they mispronounce words, although they know the meaning, and problems in communicating information they comprehend. Thus, content teachers must be patient and persistent in working with these students.

Students with socioemotional disabilities present another troublesome instructional problem. Not only is their disruptive behavior detrimental to the classroom learning environment, but it also prevents learning disabled students from functioning as contributing participants in that classroom. Students' misbehavior may range from quiet, contained hostility to outbursts that disrupt all classroom activities. Content teachers must be aware of such behaviors and determine appropriate techniques for helping these disabled students function more normally in the classroom. Such techniques may include reinforcing positive behavior and ignoring the undesired, developing with students specific guidelines of conduct (and resulting consequences when not followed), asking for parental assistance, and using peer influence to help in coping with socioemotional disorders that hinder learning for all students. Content teachers must be firm as well as understanding with these students, realizing that they need the experience of being with their peers in a mainstreamed situation while also recognizing that they may need to be phased into such a situation with only short visits initially.

Just as with the poor reader, there is no one best way to assist learning disabled students in the content classroom. Although some students respond better to audiotapes and oral discussions, other learning disabled students prefer visual instruction and printed materials. Other students respond better to a combination of instructional procedures. Still others need a structured environment with positive reinforcement and few distractions. Working with the special education resource teacher, content teachers can provide appropriate instruction for these students with such special needs.

REFLECTION

Have you observed or worked with a student diagnosed as learning disabled? How did he function in the content classroom? What could be done to make content learning a more successful experience for this student?

Educable Mentally Retarded

The EMR student is referred to as a slow learner who needs to learn much of the same information as other students, but at a slower rate. At the middle and secondary level, these students, obviously, are not put in a college prep course, but should be included in classes that help them become self-supporting adults. Courses like home economics, health, and typing are important content areas for these students.

Content teachers should recognize that these students progress in school at about one-half to three-quarters the rate of the average student, exhibit short attention spans, are easily frustrated, and often create more behavior problems in school than other students.[7] These behavior problems, however, are usually overcome as students are provided instruction on a level at which they can experience some success. Additionally, content teachers should realize that EMR students dislike reading and avoid it whenever possible. This is because they have experienced so much failure with printed materials and have such a difficult time with reading. Because of their lack of success in school and the frequent frustrations they have encountered in learning situations, these students often show poor self-concept demonstrated through negative attitudes and hostile reactions toward authority. In providing instruction to these students, the content teacher should find these suggestions helpful:

1. *Gear instruction to the level of EMR students.* They cannot achieve at the same level as other students in the regular classroom.
2. *Keep tasks uncomplicated.* New tasks must be introduced slowly and in a step-by-step manner.
3. *Provide sequential, systematic instruction.* Students must progress slowly and in a systematic way.
4. *Demonstrate new ideas whenever possible.* These students must be shown and not just told how to do a new task.
5. *Keep information brief.* Because these students have a short attention span, they tune people out quickly.
6. *Go slowly and repeat information frequently.* These students are slow learners who need much repetition in order to be successful learners. Overlearning is necessary. Much drill is also helpful.
7. *Provide relevant, concrete learning experiences.* Whenever possible, relate information to specific objects or situations to help students remember new ideas. Practical application is essential.
8. *Know students' levels of performance.* Be truthful with students and let them know when they are doing well.
9. *Use motivational materials that relate to "real-life" reading.* Newspapers, magazines, brochures, job forms, and directions are relevant reading materials.
10. *Show students how to read content materials.* Demonstrate study techniques and the application of reading skills that students are able to understand.

LAGNIAPPE

Extreme heterogeneity (grade level equivalent ranges of up to 10 grade levels) in junior high classes seems to limit the extent to which teachers can successfully adapt instruction to meet the needs of individual students. However, teachers who are effective classroom managers seem to make the adjustments necessary to neutralize these negative effects. This is significant as students are mainstreamed into regular junior and senior high school classes—are we providing less than ideal learning environments for all students in an effort to better accomodate a few? Teachers in these extremely heterogeneous classes need help!!

See Carolyn M. Evertson, Julie P. Sanford, and Edmund T. Emmer, "Effects of Class Heterogeneity in Junior High School," *American Educational Research Journal* 18 (Summer 1981):219–32.

Physically Handicapped Students

Occasionally content teachers may have a visually or auditorially impaired student mainstreamed into their classrooms. Although these students may seem to create problems for the teacher, they probably relate to content instruction more positively than learning disabled or EMR students. These students are

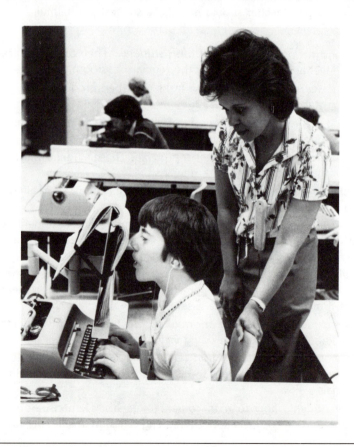

This partially sighted student participates in a regular typing class.

usually not mainstreamed until they are relatively independent and are able to function successfully with other students. Furthermore, these students' resource teachers take special pride in helping students adjust to the new classroom and in assisting the teacher in working with them. These students are mainstreamed not only for interaction with their peers, but what is more, to learn how to function in the outside world. With this goal in mind, the special education resource teacher attempts to make the transition as easy and pleasant as possible. Therefore, content teachers enjoy continuous assistance in learning how to best instruct these students.

Three basic ideas for the teacher to consider in teaching the visually impaired student are

Concreteness: Students need objects which can be manipulated in order to learn about size, shape, texture, weight, etc.

Unifying experiences: Students need systematic stimulation in order to understand how various parts relate to the total picture.

Learning by doing: Students must be involved with an activity and allowed to experience learning by touch and sound.[8]

Listening and touching are the primary means by which the visually impaired student learns. Therefore, content teachers must try to teach abstract concepts by relating ideas to known information and try to use manipulative illustrations whenever possible. For the partially sighted student, content teachers may use other resources such as magnifying lenses, large-type books, and chalkboards that are adjustable to allow a light reflection that helps in seeing the images. Additionally, three-dimensional maps, record players, dictaphones, and other specially designed equipment help teachers adjust instruction for the visually impaired learner.

Hearing impaired students often present an even greater challenge to the classroom teacher. Seldom is a totally deaf student placed in a content classroom; many hard-of-hearing students can, however, function with a little special assistance from the content teacher and a resource teacher. For hearing impaired students, reading and other language areas are most severely affected, with a seventeen-year-old reaching only about a fourth grade level in reading.[9] This low reading level, however, does not reflect the students' intelligence; thus, they can be taught many concepts in content areas using special educational procedures. Kirk and Gallagher suggest that teachers become aware of the effect of hearing aids, auditory training, speech or lipreading, oral speech remediation, speech development, and language development on students' learning.[10] The following tips in teaching hearing impaired students may be useful to the content teacher:

1. Give the student favorable seating in the classroom and allow him or her to move to the source of speech within the room; let the student turn around or have speakers turn toward the student to allow visual contact with anyone who is speaking.
2. Encourage the student to look at the speaker's lips, mouth, and face. Speechreading should help clarify many of the sounds the child cannot hear.

3. Speak naturally—neither mumbling nor overarticulating. Speak neither too fast nor too slow, too loud or too soft.

4. Keep hands away from the mouth when speaking, and make sure that books, papers, glasses, pencils, and other objects do not obstruct the visual contact.

5. Take note of the light within the room so that the overhead light or window light is not at the speaker's back. Speechreading is difficult when light shines in the speechreader's eyes. Try to prevent shadows from falling on the speaker's mouth.

6. Stand in one place while dictating words or arithmetic problems to the group, allowing the hard of hearing student to see better, as well as to give a sense of security that the teacher will be there when he or she looks up.

7. Speak in complete sentences. Single words are more difficult to speechread than are complete thoughts. Approximately 50 percent of the words in the English language look alike on the lips. Such groups of words are termed homophenous. (Example: man, pan, ban, band, mat, pat, bat, mad, pad, bad.) Phrases and sentences placing the word in context help promote visual differentiation among homophenous words.

8. Give the student assignments in advance, or give the topic which will be discussed. A list of new vocabulary to be used in an assignment also assists the student. Familiarity may help the student understand the word in context and help promote visual differentiation among homophenous words.

9. Occasionally, have the hearing impaired student repeat the assignment to some other student so you are sure the assignment has been understood.

10. Remember at all times that this is a normal student with a hearing handicap; never single out a hearing impaired student in front of the group or in any other manner encourage an attitude of being "different."

11. Understand that the student with a hearing loss may tire faster than a student with normal hearing. The demands placed upon a student in speechreading and listening are greater than for hearing people.

12. Take into consideration that many students hear better on some days than they do on others. Also, students may suffer from tinnitus (hearing noises within the head) which may make them nervous and irritable.

13. Restate a sentence, using other words that have the same meaning, when the hearing impaired individual does not understand what has been said. The reworded sentence might be more visible. (Example: Change, "Close your book," to "Shut the book," or "Please put your book away now." Look in a mirror and observe the difference.)

14. Encourage the hearing impaired student to participate in all school and community activities. This student is just as much a part of the environment as any other student.

15. Help the student to accept mistakes humorously. The deaf and the hard of hearing resent being the target of laughter just as much as anyone else. Laugh with them, not at them.

16. Encourage an understanding of and interest in the handicap of a hearing impaired student by the entire group.[11]

Content teachers having visually and auditorially handicapped students mainstreamed into their classes should find the new experience challenging; it should not be frustrating. Ask the resource teacher for help and be positive—students sense negative reactions; hence, learning becomes more difficult.

LANGUAGE-VARIED STUDENTS

Students are considered to have language variations when they are more fluent in a language other than English or when they speak in a dialect that causes communication problems. In content classes, there are many students who have learning difficulties due to language variations. Accompanying and usually complicating the language problem is a different value system. These factors often lead to attitudes that react negatively to learning. Therefore, while the language difference alone may not inhibit learning, the related elements may result in learning difficulties.

Students who speak English as a second language are called bilingual, while those who speak only their native language are monolingual. These students are considered multicultural and reflect a life-style, language, and culture that vary from those of the American student. Content teachers must approach the learning experience with these students cautiously. Any attempt to change their language means to these students that the teacher regards them as inadequate. Such an interpretation triggers negative reactions that are difficult to overcome. These students must have immediate success, positive responses, practical teaching, and acceptance from the teacher.

Because the value system, learning styles, and language of multicultural students vary from those of American students, Ramirez and Castaneda identify four major Mexican-American value clusters that must be considered by the teacher. First, strong family ties are of primary importance, with individual needs and interests being of secondary importance.[12] Second, interpersonal relationships in Mexican-American communities reflect a sensitivity to the feelings and needs of others. Cooperative efforts are perceived as more important than individual efforts. A third value cluster for these students reflects the role and status definition within the family and community. Older people enjoy greater status, with children expected to model themselves after respected members of the community. A fourth value cluster relates to the support and reinforcement provided by the Mexican-Catholic ideology. Religious commitment reinforces the importance of family ties. Thus, in teaching students with a Mexican-American background, content teachers must consider their value system as they plan instruction. Because these students are more highly motivated in a cooperative setting than in a competitive situation, instruction should include many group activities. Additionally, due to their interest in others, Mexican-American students may achieve better in a curriculum that has a human content and relates to the needs of others.

Content teachers must, therefore, learn about the culture and value system as well as the bilingual student's language when instructing. They must also consider that in order to help students learn English and the content concepts, instruction must first be provided through *listening*. This is followed by adding instruction to their *speaking* vocabulary, incorporating it into their *reading* vocabulary, and finally integrating into their *writing* vocabulary. While this seems like a slow process, language learning usually proceeds through these steps. To further assist teachers in working with multicultural students in a positive way, the teacher should

1. Become familiar with the students' culture so that cultural habits are understood.

Teachers should learn about the bilingual student's native language as well as her culture and value system.

2. Use resources within the community to help these students feel more comfortable in the classroom situation.
3. Remember that the majority of these students are academically adept—their problem is language.
4. Team students with native English-speaking students who can help interpret concepts and directions.
5. Allow students many opportunities to hear and speak English.
6. Use pictures, films, objects, etc., to help students understand concepts—their background of experience is different and they usually need additional help in learning content concepts.

Another type of language variation exists with a group of English-speaking students who, because of their background, have difficulty reading and communicating orally due to dialectical differences. These students are commonly referred to as culturally disadvantaged or culturally different. They are students who speak a nonstandard American English that creates problems when they read materials used in content classes. Their language differences, combined with background experiences that vary from those needed in content learning, cause much frustration and often create a feeling of failure. Failure leads to hostile feelings and discipline problems in the middle and secondary schools. Zintz suggests that about 25 percent of the population belongs to the lower socio-economic class that is often referred to as culturally disadvantaged, and for these students the value system is different from other students in terms of moti-vation to succeed in school, setting a high level of aspiration, desire to remain in school, and selection of college preparatory courses.[13] Content teachers must be aware and tolerant of these differences in culture, language usage, and val-ues, and remember that these students are entitled to the same respect and rec-ognition given to other students.

REFLECTION

As a content teacher, you realize that you have many language-varied stu-dents in your class. Some of the students are refugees while others are cul-turally different Americans. What would you do to make content learning a more successful experience for these students?

Laffey and Shuy suggest that research does not support the theory that a particular dialect causes reading difficulties.[14] Instead, numerous research stud-ies indicate that teacher attitudes more than dialect cause many reading problems. These research findings regarding teacher attitudes toward language-varied students, particularly those who speak nonstandard English, should be noted by content teachers.[15] The findings show that teachers not only react neg-atively toward these students, but they also rate them as lower class, less intelli-gent, and less able to achieve in an academic situation. With such teacher atti-tudes, learning for the dialectically different students in the content classroom is only more complicated. They do not have experiences that help them under-stand many of the content concepts, their language is viewed as inferior, and the teachers perceive them as unable to learn. As concluded by Harber and Beatty: "To improve the self-image and academic achievement among black, lower socioeconomic status children, teachers need to be trained to expect more from them, to judge their capabilities independent of race and socioeco-nomic status, and to understand and respect their dialect and cultural back-ground."[16] Thus, to help these students succeed in content learning, teachers must

1. *Carefully introduce concepts and vocabulary.* Because of their limited back-ground experiences, these students must be well prepared for learning in order to be successful.
2. *Help them apply study strategies and set purposes for reading content mate-rials.* Structured reading and rereading are necessary for these students to learn abstract ideas; every effort should be made, however, to provide stu-dents with materials that are interesting and have some relevance to their daily lives.
3. *Be tolerant of their language.* Language is a person's most private posses-sion—avoid ridicule.
4. *Encourage students to participate in class discussions.* A feeling of self-worth is developed as students become active in the learning process.
5. *Motivate students to learn.* The teacher's concern for the student and enthu-siasm for the content being taught should go far in motivating the student to learn content material.

Content teachers may have a better understanding of the differences between standard English and black English after reviewing Tables 10.1 and 10.2. An awareness of these differences may help teachers better comprehend language variations and become more understanding of students with dialectal problems.

Language-varied students represent a large portion of the population in some classrooms. Since there is no simple way to change their language, content teachers must accept the linguistic differences and strive to motivate these students to learn. As students experience success in content learning, attitudes improve and language differences become less obvious.

TABLE 10.1

Phonological Differences Between Standard English and Black English

Feature	Standard English	Black English
Simplification of consonant clusters	test	tes
	past	pas
th sounds		
voiceless th in initial position	think	tink or think
voiced th in initial position	the	de
voiceless th in medial position	nothing	nofin'
voiced th in medial position	brother	brovah
th in final position	tooth	toof
r and l		
in postvocalic position	sister	sistah
	nickel	nickuh
in final position	Saul	saw
Devoicing of final b, d, and g	cab	cap
	bud	but
	pig	pik
Nasalization		
ing suffix	doing	doin
i and e before a nasal	pen	pin
Stress—absence of the first syllable of a multisyllabic word when the first syllable is unstressed	about	'bout
Plural marker*	three birds	three bird or three birds
	the books	de book, de books
Possessive marker*	the boy's hat	de boy hat
Third person singular marker*	he works here	he work here
Past tense—simplification of final consonant clusters*	passed	pass
	loaned	loan

*Some authorities include these under syntactical differences.

TABLE 10.2

Syntactic Differences Between Standard English and Black English

Feature	Standard English	Black English
Linking verb	He is going.	He goin'; He is goin'.
Pronomial apposition	That teacher yells at the kids.	Dat teachah, she yell at de kid (kids).
Agreement of subject and third person singular verb	She runs home. She has a bike.	She run home. She have a bike.
Irregular verb forms	They rode their bikes.	Dey rided der bike (bikes).
Future form	I will go home.	I'm a go home.
"If" construction	I asked if he did it.	I aks did he do it.
Indefinite article	I want an apple.	I want a apple.
Negation	I don't have any.	I don't got none.
Pronoun form	We have to do it.	Us got to do it.
Copula (verb "to be")	He is here all the time. No, he isn't.	He be here. No, he isn't; No, he don't.
Prepositions	Put the cat out of the house. The dress is made of wool.	Put de cat out de house. De dress is made outta wool.

From Jean R. Harber and Jane N. Beatty, *Reading and the Black English Speaking Child* (Newark, Del.: International Reading Association, 1978), pp. 46–47. Reprinted with permission of the International Reading Association and Jean R. Harber and Jane N. Beatty.

GIFTED STUDENTS

Gifted students comprise a portion of the student population that, until recently, has not received the special assistance often needed for them to reach their full learning potential. These superior students learn quickly and on many occasions have been expected to function independently while teachers devote more time to slower students. The talents of gifted students have been better recognized during the last decade as special programs have been developed to enhance their learning. Still, within the content classroom, much more can be done to provide challenging experiences for these students.

Although viewed as superior learners, gifted students usually need to develop improved study skills, expand their vocabulary—especially technical vocabulary, develop the higher-level comprehension skills such as critical reading, and learn to skim and scan materials for more varied rates of reading. Content teachers can help strengthen these areas through the Directed Learning Activity format.

Concept and vocabulary instruction can lead gifted learners into more in-depth study and, as materials are read, they may be encouraged to read more difficult selections that contribute greater insight to follow-up discussions.

Gifted students must be challenged; they must not become frustrated or bored. They should also be encouraged to function as an integral part of the class. These students demand much from the content learning experience and are usually willing to exert all efforts necessary to attain self-satisfaction. At the same time, content teachers have a major responsibility in recognizing their potential and providing stimulating activities that encourage continued learning. Activities that demand the use of critical and creative thinking skills, like the following, appeal to these students:

1. Dramatizing stories.
   a. Doing some of the things the characters did to show insight into the mood and personality of each character.
   b. Rewriting the story as a play.
2. Making graphic representations of a story.
   a. Showing a story in serial form; writing or telling what is happening in each scene.
   b. Making a picture to illustrate an event or a description from the story.
3. Oral and written presentations of stories.
   a. Telling a story up to the point of climax.
   b. Rewriting an ending to a story.
   c. Writing about a story or book and showing why it was enjoyed or not liked.
4. Planning with the teacher for help in diagnosing the student's own reading abilities and working out a plan for developing those abilities.
5. Doing self-motivated independent research for practice in using reference materials and library reference guides, and finding information independently.
6. Working alone or with others in writing original stories and essays, analyzing authors' patterns of thought and organization, and determining new application of principles and data.
7. Practicing the scientific method of problem solving.
   a. Discovering and clearly stating problems.
   b. Planning and executing ways of determining what is true.
   c. Checking with reliable sources and determining what is true.
   d. Applying what is learned to the environment.
   e. Making use of simple records.
8. Extensive reading of library materials for information, enjoyment, and enrichment.
   a. Reading a wide variety of books.
   b. Scanning and classifying reading materials for the school library.
   c. Setting up displays of books to supplement and enrich classroom work.
9. Engaging in vocabulary study.
   a. Noting special words pertinent to each content field.
   b. Determining general words with specialized meanings.
   c. Analyzing an author's connotative use of words.
   d. Becoming aware of an author's use of sensory words.
   e. Noting and defining figures of speech.

10. Classroom discussion. Superior students learn from each other by increasing their own depth and scope of knowledge and by sharpening their vocabulary in the communicative skills which is basic to discussion.[17]

REFLECTION

If you had only the content textbook for use in any content classroom, how could it be used best to teach the poor reader? the EMR student? the learning disabled student? the bilingual student? the gifted student?

SUMMARY

The content teacher is confronted by numerous students with a variety of special requirements. Poor readers, mainstreamed students, students with language variations, and gifted students are all part of the content classroom. Their special needs must be met if the teacher expects to teach successfully the content information.

For this reason, teachers should seek the assistance of the reading teacher, special education resource teacher, or a central office supervisor if in doubt about how to proceed. Special equipment and materials plus an awareness of the student's unique characteristics also greatly facilitate content instruction.

FOR DISCUSSION

1. What do you think is the most common population of special need students in content classes? What special provisions can be made for these students?
2. Of the types of students and their special needs discussed in this chapter, which type of student would you prefer to have in your content class? Why?

OTHER SUGGESTED READINGS

Bachner, Saul. "Teaching Reading and Literature to the Disadvantaged—Part VII Specific Practices: An Assignment." *Journal of Reading* 18 (March 1975):481–85.

Baldauf, Richard B.; Dawson, Robert L.T.; Prior, John; and Propst, Ivan K. "Can Matching Cloze Be Used with Secondary ESL Pupils?" *Journal of Reading* (February 1980):435–40.

Baratz, Joan C. "A Cultural Model for Understanding Black Americans." In *Black Dialect and Reading*, ed. Bernice E. Cullinan. Urbana, Ill.: National Council of Teachers of English, 1974.

Baratz, Joan C., and Shuy, Roger W., eds. *Teaching Black Children to Read*. Washington, D.C.: Center for Applied Linguistics, 1969.

Bartel, Nettie R., and Axelrod, Judith. "Nonstandard English Usage and Reading Ability in Black Junior High Students." *Exceptional Children* 39 (May 1973):653–55.

Belch, P. J. "Improving the Reading Comprehension Scores of Secondary Level Educable Mentally Handicapped Students Through Selective Teacher Questioning." *Education and Training of the Mentally Retarded* 13 (December 1978):385–89.

Blake, Kathryn A. "Special Reading Instructional Procedures for Mentally Retarded and Learning Disabled Children: Summary, Instructional Principles, and Next Step." *Journal of Research and Development in Education* 9 (Monograph 1976):1–63.

Blanchard, Jay S. "A Comprehension Strategy for Disabled Readers in the Middle School." *Journal of Reading* 24 (January 1981):331–35.

Bryen, Diane N.; Hartman, Cheryl; and Tait, Pearla. *Variant English: An Introduction to Language Variation*. Columbus, Ohio: Charles E. Merrill, 1978.

Brooks, C. R., and Riggs, S.T. "WISC-R, WISC, and Reading Achievement Relationships Among Hearing-Impaired Children Attending Public Schools." *The Volta Review* 82 (February/March 1980):96–102.

Cheyney, Arnold B. *Teaching Reading Skills Through the Newspaper*. Newark, Del.: International Reading Association, 1971.

Childrey, John A. "Home Remedies for Reluctant Readers." In *Motivating Reluctant Readers*, ed. Alfred J. Ciani. Newark, Del.: International Reading Association, 1981.

Ching, Doris C. *Reading and the Bilingual Child*. Newark, Del.: International Reading Association, 1976.

Cohen, S. Alan. *Teach Them All to Read*. New York: Random House, 1969.

Crandall, Kathleen F. "Reading and Writing Skills and the Deaf Adolescent." *Volta Review* 80 (September 1978):319–32.

Cullinon, Bernice E., ed. *Black Dialects and Reading*. Urbana, Ill.: National Council of Teachers of English, 1974.

Dixon, Carol N. "Teaching Strategies for the Mexican American Child." *The Reading Teacher* 30 (November 1976):141–45.

Donlan, Dan. "What Research Says About Teaching Standard English to Disadvantaged Students." *Peabody Journal of Education* 51 (July 1974):261–68.

Douglas, Malcolm P. "The Development of Teaching Materials for Cultural Pluralism: The Problem of Literacy." In *Cultural Pluralism in Education: A Mandate for Change*, ed. Madelon D. Stent, William R. Hazard, and Harry N. Rivlin. New York: Appleton-Century-Crofts, 1973.

Feitelson, Dina, ed. *Mother Tongue or Second Language?* Newark, Del.: International Reading Association, 1979.

Gardner, David C., and Kurtz, Margaret A. "Teaching Technical Vocabulary to Handicapped Students." *Reading Improvement* 16 (Fall 1979):252–57.

Geoffrian, Leo D., and Schuster, Karen E. *Auditory Handicaps and Reading: An Annotated Bibliography*. Newark, Del.: International Reading Association, 1980.

Gormley, Kathleen A., and Franzen, Anne McGill. "Why Can't the Deaf Read? Comments on Asking the Wrong Question." *American Annals of the Deaf* 123 (August 1978):542–47.

Grant, Carl A., ed. *Multicultural Education: Commitments, Issues, and Applications*. Washington, D.C.: Association for Supervision and Curriculum Development, 1977.

Marwit, Samuel J., and Neumann, Gail. "Black v. White Children's Comprehension of Standard and Non-standard English Passages." *Journal of Educational Psychology* 66 (June 1974):329–32.

Mason, George E. "High Interest-Low Vocabulary Books: Their Past and Future." *Journal of Reading* 24 (April 1981):603–7.

Moore, Fernie Baca, and Parr, Gerald D. "Models of Bilingual Education: Comparisons of Effectiveness." *The Elementary School Journal* 79 (November 1978):93–97.

Moskowitz, Gertrude, and Hayman, John L. "Success Strategies of Inner City Teachers: A Year Long Study." *Journal of Educational Research* 69 (April 1976): 283–89.

Norton, Donna E. *The Effective Teaching of Language Arts*. Columbus, Ohio: Charles E. Merrill, 1980.

Otto, Sr. Jean. "A Critical Review of Approaches to Remedial Reading for Adolescents." *Journal of Reading* 23 (December 1979):244–50.

Pell, Sarah-Warner J. "A Communication Skills Project for Disadvantaged Aleut, Eskimo, and Indian Ninth and Tenth Graders." *Journal of Reading* 22 (February 1979):404–7.

Pflaster, Gail. "A Factor Analysis of Variables Related to Academic Performance of Hearing-Impaired Children in Regular Classes." *The Volta Review* 82 (February/March 1980):71–84.

Hall, William S., and Feedle, Roy O. *Culture and Language: The Black American Experience.* New York: John Wiley and Sons, 1975.

Harber, Jean R., and Bryen, Diane N. "Black English and the Task of Reading." *Review of Educational Research* 46 (Summer 1976):387–405.

Harber, Jean R., and Beatty, Jane N. *Reading and the Black English Speaking Child* (Newark, Del.: International Reading Association, 1978).

Joynes, Yvonne D.; McCormick, Sandra; and Howard, William L. "Teaching Reading Disabled Students to Read and Complete Employment Applications." *Journal of Reading* 23 (May 1980):709–14.

Knott, Gladys P. "Developing Reading Potential in Black Remedial High School Freshmen." *Reading Improvement* 16 (Winter 1979):262–69.

Komachiya, Megumi. "Using a Wide Range of Activities to Foster Second Language Growth." *Journal of Reading* 25 (February 1982):436–48.

Labov, William. *Language in the Inner City: Studies in the Black English Vernacular.* Philadelphia: University of Pennsylvania Press, 1972.

Labuda, Michael, ed. *Creative Reading for Gifted Learners: A Design for Excellence.* Newark, Del.: International Reading Association, 1974.

Litsinger, Dolores Escobar. *The Challenge of Teaching Mexican-American Students.* New York: American Book, 1973.

Marmolin, Hans; Nilsson, Lars-Goran; and Smedshammar, Hans. "The Mediated Reading Process of the Partially Sighted." *Visible Language* 13 (1979):168–83.

Rupley, William H., and Blair, Timothy R. "Mainstreaming and Reading Instruction." *The Reading Teacher* 32 (March 1979):762–65.

Shephard, David L. "Teaching Science and Mathematics to the Seriously Retarded Reader in the High School." *The Reading Teacher* 17 (October 1963):25–30.

Shuy, Roger W. "Language Variation and Literacy." In *Reading Goals for the Disadvantaged*, ed. J. Allen Figurel. Newark, Del.: International Reading Association, 1970.

Smith, Cyrus F. "Motivating the Reluctant Reader through the Top Twenty." In Alfred J. Ciani, ed., *Motivating Reluctant Readers*. Newark, Del.: International Reading Association, 1981.

Stoefen, Jill M. "Instructional Alternatives for Teaching Content Reading to Mainstreamed Hearing Impaired Students." *Journal of Reading* 24 (November 1980):141–43.

Tiedt, Pamela L., and Tiedt, Iris M. *Multicultural Teaching: A Handbook of Activities, Information, and Resources.* Boston: Allyn and Bacon, Inc., 1979.

Usova, George M. "A Synthesis of Research on Reading and the Disadvantaged." *Reading World* 18 (December 1978):176–85.

Valverde, Leonard A., ed. *Bilingual Education for Latinos.* Washington, D.C.: Association for Supervision and Curriculum Development, 1978.

Vick, Marian L. "Relevant Content for the Black Elementary School Pupil." In *Literacy for Diverse Learners: Promoting Reading Growth at All Levels,* ed. Jerry L. Johns. Newark, Del.: International Reading Association, 1973.

Wilson, Robert M., and Barnes, Marcia M. *Using Newspapers to Teach Reading Skills.* Washington, D.C.: American Newspaper Publishers Association Foundation, 1975.

Wilton, Shirley M. "Juvenile Science Fiction Involves Reluctant Readers." *Journal of Reading* 24 (April 1981):608–11.

Witty, Paul A., ed. *Reading for the Gifted and the Creative Student.* Newark, Del.: International Reading Association, 1971.

NOTES

1. Sidney P. Marland, *Education of the Gifted and Talented* (Washington, D.C.: U.S. Office of Education, 1972), p. 10.
2. Lewis M. Terman and Melita H. Oden, *The Gifted Group at Midlife: Thirty-Five Years' Follow-up of the Superior Child, Genetic Studies of Genius,* vol. 5 (Stanford, Calif.: Stanford University Press, 1959).
3. Carl B. Smith, Sharon L. Smith, and Larry Mikulecky, *Teaching Reading in Secondary School Content Subjects* (New York: Holt, Rinehart, and Winston, 1978), p. 143.
4. James N. Nichols, "Using Paragraph Frames to Help Remedial High School Students with Written Assignments," *Journal of Reading* 24 (December 1980):228–31.
5. Hap Gilliland, *A Practical Guide to Remedial Reading* (Columbus, Ohio: Charles E. Merrill, 1978), pp. 282–83.
6. Daniel P. Hallahan and James M. Kauffman, *Introduction to Learning Disabilities: A Psycho-Behavioral Approach* (Englewood Cliffs, N.J.: Prentice-Hall, 1976), p. 28.
7. Samuel A. Kirk and James J. Gallagher, *Educating Exceptional Children*, 3rd ed. (Boston: Houghton Mifflin, 1979), pp. 140–52.
8. Berthold Lowenfeld, ed. *The Visually Handicapped Child in School* (New York: John Day, 1973).
9. Raymond J. Trybus and Michael A. Kanchmer, "School Achievement Scores of Hearing Impaired Children: National Data on Achievement Status and Growth Patterns," *American Annals of the Deaf* 122 (April 1977):62–69.
10. Samuel A. Kirk and James J. Gallagher, *Educating Exceptional Children*, 3rd ed., pp. 213–23.
11. Alfred D. Larson and June B. Miller, "The Hearing Impaired," in *Exceptional Children and Youth: An Introduction*, ed. Edward L. Nuyan (Denver, Colo.: Love Publishing Company, 1978), pp. 463–65.
12. Manuel Ramirez and Alfredo Castaneda, *Cultural Democracy, BiCognitive Development and Education* (New York: Academic Press, 1974).
13. Miles V. Zintz, *Corrective Reading*, 4th ed. (Dubuque, Iowa: William C. Brown, 1981), p. 316.
14. James L. Laffey and Roger W. Shuy, eds., *Language Differences: Do They Interfere?* (Newark, Del.: International Reading Association, 1973).
15. Harris M. Cooper, Reuben M. Barron, and Charles A. Love, "The Importance of Race and Social Class Information in the Formation of Expectations about Academic Performance," *Journal of Educational Psychology* 67 (April 1975):312–19; Thomas K. Crowe and Walter H. MacGinitie, "The Influence of Students' Speech Characteristics on Teachers' Evaluations of Oral Answers," *Journal of Educational Psychology* 66 (June 1974):304–8; Patricia M. Cunningham, "Teachers' Correction Responses to Black Dialect Miscues Which Are Non-Meaning Changing," *Reading Research Quarterly* 12 (Summer 1977):637–53; James F. Ford, "Language Attitude Studies: A Review of Selected Research," *Florida FL Reporter* (Spring/Fall 1974):53–54, 100; Tom Freijo and Richard M. Jaeger, "Social Class and Race as Concomitants of Composite Halo in Teachers' Evaluative Rating of Pupils," *American Educational Research Journal* 13 (Winter 1976):1–14; Thomas H. Hawkes and Nora F. Furst, "An Investigation of the Misconceptions of Pre- and Inservice Teachers as to the Manifestation of Anxiety in Upper Elementary School Children from Different Racial-Socioeconomic Backgrounds," *Psychology in the Schools* 10 (January 1973):23–32; Mary Jensen and Lawrence B. Rosenfeld, "Influence of Mode of Presentation, Ethnicity, and Social Class on Teachers' Evaluations of Students," *Journal of Educational Psychology* 66 (August 1974):540–47; Roger W. Shuy and Frederick Williams, "Stereotyped Attitudes of Selected English

Dialect Communities," in *Language Attitudes: Current Trends and Prospects*, ed. Roger W. Shuy and Ralph W. Fasold (Washington, D.C.: Georgetown University Press, 1973), pp. 85–96.

16. Jean R. Harber and Jane N. Beatty, *Reading and the Black English Speaking Child* (Newark, Del.: International Reading Association, 1978), p. 20.

17. David L. Shepherd, *Comprehensive High School Reading Methods*, 3rd ed. (Columbus, Ohio: Charles E. Merrill, 1982), pp. 211–12.

CHAPTER ELEVEN

MOTIVATING STUDENTS THROUGH CONTENT READING

"I can't believe the fantastic projects that my tenth graders have just finished," Ms. Hankamer commented to a group of teachers. "They are so involved in this unit that I have to drive them out of the room at the end of class!"

"Something happens to them between your class and my English class," lamented Ms. Hunter. "About half of the students want to be in class and the other half couldn't care less. I've run out of ideas to get them interested in learning!"

Worrying about student interest in learning content information is common to teachers in middle and secondary schools. Many parents are also disturbed by the lack of their children's interest in learning. Why do some students do well in one content class, but not in another? Who's to blame? Is it the teacher, the student, the parents, or is it a combination of all of these? Teachers become frustrated with students for not showing interest in the content presented or for not working up to their potential. Students become frustrated with teachers for either pushing too hard or not enough. Parents become frustrated because they expect more from their children, and more from the school. (After all, parents feel that it is their tax dollars that foot the bills and pay the teachers' salaries!) As a result of these frustrations, animosities develop and everyone suffers. In truth, teachers, parents, and students alike are responsible for the lack of motivation in learning. Failure to establish effective communication, among other factors, also contributes to the problem.

Many students are intrinsically motivated—self-motivated—meaning that regardless of any outside influences they will complete the task. On the other hand, some students are extrinsically motivated, meaning they are affected by outside influences, and require additional stimuli to accomplish their goals. Because these students need help, all forces interacting with them must be of such a nature that motivation is enhanced. Thus, teachers and parents must assume their respective shares of responsibility for providing an environment that motivates these students to perform at their highest level. This chapter is devoted to defining the roles of teachers, parents, and students and their responsibilities in the motivational process.

STUDY QUESTIONS

1. What is the teacher's responsibility in the motivational process?
2. What is the value of parental involvement in the motivational process?
3. What is the role of the student as a self-motivator in this process?

VOCABULARY

Extrinsic motivation
Intrinsic motivation

Sustained silent reading

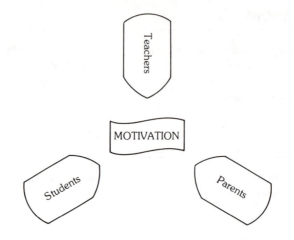

Figure 11.1

Persons Involved in the Motivational Process

TEACHER RESPONSIBILITY IN MOTIVATION

In some content classrooms the lack of motivation is a key element in poor student performances, disruptive behavior and teacher burnout. Most teachers sincerely believe they are putting forth their best efforts in providing effective instruction for their students; unfortunately, many students still remain aloof and unresponsive in the classroom. A few become so disruptive that effective instruction is severly hampered. Teachers become frustrated and often bitter. They blame their students, the students' parents, and anyone or anything that seems responsible for this situation. Worst of all, some teachers, who could make a valuable contribution, leave the profession angry and disgusted. Why does this happen? Who is responsible? What can teachers do to provide effective instruction in the content classroom—instruction that provides extrinsic stimuli to motivate students to want to learn?

First of all, an examination of the reasons that contribute to a lack of motivation should prove worthwhile. This review yields three broad categories that appear to have an effect, either positively or negatively, on motivation. These categories are environment, teacher attitude, and instruction.

Environment in this instance refers to the school. How important is this? For many students it means the difference between learning and not learning. Environment can refer to the actual school facilities, or the atmosphere prevalent in a classroom. Some students attend schools that are unkempt, overcrowded, and noisy, while other students attend schools that are clean, pleasant and quiet. In many instances, students attending the former school would be less motivated than those attending the latter; students, however, may still learn satisfactorily in a physically subpar school, if the classroom environment is conducive to learning. Furthermore, the school that is clean, pleasant, and quiet may not always provide the best learning environment if the classroom atmosphere is oppressive. Teachers control the atmosphere of a classroom. A clean, colorful, and comfortable room clearly aids leaning. When students realize that the

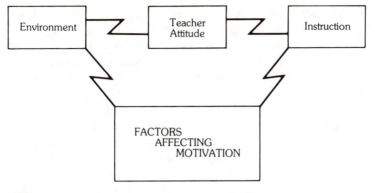

Figure 11.2

Three Factors Affecting Motivation

classroom is important to the teacher, it becomes important to them, thus motivating the desire to learn.

Most teachers are aware that they directly affect their students' behavior by the image they project in the classroom. This is an important aspect of the motivational process. Since teachers set the tone for the class, they should be conscious of their role in enhancing effective instruction. Students are quite adept at perceiving the attitude of the teacher. Negative attitudes project rigidity and a confrontational posture, while positive attitudes project flexibility and patience tempered with goodwill.

If teachers want students to feel good about learning, they must feel good about teaching. It is not unusual for students to perceive an average teacher as really outstanding because of that teacher's sincere concern for them. Enthusiasm is contagious. Teachers wishing to motivate their students to do well exude this enthusiasm that spreads throughout their classroom. As a result, students learn by emulating their teacher's behavior. Thus, attitudes not only exert a positive or negative influence on the students' desire to do their best, but also affect the teacher's performance as well. Good attitudes result in well-motivated students and positive results; poor attitudes result in poorly motivated students and negative results.

LAGNIAPPE

In 1980, 72% of the surveyed high school seniors indicated that schools should place an increased emphasis on academics as compared to 50% in 1972. Sixty-four percent of the students rated the quality of academic instruction as good or excellent as compared to 67% in 1972. Sixty percent indicated that poor teaching had interfered with their education as compared to 50% in 1972. Sixty-four percent rated the condition of the facilities as good or excellent as compared to 69% in 1972. However, fifty-five percent felt that the teachers were interested in the students in comparison to 52% in 1972.

See Theodore C. Wagenaar, "High School Seniors' Views of Themselves and Their Schools: A Trend Analysis," *Phi Delta Kappan* (September 1981).

Motivating students to do well in content classes is not easy. It requires a great deal of thought and preparation. Thus, it is not surprising that the third category affecting motivation is instruction. In the instructional process, there are three key ingredients essential for success. These are organizing and managing the content classroom, improving the student's self-concept, and enlisting the assistance of other faculty members when needed.

When organizing the content classroom for instruction, teachers need to be aware of each student's strengths and limitations. Appropriate instruction for each student is essential to providing the most motivating atmosphere. Being aware of such information as the independent and instructional reading levels of each student, strengths and/or deficiencies in the various skill areas, and the student's interest are essential in planning and implementing appropriate instruction. Knowledge of this information dictates the type of organizational format to be used in the classroom. Teachers can use various grouping patterns along with total class instruction. Achievement groups, skill groups, interest groups, as well as peer groups have a place in the content classroom. Appropriate instruction for each student ensures the opportunity for leaning. Students provided with instruction on their level and grouped to do tasks with which they can be successful are less likely to be disruptive and more likely to be motivated to learn.

Teachers exhibiting flexibility in their classrooms are perceived by students as being interested in seeing them succeed. Organization and management techniques such as grouping combined with whole-class instruction, allow more diversity in the classroom, more movement, more independence, and more opportunities for learning.

Further evidence of flexibility in the content classroom in indicated by the teacher's ability to integrate a variety of alternate activities and teaching techniques into the instructional flow. One problem that teachers constantly face is that of falling into the same routine for extended periods of time. A few teachers actually use basically the same instructional pattern for weeks or months at a time. As a result, many students become bored with the same old routine. Students like variety, and using alternative activities and teaching techniques provide that variety. Many content teachers would be amazed at the difference variety makes in motivating students to learn. Some alternate activities and techniques that can improve instruction, and result in more highly motivated students, are suggested by Mason and Mize. These include:

> *Make a question book:* This activity is designed to encourage reference material reading. Students are invited to submit questions on index cards. Under the question they should write the exact reference for locating the answer. Other students may select a question of interest, use the reference and write the answer. Students may then compile these into books of questions with each question followed by the author's name.
>
> *Read popular songs:* Using popular songs, structural analysis, vocabulary, and other reading skills can be taught. The final step may be designed as a sing-along.
>
> *Make sentence anagrams:* This activity is designed to improve comprehension by cutting sentences into separate words. After the sentences are cut, the students reassemble the words into sentences.
>
> *Help students write stories for younger children:* This is an activity in which students are asked to compile stories for younger students. They are provided

a graded word list to get them started. These stories should be kept relatively brief.

"Book Tasting Time": In order to whet appetites for reading books, students preview several books by briefly perusing them ("tasting time") to get the "flavor" of the book before going to the next one. This activity is designed to encourage students to read more books.

Make or use reading games: Many popular games such as "Scrabble" and "Password" are great motivators. Teachers may also wish to try their hand at making some games.

Interviewing: The first step in this activity is to select people from different occupations and write out an interview. This activity is designed to improve verbal and writing skills, as well as provide students with a variety of experiences.

Fun writing: In this activity teachers may allow students to write riddles, spoonerisms, or poetry as a recreational activity. They may also try some group writing activities. One activity begins by having each member of a group start a story by writing one word on a piece of paper. As the papers are passed to the right, a word is added. This continues for several minutes. At the end of the allotted time, the story is completed by the student last receiving the paper. Then the best story from the groups is chosen and read to the class.

T.V. tie-ins: The medium of television can be used as a teaching tool when planned lessons are tied into T.V. programs.[1]

Another successful motivational activity is proposed by Fader and McNeil:

> *Keeping a journal or diary:* This is a technique designed to encourage writing with students free to write anything that they wish in their journal. For some students, it is an outlet for venting their hostility toward school, teachers, and society in general. Although this is a flexible activity, the teacher may wish to recommend that a minimum of four pages a week be written. If students experience difficulty in expressing themselves, they may be allowed to copy material.[2]

Other motivational activities that may interest content teachers are:

Recreational reading: In this activity students should be encouraged to read materials inside and outside of the classroom on a regular basis. The materials read should be chosen by the student.

Uninterrupted sustained silent reading (USSR) or *Sustained Silent Reading* (SSR): This is a technique for encouraging recreational reading. A specific uninterrupted block of time is set aside during the school day for everyone to participate. It is essential that teachers, principals, and other staff members participate in this activity in order for the students to identify with adults in a reading situation. This may also be used on a smaller scale in individual classrooms.

Although the use of a variety of alternate activities and techniques to enhance instruction is necessary, teachers are also concerned about providing a variety of materials that complement the activities and techniques. Additionally, students are encouraged to read as much as possible and as often as possible. For many students, the materials not only provide the opportunity to gain knowledge through various experiences, but also offer an outlet for pent-up frustrations and hostilities.

LAGNIAPPE

Attitudes among junior high school students participating in a Sustained Silent Reading program improved significantly. They felt happier about going to the school library, more positive about reading a book, better about doing assigned reading, and were more positive about the importance of reading.

See Ruth K. J. Cline and George L. Kretke, "An Evaluation of Long-term SSR in the Junior High School," *Journal of Reading* (March 1980): 505.

The use of high interest-low vocabulary materials is necessary for some students to remain interested in the content area. Another aspect to remember in choosing materials is that they need to be relevant to the students. Nothing turns students off more quickly than a book or story that has no meaning for them. Some students need materials that relate to them on a concrete level. This means materials that are realistic and deal with issues they encounter in their everyday lives. Materials that provide variety in the content classroom are:

Every student will be able to find at least one paperback book that will appeal to him.

Paperback books: There are so many of these that it is virtually impossible *not* to find something that each student would enjoy reading.

Library books: In most instances school libraries are good sources of student materials. The public library is another source for additional materials.

Reference books: These are excellent sources of information, although some students may experience difficulty in reading them. (Some encyclopedias are easier to read than others.) Additionally, some have accompanying activity books that assist in their use.

Content textbooks: A variety of content textbooks is very helpful in providing alternate reading sources to the regular content text.

Magazines: The use of magazines is a good way to keep students involved in current events, as well as providing them with a variety of additional reading materials. Diversity is the key word here.

Newspapers: Many idea books use newspapers as motivators in content learning. Newspapers, like magazines, contain diverse information for student use.

Comics: Although some teachers may hesitate to use this resource, comics may be a key motivational tool. If this is the only material that some students can or will read, then teachers should use it as a starter and later encourage students to read other materials.

LAGNIAPPE

A survey of over **1500** persons found that **94%** of the American public age sixteen or older read magazines and newspapers, **33%** read at least a book a month, and **55%** had read at least one book in the past six months. Although **39%** of those surveyed never read a book, they do read newspapers and magazines. The most popular fiction categories were action and adventure stories, followed by historical fiction and historical romance. The top nonfiction categories were biography and autobiography, followed by cooking, home economics, and history.

See Yankelovich, Skelly and White, *The 1978 Consumer Research Study on Reading and Book Purchasing*, BISG Report no. 6, Book Industry Study Group, 1978.

Effective instruction that motivates requires manipulation of students, materials, activities, and teaching techniques. The recipients of all this flexibility and movement are the students. Above all, students need to be aware of their progress. When students complete assignments, projects, or any other tasks, immediate feedback is needed. Some teachers may prefer writing brief notes to their students while others prefer verbal feedback. A combination of the two is preferable with more emphasis on verbal communication since all students want their teachers to talk to them. Rember that students who receive immediate feedback are more likely to be motivated than those who do not.

Although effective classroom organization and management are essential in developing a motivational atmosphere, an equally important but more fragile ingredient is that of enhancing a positive self-concept. How does the teacher combat a poor self-concept and improve it? The primary element again is the teacher. Usually good teaching emphasizing individual student differences results in a positive self-concept about learning. Also, giving students opportuni-

Effective instruction requires careful coordination of students, materials, activities, and teaching techniques.

ties to work on their level with a variety of materials and activities, in a setting in which they are contributing members, definitely helps self-concept. Effective instruction, organization, and management, too, combined with the teacher's personal interest in the students, help develop a more positive self-concept. Again, the teacher is a role model. The teacher who has a positive self-concept and enjoys teaching will transmit this attitude to the student. Thus, instruction, organization, and personal concern can interrelate to help students feel more positive about themselves and their content learning.

How can teachers ensure success? Students need as many positive experiences in the classroom as possible. Nothing is gained through negative reinforcement. When students complete assignments, projects, or any other task, teachers should say, "You really worked hard and I can see that you did your best!" Perhaps the assignment was not well done, but it is probable that next time it may be better.

Another way of improving a student's self-concept is to give that student some type of responsibility. This could be anything from closing windows to helping a handicapped student complete an assignment. It is not the task, but the thought that is important. In conjunction with giving students responsibilities in the classroom, they should also be allowed to participate in making decisions. As students become involved, they begin to feel they really belong and are an integral part of the class. This reinforces their positive feelings about school, teachers, and their peers. But most important, it tells them that teachers believe in them.

Although most students are motivated when they are involved in a positive instructional environment, there are still those few who are difficult to teach. In this situation, teachers may wish to take advantage of the school's resources such as other faculty members who are available to assist in motivating difficult students. The school librarian, school counselor, reading specialist, special education resource teacher, physical education teacher, or the principal are examples. Perhaps the more effective of these in motivating some students is the physical education teacher. When the "coach" suggests that a student may be interested in reading a certain book, teachers and librarians can be sure that the book will be checked out continuously!

Many testimonials have been given by reading teachers, physical education teachers, other content teachers, and administrators to prove the suggestive powers of the physical education teacher in encouraging students to read. Thomas and Robinson[3] discuss how one coach got the students hooked on reading by bringing a crate of books to class and passing out books of interest geared to the reading level of individual students, or by asking students to stop by his office to look at books he had found for them. A similar effective motivational device used by some physical education teachers is the establishing of a "Sports Library" in a corner of the gym.[4]

No matter what techniques are used for motivating the student, the important point to remember is that instruction and motivation depend on one another.

PARENTAL INVOLVEMENT IN THE MOTIVATIONAL PROCESS

An examination of the role of teachers in the motivational process clarifies many of the issues involved; however, another essential link in the process is the parents. Parental involvement is crucial in motivating their children. What is the parents' responsibility?

Parents instill in their children the desire to learn by showing an interest in learning themselves. This, in turn, is transmitted to their children. When parents are indifferent toward school and learning, their children see no value in attending school. Such an attitude increases the difficulty of providing appropriate instruction for students, and also increases the likelihood of their failure.

Encouraging reading at home is especially important to the development of a successful learner. Responsible parents should provide good reading materials. Even children from the poorest socioeconomic backgrounds should have at least a book or magazine that gives them a chance to improve their reading skills.

Parents need to spend time with their children, providing them with both vicarious and actual experiences. Most important is the obligation of parents to provide a role model that reflects a positive approach to learning and life in general.

Also important is the responsibility of parents to become involved in school activities—to show their children that they are concerned about learning. Teachers need this parent support. Most of the really effective instructional programs exist in communities where there is good rapport between parents and teachers. In these instances, parents are visible, as well as positive, by providing ideas and experiences, and occasionally helping out in the classroom. Parents and teachers may not always agree, but it is important for both to work together to promote good instructional programs.

As with teachers, parental trust is essential in motivating students. It is another element essential to learning.

LAGNIAPPE

According to the 13th Annual Gallup Poll of the public's attitude toward the public schools, 55% of the parents with children ages 13 and older had discussed their child's progress or problems during the year with any of their teachers. Of those who had spoken with the teacher, 80% felt the teachers were interested in the child—14% were uncertain! Only 14% of the parents of children 13 or older helped with homework and only 27% of these parents placed a limit on television viewing. Parents rate lack of discipline as the number one problem facing the public school. Parents' lack of interest was rated slightly higher than teachers' lack of interest as a problem area in the public schools!

See *Phi Delta Kappan* (September 1981).

STUDENT AS A SELF-MOTIVATOR

Much of the responsibility for motivating students belongs to the teacher, and parents must accept their fair share also. But the students themselves carry a responsibility in the motivational process. They must develop the capacity to become self-motivators. How can teachers help students achieve this goal?

Difficulties with attitudes and interests frequently hamper students' potential for learning. Many students believe that all they should be responsible for is showing up in the classroom, and then it is the teacher's duty to make them want to learn. This attitude frequently reflects a poor environmental background or instability in the home. Many students, however, come from similar situations and are excellent students. They have managed to overcome these hurdles. Teachers can help students adopt a cooperative attitude and a willingness to learn by encouraging them to contribute to their own success in school. Some suggestions include:

1. *Accept responsibilities:* This is primarily the realization that learning requires a commitment. In this instance, teachers can help students accept personal responsibility for learning. It also means becoming active in the learning process, and working with peers cooperatively. Accepting responsibility is the first step toward student success.
2. *Awareness of goals:* Teachers can help students set realistic goals. Goals reflecting short-term and long-term planning are essential to success, and demonstrate a positive attitude toward learning.
3. *Awareness of progress:* Teachers should keep students aware of how successfully they meet their goals. If they are not as successful as they wish to be, less stringent goals should be set; however, if they are achieving better than expected, then more challenging goals may be set. Setting goals in conjunction with the teacher's input allows students to judge where they are in relation to where they want to be.

4. *Student involvement in learning:* Teachers should allow students to participate in decision making, encourage cooperation with teachers and peers, facilitate discussions, and assist students in adopting an interactive posture in the class.

5. *Regular reading:* In order to become more knowledgeable members of the class, students need to read regularly. Teachers can help in this effort by demonstrating their own interest in reading and by sharing what they have read. They can also suggest interesting books relating to the content being studied. Reading related activities such as Uninterrupted Sustained Silent Reading, as well as delving into a variety of materials, helps students succeed in the content classroom.

6. *Trust:* Just as teachers and parents are expected to foster an attitude of trust toward students, students in turn must learn to trust adults. Trust will evolve in time as students observe desirable teacher behavior. Trust is essential to learning.

In retrospect, motivation depends on close communication and a sense of fulfillment among teachers, students, and parents. It is intangible; it cannot be bought or sold, but must be earned. Working together, teachers, parents, and students find that learning is exciting.

REFLECTION

Identify strategies that are used in your school, or a school in which you have observed, to motivate students to read in the content classroom. Make a list of these strategies to add to those suggested in this chapter.

SUMMARY

In this chapter students are characterized as either intrinsic or extrinsic learners. Intrinsic learners are self-motivated, while extrinsic learners need outside stimuli. The latter tend to be more difficult to motivate and frequently create problems for teachers and parents.

The teacher's responsibility in motivation consists of providing an appropriate environment for learning, maintaining a positive and enthusiastic attitude toward teaching, and providing effective instruction. Other roles of the teacher include using effective classroom organization and management techniques, improving the self-concept of students, and using all available faculty resources to assist in motivating students.

Parents' involvement in motivation include developing and maintaining a positive attitude toward the school environment, projecting a positive image toward reading, providing a variety of experiences for their children, and supporting the school and teachers.

Teachers help students become self-motivators by encouraging them to develop a positive attitude toward learning, to accept responsibility, to know their goals, to keep abreast of their progress, to become involved in learning, to read regularly, and to develop a sense of trust with their parents and teachers.

FOR DISCUSSION

1. As a content teacher, what do you see as the major motivational strategies that you could use in your class?
2. What do you think can be done to get parents more involved in the middle and secondary school programs? What impact do you think this would have on motivation?
3. Why do you think many secondary students become disinterested in learning content information? What can be done to correct this problem?

OTHER SUGGESTED READINGS

Arnoldsen, Larry M. "Reading Made Necessary, Naturally!" *Journal of Reading* 25 (March 1982):538–42.

Betts, Emmett Albert. "Capture Reading Motivation." *Reading Improvement* 13 (1976):41–46.

Ciani, Alfred J., ed. *Motivating Reluctant Readers.* Newark, Del.: International Reading Association, 1981.

Colwell, Clyde G. "Humor as a Motivational and Remedial Technique." *Journal of Reading* 24 (March 1981):484–86.

Drew, Walter F.; Olds, Anita R.; and Olds, Henry F. *Motivating Today's Students.* Palo Alto, Calif.: Learning Handbooks, 1974.

Forgan, Harry W., and Mangrum, Charles T. *Teaching Content Area Reading Skills,* 2nd ed. Columbus, Ohio: Charles E. Merrill, 1981. Module 9.

Gentile, Lance M., and McMillan, Merna M. "Why Won't Teenagers Read?" *Journal of Reading* 20 (May 1977):649–54.

Gold, Patricia Cohen, and Yellin, David. "Be the Focus: A Psychoeducational Technique for Use with Unmotivated Learners." *Journal of Reading* 25 (March 1982):550–52.

Guerra, Cathy L., and Payne, DeLores B. "Using Popular Books and Magazines to Interest Students in General Science." *Journal of Reading* 24 (April 1981):583–86.

Haimowitz, Benjamin. "Motivating Reluctant Readers in Innercity Classes." *Journal of Reading* 21 (December 1977):227–30.

Heathington, Betty S. "What to Do about Reading Motivation in the Middle School." *Journal of Reading* 22 (May 1979):709–13.

Koenke, Karl. "Motivation and Reading." *Language Arts* 55 (November/December 1978):998–1002.

Lamberg, Walter J., and Lamb, Charles E. *Reading Instruction in the Content Areas.* Chicago: Rand McNally, 1980. Chapter 20.

Lunstrum, John P. "Building Motivation Through the Use of Controversy." *Journal of Reading* 24 (May 1981):687–91.

Mathewson, Grover C. "The Moderating Effect of Extrinsic Motivation Upon the Attitude/Comprehension Relationship in Reading." *Reading Comprehension at Four Linguistic Levels,* ed. Clifford Pennock. Newark, Del.: International Reading Association, 1979.

Noland, Ronald G., and Craft, Lynda H. "Methods to Motivate the Reluctant Reader." *Journal of Reading* 19 (February 1976):387–91.

Tierney, Robert J. "Motivating the Superior Reader." *Journal of Research and Development in Education* 11 (Spring 1978):75–79.

NOTES

1. George E. Mason and John M. Mize, "Twenty-two Sets of Methods and Materials for Stimulating Teenage Reading," *Journal of Reading* 21 (May 1978):735–41.
2. Daniel Fader and Elton B. McNeil, *Hooked on Books: Program and Proof* (New York: Berkley, 1976), pp. 35–44.
3. Ellen Lamar Thomas and H. Alan Robinson, *Improving Reading in Every Class* (Boston: Allyn and Bacon, 1972), pp. 465–71.
4. Sanford Patlak, "Physical Education and Reading: Questions and Answers," in *Fusing Reading Skills and Content*, ed. H. Alan Robinson and Ellen Lamar Thomas (Newark, Del.: International Reading Association, 1969), pp. 81–88.

STEP FIVE

RETEACH OR RECYCLE

Following instruction, content teachers evaluate student learning to determine if the concepts have been understood. If the teacher is satisfied with the evaluation, the class usually proceeds to a new set of concepts and the model presented in this text is repeated or recycled. If the content teacher is not satisfied with the evaluation results, however, the necessary concepts must be retaught until the students demonstrate an understanding. In Step V, ideas are suggested for reteaching identified concepts, and a review of the model is provided for use in recycling for teaching new concepts. After reading the chapters in Step IV, Chapters 5-11, and using the model to incorporate reading into content instruction, content teachers may find a rereading of Chapters 5 and 6, as well as Chapter 9, to be extremely helpful. As teachers use this model for content instruction, adjustments must be made in order for individual teaching styles to be complemented. Thus, in recycling, once content teachers have used the model as outlined, they may then adjust it to better meet their individual needs and the specific needs of their students.

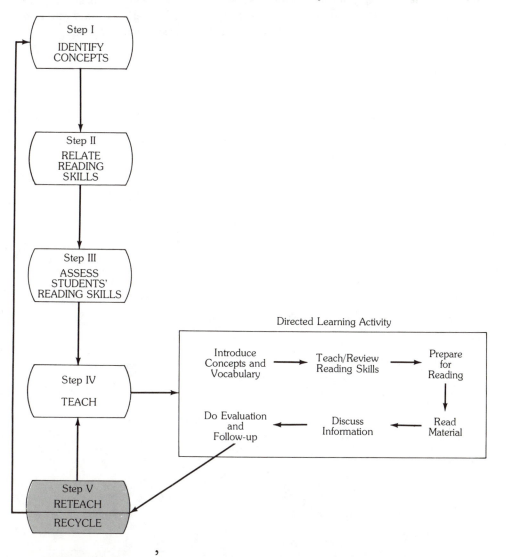

Step I
IDENTIFY
CONCEPTS

Step II
RELATE
READING
SKILLS

Step III
ASSESS
STUDENTS'
READING SKILLS

Step IV
TEACH

Directed Learning Activity

Introduce Concepts and Vocabulary → Teach/Review Reading Skills → Prepare for Reading

Do Evaluation and Follow-up ← Discuss Information ← Read Material

Step V
RETEACH
RECYCLE

CHAPTER TWELVE

PUTTING IT ALL TOGETHER

As content teachers met to discuss the successes and disappointments of incorporating reading instruction into their content teaching, they shared ideas that demonstrated they understood the model and the learning process. Ms. Barckley, a central office supervisor, suggested that the group organize and summarize their questions, suggestions, and ideas for new content teachers struggling to better meet students' needs in the content classroom. The following questions (see "Study Questions") were identified.

Using these questions, the content teachers applied their experiences and made suggestions to help others who incorporate this model into their content classes.

STUDY QUESTIONS

1. What can the content teacher do when students fail to learn content concepts after instruction?

2. What does the teacher do when most of the students learn the concepts, but a few do not understand?

3. How do the different steps in this model for content instruction interrelate?

4. When are individual teaching styles considered in this model?

RETEACHING: A NECESSARY PART OF INSTRUCTION

Concepts and vocabulary were introduced, related reading skills were reviewed, appropriate materials were used for reading content information, and an adequate discussion of the various concepts was conducted. Yet when test papers were graded, Mr. Larimer, the science teacher, was disappointed with the results. All of this work and students still did not understand the concepts. Although some learned more than others and everyone seemed to understand a few of the concepts, there remained several critical concepts that a majority of the students did not comprehend. What is the content teacher to do? One word answers the question—RETEACH! But how?

In reteaching content concepts, teachers must use test and other evaluative data, such as results of class discussion, as assessment or diagnostic information. Such information provides clues on what concepts or parts of concepts must be retaught. If, for example, students do not understand the concept, "Two or more chemical elements combine to form a compound," the teacher must then analyze the concept to determine what must be retaught. Is it the vocabulary or is it the application of the concept in a laboratory situation? After identifying what must be retaught, teachers can proceed with instruction. Failure to understand concepts usually occurs because of one or more of the following reasons:

1. *Lack of background understanding.* Students who have had no prior experiences to relate to the concepts being learned need more initial instruction. For example, in teaching the concept, "Volcanic eruptions cause many changes in the earth's surface," to students who have never seen mountains or rock formations, teachers must provide concept-related experiences before the new concept can be understood. For suggestions on concept instruction, review Chapters 2 and 5.
2. *Difficult vocabulary.* Because students frequently have not had experiences with the technical and specialized vocabulary of many content areas, they may not learn the concepts because of not understanding the words. In this instance, additional vocabulary instruction is sometimes all that is needed. Suggestions on content vocabulary instruction are given in Chapters 3 and 5.
3. *Inability to apply reading skills to content materials.* If students are unable to apply appropriate reading skills to content materials, they probably will not understand them. Thus, content teachers must remedy this deficiency. Information on reading skill development is given in Chapters 3 and 5, with specialized information relating specific skills to different content areas given in the following section, "Special Notes for Special Folks."
4. *Material is too difficult.* When students are assigned content materials in which they have difficulty recognizing words and understanding the subject, little content learning occurs. If teachers suspect this as a problem, different materials must be used appropriate to students' reading levels. Suggestions on material selection and its use are given in Chapter 8.
5. *Poor discussion strategies.* Sometimes in content discussions, limited participation occurs because the wrong questions may be asked or a few students tend to monopolize the discussion. When this happens, other students tend to tune out the discussion, daydream, or listen to only parts of the discussion and reach erroneous conclusions. Poor questioning strategies such as asking

only for short answers do not promote discussions. Instead, they contribute to confusion and possibly a misunderstanding of information. Ideas, too, are not expanded to form relationships often necessary to understand content information. When teachers suspect that this is causing a problem in content learning, they should go back to a beginning level to develop the questioning and discussion strategies outlined in Chapter 5.

6. *Poor evaluation procedures.* A frequent student complaint is that teachers do not test what is taught. Teachers must, therefore, carefully review their evaluation tools to be sure that concepts and related information are assessed. If evaluation instruments are weak, reteaching will not solve the problem! Evaluate your exams and help students develop the test-taking skills outlined in Chapter 5.

Content teachers may find that students are more amenable to reviewing concepts if they are involved in the evaluation and realize that certain concepts have not been understood. When concepts are initially introduced and students have an idea of what they are expected to learn, a criterion is established that can be used as a self-evaluation procedure. As students conduct their own needs-assessment and realize they do not understand the concepts, content teachers may use different grouping procedures, such as peer tutoring, along with alternative content materials in reteaching.

Teachers should not, in reteaching content information, use ideas and materials identical to those in the initial teaching. Repeating the same process with the same materials does not always improve learning. Identifying areas of need and using different strategies and materials are more likely to result in improved learning.

Content teachers are frequently concerned about a few students who do not understand concepts when others in the class are ready to study new concepts. How can this be managed? This is an ever-present problem with no easy answer.

First, decide how important the unlearned concept is to future learning. If the student can proceed with the class in learning new concepts without previous information, this should be done; if not, special time must be used to reteach. For essential concepts, determine a way to reteach. The content teacher must proceed with new concepts for the class while at the same time reteaching old concepts to one or two students. This is when time and classroom management become critical. The teacher may try to

Identify materials that the few students can study on their own to understand the information.

Provide tapes or films that students can use to review concepts.

Use the time to reteach concepts to the few students while other students are reading new materials.

Elicit parental or other volunteer assistance to help students at home or at school.

Group students so they can help one another, and use study guides or similar strategies for reteaching.

Obtain assistance from special teachers such as the reading teacher or resource teacher.

Content teachers should find one or more of these ideas useful in reteaching. For nonessential concepts, proceed to teach these few students with the class. If possible, these students should continue to learn the new concepts being taught. This keeps them from lagging behind continuously. At the same time, the unlearned concepts must not be overlooked. Teachers should incorporate a review of this information into other lessons. Eventually, this information becomes essential for learning other concepts!

Reteaching is always necessary in any instructional situation. All students do not learn at the same rate or in the same way; therefore, reteaching is required. Sometimes reteaching must be dealt with several times. Try to be patient, carefully assess the problem, and logically decide what can be done, remembering that many elements affect learning.

REFLECTION

Identify a student in a content classroom who has not learned the concepts that were taught. Using the evaluative data and your observations, tell what you think needs to be retaught and how you would go about reteaching.

RECYCLE: DO IT AGAIN!

When concepts are learned, new concepts must be identified and taught. Content teachers should follow this same basic model for each new set of concepts to be learned. After working through the model several times, however, content teachers may wish to make adjustments so they feel more comfortable with the instructional process. This is expected and encouraged as long as planning and organized instructional procedures are used.

The steps included in this model are interwoven, with one step leading to another. In order to adapt or adopt this model for content reading instruction, teachers must understand these interrelationships.

Step I: Identify Concepts. This initial step provides the basis for content instruction. The content teacher must first identify what is to be learned before any instruction is begun.

Step II: Relate Reading Skills. In order to incorporate reading into content teaching, teachers must be aware of and identify the reading skills that students need to apply in order to learn the content information. Therefore, the necessary reading skills are identified for each concept. Although this step may be considered unnecessary, learning does not occur in a content classroom unless students apply the appropriate reading skills.

Step III: Assess Students' Reading Skills. Again, content teachers often view assessment prior to instruction as an unnecessary part of instruction. However, by identifying needs and providing instruction based on these needs, content teachers find that less reteaching is necessary and time is actually saved.

Step IV: Teach. Instruction is the major concern for all content teachers. Good instruction requires careful planning such as outlined in Steps I-III. As content teachers begin instruction, they should follow a structured procedure, such as the Directed Learning Activity, to be sure that preteaching is done as a part of the instructional process. In following the Directed Learning Activity format, these parts should be included:

1. *Introduce concepts and vocabulary.* Preteaching is necessary in order for students to develop a grasp of what is going to be learned and to understand the vocabulary used with the concepts. This develops a readiness for learning.
2. *Teach or review reading skills.* Using the assessment data on skills identified as important for learning concepts, content teachers must show students how to relate their reading skill to content learning. While content teachers sometimes believe that students do not know how to read, the problem is usually that they cannot relate their knowledge to the content material. Only content teachers can show them how to do this.
3. *Prepare for reading.* Students should be given a purpose for reading content material or led to develop their own purposes for reading. Regardless, they should have a reason for reading the materials. Content teachers may introduce study strategies such as SQ3R or use study guides to help students read the materials.
4. *Read material.* Content teachers should provide students with materials that are appropriate to their reading levels and which allow them to learn about the concepts. All students will probably not read the same materials; however, each should be able to contribute to the class discussion.
5. *Discuss information.* Following a silent reading of different materials, the teacher should guide class or small group discussions that serve to encourage learning from one another and allow each student to participate. Careful questioning strategies must be used in discussions to assure that all important aspects of a topic are covered.

Step V: Reteach or Recycle. Using the evaluation information, teachers must determine if concepts should be retaught or if students are ready to move to new concepts. New concepts may be taught by repeating this five-step process.

As this five-step model for content reading instruction is recycled when new concepts are taught, teachers should find it beneficial to improving learning in their content classes.

LAGNIAPPE

If we think of it, all that a University, or final highest school can do for us, is still but what the first school began doing—teach us to *read*.

Thomas Carlyle, *The Hero as Man of Letters*

SUMMARY

The model for content reading instruction is reviewed in this chapter, along with considerations for reteaching unlearned concepts. Content teachers must consider the steps as they plan for instruction and should adopt or adapt these procedures in their classrooms in order to enhance content learning. Content learning cannot occur unless students can read content materials. Therefore, content teachers must incorporate the necessary reading instruction into their teaching and realize that every teacher is indeed a teacher of reading.

FOR DISCUSSION

1. What do you view as the most essential elements in this model? The least essential? Why do you believe as you do?
2. Is reteaching necessary in the middle or secondary content class? Why or why not? Is reteaching possible at this level? Why or why not?
3. How can individual teaching styles be considered when this model is used in content instruction?

SPECIAL NOTES FOR SPECIAL FOLKS

ADDITIONAL SUGGESTIONS ESPECIALLY FOR . . .

. . . all teachers in the middle and secondary schools. A few notes are provided in this section to give more specialized information in each of the content areas, as well as to the reading specialist working with content teachers. Suggestions are also given for sources of information that provide other ideas for use in the different content areas. So, these special notes are for special content folks and provide additional suggestions especially for . . . YOU!

The Social Studies Teacher

Integrating social studies and reading requires careful thought and planning by the content teacher. Plans must be carefully constructed to effectively use reading techniques for enhancing content instruction. Because of the special nature of social studies material, many reading techniques lend themselves naturally to this area. Social studies materials are written in an expository style that is characterized by precise factual writing, a lack of descriptive words, and quite often, a preponderance of technical terms that the student must understand in order to comprehend the material. Clearly the use of study strategies, readiness techniques such as advance organizers and structured overviews, as well as study guides, facilitate the student's learning process. Thus, reading strategies become tools for successfully teaching social studies material. Shepherd describes this process which combines the teaching of content and the skills of reading as "fusion".[1]

This fusion or integration of social studies and reading skills results in increased efficiency in learning social studies content as well as improving reading skills.[2]

Although many reading skills must be applied as different social studies materials are read, some skills are used more frequently. These include:

1. *Sequencing of information:* In history, events are usually presented in a chronological order requiring that students recognize the sequence and remember the facts in order.
2. *Cause-effect relationships:* History, geography, and sociology materials require that students recognize both stated and inferred cause-effect relationships. Social studies information may give a cause of an event and expect the reader to infer or conclude the effect (or possibly provide the effect or result of a series of incidents and expect the reader to synthesize the information to determine the cause).

3. *Comparisons and contrasts:* Students are asked to consider likenesses and differences in governments, people, culture, countries, etc., in the social studies materials they read. This is an essential skill that relates information in an organized way.

4. *Fact and opinion:* In reading current events as well as social studies text materials, and listening to accounts of historical events, students must become evaluative thinkers. This process begins as they distinguish facts from opinions and must continue as they detect *propaganda techniques* being used in editorials and in the analysis of political systems.

5. *Reading maps, charts, and other pictorial information:* Geography materials require the careful reading of maps and the relating of this information to the narrative. Many charts, tables, and diagrams are presented in history, psychology, sociology, and political science materials. Students must learn to read these pictorial illustrations and to interrelate the content to the text narrative.

When students encounter social studies printed materials, teachers can predict some of the difficulties they will experience. Although all social studies materials are different, the same general problems exist, namely, the organization of the materials, readability, relevance of and interest in the content, and the abstractness of the concepts and vocabulary. Awareness of these difficulties assists social studies teachers in helping students improve their content learning.

Social studies materials are filled with terms that relate to concepts that can best be understood through experience, and that are comprehended based on previous experiences. Because all students have not had the same experiences, and teachers cannot provide firsthand all of the experiences necessary for social studies learning, many vicarious experiences must be used as new concepts are introduced. Films, pictures, resource people, books, etc., help students develop the background understanding needed to learn new concepts.

Additional information on incorporating reading into social studies instruction can be found in the following sources:

Arnold, Marie J., and Ingraham, Murray J. "Using ECRI Techniques to Improve Reading Skills in Social Studies." *Reading Horizons* 17 (Winter 1977):137–140.

Capron, Barbara; Charles, Cheryl; and Kleiman, Stanley. "Curriculum Reform and Social Studies Textbooks." *Social Education* 8 (April 1973):280–88.

Donlan, Dan. "Locating Main Ideas in History Textbooks." *Journal of Reading* 24 (November 1980):135–40.

Johnson, Roger, and Vardian, Ellen B. "Reading Readability and the Social Studies." *The Reading Teacher* 26 (February 1973):483–88.

Frankel, Jill C. "Reading Skills through Social Studies Content v Student Involvement." *Journal of Reading* 18 (October 1974):23–26.

Lunstrum, John P. "Reading in the Social Studies: A Preliminary Study of Recent Research." *Social Education* (January 1976):10–18.

Lunstrum, John P., and Taylor, Bob L. *Teaching Reading in the Social Studies.* Newark, Del.: International Reading Association, 1978.

Mize, John M. "A Directed Strategy for Teaching Critical Reading and Decision Making." *Journal of Reading* 22 (November 1978):144–48.

Wilson, Cathy R., and Hammill, Carol. "Inferencing and Comprehension in Ninth Graders' Reading Geography Textbooks." *Journal of Reading* 25 (February 1982):424–28.

The Mathematics Teacher

For years, the importance of reading in mathematics has been discussed. Glennon and Callahan suggested that the four factors most important to success in math are

1. general reading skills;
2. problem-solving reading skills;
3. mechanical computation and mathematical understanding of the concepts of quantity, the number system, as well as arithmetical relationships; and
4. a spatial factor involving the ability to visualize and conceptualize as well as to clarify word meanings.[3]

Thus, the application of reading skills must be encouraged as students study math materials.

To read math materials, students must use a variety of skills. They must, of course, identify the words and understand the ideas. However, reading skills are considered critical to understanding the different math concepts. These include:

1. *Following directions:* If all other reading skills are correctly applied in studying math materials, but students fail to use their skill in following written directions, the problem will be solved incorrectly. Following directions is essential in computing problems.
2. *Interpreting symbols:* Understanding mathematics information requires students to associate symbols or abbreviations used in directions and problems with the appropriate term. Awareness of the unique features of math's technical vocabulary is basic to understanding the information.
3. *Perceiving relationships:* As students attempt to solve word problems in math, they must learn to recognize the relationships among various numbers and directions. Math problems cannot be solved through a literal interpretation—students must see the interrelationships of the various components.
4. *Problem solving:* In reading math materials, students continuously use their problem-solving skills. To understand examples, as well as to compute equations and word problems, students need to know and follow the steps in problem solving.
5. *Determining relevant and irrelevant information:* To compute word problems, students must sort out essential information for problem solving from verbiage. Students who think that all numbers contained in a math problem must be used tend to get confused and lose sight of what the problem asks them to do.

Another consideration to help students interpret mathematical information is the material's readability. Math materials are usually written concisely, being packed with details, each of which must be understood to compute the problem. The terse presentation is compounded by the unstated relationships and imprecise language that must be interpreted by the reader. Although many concepts are explained, knowledge of others is assumed. Long sentences, hidden concepts, unstated relationships, and technical vocabulary combine to form materials that are difficult to read. Because math materials use many symbols and charts, teachers find it difficult to use a readability formula on parts of the materials.

Kane, Byrne, and Hater have studied the use of readability formulas with math materials and have developed a formula that may be used with materials containing numerals and equations.[4] Hater and Kane have also suggested the use of the cloze procedure to determine the readability of the mathematics text.[5] Regardless of the procedure used, teachers should remember that although numbers, symbols, and short paragraphs may appear easy to read, mathematics materials are indeed quite difficult.

More information on incorporating reading instruction into the mathematics classroom can be found in the following sources:

Aaron, Ira E. "Reading in Mathematics." *Journal of Reading* 6 (May 1965):391–395, 401.

Aiken, Lewis R. "Language Factors in Learning Mathematics." *Review of Educational Research* 2 (Summer 1972):359–85.

Blankenship, Colleen S., and Lovitt, Thomas C. "Story Problems: Merely Confusing or Downright Befuddling?" *Journal for Research in Mathematics Education* 7 (November 1976):290–98.

Call, Russell J., and Wiggin, Neal A. "Reading and Mathematics." *Mathematics Teacher* 59 (February 1966):149–51.

Catterson, John H. "Techniques for Improving Comprehension in Mathematics." In *Reading in the Middle School*, ed. G. G. Duffy. Newark, Del.: International Reading Association, 1975, pp. 153–65.

Cohen, S. Alan, and Stover, Georgia. "Effects of Teaching Sixth-Grade Students to Modify Format Variables of Math Word Problems." *Reading Research Quarterly* 16 (1981):175–200.

Earle, Richard A. *Teaching Reading and Mathematics*. Newark, Del.: International Reading Association, 1976.

Easp, N. Wesley. "Observations on Teaching Mathematics." *Journal of Reading* 13 (April 1970):529–32.

Feeman, G. E. "Reading and Mathematics." *Arithmetic Teacher* 20 (November 1973):523–29.

Lees, Fred. "Mathematics and Reading." *Journal of Reading* 19 (May 1976):621–26.

Morris, Robert W. "The Role of Language in Learning Mathematics." *Prospects* 8 (1978):73–81.

Pachtman, Andrew B., and Riley, James D. "Teaching the Vocabulary of Mathematics Through Interaction, Exposure, and Structures." *Journal of Reading* 22 (December 1978):240–44.

Riley, James D., and Pachtman, Andrew B. "Reading Mathematical Word Problems: Telling Them What to Do is Not Telling Them How to Do It." *Journal of Reading* 21 (March 1978):531–34.

The English Teacher

English teachers frequently find their content area identified as the focal point around which other areas of the curriculum revolve. They are expected to provide the student with many of those experiences necessary for learning other content area materials. Additionally, they are expected to teach students how to use language, how to write effectively and correctly, and how to apply certain study skills in order to enhance learning. As a result, there are frequent attempts to delegate the responsibility for teaching reading skills to these teachers; however, English teachers have rebuffed these advances for the most part.

Literature is the primary focus for many English teachers. Some attention is given to reinforcing grammatical principles, writing compositions, and personal reading, but literature receives the most attention. The reason is that English teachers consider literature the core of their curriculum; it represents their content. Because of this emphasis, integrating reading in English becomes even more important, since studying literature is primarily a reading task. This is the area in which many students need help in dealing with printed material.

When students come to the English teacher, they are often conditioned to relate to and to work in the cognitive domain; however, literature requires that students relate effectively to information. Students must react emotionally when reading the material. For many students, this is difficult since they are used to looking for facts, analyzing the information read, and reading for literal meaning. Students have also been taught to understand the mechanics of the materials, but not to be involved with them in an affective sense. Teachers wanting students to become emotionally involved with literature must first show them how to appreciate it. Since enthusiasm is contagious, teachers must demonstrate that they themselves are interested in their subject. Discussions and readings on appreciation also develop an emotional feeling for literature.

Reading poetry represents special problems to students that other forms of literature do not. These difficulties include format, language patterns, attention to rhythm to the exclusion of comprehension, and abstractions. Poetry is compressed with the poet's point of view expressed succinctly. The readability of poetry is affected by the format, since students encounter longer sentences, irregular punctuation, the capitalization of each line, and the use of interrupting thoughts dispersed throughout the selection.[6]

Another student problem in reading poetry involves language patterns. In poetry, language patterns are more difficult to understand than vocabulary. These patterns include dialectical language, rare and elegant language, figurative language, words used differently than normally expected, and unfamiliar words.[7] Although these poetic patterns enhance elegance and style, they create problems for the uninitiated reader.

As noted in Table 3.1 (Chapter 3), all reading skills are used as students read literature. Some of the most essential skills unique to literature include:

1. *Noting character traits and actions:* Recognizing the personalities, and understanding the actions of characters, in short stories, poetry, and plays are essential to comprehending literature. Students often note who the characters are, but sometimes fail to associate actions and traits with them. Understanding this relationship is critical to the comprehension of the work.
2. *Figurative language:* Poetry commonly uses figurative language in communicating ideas and feelings. Students usually have no difficulty in recognizing the words used in these figurative expressions. They do, however, experience difficulty in associating meaning with the words. This is sometimes due to the multiple meanings of words, different backgrounds of the students and their lack of association with some expressions, and possibly even a difference in the times. (Many figures of speech used by today's teenagers are totally unfamiliar to their parents and teachers with the inverse also being

true). Therefore, some direct teaching on how to interpret figurative language is essential.

3. *Using reference materials:* English classes involve students in many writing activities, some of which require the use of reference materials. Students should be taught to use periodical indexes, the synthesis of ideas from various sources, footnoting procedures, and techniques for locating information. This requires that students understand how to read the reference materials and use them in writing.

4. *Interpreting mood:* Authors portray varying moods in literature. Hence, part of enjoying reading involves the identification of the author's mood and relating to it. Teachers should help students determine the moods reflected in various writing styles as well as in the personalities of the characters. Applying this reading skill brings more enjoyment to reading.

Additional information is found in the following sources:

Blanc, Robert A. "Cloze-Plus as an Alternative to Guides for Understanding and Appreciating Poetry." *Journal of Reading* 21 (December 1977):215–18.

Carter, B. Betty. "Helping Seventh Graders to Understand Figurative Expressions." *Journal of Reading* 20 (April 1977):559–62.

Ciani, Alfred J. "Recent Adolescent Literature: An Alternative to the Serials." In *Motivating Reluctant Readers*, ed. Alfred J. Ciani. Newark, Del.: International Reading Association, 1981.

McAuliffe, Sheila, and Brancard, Ruth. "An Experience Based Approach to Evaluating Literature." *Journal of Reading* 25 (March 1982):501–4.

McKay, J. W. "Developing Reading Skills through Literature." In *Reaching Children and Young People through Literature*, ed. Helen W. Painter. Newark, Del.: International Reading Association, 1971.

McKenna, Michael C. "A Modified Maze Approach to Teaching Poetry." *Journal of Reading* 24 (February 1981):391–94.

Readence, John E., and Moore, David. "Responding to Literature: An Alternative to Questioning." *Journal of Reading* (November 1979):107–11.

Stotsky, Sandra. "The Role of Writing in Developmental Reading." *Journal of Reading* 25 (January 1982):330–40.

Strickland, Dorothy S., ed. *The Role of Literature in Reading Instruction*. Newark, Del.: International Reading Association, 1981.

Twining, James E. "Reading and Literature: The Heterogenous Class: *Journal of Reading* 18 (March 1975):475–80.

The Science Teacher

Historically, science has been known as one of the most difficult areas in the middle and secondary school curriculum. One reason for this is that the vocabulary and concepts in the science program are not a part of the experiential backgrounds of many students. Unfamiliarity combined with hard-to-understand textbooks causes some students to believe that science is an area too difficult for them to enjoy learning. To repudiate this negative feeling toward one of the more exciting content areas in the curriculum, and to develop more student confidence in studying science, teachers must recognize the parts of the science program that seem to be most troublesome and adjust their teaching accordingly.

Shepherd suggests three basic types of reading done by students in science.[8] The first involves technical textbooks and lab manuals. These materials tend to frustrate unprepared students. Reading these materials requires careful, analytical thinking and a slow reading rate. A second type of scientific reading involves scientific journals, popular science magazines, and books on scientific research. Depending on the purposes for reading these materials and the content, this reading may be easier or more difficult. However, students who become involved with reading these supplementary materials are usually more interested in science; thus, the reading often seems easier. The third type of reading involves the nontechnical that appears in newspapers and magazine reports. These materials are the easiest to read and present few difficulties for the average student.

Thus, in reading the technical scientific information used in many science classrooms, students may experience difficulty in understanding the information because of

Organization of the text
Complex vocabulary
Overall readability
Variety in materials
Wide use of illustrations and typographical aids
Necessity to apply higher level thinking skills
Boring style used in many of the textbooks

Any or all of these problems may become factors that make reading science more difficult.

Among the most frequently used reading skills, the science teacher finds the following necessary in most lessons:

1. *Structural analysis:* Because students are often unfamiliar with scientific terms, teachers find it necessary to help them determine word pronunciation as well as meaning by looking at word parts like syllables. Structural analysis may also be used in teaching the meaning of prefixes and suffixes.
2. *Contextual analysis:* Science materials writers recognize that the science vocabulary is difficult for students to learn. Therefore, the new terms are commonly defined, directly or indirectly, within the text. This does not help students in pronouncing the words, but it does aid in comprehension. Thus, the science teacher should encourage the use of context to provide meaning for unknown words.
3. *Cause-effect relationships:* Whether students are studying chemical reactions, changes in the weather, or growing plants, they are required to note why something happens as well as the result. The result is often obvious, but the process or reasons for the results are sometimes not as apparent. Therefore, if the science teacher expects this kind of understanding, the skill of identifying stated and inferred cause-effect relationships is essential.
4. *Interpreting symbols:* In chemistry and physics, printed materials display numerous symbols and abbreviations. Teachers must provide instruction in interpreting them since they consist largely of letters rather than words.
5. *Reading charts and tables:* All science materials are filled with diagrams of different types which must be interpreted and related to the text narrative.

These illustrations frequently serve to simplify the text's narrative and aid in the understanding of the concepts.

6. *Problem solving:* Just as in mathematics, students are expected to find solutions to problems or experiments. To use this skill as they read, students should be familiar with the specific steps involved in scientific inquiry. These are outlined in Chapter 3.

Further information on reading science materials can be found in the following sources:

Dole, Janice A., and Johnson, Virginia R. "Beyond the Textbook: Science Literature for Young People." *Journal of Reading* 24 (April 1981):579–82.

Guerra, Cathy L., and Payne, DeLores B. "Using Popular Books and Magazines to Interest Students in General Science." *Journal of Reading* 24 (April 1981):583–86.

Ley, Terry C.; Henry, Loren L.; and Rowsey, Robert E. "Eighth Graders' Performance in Reading and Computing for Science-Related Word Problems." *Journal of Reading* (December 1979):222–28.

Thelen, Judith. *Improving Reading in Science.* Newark, Del.: International Reading Association, 1976.

The Business Education Teacher

Business education encompasses many different courses, each of which is unique in some manner. Included in this general area of business education are bookkeeping, business English, business law, typing, and shorthand. These courses attract good readers and poor ones. Business education teachers must, therefore, be adept at assisting students by providing differentiated levels of instruction and allowing them to progress at their own rate. Reading business education materials is difficult for students because of the wide range of reading levels as well as readability levels of the materials, the variety of organizational patterns, the specialized vocabulary and concepts, and the wide variety of materials—texts, brochures, forms, etc.—used in the courses.

The different areas of business education require the use of various reading skills. However, skills common to all areas include:

1. *Noting details:* In all areas of business education, students must read carefully to remember the details in the materials. Bookkeeping requires a careful note of figures, while typing requires an exactness in going from one document to the development of another. Similarly, in shorthand, the student must distinguish the minor differences in directions for forming as well as transcribing the symbols used in shorthand.

2. *Following directions:* Business education materials are filled with directions and problems to be solved. To accomplish these tasks, the reader must learn carefully to read all directions and to follow them exactly. Because business education courses train students in marketable skill areas, and because employers expect them to follow directions in the business world, teachers in business education classes should consider this skill of paramount importance.

3. *Noting symbols and abbreviations:* Students find many abbreviations and symbols used in all business education courses. In business English, abbreviations are used in letter writing as well as in completing order forms. In typing, writers often use abbreviations and symbols that the typist must interpret in order to type the entire word and to follow directions. Bookkeeping also uses symbols in keeping ledger sheets, and shorthand is an abbreviated writing system that must be translated to communicate information.

As in the other content areas, interest is a factor that affects learning in business education. In contrast to other academic areas, however, many students are enrolled by choice, thus increasing the probability of a high-interest level in learning. Because of this positive aspect, many students perform at a higher level than they might otherwise in social studies, English, math, or science. Teachers must be aware of these interests as well as that many students may experience reading problems. Reading difficulties can cause students to quickly lose their interest and develop a defeated attitude because of being unable to learn employment skills material. These difficulties must be acknowledged by business education teachers in order to assist students in more successfully learning the important concepts presented in the various business classes.

Other information on developing reading skills through business education can be found in these sources:

Afflerbach, Peter P.; Allington, Richard L.; and Walmsley, Sean A. "A Basic Vocabulary of U. S. Federal Social Program Applications and Forms." *Journal of Reading* 8 (January 1980):332–36.

Ahrent, Kenneth, and Haselton, Shirley S. "Essential Reading Skills in Bookkeeping." *Journal of Reading* 16 (January 1973):314–17.

Danneman, Jean. "Reading: The Road to Shorthand Skill." *Business Education World* 40 (January 1960):26.

Haehn, Faynelle. "Let's Have a 'Read-In' in Typewriting." In *Fusing Reading Skills and Content*, ed. H. Alan Robinson and Ellen Lamar Thomas. Newark, Del.: International Reading Association, 1969.

Heinemann, Susan Turk. "Can Job-Related Performance Tasks Be Used to Diagnose Secretaries' Reading and Writing Skills? *Journal of Reading* (December 1979):239–43.

Pyrczak, Fred. "Effects of Abbreviations on Comprehension of Classified Employment Advertisements." *Journal of Reading* 24 (December 1980):249–52.

The Vocational Education Teacher

Vocational education encompasses a number of specialized fields that are unique in that they tend to attract one population of students interested in learning job-related skills and another population interested in learning how to become more self-sufficient. Courses included are industrial arts, vocational agriculture, and home economics.

Just as in business education, vocational education courses are composed of diverse student populations with different reading levels. This creates a problem for vocational teachers. Some students are able to grasp the vocabulary and concepts almost immediately, while others must receive continuous reinforcement. Thus, teachers must become adept at providing differentiated levels of instruction for students and allowing them to progress at their own rate. Teachers must also be aware that some students become frustrated in vocational education courses because although able to perform the tasks required, they cannot read the directions that allow them to expand their ideas.

In reading vocational education materials, students frequently use the following skills:

1. *Following directions:* As in business education courses, students in vocational education are receiving training to enter a skill area. Thus, they must learn to read and follow all directions carefully. Without this skill, their success in mastering a particular trade will be limited.
2. *Sequence:* Incorporated into the skill of following directions is that of sequence. In reading construction, cooking, or farming information, students must recognize the sequence of information, and follow it as they perform.
3. *Cause-effect relationships:* As students study areas of agriculture including farming and home economics, they are constantly asked to read information to determine what will happen in various situations, e.g., when too much flour is put in a cake batter, or a special liquid fertilizer with heavy nitrogen content was used to grow soybeans in a specific region. The ability to read information and to note the different relationships of ideas is essential in studying vocational education.
4. *Reading maps, tables, and charts:* All areas of vocational education require that students study illustrations related to the subject matter. These include patterns used in sewing, contour maps in farming, various charts indicating measures, etc., that help in understanding the concepts.
5. *Interpreting symbols and abbreviations:* Whether reading recipes, directions for construction, or noting ingredients in fertilizers, students are expected to recognize and interpret different symbols and abbreviations. Some abbreviations are mathematical, others are related to science. If concepts are to be learned, the vocational education teacher must provide the necessary instruction.

In many instances, students in vocational education are receiving the only training they will receive before entering the job market; thus, it is essential that these students learn to apply as many reading skills as possible for present and future use.

Vocational teachers should realize that students may experience problems in trying to read vocational education materials. These include:

1. Extreme ranges of *readability levels* in vocational education materials used, in conjunction with wide ranges of student reading levels.
2. *Much technical and specialized vocabulary,* as well as complex concepts in the materials and discussions.
3. The use of a *variety of materials.*
4. A positive, high *interest* level among students unless unrealistic goals have been set by the students for themselves; this can then become a negative factor.
5. A variety of *organizational patterns* in the materials.

Additional ideas can be found in the following materials:

Bosanko, Robert J. "They Learn to Read in Auto I, Honest! *Journal of Reading* 19 (October 1975):33—35.

Carney, John J., and Losinger, William. "Reading and Content in Technical-Vocational Education." *Journal of Reading* 20 (October 1976):14—17.

Ciani, Alfred, and Hogue, Donald. "How to Help Industrial Arts Students with Reading." *Industrial Education* 65 (October 1976):32—33.

Clark, Andrew K. "Readability of Industrial Education Textbooks." *Journal of Industrial Teacher Education* 16 (1978):13—23.

Conroy, Michael. "Instructional Sheets for Students with Reading Difficulties." *Industrial Education* 68 (November 1979):32—34.

Frederick, E. Coston. "Reading and Vocational Education." In *Fusing Reading Skills and Content*, ed. H. Alan Robinson and Ellen Lamar Thomas. Newark, Del.: International Reading Association, 1969.

Johnson, Joyce D. "The Reading Teacher in the Vocational Classroom." *Journal of Reading* 17 (October 1974):27—29.

Lee, Howard D. "Dealing with Reading in Industrial Arts." *Journal of Reading* 24 (May 1981):663—66.

Szymkowicz, Dorothy. "Home Economics and Reading." In *Fusing Reading Skills and Content*, ed. H. Alan Robinson and Ellen Lamar Thomas. Newark, Del.: International Reading Association, 1969.

Young, Edith M., and Rodenborn, Leo V. "Improving Communication Skills in Vocational Courses." *Journal of Reading* 19 (February 1976):373—77.

The Physical Education Teacher

Although physical education is often viewed as a content area in which more emphasis is placed on physical activities than on reading information, physical education teachers can include instruction that requires reading. Furthermore, the physical education teacher or coach can be an important motivating factor in helping students become interested in reading.

Reading physical education materials requires the continuous application of several reading skills. These include:

1. *Following directions:* If students are to perform any physical activity, whether an individual or team sport, directions must be followed. Many physical education teachers give directions orally; however, by using written directions, these teachers could greatly enhance the students' reading skills. Since students want to participate in the activities, they should realize that the only successful way to do so is to read the directions—a built-in motivational technique.

2. *Reading charts and diagrams:* To help students understand different sports better, physical education teachers frequently use materials containing charts and diagrams of the tennis court, or possibly strokes used in swimming. If students are to understand the concepts being presented, they must be able to interpret the illustrations.

3. *Perceiving relationships:* How is the trajectory of a basketball shot from the top of the key related to scoring two points? How is the type of shoe worn by the runner related to his speed? These and other relationships must be noted as physical education materials are read and activities performed. Just noting the details will not present a complete understanding of the information.

4. *Noting details:* Many details are presented in physical education materials. What is the distance from one base to another on the baseball field? How many sets in a tennis game? Similar details are important in understanding the directions for all physical education activities.
5. *Contrast and comparisons:* As students read about the different sports and activities included in physical education materials, they must make some comparisons of the information to note likenesses and differences in the directions. This differentiation will help them in remembering the activity.

Gentile suggests that sports and content area reading fit together for several reasons.

> Students have experiences in participating in sports as well as in watching athletic events on television. Thus, these experiences provide them with a background of information that can serve as a basis to develop higher level reading skills.
>
> Sports and reading skill development can promote independence, aggressiveness, assertiveness, an ambitious desire for achievement, success, prestige, self-discipline, and a sense of mastery.
>
> The two areas require sound coaching/teaching methods; good models; structured, consistent, and individualized guidance; continuous reinforcement; sequential acquisition of fundamental skills; plenty of practice; and a lifetime of development.
>
> Because of the intense interest in athletics, the many sports publications can be used to develop reading skills in all content areas.[9]

Additional ideas on relating reading and physical education can be found in the following sources:

Gentile, Lance M. *Using Sport and Physical Education to Strengthen Reading Skills.* Newark, Del.: International Reading Association, 1980.
Grubaugh, Steven, and Molesworth, Roy. "Teaching Vocabulary and Developing Concepts in Health." *Journal of Reading* (February 1980):420–23.
Maring, Gerald H., and Ritson, Robert. "Reading Improvement in the Gymnasium." *Journal of Reading* 24 (October 1980):27–31.
Patlak, Sanford. "Physical Education and Reading: Questions and Answers." In *Fusing Reading Skills and Content*, ed. H. Alan Robinson and Ellen Lamar Thomas. Newark, Del.: International Reading Association, 1969.

The Music and Art Teachers

Just as the physical education teacher can motivate students to read, the art and music teachers likewise have some students who are successful with their content, but have been unsuccessful in courses requiring a great deal of reading. Art and music usually are not thought of as reading courses, but rather as classes that may teach the skills, history and appreciation of the area. However, as students become involved in the psychomotor activities in these classes and begin to enter the affective domain of fine arts appreciation, teachers can also develop some cognitive skills that will enhance the other areas. For example, as students work with color and the effect of color on emotions in an art class, examples of such art work and printed descriptions could be used to further the students' understanding. Students who enjoy art and music, but who do not enjoy reading, may be motivated to read through these classes.

As students read music and art materials, they employ many reading skills continuously. Sometimes these skills are used directly in reading the printed materials, and sometimes they are used as the students listen or view the work of different composers or artists. These skills include:

1. *Mood:* Words in a song as well as the melody that accompanies the words serve to set a mood for the listener. In viewing works of art, students respond to the mood that is presented through color, lines, or medium. While the skill of understanding mood is not strictly controlled by interpreting words, teachers in these context areas can develop this skill using nonverbal procedures initially and then helping students transfer this skill to understanding the mood portrayed by words and ideas in text materials. The motivational factor that these teachers have at their disposal can help reading make sense for some students.
2. *Contrast and comparisons:* As students learn to visualize and auditorially determine likenesses and differences in these areas of fine arts, they can also develop the reading skill of comparing and contrasting. This skill can be applied as they read about different composers or periods of history.
3. *Interpreting symbols:* In reading music, a basic skill involves the ability to translate a musical notation into a meaningful unit. Reading symbols is one type of decoding strategy with which students who have been poor readers find success. As they experience success in this area, they begin to learn words to go with their music. Results are—better readers.

Thomas and Robinson suggest some special study techniques for learning the vocabulary of music that can also be applied to studying art materials.

Look for new words that are often set off in boldface or italic type.
Consider new terms as they are presented and reread as necessary.
Use textbook aids such as the glossary, the dictionary, and the index.
Consider words in relation to corresponding illustrations when possible.
Use pencil and paper to review examples and create new ones.
Ask questions to clarify terms.
Use the new terms in class discussions and writing.[10]

Other ideas for developing reading through art and music are found in these sources:

Earle, Richard, and Penney, Linda S. "Reading the Words in Music Class." *Music Education Journal* 59 (December 1972):55–56.
Erickson, Robert D. "The Art Room Book Collection." In *Fusing Reading Skills and Content*, ed. H. Alan Robinson and Ellen Lamar Thomas. Newark, Del.: International Reading Association, 1969.
Tirro, Frank, "Reading Techniques in the Teaching of Music." In *Fusing Reading Skills and Content*, ed. H. Alan Robinson and Ellen Lamar Thomas. Newark, Del.: International Reading Association, 1969, 103–7.

Wulffson, Don L. "Music to Teach Reading." *Journal of Reading* 14 (December 1970):179–82.

The Foreign Language Teacher

In reading passages written in a foreign language, students often have difficulty in comprehending the long, complex sentences in an unfamiliar language. Brown recommends that students be helped with this difficulty by using sentence-combining techniques.[11] This technique takes a series of short sentences and combines them to form the complex sentences that are often found in reading. Other researchers such as O'Hare and Strong have used this technique to enhance composition and the understanding of grammar.[12] This technique has been highly successful with junior high students. The technique may use a picture and a series of questions that produce short sentence responses. These responses are then pulled together to form a longer sentence. Following this process, students can better comprehend the sentence, having analyzed the components.

Reading a foreign language is similar to reading an English or social studies book with one exception—the language is different. Thus, foreign language teachers must concentrate initially on developing a vocabulary. Once the students learn even a minimum vocabulary, they can begin to read sentences or passages. To become proficient in a new language, students must be given opportunities to read, write and speak the language as well as to listen to it. Learning to read a foreign language requires the integration of all communication skills.

Several tips that students should consider in identifying new foreign language words are:

Does the context give a clue as to the meaning of the word?
Does the word (or group of words) look like some word or expression you already know?
Can you discover a clue in a familiar part?
If the previous tips have not yielded all the meaning you want, turn to the vocabulary section or use a foreign language dictionary.[13]

One specific reading skill that is unique in reading foreign language material is the use of cognates. Cognates are words that resemble the English translation of the word and serve as clues in decoding the language. Students should be cautioned not to overrely on this form of translation because some words may appear to be a cognate and yet have a very different translation.

Other reading skills used in reading foreign language materials are those identified in English and social studies.

Further information on reading in foreign languages is found in the following sources:

Carsello, Carmen J., and Bartell, Donald E. "Increasing Rate of Reading a Foreign Language." *Journal of Reading* 14 (December 1970):171–72.
Combs, Warren E. "Sentence-Combining Practice Aids Reading Comprehension." *Journal of Reading* 21 (October 1977):18–24.

Finstein, Milton. "Reading Skills and French." In *Fusing Reading Skills and Content*, ed. H. Alan Robinson and Ellen Lamar Thomas. Newark, Del.: International Reading Association, 1969.

Hayden, Louise. "Dialogues in Action: A Multisensory Approach to Language and Content Learning." *Journal of Reading* 22 (October 1978):55–59.

Preston, Ralph C. "Give the Student Tips on How to Get the Most from Foreign Language Books." In *Improving Reading in Secondary Schools: Selected Readings*, ed. Lawrence E. Hafner. New York: Macmillan, 1967.

Richaudeau, François. "Some French Work on Prose Readability and Syntax." *Journal of Reading* 24 (March 1981):503–8.

The Reading Specialist

The reading specialist has an important role in assisting content teachers as they incorporate reading instruction into their content teaching. Sometimes indifference is encountered. This attitude is caused by a lack of understanding of content reading instruction. Just as a reading specialist takes many reading courses to gain a greater understanding of how to teach reading, the science teacher is prepared to become a science specialist by taking numerous science courses.

Preparation programs, until recently, provided no instruction for the content teacher on how to help a student read content material. Thus, many teachers are unsure of what should be done, just as reading specialists would be unsure of what is needed when teaching an unfamiliar content area. Therefore, in order to help the content teacher feel more comfortable with this curriculum change, and to know what to do in order to implement such a change, someone must provide the necessary assistance. This may be the reading specialist, the administrator, another content teacher, a consultant, or anyone who has the specific knowledge and can communicate the information in a professional manner.

Thus, a major consideration in incorporating reading into content classes in the middle and secondary curricula is that of helping the content teachers to see the need as well as to understand how to include reading development as a means of enhancing the content subject.

In thinking about incorporating reading into content areas, consideration must be given to coordination within the curriculum. Coordination requires cooperation and without this ingredient, content reading instruction may result in duplication of effort as each teacher goes a separate way.

Administrators as well as teachers must be aware of the importance of coordination, and facilitate it through area or team discussions on ways to assist students in content reading. The administrator and/or reading specialist should be the leader in seeing that coordination occurs within the school.

Coordination must begin with a good working relationship between the reading specialist and the principal. The reading specialist is responsible not only for assisting the teachers in coordinating their efforts, but also for integrating those recommendations that the principal believes are essential to a good program. Thus, without an efficient working arrangement and a high degree of confidence between the principal and the reading specialist, the possibility of real coordination among teachers is slight. The working relationship between the administration and the reading specialist should serve as a model for others in the school.

The development of a plan for content reading requires an exchange of ideas as well as coordination. The steps that should be considered in the development of such a plan are:

1. The formation of a small group of teachers, the reading specialist, and the principal to discuss the reading needs of the school.
2. After completion of the needs assessment, recommendations are made to the faculty who will then assist in the formulation of goals for the content reading program within the philosophical framework of the school.
3. Using the agreed upon goals, the faculty committee develops specific objectives and activities to assist in meeting the goals.
4. The committee should discuss the objectives and activities with the faculty and make modifications as necessary.
5. Finally, timelines and responsibilities for achieving the various goals and objectives must be determined prior to implementing the content reading plan.

To assist the faculty in successfully achieving its goals, the administration must provide the necessary staff development. The school reading specialist may assist with in-service workshops and demonstrations. Assistance from consultants outside the school may also be needed. The objective of all staff development is to upgrade the teachers' skills in successfully integrating reading into their content classroom. Thus, the sessions must appeal to the content teacher by presenting practical suggestions for improving classroom instruction. Failure to provide quality staff development will cause content teachers to lose enthusiasm for content reading and create a loss of support for implementing a content reading program.

NOTES

1. David L. Shepherd, *Comprehensive High School Reading Methods*, 3rd ed. (Columbus, Ohio: Charles E. Merrill, 1978), p. 204.
2. Richard T. Vacca, "The Development of a Functional Reading Strategy: Implications for Content Area Instruction," *The Journal of Educational Research* 69 (November 1975):108–12; Raymond Duscher, "How to Help Social Studies Students Read Better," *The Social Studies* 66 (November 1975):261.
3. V. J. Glennon and L. G. Callahan, *Elementary School Mathematics: A Guide to Current Research* (Washington, D.C.: Association for Supervision and Curriculum Development, 1968).
4. Robert B. Kane, Mary Ann Byrne, and Mary Ann Hater, *Helping Children Read Mathematics* (New York: American Book, 1974).
5. Mary Ann Hater and Robert B. Kane, "The Cloze Procedure as a Measure of the Reading Comprehensibility and Difficulty of Mathematical English," 1970. (ERIC ED040 881)
6. Lawrence E. Hafner, *Developmental Reading in Middle and Secondary Schools: Foundations, Strategies, and Skills for Teaching* (New York: Macmillan, 1977), p. 348.
7. Lawrence E. Hafner, *Developmental Reading in Middle and Secondary Schools: Foundations, Strategies, and Skills for Teaching*, pp. 348–49.
8. David L. Shepherd, *Comprehensive High School Reading Methods*, 3rd ed., p. 284.

9. Lance M. Gentile, "Using Sports to Strengthen Content Area Reading Skills," *Journal of Reading* 24 (December 1980):245–56.

10. Ellen Lamar Thomas and H. Alan Robinson, *Improving Reading in Every Class*, abr. 2nd ed. (Boston: Allyn and Bacon, 1977).

11. T. Grant Brown, "How to Apply Linguistics to Language Learning Without Scotch Tape." Unpublished study. Tallahassee, Fla.: Florida State University, 1975.

12. Frank O'Hare, "The Effect of Sentence-Combining Practice Not Dependent on Formal Knowledge of a Grammar on the Writing of Seventh Graders." Ph.D. dissertation, Florida State University, 1971; Frank O'Hare, *Sentencecraft: An Elective Course In Writing* (New York: Ginn, 1975); William Strong, *Sentence Combining: A Composing Book* (New York: Random House, 1973).

13. Ellen Lamar Thomas and H. Alan Robinson, *Improving Reading in Every Class*, pp. 398–401.

APPENDIX A
CONTENT READING ACTIVITIES

Understanding Symbols

Provide students with a list of symbols that must be understood to read music materials. They should be asked to match the symbol with its meaning.

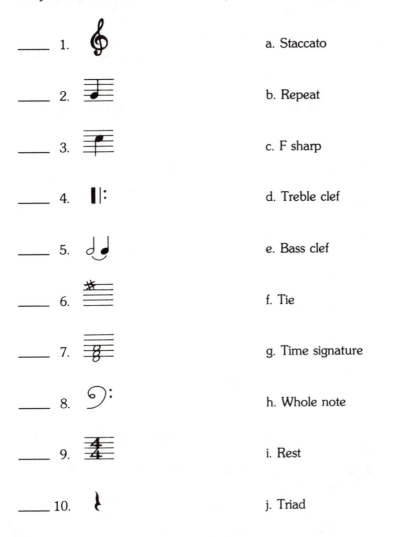

_____ 1.   a. Staccato

_____ 2.   b. Repeat

_____ 3.   c. F sharp

_____ 4.   d. Treble clef

_____ 5.   e. Bass clef

_____ 6.   f. Tie

_____ 7.   g. Time signature

_____ 8.   h. Whole note

_____ 9.   i. Rest

_____ 10.   j. Triad

WORD IDENTIFICATION

Contextual Analysis

Give students a passage from a sports story or directions to a game and leave out some of the words. Have the students fill in the blanks by using context clues.

> The _____ plays directly _____ the center and handles
> the _____ every play. The fullback is _____ him with the
> left _____ three long steps to his left. The _____ halfback
> plays just _____ his own end and close to the line of
> _____ .

This activity may be modified by giving the students the words that fill the blanks at the bottom of the page.

Physical Education and Reading: A Winning Team (Tallahassee, Fla.: Florida Department of Education, 1975), p. 8.

WORD IDENTIFICATION

Sight Words

Using a word search game and definitions of the words, ask students to circle the words.

B	H	A	S	T	H	M	A
U	A	L	A	H	A	O	C
L	Y	L	P	I	I	L	N
L	F	E	E	N	R	E	E
E	E	R	A	S	H	S	T
Y	V	G	L	A	N	D	S
L	E	I	H	I	V	E	S
I	R	E	C	E	L	L	S
O	K	S	K	I	N	P	M

1. An allergic disorder of respiration, characterized by wheezing and a feeling of constriction in the chest.
2. A state of hypersensitivity to certain things such as pollen, foods, animals, etc.
3. The structural unit of plant and animal life.

4. An affection of the mucous membranes of the eyes and respiratory tract caused by an allergic response to the pollen of certain plants.
5. An eruption on the skin.
6. The external covering of the body.
7. Fine filaments growing from the skin of man and animals.
8. A description of a type of skin.
9. A small congenital spot on the human skin.
10. An inflammatory disease of the sebaceous glands.
11. A cell, group of cells, or organ producing a secretion.
12. Any of various eruptive conditions of the skin.

WORD IDENTIFICATION

Structural and Contextual Analysis

Prior to assigning the students a section of a chapter to read, ask them to preview that section of the chapter to be assigned. As they are previewing the reading assignment, they are to locate and write on a sheet of paper all of the technical words they find. When they have completed this task, ask each student to check the glossary or use contextual analysis to determine the meaning of each term and write it on their paper. Ask students to identify orally these technical words, place them on the board as they are identified, and to define them. Then go over each term with the class. After this preview activity is completed, allow the students to read the assignment.

WORD IDENTIFICATION

Structural Analysis

Make flash cards that have printed mathematical roots and prefixes. As the card is flashed, have the students name as many mathematical words as they can that contain the prefixes or roots. Write the words on the board and discuss each word, giving a definition and using the word in a sentence.

Some possible prefixes and root words are

tri-	-angle
poly-	-circle
sub-	-lateral
circum-	-sect
bi-	-set

VOCABULARY

Matching Terms and Definitions: English

Ask students to match the word on the left with its meaning on the right by drawing a line from the word to its meaning.

1. Conjunction
2. Adverb
3. Adjective
4. Predicate Adjective
5. Direct Object

a. A word that modifies a noun or a pronoun.
b. A word that completes the verb and describes the subject.
c. A word that connects other words or groups of words.
d. A word that answers the question "what?" or "whom?" after an action verb.
e. A word that modifies a verb, an adjective, or an adverb.

VOCABULARY

Picture Clues for Meaning

In teaching concepts such as texture or architectual styles, the students could find examples representing the concepts and vocabulary and develop a collage. The vocabulary word can be displayed on the poster with numerous examples surrounding it. This type of activity is actually using picture clues for meaning.

VOCABULARY

Identifying Unfamiliar Words: Physical Education

Give the students a page designed like the one below and information to study related to the topic. Ask them to identify an unfamiliar word or a word directly related to the topic that begins with the capitalized letter. They are then to look up or provide an appropriate definition.

Topic	Word	Definition
F	Flanker	An offensive maneuver in which a player lines up nearer the sideline than a designated opponent.
O		
O		
T		
B		
A		
L		
L		

VOCABULARY

Demonstrating Meaning: Physical Education

The students are given a list of vocabulary words related to any sport (in this case track and field is used) and asked to match the meaning to the word. When this is complete, students are then asked to demonstrate or describe each term.

_____ 1. Baton
_____ 2. Heat
_____ 3. Hurdle
_____ 4. Scratch line
_____ 5. Starting blocks

a. A step in running.
b. Devices in which the feet are placed to aid the runner in starting.
c. A wooden or metal obstacle over which the runners must leap in certain races.
d. A hollow cylinder carried by one runner and given to the next in a relay race.
e. A line over which the athlete must not step during a trial.
f. Preliminary races in which the winners qualify for semifinals or finals.

COMPREHENSION

Following Directions: Woodworking

After providing appropriate data to students, ask them to plan a bill of materials and compute the cost of the project. Before planning the bill of material, the teacher should go over the following terms with the students, then ask them to match the vocabulary on the left side of the page with its definition on the right.

1. Bill of material
2. Board foot
3. Running foot
4. Rough lumber
5. Surfaced lumber
6. Dimension

a. A foot length of lumber regardless of thickness and width of the lumber
b. Lumber that has run through a planer
c. An itemized list of number of pieces of lumber needed and dimension of each
d. Size of lumber
e. A piece of lumber one inch thick, twelve inches wide and twelve inches long
f. Lumber that has not been dressed

Bill of Materials

Name of Buyer:

Address of Buyer:

Date:

Name of Project:

Pieces of Lumber: Finish:

Kinds of Wood: Bd. Ft.:

Dimensions: Cost per Piece:

COMPREHENSION

Following Directions: Letter Writing

In order to assist students in using the correct form for writing a business letter, give them an outline of both the block and indented styles. Ask students to write letters using both. When they finish, ask them which of the two styles appears to be more practical to use.

Block Style

2929 Ohio Avenue
Miami, Florida 30216
March 5, 1981

The University of New Mexico
100 Inca Plaza
Albuquerque, New Mexico 50912

To Whom It May Concern:

_____
_____
_____
_____ .

Sincerely,

Marie Topaz

Indented Style

2929 Ohio Avenue
Miami, Florida 30216
March 5, 1981

The University of New Mexico
  100 Inca Plaza
    Albuquerque, New Mexico 50912

To Whom It May Concern:

_____
_____
_____
_____ .

Sincerely,

Marie Topaz

COMPREHENSION

Fact and Opinion

Ask each student to read the following commercial passage. After they have read the message, ask them to list in one column factual information and in the other column, opinions.

Why You Should Vote for the Democrats

Everyone knows that the Democratic Party is the party of the common man and always has been. Thomas Jefferson founded the Democratic Party for the purpose of giving these people a forum. Democrats favor high wages, low taxes, social reforms, and strong defense. Republicans on the other hand are affluent, arrogant, and believe that every person should pay his own way through life. They favor abolishing social reforms, fiscal policies that will raise taxes and lower net income, and an aggressive defense posture that threatens world peace. Vote for peace, prosperity, and the people! Vote for the Democratic Party!

Details:
Now ask the students to answer the following questions about the message:

Who founded the Democratic Party?
What do the Democrats favor?
What do the Republicans favor?

Main Idea:
Ask students to identify the main idea in this message.

COMPREHENSION

Discussing Fiction

Ask students to read the book, *All Quiet on the Western Front.* Ask them to answer the following questions after reading the book. They should be prepared to discuss their answers in class.

1. What was the author's purpose in writing this book?
2. What was the mood of the book and how did you react to it?
3. What conclusions did you draw after reading the book?
4. Briefly summarize the main events in the book.

COMPREHENSION

Math Word Problem

Problem:
An airplane leaves the airport at 4 p.m. traveling due north at the speed of 400 mph. At 4:30 p.m. another airplane leaves the airport traveling due east at 300 mph. Find an

equation to express the distance between the airplanes in terms of the time after the second airplane took off.

Details:
1. What is the situation?
2. What is being asked for?
3. Are the numbers important to remember?

Paraphrasing:
What is necessary to remember about this problem in order to determine an equation?

Summarizing/Synthesizing:
1. Plane 1 leaves at 4:00 traveling at 400 mph.
2. Plane 2 leaves at 4:30 traveling at 300 mph.
3. Equation needed to express distance between planes in terms of time.

COMPREHENSION

Problem Solving:Geometry

Problem:
Draw a pair of parallel lines. On each of the lines make a segment congruent to AB. Label one segment CD and the other EF. Join the end points of the segments so that the lines do not cross. What kind of figure do you have?

Following Directions:
Identify the steps to be followed and the order. Do each step as outlined in the problem.

Details:
1. What is to be drawn?
2. How are the lines to be drawn?
3. How are they to be labeled?

Predicting:
What type of figure will be drawn?

Comparing/Contrasting:
How does this figure compare to those that have been recently studied?

Conclusion:
Is this figure corectly drawn?

COMPREHENSION

Guided Reading

Direct students to read the selection using questions such as those below to guide their reading and for discussion.

> There are two separate types of tennis—singles and doubles. The singles game has two opposing participants. The doubles game has four participants. The doubles game has four participants with two individuals competing against the other two. The course used for playing doubles is nine feet wider than the sin-

gles court—four and a half feet on each side. The basic rules are the same for both types. However, in doubles, each player serves a game in his turn, with the member of one team serving and then a member of the other team. Also in a doubles game, each player has a position that should be followed during the entire game.

Details:
1. What are the two types of tennis?
2. How many players participate in singles? In doubles?

Relationships:
1. How is a doubles game similar to and different from the singles game?
2. If a player does not play a position in a game, what effect may this have on the game?

STUDY SKILLS

Study Strategy PARS

Using the study strategy PARS, the teacher helps students apply it to *The Complete Book of Running,* by James F. Fixx.

1. The students should first preview the book by skimming and scanning to get a general sense of movement and organization and its important headings and concepts.
2. Students should then ask questions before reading such as:

   What happens to your mind when running?
   What is the best way to start running?
   How do you fit running into your life?

3. The next step is to read, keeping the preceding questions in mind.
4. In the final step, the student should summarize the reading by checking information gained against the preestablished questions

STUDY SKILLS

Organizational Skills

Outlining:
After the students read the following passage, ask them to develop an outline of the major events in the passage.

Everyone knows that liberals are interested in helping their fellow man. They tend to be members of the Democratic Party, favor expensive social programs, peaceful solutions to crisis situations, and are more tolerant of differences among people. Conservatives on the other hand, are more self-centered and less tolerant of unproductive people. They are generally Republicans and favor limiting social programs, helping large corporations, maintaining a strong defense, and cutting taxes. Liberals believe conservatives to be intolerant of others and more likely to get involved in aggressive activities that threaten peace. Conservatives think liberals are "bleeding heart" intellectuals and spendthrifts.

Underlining:
After the students read the passage, ask them to underline the important points in the passage.

STUDY SKILLS

Book Parts

Direct students to use the textbook to answer these questions. They must read the information carefully in order to completely answer some of the questions. Advise them to take their time and get acquainted with the new textbook.

1. On what page does the glossary begin?
2. What is the title of your book?
3. What do the authors hope to accomplish in this book? (Read the foreword.)
4. How many authors are there? Who are they and where are they from?
5. How many chapters does the book contain?
6. What chapters deal with nonmetric and metric geometry?
7. Where can you find a table of mathematical symbols? What is the meaning of 41?
8. On what pages could you find information on isosceles triangles?
9. Does this book have an answer key?
10. What is included in the "Chapter Supplement" at the end of each chapter?

STUDY SKILLS

Reading Charts and Diagrams

Using a diagram such as the one below, help students learn to read the diagram by asking specific questions such as those listed below the diagram.

Football Field

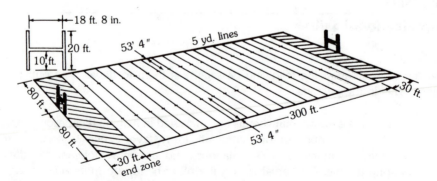

1. How long is a football field?
2. How wide is a football field?
3. What is the distance between the yard lines on the field?

4. What is the length of the end zone?
5. How high is the goal post?
6. How far is the crossbar from the ground?
7. How wide is the goal post?

STUDY SKILLS

Understanding Symbols and Abbreviations

Ask students to identfiy the following symbols and abbreviations.

1. O.A.S.
2. WHO
3. VJ Day
4. ⬭(10)
5. NATO

6. OPEC
7. ┼┼┼┼┼┼┼┼
8. SEATO
9. U.S.S.R
10. UNESCO

STUDY SKILLS

Understanding Charts and Tables

Using a chart such as the one below, students should be shown how to read it by posing a series of questions. Teachers can further the learning of health information by developing the skill of reading diagrams or charts.

Vitamin	Source
Carotene	milk, butter, egg yolk, yellow vegetables, fish oils
B_1(thiamin)	green vegetables, hole cereals, pork, liver, beef
B_2(riboflavin)	milk, meat
Niacin (nicotinic acid)	milk, meat
B_6	meat, grain, vegetables
B_{12}	meat, especially liver
C (ascorbic acid)	citrus fruits, tomato juice, raw tomatoes
D	fish oils, butter, egg yolk
E (tocopheral)	wheat germ oil, vegetable oils

1. If a person eats a lot of meat, what vitamins are provided?
2. To prevent colds, many people eat much food with Vitamin C. What are some examples of foods containing Vitamin C?
3. Riboflavin is another name for what vitamin?
4. If a person does not eat vegetables, which vitamins may be missing in his/her diet?

CONSTRUCTING, ADMINISTERING AND INTERPRETING AN INFORMAL READING INVENTORY (IRI)

CONSTRUCTION OF AN IRI

An IRI consists of a series of graded passages of approximately 100 to 200 words selected from content texbooks or written by the teacher using content area themes. Lower-level passages may have fewer than 100 words while higher-level passages may have more than 200 words. The specific tasks involved in developing an IRI for use in the content classroom include:

Task 1: Two passages of approximately 100 to 200 words should be selected for each level. Middle school or junior high content teachers may wish to have a range from second through tenth grade level for their passages. Senior high school teachers should have passages that range from fourth to college level.

Passages should be selected to reflect the kind of content material that the students are going to encounter in the classroom. More accurate and complete diagnosis of the students' capabilities are obtained with appropriate passages. Therefore, examine the material chosen for the IRI carefully in order to ensure a better instrument that will yield optimum results from the assessment procedure.

In developing or selecting the passages, the content teachers must also attempt to determine the approximate level of each passage. Because these passages are used to ascertain the reading level of a student in a particular content area, the passages must progress from easier to more difficult selections and be assigned an estimated level. Readability formulas are often used to determine the approximate level of each passage. The concept of readability is discussed in Chapter 8.

Task 2: Develop comprehension questions for each of the passages. After the passages have been selected from content material, and the accuracy of the readability level of each passage has been determined, the next step is to develop a series of comprehension questions for each passage. Many teachers prefer to have a range of five to ten questions for this purpose. No fewer than five or more than ten questions should be used because fewer than five will limit the information on comprehension and more than ten will take too much time.

There are three levels of understanding that the questions should measure: literal, interpretive, and critical. Various reading skills should be assessed by the questions. Samples of various types of questions are provided in Chapter 3. Specific information on questioning strategies is in Chapter 5.

Task 3: Develop marking sheets for use while administering the inventory. Marking sheets are necessary for the teacher to use in recording student errors made during the administration of the IRI. The marking sheets should consist of copies of the passages with the comprehension questions below each passage.

Task 4: Type the passages that the student will read. Each passage should be typed on a separate sheet of paper or a large index card. The reason for this is that the materials have come from many different sources and a similar format of pages or cards is easier to manage.

Following these four tasks closely will assist in constructing an IRI. However, after the instrument has been constructed, the most important tasks remain—administration and interpretation.

ADMINISTRATION OF THE IRI

Although the IRI is an individually administered instrument, the content teacher should find that it can be easily and quickly administered. In order to administer an IRI, the teacher needs the appropriate passages for the student, and copies of the passages that contain the comprehension questions and on which the teacher can mark errors. After these materials are compiled, the teacher is ready to administer the IRI to determine the student's independent, instructional, and frustration levels in reading.

The Basic Steps that should be followed in administering an IRI are:

1. Establish rapport with the student. The teacher needs to discuss with the student what is taking place and to develop readiness for reading each of the selections.
2. The first selection chosen for the student should be approximately two grade levels below the student's estimated instructional level. The teacher should then introduce the selection and set a purpose for reading.
3. The paragraph is read aloud by the student. On the marking sheet, the teacher indicates the student's oral reading errors. The following marking symbols are suggested:

for words pronounced by the teacher—   over the word
mispronunciation—   over the word with the word written above as mispronounced
substitution—   through the word with new word written above
omission—   circle around the words or sounds omitted
repetition—   over the word
insertion—   with word written in

A sample marked paragraph is provided.

4. After the oral reading, the teacher asks comprehension questions and indicates correct and incorrect responses on the marking sheet.

5. The various errors are counted by the teacher, including words pronounced for the student, mispronunciations, substitutions, omissions, insertions, and repetitions. By using the criteria presented in Chapter 4, the teacher determines if the selection is on the student's independent, instructional, or frustration level.

6. The second passage at the same level is used for silent reading. The passage is introduced to the student by giving a purpose for reading.

7. As the student reads silently, the teacher records any words that the student may ask.

8. Following the silent reading, the teacher asks the comprehension questions and records the correct and incorrect answers on the marking sheet. This particular section of the IRI is extremely important to the content teacher because much of the reading required of students in content classes is done silently. Thus, this part of the IRI must be analyzed carefully.

9. The words asked by the student during the silent reading portion of the IRI are counted, and using the criteria for word identification, satisfactory or unsatisfactory performance is noted. Again using the criteria for comprehension in Chapter 4, the teacher determines if the student's comprehension level is on the independent, instructional, or frustration level. After the independent reading level has been established, the student reads more difficult selections in an attempt to determine instructional and frustration levels. In instances where the material is too easy for the student, several levels may be skipped. When errors on either the word identification, the oral reading, or the comprehension sections indicate the frustration level, the teacher must select an easier passage, or stop the test if the independent and instructional levels have been determined.

SAMPLE IRI PASSAGE

Green plants are not the only living things that are able to make food. Several other forms of life, such as certain algae and some bacteria, can also make food. Biologists refer to all living things that make their own food as producers. The food manufactured by producers is used by the producers themselves and by other members of the community. Living things unable to produce their own food are called consumers.

Most producers use sunlight to produce their food by a complex process. This process is known as photosynthesis, meaning "put together with light." Just as consumers have many ways of getting food, producers have many adaptations to aid photosynthesis. For example, the number of leaves and their arrangement on the plant help trap sunlight.

From Raymond F. Oram, et al., *Biology Living Systems*, 3rd ed. (Columbus, Ohio: Charles E. Merrill, 1979), p. 7.

_✓_ 1. What do biologists call those living things that make their own food? (Producers)

_✓_ 2. How does sunlight affect the production of food? (It aids the producers through photosynthesis.)

_✓_ 3. What are living things that are unable to produce their own food called? (Consumers)

_✗_ 4. How does the acquisition and production of food affect your life? (Any logical answer is acceptable.)

_✗_ 5. What is the shape of most tree leaves? Why do you think this is true? (Most leaves are broad and flat so that they have more surface area available for light absorption.)

INTERPRETATION OF AN IRI

Although most content teachers do not have time to conduct an in-depth analysis of each student's IRI results, there are some areas that are especially worth noting. Certainly, the primary reason for giving a content-oriented IRI is to ascertain the student's independent, instructional, and frustration reading levels. With this information the teacher can provide material appropriate to each student's reading level. Other areas of concern are structural analysis, contextual analysis, vocabulary knowledge, and comprehension.

In looking at structural analysis skills such as syllabication, prefixes, suffixes, and inflectional endings, the teacher is able to determine the extent to which students are able to identify words by observing word parts. This type of information gives the teacher a skill area on which to focus instruction to aid identification of new content words.

Contextual analysis involves the use of context clues in reading material. Strengths and weaknesses in this skill area indicate to the teacher the extent to which students are able to use syntactical cues and the words surrounding unknown words in a passage to gain meaning from the passage and to decode the unknown word.

Another important area of concern to the teacher is vocabulary knowledge. Information from the IRI may indicate the student's knowledge of general vocabulary and also specialized and technical vocabulary. Awareness of skills in this area enables the teacher to plan instructional strategies for teaching vocabulary to each student.

Since the primary objective in reading is comprehension, the content teacher must carefully analyze errors in this area. Attention should be given to the student's ability to answer questions at all three levels of questions—literal, interpretive, and critical. A review of the errors will indicate problem areas in comprehension. The teacher can then plan for instruction to strengthen the deficient skills. Another consideration in analyzing comprehension is the effect of vocabulary on comprehension. Often deficiencies in vocabulary contribute to errors in comprehension; thus, the teacher must determine if vocabulary knowledge enhances or hinders comprehension for an individual student.

APPENDIX C

INFORMAL DIAGNOSTIC ASSESSMENTS

Burns, Paul C., and Roe, Betty D. *Informal Reading Assessment*. Chicago, Ill.: Rand McNally, 1980.
A series of Graded Word Lists and Graded Passages intended for use with individual students, Preprimer to Twelfth Grade.

Ekwall, Eldon C. *Ekwall Reading Inventory*. Boston, Mass.: Allyn and Bacon, 1979.
A set of reading passages ranging from preprimer through ninth grade level in difficulty, designed to measure individual students' oral and silent reading grade levels.

Jacobs, H. Donald, and Searfoss, Lyndon W. *Diagnostic Reading Inventory*, 2nd ed. Dubuque, Iowa: Kendall/Hunt, 1979.
Designed for use by reading teachers who have previous experience with reading inventories. It is to be individually administered to a student, third grade and above, who has already been identified as having reading problems.

Johns, Jerry L. *Advanced Reading Inventory*. Dubuque, Iowa: William C. Brown, 1981.
Reading inventory and cloze tests that may be used with individuals or with groups, grade seven through college.

Johns, Jerry L. *Basic Reading Inventory*, 2nd ed. Dubuque, Iowa: Kendall/Hunt, 1981.
Graded Word Lists and Graded Passages to be used in determining an individual's Independent Reading Level, Frustration Level, and Listening Level, Preprimer–Grade Eight.

McWilliams, Lana, and Rakes, Thomas A. *Content Inventories, English, Social Studies, Science*. Dubuque, Iowa: Kendall/Hunt, 1979.
Contains cloze placement tests, group reading inventories, and skills and attitude survey instruments useful in screening groups of students to determine general reading and study skill abilities in specific subject content.

Rinsky, Lee Ann, and de Fossard, Esta. *The Contemporary Classroom Reading Inventory*. Dubuque, Iowa: Gorsuch Scarisbrick, 1981.
Three selections: one fiction, one social studies, one science for each grade level four through nine. Includes supplementary cloze tests which may be administered to the entire class as well as individual reading inventories.

Searfoss, Lyndon W., and Jacobs, H. Donald. *Decoding Inventory*. Dubuque, Iowa: Kendall/Hunt, 1979.
A screening measure designed to assess individual student performance in auditory and visual discrimination phonics, structural analysis, and use of content clues. Level one, grades one through three; Level two, grades four and above.

Silvaroli, Nicholas. *Classroom Reading Inventory*, 3rd ed. Dubuque, Iowa: William C. Brown, 1976.

Contains graded word lists and paragraphs to be used with an individual and a spelling survey used with a group (grades two through ten).

Sucher, Floyd, and Allred, Ruel A. *Sucher-Allred Reading Placement Inventory*. Oklahoma City, Okla.: The Economy Company, 1973.

Word-Recognition Tests and Oral Reading Tests, primer through grade nine, to be used to enable the teacher to identify individual reading levels, common word-recognition and comprehension errors in oral reading, and to place a student appropriately for reading instruction.

Woods, Mary Lynn, and Moe, Alden J. *Analytical Reading Inventory*, 2nd ed. Columbus, Ohio: Charles E. Merrill, 1981.

Designed to be used individually in order to enable the teacher to identify strengths and weaknesses in word recognition skills and examine comprehension strategies, as well as determine reading level, grades two through nine.

Compiled by Julia M. Seal, St. Tammany Parish Schools, Louisiana.

STRUCTURED OVERVIEWS, PATTERN GUIDES, CONCEPT GUIDES, AND THREE-LEVEL STUDY GUIDES

A Structured Overview in English

Questions to Guide Students in Understanding the Structured Overview

1. Who is the main character in this story?
2. Who is Aunt Polly?
3. What is Tom Sawyer's task for this particular day?
4. Do you think Tom would rather do something other than work? What?
5. What kinds of rewards does Tom offer his friends to get them to take over the white-washing job?
6. Do you think Aunt Polly really believed that Tom whitewashed the fence without any help at all? Why do you think as you do?

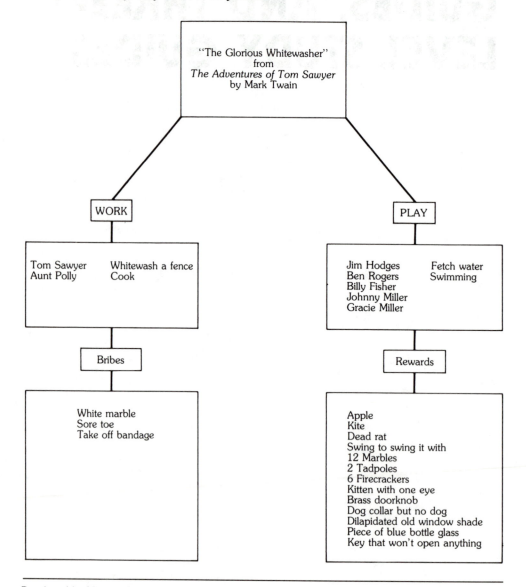

Structured Overview in Biology

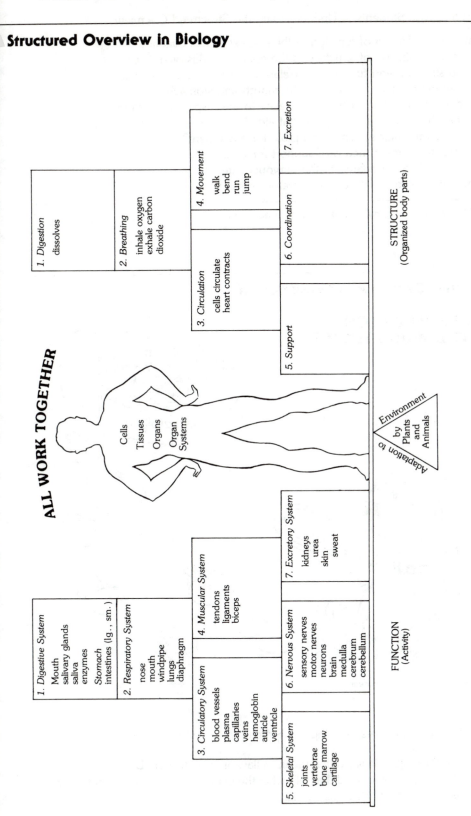

Questions to Guide Students in Understanding the Structured Overview

1. What is the definition of function in the context of this overview?
2. What is the definition of structure in the context of this overview?
3. How do structure and function interrelate to ensure man's survival?
4. What are the primary functions of the mouth and stomach?
5. How does the function of breathing relate to the respiratory system?
6. What are the various components that aid circulation?
7. Why is the muscular system responsible for movement?
8. What are the primary means of support for your body?
9. How is coordination related to the nervous system?
10. What is the responsibility of the excretory system?

Developed by Frances Swaggerty, Livingston Parish School System, Louisiana.

A Structured Overview in Consumerism

CLUES TO WATCH
IN THE MARKETPLACE

Illustration idea by Corinne Pearce.

Questions to Guide Students in Using the Structured Overview

1. Identify the three-syllable word that means a flaw or imperfection. D_____
2. Identify the three-syllable word that tells what the person is called who spends money for goods and services. C_____

3. Identify the two words that refer to any place where a consumer spends money for goods and services. M_____   P_____
4. Identify the two-syllable word that means to hint at. I_____
5. Identify the three-syllable word that means an agreement between two or more persons, almost always involving sales or business agreements. C_____
6. Whom does consumer law protect?
7. After making a purchase from a door-to-door salesman, does the consumer have the right to cancel the sale and expect a refund, if he changes his mind about wanting the item?
8. When a consumer breaks her contract, what can the seller do?
9. If buyers and sellers disagree in the marketplace, how can they settle their differences?

Adapted from Miriam B. Gurley, Orange County Schools, Florida.

Pattern Guide for Relationship in Social Studies

How Bananas Grow

Place the ideas in the right order. Match the letter with the correct number.

Field Preparation and Planting

Time	*Idea*
1.	a. hoe the ground
2.	b. cut down old plants
3.	c. plant the roots
·4.	d. dig small holes

Plant Growing

Time	*Idea*
1.	a. a bunch of bananas grow
2.	b. plants grow to be small trees
3.	c. one large purple blossom blooms

Complete the sentence about the banana planting and gathering schedule

Every week or two they_____
Every day they_____

A Fishing Trip

Place the ideas in the right order. Match the letter with the correct number.

Time	*Idea*
1.	a. carried the baskettrap to the river
2.	b. gathered stones and brush
3.	c. mended the fishnet
4.	d. put the baskettrap in the river
5.	e. fished in the dugout with a fishnet

6.   f. placed the stones and brush by a rock in
7.   the river
                                      g. put stones on the trap

Developed by Frances Swaggerty, Livingston Parish School System, Louisiana.

A Pattern Guide for Relationship in Cultural Life-styles

Our chapter on the Middle East and Northern Africa gives an excellent comparison of three lifestyles: Nomadic, Farming, and City Dwelling. Read the material on pages 88–98 to discover the differences in these three ways of life. Complete the following comparison by stating what each life-style would have for all seven categories. The first is done for you as an example.

	Nomadic	Farming	City Dwelling
1. Housing	Temporary dwellings (tents) Live with clans in a tribe Change location very often	Brick houses or tiny huts No modern conveniences	Modern homes and apartment buildings for middle class Shacks and run-down homes for poor
2. Occupations			
3. Education			
4. Travel			
5. Social & Cultural Activities			
6. Economic Prosperity			
7. Products for Sale or Trade			

Developed by Beth Tope, Louisiana Department of Education, Baton Rouge, Louisiana.

A Pattern Guide for Relationship in Literature

The Glorious Whitewasher

Consider Tom Sawyer's attitude toward the following characters and concepts. Note that the columns ask you to consider his attitudes to these things twice—the way he is at the beginning of the story and the way you think he is at the end of the story.

At the beginning of the story what is Tom's attitude toward:		At the end of the story what is Tom's attitude toward:
	Aunt Polly	
	Ben Rogers	
	Bribes	
	Work	
	Himself	

Developed by Mary D. Daniel, Ascension Parish School System, Louisiana.

Concept Guide in Math

Topic: Variables and Open Sentences

Part I: As you preview pages 8–12 in your text, match the statement on the right side of the page with the term on the left side of the page.

_____ 1. Variable
_____ 2. Domain
_____ 3. Values
_____ 4. Constant
_____ 5. Open sentence
_____ 6. Solution set

a. Members of the domain of a variable.
b. A sentence containing a variable.
c. Each symbol.
d. A variable having just one value.
e. The subset of the domain of the variable for which the sentence is true.
f. The set whose elements may serve as replacements for the variable.

Part II: Put the symbols in the list below in their proper sequence under Solution Set.

$$N \qquad \{5\} \qquad 0 \qquad \{1,2,3\}$$

Open Sentence

$x + 3 = 8$
$x + 2 = 2 + x$
$z + 2 = z + 1$
$4 - n \in N$

Solution Set

Concept Guide in Social Studies

Topic: Industrial Growth in the late 1800s and early 1900s

Part I: As you preview pages 632−636 in your text, complete these statements.

1. A system of manufacturing large numbers of items exactly alike is _____.
2. A _____ is a company with individual stockholders, directors, and managers with dividends paid according to the number of shares an individual retains.
3. Corporations created _____ in an attempt to avoid competition.

Part II: Put the words in the list below into their proper group based on their relationship to the concept.

assembly line	Henry Ford	Adam Smith
capital	division of labor	J. P. Morgan
cartels	conveyor belt	raw materials
laissez-faire	Eli Whitney	natural monopoly
joint-stock companies	industrialization	Standard Oil
Sherman Antitrust Act	interchangeable parts	

	Mass Production	Corporation	Monopolies
1.	_____	_____	_____
2.	_____	_____	_____
3.	_____	_____	_____
5.	_____	_____	_____
6.	_____	_____	_____
7.	_____	_____	_____
8.	_____	_____	_____
9.	_____	_____	_____
10.	_____	_____	_____

Three-Level Study Guide in Physics

As you read pages 108−113, "Atomic Theory," use these questions to guide your reading. Answer the questions as you read.

Literal
1. When was the first atomic theory proposed, and by whom?
2. State the Law of Conservation of Mass.
3. List the key parts of Dalton's hypothesis.

Interpretive
4. What would Dalton have said about the mass of all oxygen atoms in a sample of water?
5. Which two of Dalton's hypotheses is not considered entirely correct now? Why?
6. How did Avogadro explain Gay-Lussac's observations on gases?

Application
7. How would you show the Law of Conservation of Mass with a burning candle?

8. How does the existence of carbon monoxide (CO) and carbon dioxide (CO_2) demonstrate the law of multiple proportions?
9. N_2 and H_3 combine to form NH_3. Write a balanced equation for this reaction and explain how this supports Gay-Lussac's observations on the combining volumes of gases.

Developed by Mary Hamilton, East Baton Rouge Parish School System, Louisiana.

Three-Level Study Guide in Music

The Time Signature

Level I (Literal)
1. What does the top number in a Time Signature mean?
2. How many bottom numbers are there in a Time Signature?
3. What is the purpose of a Time Signature?

Level II (Interpretive)
1. If the quarter note doubles in value, what happens to all of the other notes and rest?
2. Why must there be a number in the bottom of the Time Signature when an 8th note gets one beat?
3. Why do rests have the same value as notes with the same name?

Level III (Application)
1. Write four measures of 4/4 time—no two measures may be alike rhythmically.
2. Write four measures of 3/4 time—each different in rhythm.
3. Given four measures (incomplete), fill in each measure with the one note that correctly completes the measure according to the Time Signature.

Adapted from E. Tyrrell Owen, Orange County Schools, Florida.

Three-Level Study Guide in Literature

Level I (Literal):
Listed below are vocabulary words from the story. Place each word from the story in the sentences.

whitewash	paintbrush	particular	reckon
tackled	core	collected	awfully
marbles	brass	doorknob	collar
adventure	support	childhood	sense

1. "... and you take this bucket of _____ and this _____ and don't come in till you're finished."
2. "I'll give you the _____ of my apple."
3. "No, I _____ it wouldn't do, Aunt Polly is so _____ about this fence."
4. "Tom had _____ more things—twelve _____, a _____, and a dog _____.''

5. Mark Twain had a difficult _____, still he had time for _____ with his friends.
6. Mark had to go to work to help _____ the family.
7. Mark Twain wrote with a great _____ of humor.

Level II (Interpretive)
Answer the following questions in complete sentences.

1. Why did Tom's friends want to whitewash the fence?
2. Did anything Tom said influence them? What?
3. How do you think Tom felt after the job was done?

Level III (Application):
Answer the following questions and explain what you mean.

1. Would you like to be a friend of someone like Tom?
2. How would you feel if you had been one of those who were tricked?
3. Would you think the trick was funny, mean, or what?
4. Explain the circumstances that involved changing work into play.

Developed by Mary D. Daniel, Ascension Parish School System, Louisiana.

APPENDIX E

ACTIVITY BOOKS FOR USE IN CONTENT TEACHING

Abruscato, Joe, and Hassard, Jack. *Earthpeople Activity Book*. Santa Monica, Calif.: Goodyear, 1978.

Abruscato, Joe, and Hassard, Jack. *The Whole Cosmos Catalog of Science Activities*. Santa Monica, Calif.: Goodyear.

Adams, Anne H., et al. *Mainstreaming Language Arts and Social Studies: Special Ideas and Activities for the Whole Class*. Santa Monica, Calif.: Goodyear, 1977.

Adams, Anne; Flowers, Anne; and Woods, Elsie. *Reading for Survival in Today's Society*, vols. 1–20. Santa Monica, Calif.: Goodyear, 1977.

Barnard, J. Darrell. *Ideas for Teaching Science in the Junior High School*. Washington, D.C.: National Science Teachers Association, 1963.

Beach, Don M. *Reaching Teenagers: Learning Centers for the Secondary Classroom*. Santa Monica, Calif.: Goodyear, 1977.

Bee, Clifford P. *Learning Centers for Secondary Level Students*. Santa Monica, Calif.: Goodyear, 1980.

Benson, John William. *Social Studies Starters: Games Students Like to Play*. Belmont, Calif.: Pitman Learning, 1974.

Berger, Allen, and Smith, Blanche H., eds. *Classroom Practices in Teaching English*. Urbana, Ill.: National Council of Teachers of English, 1974.

Blackburn, Jack E., and Powell, W. Conrad. *One at a Time All at Once: The Creative Teacher's Guide to Individualized Instruction Without Anarchy*. Santa Monica, Calif.: Goodyear, 1976.

Brown, Thomas, et al. *Teaching Secondary English: Alternative Approaches*. Columbus, Ohio: Charles E. Merrill, 1975.

Christian, Barbara. *Creative Escapes: Adventures in Writing for Grades 7–12*. Belmont, Calif.: Pitman Learning, 1980.

Churchill, E. Richard, and Churchill, Linda R. *Enriched Social Studies Teaching: Through the Use of Games and Activities*. Belmont, Calif.: Pitman Learning, 1973.

Criscuolo, Nicholas. *100 Individualized Activities for Reading*. Belmont, Calif.: Pitman Learning, 1974.

Culp, Mary Beth, and Spann, Syliva. *Me? Teach Reading? Activities for Secondary Content Area Teachers*. Santa Monica, Calif.: Goodyear, 1977.

Educational Service, Inc. *Focus—A Handbook for Teachers of Intermediate Social Studies*, ed. Susan W. Brackenridge. Stevensville, Mich.: Educational Service, Inc., 1977.

Florida Department of Education. *Physical Education and Reading: A Winning Team*. Tallahassee, Fla., 1975.

Florida Department of Education. *Reading the Language of Mathematics*. Tallahassee, Fla., n.d.

Florida Department of Education. *Science and Reading*. Tallahassee, Florida, n.d.

▷Florida Department of Education. *Social Studies and Reading*. Tallahassee, Florida, n.d.

Forte, Imogene; Frank, Marjorie; and MacKenzie, Joy. *Kids' Stuff Reading and Language Experiences, Intermediate—Jr. High*. Nashville, Tenn.: Incentive Publications, 1973.

Hoover, Sharon. *Reading Ideas*. Dansville, N.Y.: The Instructor Publications, 1981.

Johnson, Marjorie S.; Lackman, Thomas W.; and Reisboard, Richard J. *Critical Reading, a Teaching Guide*. Dansville, N.Y.: The Instructor Publications, 1977.

Kohl, Herbert R. *Math, Writing, and Games in the Open Classroom*. New York: Vintage Books, 1974.

McIntyre, Virgie M. *Reading Strategies and Enrichment Activities for Grades 4–9*. Columbus, Ohio: Charles E. Merrill, 1977.

Mallett, Jerry J. *Make-and-Play Reading Games for the Intermediate Grades*. West Nyack, New York: Center for Applied Research in Education, 1976.

Metzner, Seymour. *77 Games for Reading Groups*. Belmont, Calif.: Fearon, 1973.

Miller, Robert D. *Spelling Games and Puzzles for Junior High*. Belmont, Calif.: Fearon, 1976.

Morlan, John E. *Classroom Learning Centers*. Belmont Calif.: Fearon-Pitman, 1974.

Piercy, Dorothy. *Reading Activities in Content Areas*. Boston.: Allyn and Bacon, 1976.

Platts, Mary E. *Anchor—Handbook of Classroom Ideas to Motivate the Teaching of Intermediate Language Arts*. Stevensville, Mich.: Educational Service, Inc., 1970.

Platts, Mary E. *Challenge—Suggested Activities to Motivate the Teaching of Mathematics in the Intermediate Grades*. Stevensville, Mich.: Educational Services, Inc., 1977.

Platts, Mary E. *Craft—A Handbook for Teachers of Intermediate Art*. Stevensville, Mich.: Educational Service, Inc., 1977.

Platts, Mary E. *Inquire—A Handbook for Teachers of Intermediate Science*. Stevensville, Mich.: Educational Service, Inc., 1975.

Sawyer, W. E. *Mathematician's Delight*. Baltimore, Md.: Penguin Books, 1959.

Schaff, Joanne. *New Dimensions in English*. Santa Monica, Calif.: Goodyear.

Schneider, Maxine Springer. *Science Projects for the Intermediate Grades*. Belmont, Calif.: Pitman Learning, 1973.

Schrank, Jeffrey. *Teaching Human Beings: 101 Subversive Activities for the Classroom*. Boston: Beacon Press, 1972.

Short, J. Rodney, and Dickerson, Beverly. *The Newspaper: An Alternative Textbook*. Belmont, Calif.: Pitman Learning, 1980.

Smith, Carl B., and Elliott, Peggy G. *Reading Activities for Middle and Secondary Schools: A Handbook for Teachers*. New York: Holt, Rinehart, and Winston, 1979.

Smuin, Stephen K. *Turn-Ons! 185 Strategies for the Secondary Classroom*. Belmont, Calif.: Pitman Learning, 1978.

Compiled by Julia M. Seal, St. Tammany Parish Schools, Louisiana.

GLOSSARY

Achievement groups. A classroom organizational technique by which students are instructed based upon their level of reading proficiency.

Advance organizer. A short reading selection that precedes a longer selection to be read, written with a higher level of generality to prepare the reader for comprehending the ideas of the longer selection.

Bilingual. A term used to describe students who speak two or more languages of which English is usually the second language.

Classroom organization. The procedure by which teachers serve to plan and coordinate instruction, with the students functioning more independently as reinforcement and enrichment activities are used to enhance learning.

Cloze technique. An informal diagnostic procedure consisting of a 250–300 word passage from which every fifth word is deleted. As a diagnostic tool its primary purposes are to determine the students' instructional and independent reading levels. It also has secondary instructional applicability.

Comprehension. The association of meaning to recognizable words and understanding of phrases, sentences, and paragraphs.

Concept development. The understanding of information and ideas in order to categorize and better comprehend daily events.

Concept identification. A planning stage in which the teacher selects the ideas that are most important in a chapter or unit of study.

Concepts. Abstract ideas generalized from several pieces of related specific information. They are theories, ideas, views, or goals.

Concept teaching. The identification of ideas essential to understanding content information, and the provision of instruction to insure learning this information.

Content reading. An instructional procedure whereby all aspects of reading are integrated into the various subject matter areas.

Content teaching. A general term that means instruction in any subject area, whether science, mathematics, home economics, or social studies.

Contextual analysis. The use of other words in a sentence or passage to determine the pronunciation or meaning of an unknown word.

Critical reading skills. The highest level of the hierarchy in which the reader must analyze and evaluate what is read.

Deductive teaching. Teaching by moving from a general idea to the specific. It is characterized by the teacher's giving information to the student.

Developmental reading. A total school program designed to help each student reach his maximum reading potential.

Dialectical Differences. Term applied to students who speak a nonstandard American English that creates problems when they encounter reading materials.

Directed Learning Activity. An organizational format for incorporating reading instruction and management techniques into a content classroom.

Educable Mentally Retarded. A slow learner who needs to learn much of the same information as other students, but at a reduced rate.

EVOKER. A study strategy developed by Walter Pauk to assist in reading prose, poetry, and drama. Its steps are: explore, vocabulary, oral reading, key ideas, evaluation, and recapitulation.

FOG. Gunning's readability formula based on determining the reading level of a selection by using its sentence length and number of words with three or more syllables.

Fry Readability Graph. Edward Fry's chart that bases its prediction of difficulty on the length of sentences and the number of syllables in a selection.

General vocabulary. Words that are used in normal communication and frequently appear in various content areas.

Gifted. Students who, by virtue of outstanding abilities, are capable of high performance.

Guided Lecture Procedure. A procedure developed by Kelly and Holmes designed to improve notetaking skills by becoming better listeners. To enhance listening, the students are given a purpose for listening, recapitulate the lecture periodically, and outline their notes according to major concepts, details, and conclusions.

Heterogeneous. A word taken from the Greek term meaning *different*. Used in reading to describe a randomly formed group.

Homogeneous. A word taken from the Greek term meaning *same*. Usually used in reading to define a group formed on the basis of similarities of knowledge.

Individualization. Students are given assignments on their own instructional level and are engaged in tasks that meet their specific needs.

Inductive teaching. Teaching that involves moving from specific facts to general ideas. Students are provided with examples that encourage obtaining information through reasoning.

Instruction. A procedure for teaching students specific information in an appropriate environment for learning.

Interest groups. An organizational plan by which students with similar interests are allowed to work together in order to explore their interests in greater depth.

Interpretive comprehension. The process of assimilating information in an effort to infer the author's meaning.

Language-varied. Description applied to a student who is more fluent in a language other than English or who speaks in a dialect that causes communication problems.

Learning disabled. Students who exhibit a dysfunction in one or more of the basic neurological or psychological processes involved in understanding or using spoken or written language.

Learning hierarchy. The grouping of information in order to plan instruction according to a specified sequence.

Literal comprehension. The location of explicitly stated information in content materials.

Mainstreamed. A student who may function in the regular classroom part time and with a special education resource teacher part time. These students are sometimes classified as learning disabled, educable mentally retarded (EMR), or physically handicapped.

Management. The total process of selecting, organizing, and presenting content materials to the students.

Material evaluation. The determination by content teachers of the appropriateness of their materials in meeting students' instructional needs.

Monolingual. Students who speak only one language.

Multicultural. Students in the middle and secondary school population who have an experiential background, as well as a language, representative of another nationality or area.

Nonspecific words. Words that have a precise meaning in one content area, and change meaning in another content.

Organizational patterns. The structure in which content materials are arranged. These include enumeration, relationship, persuasive, and problem-solving patterns.

Organizational skills. Study skills needed to synthesize and evaluate the material read so that it can be arranged into a workable format. These skills include outlining, underlining, and notetaking.

PANORAMA. A three-stage, eight-step study strategy developed by Peter Edwards. The eight steps are: purpose, adapting rate to material, need to pose questions, overview, read and relate, annotate, memorize, and assess.

PARS. A modified, simplified study strategy developed by Carl Smith and Peggy Elliot. The steps are: preview, ask questions, read, and summarize.

Peer grouping. Involves students working together who are on the same grade level, but do not have the same reading levels.

Physically handicapped. For the purpose of this text, the physically handicapped are considered to be students with visual and auditory impairments.

Poor reader. Students who do not read at the grade level to which they are assigned.

PQ4R. A study strategy developed by H. Alan Robinson and Ellen L. Thomas. The steps are: preview, question, read, reflect, recite, and review.

PQRST. A study strategy developed by George Spache and Paul Berg that is usually applied to social studies and science materials. The steps are: preview, question, read, state, and test.

Prerequisite concepts. Ideas that are essential for the learning of other information.

Raygor Readability Estimate. Alton Raygor's readability chart that uses sentence length and long words (those with six or more letters) to determine the difficulty of a passage.

Readability. The determination of the approximate grade level at which various materials are written.

Reading instruction. The teaching and application of skills necessary to understand printed information.

Reading skills. Skills that involve the learning of procedures or strategies necessary for decoding and understanding the meaning of printed symbols.

REAP. A study strategy developed by Marilyn Eanet and Anthony Manzo for use in reading and in content area classrooms. The steps are: read, encode, annotate, and ponder.

Reference skills. Skills that are concerned with locating information in various sources.

Semantic context clues. Clues inherent in surrounding words that provide the definition or give sufficient clues so as to reveal the entire meaning of an unknown word.

Skills groups.   Using reading skills for the purpose of student placement in an individual situation.

SMOG.   McLaughlin's readability formula that is predicated on the theory that the difficulty of a selection can be determined by the number of polysyllabic words it contains.

Specialized study skills.   Specific reading and study strategies such as skimming, scanning, using parts of the book, reading illustrations, and adjusting rate to purpose.

Specialized vocabulary.   Words that change in meaning from one content area to another.

SQRQCQ.   A study strategy developed by Leo Fay to aid students in studying mathematical materials. The six steps are: survey, question, read, question, compute, and question.

SQ3R.   A study strategy developed by Robinson involving these five steps: survey, question, read, recite, and review.

Structural analysis skills.   A form of word recognition involving decoding plural forms, analyzing prefixes and suffixes, studying inflectional endings, and using syllabication generalizations; also used as an aid in meaning.

Structural overview.   A graphic technique for identifying vocabulary and concepts essential to learning content area materials.

Study guides.   Teacher directed aids (usually written) to help students through their content materials.

Study skills.   Functional skills necessary for understanding content materials. This skill area includes reference skills, organizational skills, and specialized study skills.

Study strategies.   Procedures followed in previewing and reading content materials.

Syllabication.   A structural analysis skill, based on examining word parts, to assist in recognizing unknown words.

Syntactic context clues.   Clues, such as inflectional endings, that reveal the meaning of an unknown word by demonstrating its order or function.

Technical vocabulary.   Words essential to the understanding of a specific content area. These words relate to only one content area and are crucial to the understanding of concepts in that area.

Total class instruction.   Teaching the entire class with no differentiation for individual needs.

Undercutting.   Rewriting content materials in order to lower the readability level and provide instructional materials to a more diverse population.

Vocabulary guide.   A special strategy for assisting students in learning and reviewing new content terms.

Word identification skills.   Use of prior memory or a decoding process by the reader to assist in the recognition of words and the association of meaning with these identified symbols. Frequently referred to as word recognition skills.

Glossary complied by Harley F. Anton, Louisiana State University.

BIBLIOGRAPHY

Anderson, Richard C.; Picher, James W.; and Shirey, Larry L. *Effect of the Reader's Schema at Different Points in Time.* Technical Report no. 119. Cambridge, Mass.: Bolt, Berenek, and Newman; Urbana-Champaign, Ill.: Center for the Study of Reading, University of Illinois, 1979.

Anderson, Richard; Spiro, Rand; and Anderson, Mark. *Schemata as Scaffolding for the Representation of Information in Connected Discourse.* Technical Report no. 24. Urbana-Champaign, Ill.: Center for the Study of Reading, University of Illinois, 1977.

Armbruster, Bonnie B., and Anderson, Thomas H. "Research Synthesis on Study Skills." *Educational Leadership* 39 (November 1981):154.

Artley, A. Sterl. "A Study of Certain Relationships Existing Between General Reading Comprehension and Reading Comprehension in Specific Subject-Matter Areas." *Journal of Educational Research* 37 (February 1944):464–73.

Ausubel, David P. *Educational Psychology: A Cognitive View.* New York: Holt, Rinehart, and Winston, 1968.

Ausubel, David P. "The Use of Advance Organizers in the Learning and Retention of Meaningful Verbal Material." *Journal of Educational Psychology* 51 (1960):267–72.

Baez, Joan. *David's Album.* Vanguard, 1969.

Barrett, Thomas C. "Taxonomy of Cognitive and Affective Dimensions of Reading Comprehension." "What is Reading? Some Current Concepts." In *Innovation and Change in Reading Instruction,* ed. Theodore Clymer. Sixty-seventh Yearbook, National Society for the Study of Education, Part II. Chicago: University of Chicago Press, 1968.

Barron, Richard F. "The Effects of Advance Organizers and Grade Level Upon the Reception, Learning, and Retention of General Science Content." In *Investigations Relating To Mature Reading,* ed. Frank P. Green, Twenty-first Yearbook of the National Reading Conference. Milwaukee, Wis.: National Reading Conference, 1972.

Betts, Emmett A. *Foundations of Reading Instruction.* New York: American Book Company, 1957.

Bloom, Benjamin S. et. al., eds. *Taxonomy of Educational Objectives: Handbook 1— Cognitive Domain.* New York: David McKay, 1956.

Bormuth, John. "The Cloze Readability Procedure." *Elementary English* 45 (April 1968):429–36.

Boyd, R. D. "Growth of Phonic Skills in Reading." *Clinical Studies in Reading III,* ed. Helen M. Robinson. Supplemental Education Monographs, no. 97. Chicago: University of Chicago Press, 1969.

Brown, T. Grant. "How to Apply Linguistics to Language Learning Without Scotch Tape." Unpublished study. Tallahassee, Fla.: Florida State University, 1975.

Bruner, Jerome S.; Goodnow, J. J.; and Austin, G. A. *A Study of Thinking.* New York: John Wiley, 1956.

Burmeister, Lou E. *Reading Strategies for Secondary School Teachers.* Reading, Mass.: Addison-Wesley, 1978.

Burton, D. L. "Some Trends and Emphasis in High School Reading and Literature."In *Changing Concepts of Reading Instruction,* ed. J. A. Figurel. Newark, Del.: International Reading Association, 1961.

Call, Russell J., and Wiggins, Neal A. "Reading and Mathematics." *Mathematics Teacher* 59 (February 1966):149–51.

Campbell, Anne. "How Readability Formulas Fall Short in Matching Student to Text in the Content Areas." *Journal of Reading* 22 (May 1979):683–89.

Certification Requirements in Reading, 3rd ed. Newark, Del.: International Reading Association, 1981.

Cheek, Martha Collins, and Cheek, Earl H. "Diagnosis—A Part of Content Area Reading." *Reading Horizons* 19 (Summer 1979):308–13.

Cheek, Martha Collins, and Cheek, Earl H., Jr. *Diagnostic-Prescriptive Reading Instruction: A Guide for Classroom Teachers.* Dubuque, Iowa: William C. Brown, 1980.

Clegg, Ambrose A. "Classroom Questions." *The Encyclopedia of Education,* vol. 2. New York: Macmillan, 1971.

Cooney, Thomas J.; Davis, Edward J.; and Henderson, K.B. *Dynamics of Teaching Secondary School Mathematics.* Boston: Houghton Mifflin, 1975.

Cooper, Harris M.; Barron, Reuben M.; and Love, Charles A. "The Importance of Race and Social Class Information in the Formation of Expectations about Academic Performance." *Journal of Educational Psychology* 67 (April 1975):312–19.

Copperman, Paul. "The Achievement Decline of the 1970's." *Phi Delta Kappan* 60 (June 1979):736–39.

Crowe, Thomas K., and MacGinitie, Walter H. "The Influence of Students' Speech Characteristics on Teachers' Evaluations of Oral Answers." *Journal of Educational Psychology* 66 (June 1974):304–8.

Cunningham, Patricia M. "Teachers' Correction Responses to Black Dialect Miscues Which Are Non-Meaning Changing." *Reading Research Quarterly* 12 (Summer 1977):637–53.

Cushenberry, Donald C. "Principles for Establishing Effective Secondary Reading Programs." *Reading Horizons* 19 (Summer 1979):320–23.

Davis, Frederick B. "Research in Comprehension in Reading." *Reading Research Quarterly* 3 (1968):499–545.

D'Angelo, F. J. "Paradigms as Structural Counterparts of Topoi." In *Linquistics, Stylistics, and the Teaching of Composition,* ed. D. McQuade. Akron, Ohio: University of Akron Press, 1979.

Dawkins, J. *Syntax and Readability.* Newark Del.: International Reading Association, 1975.

Dechant, Emerald. *Improving The Teaching of Reading.* Englewood Cliffs, N. J.: Prentice-Hall, 1970.

Donlan, Dan. "How To Play 29 Questions." *Journal of Reading* 21 (March 1978):535–41.

Dunn, Rita, and Dunn, Kenneth. *Teaching Students Through Their Individual Learning Styles: A Practical Approach.* Reston, Virginia: Reston, 1978.

Durkin, Dolores. "What Classroom Observations Reveal About Reading Comprehension Instruction." *Reading Research Quarterly* 14 (1978/79):481–533.

Duscher, Raymond. "How to Help Social Studies Students Read Better." *The Social Studies* 66 (November 1975):261.

Eanet, Marily G., and Manzo, Anthony V. "REAP—A Strategy for Improving Reading/Writing/Study Skills." *Journal of Reading* 19 (May 1976):647–52.

Earle, Richard A. "Use of the Structured Overview in Mathematics Classes." In *Research in Reading in the Content Areas: First Year Report,* ed. Harold L. Herber and Peter L. Sanders. Syracuse, N.Y.: Reading and Language Arts Center, Syracuse University, 1969.

Edwards, Peter. "Panorama: A Study Technique." *Journal of Reading* 17 (November 1973):132–35.

Education Commission of the States. *National Assessment of Educational Progress: A Project of the Education Commission of the States.* Washington, D.C.: National Center for Educational Statistics, 1971.

Eggen, Paul D.; Kauchak, Donald P.; and Harder, Robert J. *Strategies for Teachers.* Englewood Cliffs, N. Y.: Prentice-Hall, 1979.

Estes, Thomas H.; Mills, Daniel C.; and Barron, Richard J. "Three Methods of Introducing Students to a Reading-Learning Task in Two Content Subjects." In *Research in Reading in the Content Areas: First Year Report,* ed. Harold L. Herber and Peter L. Sanders. Syracuse, N.Y.: Reading and Language Arts Center, Syracuse University, 1969.

Estes, Thomas H., and Vaughan, Joseph L. "Reading Interests and Comprehension: Implications." *The Reading Teacher* 27 (November 1973):149–53.

Estes, Thomas H., and Vaughan, Joseph L. *Reading and Learning in the Content Classroom.* Boston: Allyn and Bacon, 1978.

Fader, Daniel, and McNeil, Elton B. *Hooked on Books: Program and Proof.* New York: Berkley, 1976.

Farr, Roger; Fay, Leo; and Negley, Harold. *Then and Now: Reading Achievement in Indiana (1944–45 and 1976).* Bloomington, Ind.: School of Education, Indiana University, 1978.

Fay, Leo. "Reading Study Skills: Math and Science." In *Reading and Inquiry,* ed. J. Allen Figurel. Newark, Del.: International Reading Association, 1965.

Fisher, Donald. *Functional Literacy and the Schools.* Washington, D.C.: National Institute of Education, 1978.

Ford, James F. "Language Attitude Studies: A Review of Selected Research." *Florida FL Reporter* (Spring/Fall 1974):53–54, 100.

Forgan, Harry W., and Mangrum, Charles T. *Teaching Content Area Reading Skills.* 2nd ed. Columbus, Ohio: Charles E. Merrill, 1981.

Freijo, Tom, and Jaeger, Richard M. "Social Class and Race as Concomitants of Composite Halo in Teachers' Evaluative Rating of Pupils." *American Educational Research Journal* 13 (Winter 1976):1–14.

Fry, Edward. "Fry's Readability Graph: Clarifications, Validity, and Extension to Level 17." *Journal of Reading* 21 (December 1977):242–52.

Gagné, Robert M. *The Conditions of Learning,* 3rd ed. New York: Holt, Rinehart, and Winston, 1977.

Gagné, Robert M., and Briggs, Leslie J. *Principles of Instructional Design,* 2nd. ed. New York: Holt, Rinehart, and Winston, 1979.

Gentile, Lance M. "Using Sports to Strengthen Content Area Reading Skills." *Journal of Reading* 24 (December 1980):245–48.

Gilliland, Hap; *A Practical Guide to Remedial Reading.* Columbus, Ohio: Charles E. Merrill, 1978.

Glass, Gerald G., and Burton, Elizabeth H. "How do they Decode? Verbalizations and Observed Behaviors of Successful Decoders." *Education* 94 (September/October 1973):58–64.

Glennon, V. J., and Callahan, L. G. *Elementary School Mathematics: A Guide to Current Research.* Washington, D.C.: Association for Supervision and Curriculum Development, 1968.

Goodman, Kenneth S. "A Linguistic Study of Cues and Miscues in Reading." *Elementary English* 42 (1965):639–43.

Goodman, Kenneth S. "Behind the Eye: What Happens in Reading." *Theoretical Models and Processes of Reading,* ed. Harry Singer and Robert Ruddell. Newark, Del.: International Reading Association, 1976.

Grant, Patricia L. "The Cloze Procedure as an Instructional Device." *Journal of Reading* 22 (May 1979):699–705.

Gray, William S. "Looking Ahead in Reading." *Educational Digest* 26 (February 1961):26–28.

Guice, Billy M. "The Use of the Cloze Procedure for Improving Reading Comprehension of College Students." *Journal of Reading Behavior* 1 (Summer 1969):81–92.

Gunning, Robert. "The Fog Index After Twenty Years." *Journal of Business Communication* 6 (Winter 1968):3–13.

Guszak, Frank J. "Teaching, Questioning, and Reading." *The Reading Teacher* 21 (December 1968):227–34.

Hafner, Lawrence E. *Developmental Reading in Middle and Secondary Schools: Foundations, Strategies, and Skills for Teaching.* New York: Macmillan, 1977.

Hallahan, Daniel P., and Kauffman, James M. *Introduction To Learning Disabilities: A Psychobehavioral Approach.* Englewood Cliffs, N. J.: Prentice-Hall, 1976.

Harber, Jean R., and Beatty, Jane N. *Reading and the Black English Speaking Child.* Newark, Del.: International Reading Association, 1978.

Hater, Mary Ann, and Kane, Robert B. "The Cloze Procedure as a Measure of the Reading Comprehensibility and Difficulty of Mathematical English," 1970. (ED040881)

Hawkes, Thomas H., and Furst, Norma F. "An Investigation of the Misconceptions of Pre- and Inservice Teachers as to the Manifestation of Anxiety in Upper Elementary School Children from Different Racial-Socioeconomic Backgrounds." *Psychology in the Schools* 10 (January 1973):23–32.

Herber, Harold L. *Teaching Reading in the Content Areas*, 2nd ed. Englewood Cliffs, N. J.: Prentice-Hall, 1978.

Herber, Harold L. "Teaching Reading and Physics Simultaneously." In *Improvements of Reading Through Classroom Practice.* Newark, Del.: International Reading Association, 1964.

Herber, Harold L., and Nelson, Joan B. "Questioning is Not the Answer." *Journal of Reading* 18 (April 1975):512–17.

.Hittleman, Daniel R. "Seeking a Psycholinguistic Definition of Readability." *The Reading Teacher* 26 (May 1973):783–89.

Hittleman, Daniel R. "Readability Formulas and Cloze: Selecting Instructional Materials." *Journal of Reading* 22 (November 1978);117–21.

Iran-Nejad, Asghar. *The Scheme: A Structural or Functional Pattern.* Technical Report no. 159. Cambridge, Mass.: Bolt, Beranek, and Newman; Urbana, Ill.: Center for the Study of Reading, February 1980.

Irwin, Judith Westphal, and Davis, Carol A. "Assessing Readability: The Checklist Approach." *Journal of Reading* 24 (November 1980):124–30

Jackson, James E. "Reading in the Secondary School: A Survey of Teachers." *Journal of Reading* 23 (December 1979):229–32.

Jensen, Mary, and Rosenfeld, Lawrence B. "Influence of Mode of Presentation, Ethnicity, and Social Class on Teachers' Evaluations of Students."*Journal of Educational Psychology* 66 (August 1974):540–47.

Johns, Jerry L. *Advanced Reading Inventory.* Dubuque, Iowa: William C. Brown, 1981.

Jongsma, Eugene R. "The Cloze Procedure: A Survey of the Research." Bloomington, Ind.: Indiana University, 1971. (ED050893)

Kane, Robert B,; Byrne, Mary Ann, and Hater, Mary Anne. *Helping Children Read Mathematics.* New York: American Book Company, 1974.

Karahalios, Sue M.; Tonjes, Marian J.; and Towner, John C. "Using Advanced Organizers to Improve Comprehension of a Content Text." *Journal of Reading* 22 (May 1979):706–8.

Karlin, Robert. "What Does Research in Reading Reveal About Reading and the High School Student?" In *What We Know About High School Reading,* ed. M. Agnella Gunn. Urbana, Ill.: National Council of Teachers of English, 1969.

Kelly, Brenda Wright, and Holmes, Janis. "The Guided Lecture Procedure." *Journal of Reading* 22 (April 1979):602–4.

Kintsch, W., and Van Dijk, T.A. "Toward a Model of Text Comprehension and Production." *Psychological Review* 85 (1978):363–94.

Kirk, Samuel A., and Gallagher, James J. *Educating Exceptional Children,* 3rd ed. Boston: Houghton Mifflin, 1979.

Klare, George, "Assessing Readability." *Reading Research Quarterly* 10 (1974-75):62–102.

Klein, Helen Altman; Klein, Gary A.; and Vigoda, Christy Hopkins. "The Utilization of Contextual Information by High School Students." In *Reading: Convention and Inquiry,* ed. George H. McNinch and Wallace D. Miller. Twenty-fourth Yearbook of the National Reading Conference, 1975.

Laffey, James L., and Shuy, Roger W., eds. *Language Differences: Do They Interfere?* Newark, Del.: International Reading Association, 1973.

Lahey, Benjamin B., and Johnson, Martha S. *Psychology and Instruction.* Glenview, Ill.: Scott, Foresman, 1978.

Lamberg, Walter J., and Lamb, Charles E. *Reading Instruction in the Content Areas.* Chicago: Rand McNally, 1980.

Larson, Alfred D., and Miller, June B. "The Hearing Impaired." In *Exceptional Children and Youth: An Introduction,* ed. Edward L. Nyan. Denver, Colo.: Love, 1978.

Lessenger, W. E. "Reading Difficulties in Arithmetical Computations." *Journal of Educational Research* 11 (1925):287–91.

Leary, Bernice E. "Meeting Specific Reading Problems In The Content Fields." *Reading In The High School and College.* Forty-seventh Yearbook, National Society for the Study of Education, Part II. Chicago: University of Chicago Press, 1948.

Lovelace, Terry L., and McKnight, Conrad K. "The Effects of Reading Instruction on Calculus Students' Problem Solving." *Journal of Reading* 23 (January 1980):305–8.

Lowenfeld, Berthold, ed. *The Visually Handicapped Child in School.* New York: John Day, 1973.

Mangieri, John N. "Characteristics of an Effectively Organized Classroom." *Making Reading Possible Through Effective Classroom Management,* ed. Dianne Lapp. Newark, Del.: International Reading Association, 1980.

Manzo, Anthony V., and Sherk, John K. "Some Generalizations and Strategies for Guiding Vocabulary Learning." *Journal of Reading Behavior* 4 (Winter 1971/72):81–82.

Marland, Sidney P. *Education of the Gifted and Talented.* Washington, D.C.: U.S. Office of Education, 1972.

Marsh, George; Desberg, Peter; and Cooper, James. "Developmental Changes in Reading Strategies." *Journal of Reading Behavior* 9 (Winter 1977):391–94.

Marzano, Robert J.; Case, Norma; Deboog, Anna; and Prochruk, Kathy. "Are Syllabication and Reading Ability Related?" *Journal of Reading* 19 (April 1976):545–47.

Mason, George E., and Mize, John M. "Twenty-two Sets of Methods and Materials for Stimulating Teenage Reading." *Journal of Reading* 21 (May 1978):735–41.

McCallister, James M. "Using Paragraph Clues as Aids to Understanding." *Journal of Reading* 8 (October 1964):11–16.

McCallister, James M. "Determining the Types of Reading in Studying Content Subjects." *School Review* 40 (February 1932):115–23.

McFeely, Donald C. "Syllabication Usefulness in a Basal and Social Studies Vocabulary." *The Reading Teacher* 27 (May 1974):809–14.

McGuire, Marion, and Bumpus, Mary. *The Croft Inservice Program: Reading Comprehension Skills.* New London Conn.: Croft Educational Services, 1971.

McLaughlin, G. Harry. "SMOG Grading—a New Readability Formula." *Journal of Reading* 12 (May 1969):639–46.

Melnik, Amelia. "Questions: An Instructional-Diagnostic Tool." *Journal of Reading* 11 (April 1968):509–12, 578–81.

Meyer, Bonnie J. F. "Organizational Patterns in Prose and Their Use in Reading." In *Reading Research Studies and Application*, ed. M. Kamil and A. Moe. Twenty-eighth Yearbook of the National Reading Conference. Clemson, S.C.: National Reading Conference, 1979.

Meyer, Bonnie J. F. "Structure of Prose: Implications for Teachers of Reading." Research Report no. 3. Tempe, Ariz.: Department of Educational Psychology, Arizona State University, 1979.

Meyer, Bonnie J. F.; Brandt, David M.; and Bluth, George J. "Use of Top Level Structure in Text: Keys for Reading Comprehension of Ninth Grade Students." *Reading Research Quarterly* 16 (1980):72–103.

Micklos, John J. "The Facts, Please, about Reading Achievement in American Schools." *Journal of Reading* 24 (October 1980):41–45.

Nelson, Joan. "Readability: Some Cautions for the Content Area Teacher." *Journal of Reading* 21 (April 1978):620–25.

Neville, Mary H., and Pugh, A. K. "Reading While Listening: The Value of Teacher Involvement." *English Language Teaching* 33 (October 1978):45–50.

Nichols, James N. "Using Paragraph Frames to Help Remedial High School Students with Written Assignments." *Journal of Reading* 24 (December 1980):228–31.

Norwell, George W. "Wide Individual Reading Compared With The Traditional Plan of Studying Literature." *School Review* 49 (October 1941):603–13.

Niles, Olive S. "Organization Perceived." In *Perspectives in Reading: Developing Study Skills in Secondary Schools*, ed. Harold H. Herber. Newark, Del.: International Reading Association, 1974.

O'Hare, Frank. *Sentencecraft: An Elective Course in Writing*. New York: Ginn and Company, 1975.

O'Hare, Frank. "The Effect of Sentence-Combining Practice Not Dependent on Formal Knowledge of a Grammar on the Writing of Seventh Graders." Ph.D. dissertation, Florida State University, 1971.

Orlich, Donald et al. *Teaching Strategies: A Guide To Better Instruction*. Lexington, Mass.: D. C. Heath, 1980.

O'Rourke, William J. "Research on the Attitude of Secondary Teachers Toward Teaching Reading in Content Classrooms." *Journal of Reading* 23 (January 1980):337–39.

Palmer, William S. "Toward a Realistic Rationale for Teaching Reading in Secondary School." *Journal of Reading* 22 (December 1978):236–39.

Patlak, Sanford. "Physical Education and Reading: Questions and Answers." In *Fusing Reading Skills and Content*, ed. H. Alan Robinson and Ellen Lamar Thomas. Newark, Del.: International Reading Association, 1969.

Paulk, Walter. *How to Study in College*. Boston: Houghton Mifflin, 1974.

Paulk, Walter. "On Scholarship: Advice to High School Students." *The Reading Teacher* 17 (November 1963):73–78.

Pearson, P. David. "The Effects of Grammatical Complexity on Children's Comprehension Recall and Conception of Certain Semantic Relations." *Reading Research Quarterly* 10 (1974/75):155–92.

Pearson, P. David, and Johnson, Dale D. *Teaching Reading Comprehension*. New York: Holt, Rinehart, and Winston, 1978.

Piaget, Jean. *Science of Education and the Psychology of the Child*. New York: Viking, 1971.

Plattor, Emma E., and Woestehoff, Ellsworth S. "Specific Reading Disabilities of Disadvantaged Children." In *Reading Difficulties: Diagnosis, Correction, and Remediation*, ed. William Durr. Newark, Del.: International Reading Association, 1970.

Ramirez, Manuel, and Castaneda, Alfredo. *Cultural Democracy, BiCognitive Development and Education*. New York: Academic Press, 1974.

Raygor, Alton L. "The Raygor Readability Estimate: A Quick and Easy Way to Determine Difficulty." In *Reading: Theory, Research, and Practice*, ed. P. David Pearson. Twenty-sixth Yearbook of the National Reading Conference. Clemson, S.C.: National Reading Conference, 1977.

Readence, John F., and Moore, David. "Differentiating Text Assignments in Content Areas: Slicing the Task." *Reading Horizons* 20 (Winter 1980):112–17.

Robinson, Francis P. *Effective Study*, rev. ed. New York: Harper and Row, 1961.

Robinson, H. Alan. *Teaching Reading and Study Strategies*, 2nd ed. Boston: Allyn and Bacon, 1978.

Roe, Betty D.; Stoodt, Barbara D.; and Burns, Paul C. *Reading Instruction in the Secondary School*, rev. ed. Chicago: Rand McNally, 1978.

Rowe, Mary Budd "Wait-Time and Rewords as Instructional Variables, Their Influence on Language, Logic, and Fate Control: Part I, Fate Control." *Journal of Research in Science Teaching* 11 (1974):81–94.

Ruddell, Robert. "Language Acquisition and the Reading Process." *Theoretical Models and Processes of Reading*, ed. Harry Singer and Robert Ruddell. Newark, Del.: International Reading Association, 1976.

Rumelhart, David. *Schemata: The Building Block of Cognition*. Technical Report no. 79. San Diego: Center for Human Information Processing, University of California, 1978.

Samuels, S. Jay; Begy, Gerald; and Chen, Chaur Ching. "Comparison of Word Recognition Speed and Strategies of Less Skilled and More Highly Skilled Readers." *Reading Research Quarterly* 11 (1975-76):72–76.

Sanders, Norris M. *Classroom Questions—What Kinds?* New York: Harper and Row, 1966.

Schell, Leo M. "Teaching Structural Analysis." *The Reading Teacher* 21 (November 1968):133–37.

Shavelson, R. J. "Learning from Physics Instruction." *Journal of Research in Science Teaching* 10 (1973):101–11.

Shepherd, David L. *Comprehensive High School Reading Methods*, 2nd ed. Columbus, Ohio: Charles E. Merrill, 1978.

Shepherd David L. *Comprehensive High School Reading Methods*, 3rd ed. Columbus, Ohio: Charles E. Merrill, 1982.

Sheridan, E. Marcia. *A Review of Research on Schema Theory and its Implications for Reading Instruction in Secondary Schools*. South Bend, Ind.: Indiana University at South Bend, 1978.

Shuy, Roger W., and Williams, Frederick. "Stereotyped Attitudes of Selected English Dialect Communities." In *Language Attitudes: Current Trends and Prospects*, ed. Roger W. Shuy and Ralph W. Fasold. Washington, D.C.: Georgetown University Press, 1973.

Singer, Harry, and Donlan, Dan. *Reading and Learning from Text*. Boston: Little, Brown, 1980.

Smith, Carl B., and Elliot, Peggy. *Reading Activities for Middle and Secondary Schools*. New York: Holt, Rinehart, and Winston, 1979.

Smith, Carl B.; Smith, Sharon L.; and Mikulecky, Larry. *Teaching Reading in Secondary School Content Subjects*. New York: Holt, Rinehart, and Winston, 1978.

Smith, Edwin H. *Literacy Education for Adolescents and Adults*. San Francisco: Boyd and Fraser, 1970.

Smith, Edwin H.; Guice, Billy M.; and Cheek, Martha C. "Informal Reading Inventories for the Content Areas: Science and Mathematics." *Elementary English* 49 (May 1973):659–66.

Smith, Frank. *Understanding Reading*, 2nd ed. New York: Holt, Rinehart, and Winston, 1978.

Smith, Kenneth J. "A Combination of Strategies for Decoding." In *Reading Between and Beyond the Lines*, ed. Malcolm P. Douglas. Claremont Reading Conference Thirty-seventh Yearbook, 1973.

Smith, Nila Banton. *American Reading Instruction*. Newark, Del.: International Reading Association, 1965.

Smith, Nila Banton. "Patterns of Writing in Different Subject Areas, Part I." *Journal of Reading* 8 (October 1964):31–37.

Smith, Nila Banton. "Patterns of Writing in Different Subject Areas, Part II." *Journal of Reading* 8 (November 1964):97–102.

Spache, George D. *Diagnosing and Correcting Reading Disabilites*. Boston: Allyn and Bacon, 1976.

Spache, George D. "Who Is Responsible for Reading in the Content Fields?" In *Toward Better Reading*. Champaign, Ill.: Garrard, 1963.

Spache, George D., and Berg, Paul C. *The Art of Efficient Reading*. New York: Macmillan, 1966.

Stauffer, Russell G. *Teaching Reading as a Thinking Process*. New York: Harper and Row, 1969.

Steffensen, Margaret S.; Joag-Dev, Chitra; and Anderson, Richard C. "A Cross-Cultural Perspective on Reading Comprehension." *Reading Research Quarterly* 15 (1979):10–29.

Strang, Ruth. "Progress in the Teaching of Reading in High School and College." *The Reading Teacher* 16 (December 1962):173.

Strong, William. *Sentence Combining: A Company Book*. New York: Random House, 1973.

Sullivan, Kathryn. "Vocabulary Instruction in Mathematics: Do the "Little" Words Count?" Unpublished paper. 1981.

Summers, Edward G. "Information Characteristics of the *Journal of Reading* (1957/1977)." *Journal of Reading* 23 (October 1979):39–49.

Swenson, Esther J. "A Study of the Relationships Among Various Types of Reading Scores on General and Science Material." *Journal of Educational Research* 36 (1942):81–90.

Taba, Hilda. "The Teaching of Thinking." *Eelmentary English* 42 (May 1965):534.

Taylor, Wilson L. "Cloze Procedure: A New Tool for Measuring Readability." *Journalism Quarterly* 39 (Fall 1953):415–33.

Taylor, Marilyn. "Using Photos to Teach Comprehension Skills." *Journal of Reading* 21 (March 1978):514–17.

Terman, Lewis M., and Oden, Melita H. *The Gifted Group at Midlife: Thirty-Five Years' Follow-Up of the Superior Child, Genetic Studies of Genius*, vol. 5. Stanford, Calif.: Stanford University Press, 1959.

Thelen, Judith. *Improving Reading in Science*. Newark, Del.: International Reading Association, 1976.

Thomas, Ellen Lamar, and Robinson, H. Alan. *Improving Reading in Every Class*. Boston: Allyn and Bacon, 1972.

Thomas, Ellen Lamar, and Robinson, H. Alan. *Improving Reading in Every Class*, abr. 2nd ed. Boston: Allyn and Bacon, 1977.

Thorndike, Edward. "Reading and Reasoning: A Study of Mistakes in Paragraph Reading." *Journal of Educational Psychology* 8 (1977):323–32.

Tierney, Robert J., and Lapp, Diane, eds. *National Assessment of Educational Progress in Reading*. Newark, Del.: International Reading Association, 1979.

Tierney, Robery J.; Readance, John E.; and Dishner, Ernest. *Reading Strategies and Practices*. Boston: Allyn and Bacon, 1980.

Toffler, Alvin. *Future Shock*. New York: Bantam, 1970.

Trybus, Raymond J.; and Kanchmer, Michael A. "School Achievement Scores of Hearing Impaired Children: National Data on Achievement Status and Growth Patterns." *American Annals of the Deaf* 122 (April 1977):62–69.

Vacca, Richard T. *Content Area Reading*. Boston: Little, Brown, 1981.

Vacca, Richard T. "The Development of a Functional Reading Strategy: Implications for Content Area Instruction." *The Journal of Educational Research* 69 (November 1975):108–12.

Van Dijk, T.A. "Relevance Assignments in Discourse Comprehension." *Discourse Processes* 2 (1979):113–26.

Vaughan, Joseph L. "A Scale to Measure Attitudes toward Teaching Reading in Content Classrooms." *Journal of Reading* 20 (April 1977):605–9.

Vaughan, Joseph L., and Gaus, Paula J. "Secondary Reading Inventory: A Modest Proposal." *Journal of Reading* 21 (May 1978):716–20.

Waugh, Ruth F., and Howell, K.W. "Teaching Modern Syllabication." *The Reading Teacher* 29 (October 1975):20–25.

Weaver, Phyllis. *Research Within Reach*. Newark, Del.: International Reading Association, 1978.

Webster's New Collegiate Dictionary. Springfield, Mass.: G. C. Merriam Company, 1981.

Wong, B. Y. L., and Jones, W. *Increasing Metacomprehension in Learning Disabled and Normally-Achieving Students Through Self-Questioning Training*. Burnaby, B.C., Canada: Simon Fraser University, 1981.

Zintz, Miles V. *Corrective Reading*, 4th ed. Dubuque, Iowa: William C. Brown, 1981.

NAME INDEX

SUBJECT INDEX

Abbreviations, 60–62, 68
Achievement grouping, 235, 238, 397
Achievement tests, 115–19
Acronyms, 62, 68
Advanced Reading Inventory, 137
Advance organizers, 148, 397
Analysis
    contextual, 51, 54–60, 162
    discourse, 202
    structural, 51
Application level, 64
Art
    comprehension, 69, 76, 82
    specialized information, 360–62
    study skills, 92, 96
Assessment, 19, 110
Assignments, differentiated, 265–66
Attitude, 8
Audiotape, 264–65

Bilingual student, 313, 397
Biology, 79–80
Black dialect, 318–19
Business education
    comprehension, 70
    lesson, 294–95
    specialized information, 356–57
    word identification, 57

California Achievement Test, 117
California Short Form Test of Mental Maturity, 119
Cause-effect relationships, 76, 77
    examples, 170
    identified, 72–74
Charts and tables, understanding, 101
Checklist, 124
    developing, 125
    sample observation, 127–28
Chunking information, 219

Classroom
    content, components, 9
    facilities, arrangement, 242–44, 245
    management, 240–42, 399
    organization, 230–40, 397
Class size, 114
Cloze procedure, 131–33, 397
    development, 132
    instructional device, 168–69
    sample, 134–35, 146
Cognates, 62–63, 362
Cognitive development, 4, 91
Compact presentation, 12, 67
Comparison and contrast, 68, 74, 75
Comprehension, 7
    defined, 64, 395
    factors influencing, 64–65
    holistic process, 202
    levels, 64
    skills, 11, 44, 66–88, 108
    summary skills chart, 47–48
    teaching, 169–70
Comprehension skills
    critical, 82–88, 190
    interpretive, 75–82
    literal, 66, 68, 75
    teaching, 169–70
    See also specific skill areas.
Comprehensive Test of Basic Skills, 117
Concept Attainment Model, 151
Concept Guides, 183, 219–22, 391–92
Concepts
    combined to form rules, 30, 32
    defined, 26, 36, 393
    development, 146, 148–49, 395
    factors affecting, 12, 70, 344–45
    identification, 18, 24, 30–37, 397
    key, 158
    learning, 20, 28
    load, 257

Earl H. Cheek is an Associate Professor in Reading in the College of Education at Louisiana State University. He received his B.S. in Secondary Education from the University of Georgia and M.Ed. in Secondary Education from Mercer University. Dr. Cheek received his Ph.D. in Reading from the Florida State University. He is a former secondary teacher, middle school teacher, and elementary school reading specialist. He coauthored *Diagnostic-Prescriptive Reading Instruction: A Guide for Classroom Teachers* (1980) and is the author of numerous articles in professional journals. Dr. Cheek is active in various professional organizations including the International Reading Association and the National Council for the Accreditation of Teacher Education. He is currently a member of the Professional Standards and Ethics Committee of I.R.A.

Martha Collins Cheek is an Associate Professor in Reading in the College of Education at Louisiana State University. She has been an elementary classroom teacher, an elementary and middle school reading specialist, and a state consultant for reading. Dr. Cheek received her B.S. in Elementary Education from the University of Georgia and her M.Ed. in Reading from Mercer University. Her Ph.D. was awarded in Reading at the Florida State University. In addition to coauthoring a college textbook on diagnostic-prescriptive reading instruction, Dr. Cheek is the author of articles in professional journals. She is active in various professional organizations including the International Reading Association, in which she is currently on the Publications Committee and an officer in the special interest group, Professors of Reading Teacher Educators.